Empire and Neoliberalism in Asia

The post-Cold-War era has been primarily characterized by an international order dominated by one superpower, the USA. With the demise of the Soviet Union, the unilateral pursuit of US economic, political and security interests became more possible than ever, but how have these developments affected countries in the Asian region?

Empire and Neoliberalism in Asia analyses the overall effect of US primacy on social and political conflicts in Asia, discussing how the post-Cold-War US agenda does not promote democratization in the region, in contradiction to one of the major proclaimed aims of the proponents of the Pax Americana. The team of renowned scholars argue that the US agenda can strengthen anti-democratic impulses in Asian societies, exacerbating and complicating existing domestic conflicts and struggles. The book also examines how the requirements of the 'War on Terror' intersect with, and reinforce, those of transnationalized sections of US capital.

Empire and Neoliberalism in Asia uniquely brings together general theorists and area studies specialists, to give a multi-disciplinary look at the ramifications of the American Empire for the Asian region that will interest scholars of Asian politics, international relations, political economy, development studies and sociology.

Vedi R. Hadiz is Associate Professor at the Department of Sociology, National University of Singapore. His books include *Workers and the State in New Order Indonesia* (Routledge, 1997); *Reorganising Power in Indonesia: The Politics of Oligarchy in an Age of Markets* (co-author, RoutledgeCurzon, 2004); *The Politics of Economic Development in Indonesia: Contending Perspectives* (co-editor, Routledge, 1997); and *Indonesian Politics and Society: A Reader* (co-editor, RoutledgeCurzon, 2003).

Politics in Asia series
Formerly edited by Michael Leifer, London School of Economics

ASEAN and the Security of South-East Asia
Michael Leifer

China's Policy towards Territorial Disputes
The Case of the South China Sea Islands
Chi-kin Lo

India and Southeast Asia
Indian Perceptions and Policies
Mohammed Ayoob

Gorbachev and Southeast Asia
Leszek Buszynski

Indonesian Politics under Suharto
Order, Development and Pressure for Change
Michael R.J. Vatikiotis

The State and Ethnic Politics in Southeast Asia
David Brown

The Politics of Nation Building and Citizenship in Singapore
Michael Hill and Lian Kwen Fee

Politics in Indonesia
Democracy, Islam and the Ideology of Tolerance
Douglas E. Ramage

Communitarian Ideology and Democracy in Singapore
Beng-Huat Chua

The Challenge of Democracy in Nepal
Louise Brown

Japan's Asia Policy
Wolf Mendl

The International Politics of the Asia-Pacific, 1945-1995
Michael Yahuda

Political Change in Southeast Asia
Trimming the Banyan Tree
Michael R..J. Vatikiotis

Hong Kong
China's Challenge
Michael Yahuda

Korea versus Korea
A Case of Contested Legitimacy
B. K. Gills

Taiwan and Chinese Nationalism
National Identity and Status in International Society
Christopher Hughes

Managing Political Change in Singapore
The Elected Presidency

Kevin Y.L. Tan and Lam Peng Er

Islam in Malaysian Foreign Policy
Shanti Nair

Political Change in Thailand
Democracy and Participation
Kevin Hewison

The Politics of NGOs in Southeast Asia
Participation and Protest in the Philippines
Gerard Clarke

Malaysian Politics Under Mahathir
R. S. Milne and Diane K. Mauzy

Indonesia and China
The Politics of a Troubled Relationship
Rizal Sukma

Arming the Two Koreas
State, Capital and Military Power
Taik-young Hamm

Engaging China
The Management of an Emerging Power
Edited by Alastair Iain Johnston and Robert S. Ross

Singapore's Foreign Policy
Coping with Vulnerability
Michael Leifer

Philippine Politics and Society in the Twentieth Century
Colonial Legacies, Post-Colonial Trajectories
Eva-Lotta E. Hedman and John T. Sidel

Constructing a Security Community in Southeast Asia
ASEAN and the Problem of Regional Order
Amitav Acharya

Monarchy in South East Asia
The Faces of Tradition in Transition
Roger Kershaw

Korea After the Crash
The Politics of Economic Recovery
Brian Bridges

The Future of North Korea
Edited by Tsuneo Akaha

The International Relations of Japan and South East Asia
Forging a New Regionalism
Sueo Sudo

Power and Change in Central Asia
Edited by Sally N Cummings

The Politics of Human Rights in Southeast Asia
Philip Eldridge

Political Business in East Asia
Edited by Edmund Terence Gomez

Singapore Politics under the People's Action Party
Diane K Mauzy and R S Milne

Media and Politics in Pacific Asia
Duncan McCargo

Japanese Governance
Beyond Japan Inc
Edited by Jennifer Amyx and Peter Drysdale

China and the Internet
Politics of the Digital Leap Forward
Edited by Christopher R. Hughes and Gudrun Wacker

Challenging Authoritarianism in Southeast Asia
Comparing Indonesia and Malaysia
Edited by Ariel Heryanto and Sumit K. Mandal

Cooperative Security and the Balance of Power in ASEAN and the ARF
Ralf Emmers

Islam in Indonesian Foreign Policy
Rizal Sukma

Media, War and Terrorism
Responses from the Middle East and Asia
Edited by Peter Van der Veer and Shoma Munshi

China, Arms Control and Nonproliferation
Wendy Frieman

Communitarian Politics in Asia
Edited by Chua Beng Huat

East Timor, Australia and Regional Order
Intervention and its aftermath in Southeast Asia
James Cotton

Domestic Politics, International Bargaining and China's Territorial Disputes
Chien-peng Chung

Democratic Development in East Asia
Becky Shelley

International Politics of the Asia-Pacific since 1945
Michael Yahuda

Asian States
Beyond the Developmental Perspective
Edited by Richard Boyd and Tak-Wing Ngo

Civil Life, Globalization, and Political Change in Asia
Organizing between family and state
Edited by Robert P. Weller

Realism and Interdependence in Singapore's Foreign Policy
Narayanan Ganesan

Party Politics in Taiwan
Party change and the democratic evolution of Taiwan, 1991-2004
Dafydd Fell

State Terrorism and Political Identity in Indonesia
Fatally Belonging
Ariel Heryanto

China's Rise, Taiwan's Dilemma's and International Peace
Edited by Edward Friedman

Japan and China in the World Political Economy
Edited by Saadia M. Pekkanen and Kellee S. Tsai

Order and Security in Southeast Asia
Essays in Memory of Michael Leifer

Edited by Joseph Chinyong Liow and Ralf Emmers

State Making in Asia
Edited by Richard Boyd and Tak-Wing Ngo

US-China Relations in the 21st Century
Power Transition and Peace
Zhiqun Zhu

Empire and Neoliberalism in Asia
Edited by Vedi R. Hadiz

Empire and Neoliberalism in Asia

Edited by Vedi R. Hadiz

Routledge
Taylor & Francis Group

LONDON AND NEW YORK

First published 2006
by Routledge
2 Park Square, Milton Park, Abingdon, Oxon, OX14 4RN

Simultaneously published in the USA and Canada
by Routledge
711 Third Avenue, New York NY 10017

Routledge is an imprint of the Taylor & Francis Group, an informa business

© 2006 Editorial selection, ©Vedi R. Hadiz, © the contributors

Typeset in Times New Roman by Taylor & Francis Books

British Library Cataloguing in Publication Data
A catalogue record for this book is available from the British Library

Library of Congress Cataloging-in-Publication Data

ISBN: 0–415–39080–X ISBN13: 978–0–415–39080–4 (hbk)
ISBN: 0–415–39081–8 ISBN13: 978–0–415–39081–1 (pbk)

For Lina and Karla

Contents

List of illustations   xiii
Notes on contributors   xiv
Acknowledgements   xvii

Introduction   1
VEDI R. HADIZ

PART I
Theoretical issues and the international context   21

1   The pole and the triangle: US power and the
    triangle of the Americas, Asia and Europe   23
    GÖRAN THERBORN

2   Beyond new imperialism: State and
    transnational regulatory governance in East Asia   38
    KANISHKA JAYASURIYA

3   The reordering of Pax Americana: how does Southeast
    Asia fit in?   52
    RICHARD ROBISON

4   The rise of the 'neocons' and the evolution of US
    foreign policy   69
    MARK BEESON

5   International conflicts and Asia at the end of the fossil
    energy regime   83
    ELMAR ALTVATER

PART II
Asia: social conflict, power and the American Empire   **103**

6 Neoliberal globalization, conflict and security:
   new life for authoritarianism in Asia?   105
   GARRY RODAN AND KEVIN HEWISON

7 Indonesia: order and terror in a time of empire   123
   VEDI R. HADIZ

8 Islamic opposition in Malaysia: political idiom, moral economy
   and religious governance   139
   KHOO BOO TEIK

9 The American Empire and the southern Philippine
   periphery: an aberrant case?   156
   PATRICIO N. ABINALES

10 Fostering 'authoritarian democracy':
   the effect of violent solutions in Southern Thailand   169
   CHAIWAT SATHA-ANAND

11 China's response to US neoconservatism   188
   ZHIYUAN CUI

12 The post-Cold-War world order and domestic conflict
   in South Korea: neoliberal and armed globalization   202
   SONN HOCHUL

13 The USA, China and identity politics in Taiwan   218
   LEE WEN-CHIH AND YANG DER-RUEY

14 US imperialism and Bengali nationalism   232
   HABIBUL HAQUE KHONDKER

15 Hindu fundamentalist politics in India:
   the alliance with the American Empire in South Asia   247
   ANAND TELTUMBDE

Bibliography   262
Index   297

Illustrations

Figures
11.1 China's GDP, 1978–2002   188
12.1 Rise of Anti-Americanism in Korea   214

Tables
5.1   Level and growth rates of per capita GNP
      in different world regions   87
5.2   Real growth rates and real interest rates   89
5.3   Reserves and annual production of mineral oil and gas   93
5.4   Imports of fuels and export revenues of selected countries   95
5.5   Flows of oil   96
8.1   Governments of Kelantan   144
8.2   Governments of Trengganu   144
11.1 The share of exports by foreign invested enterprises in China   189
12.1 Share of foreign capital in Korean stock market   204
12.2 Major poverty indicators   207
12.3 International comparison of Gini index   208
12.4 Annual working days lost due to labour disputes   209
12.5 Number of workers prosecuted after labour disputes   210
12.6 Proportion of casual workers to the total number of workers   211

Contributors

Patricio N. Abinales is Associate Professor at the Center for Southeast Asian Studies, Kyoto University. His latest book is *State and Society in the Philippines* (Rowman and Littlefield, 2004) which he co-authored with Donna J. Amoroso.

Elmar Altvater is Professor at the Department of Political and Social Sciences, Free University of Berlin. He is co-editor of *PROKLA – Zeitschrift für kritische Sozialwissenschaft* and a member of a European network of excellence on 'Global Governance, Regionalisation and Regulation: the Role of the EU'. He publishes on globalization, financial markets, politics, environmental governance, and the informalization of labour.

Mark Beeson is Senior Lecturer in the School of Political Science and International Relations at the University of Queensland. His latest book is *Contemporary Southeast Asia: Regional Dynamics, National Differences* (Palgrave, 2004).

Chaiwat Satha-Anand is Professor of Political Science at Thammasat University, Bangkok, and director of the Thai Peace Information Centre. He is also a former vice-rector of Thammasat University. He has published numerous books and articles in Thailand and abroad on politics, religion, the military, non-violence, and other issues.

Zhiyuan Cui is Professor at the School of Public Policy and Management, Tsinghua University, Beijing. He has also taught at Shanghai Jiaotong University, Shanghai, and the Massachusetts Institute of Technology. He was Senior Visiting Fellow at Harvard Law School in 2003. He has written extensively on Chinese politics and economics and issues of social and political theory.

Vedi R. Hadiz is Associate Professor in the Department of Sociology, National University of Singapore. He is the author of *Workers and the State in New Order Indonesia* (Routledge, 1997) and co-author (with Richard Robison) of *Reorganising Power in Indonesia: The Politics of Oligarchy in an Age of Markets* (RoutledgeCurzon, 2004). His research focuses on Indonesian and Southeast Asian politics, society and economy.

Kevin Hewison is Director of the Carolina Asia Center and Professor in the Department of Asian Studies, University of North Carolina at Chapel Hill. His most recent publications have been on the political economy of migrant labour in Asia.

Kanishka Jayasuriya is currently Principal Senior Research Fellow at the Asia Research Centre (ARC), Murdoch University. He is the author of *Reconstituting the Global Liberal Order* (Routledge, 2005) and *Statecraft, Welfare and the Politics of Inclusion* (Macmillan/Palgrave, 2006). His current research examines challenges and tensions within the neo-liberal market model and the emergence of new social contracts and strategies and forms of regulatory statecraft.

Habibul Haque Khondker was educated in Dhaka, Ottawa, and Pittsburgh. He is Professor, Department of Social and Behavioral Sciences, College of Arts and Sciences, Zayed University, Abu Dhabi, U.A.E. His research interest is in globalization studies. His works have been published in *Armed Forces and Society*, *British Journal of Sociology*, *Current Sociology*, *Economic and Political Weekly*, *International Sociology* and *South Asia* among other publications.

Khoo Boo Teik is Associate Professor, School of Social Sciences, Universiti Sains Malaysia. He is the author of *Paradoxes of Mahathirism: An Intellectual Biography of Mahathir Mohamad* (OUP SE Asia, 1995) and *Beyond Mahathir: Malaysian Politics and its Discontents* (Zed Books, 2003). The latter has been translated into Chinese (*Chaoyue Mahadi*, 2004). He is co-editor of *Democracy in Malaysia: Discourses and Practices* (Curzon Press, 2002).

Lee Wen-Chih is an Associate Professor at the Department of Public Policy and Administration in National Chi-Nan University, Taiwan. He served as the Director of the Political Research Committee at the Center for Southeast Asian Studies here from 1998 to 2004. His current research topics are the impact of globalization on the political economy of the Asia–Pacific and national security strategies for Taiwan.

Richard Robison is Professor of Political Economy at the Institute of Social Studies in The Hague, Netherlands. His most recent publications include (with Vedi Hadiz) *Reorganising Power in Indonesia: the Politics of Oligarchy in an Age of Markets* (Routledge, 2004) and contributions on neo-liberalism and the politics of markets in *Critical Asian Studies*, *Journal of Development Studies* and *New Political Economy*.

Garry Rodan is Director of the Asia Research Centre and Professor of Politics and International Studies at Murdoch University, Perth, Australia.

He has written on capitalist development and political regimes, the political economy of international media, and the political impact of the Internet in East and Southeast Asia. His latest authored book is *Transparency and Authoritarian Rule in Southeast Asia* (RoutledgeCurzon, 2004).

Sonn Hochul is Professor of Political Science at Sogang University and co-chairperson of the National Association of Professors for Democratic Society, Korea. He is the author of 'The Late Blooming of South Korean Labor Movements' (*Monthly Review*, July 1997), *Modern Korean Politics: Theory and History 1945–2003* (Sahwi-pyongron, 2003, in Korean), *Political Science of Modernity and Post-Modernity* (Munhwa-gwahak, 2002, in Korean), *Korean Politics in the Age of Neo-Liberalism* (Pureunsup, 1999, in Korean).

Anand Teltumbde is a noted human rights activist associated with the Indian People's Human Rights Commission. He has written extensively on contemporary issues in support of various people's movements in India. His writings are widely translated into various Indian languages. His recent books include *Hindutva and Dalits: Perspectives for Understanding Communal Praxis* (Samya, 2005) and *Anti-Imperialism and Annihilation of Castes* (Ramai, 2005).

Göran Therborn is Director of the Swedish Collegium for Advanced Study in the Social Sciences, and University Professor of Sociology at Uppsala University. His latest books include: *Between Sex and Power: Family in the World, 1900–2000* (Routledge, 2004); *Asia and Europe in Globalization* (co-editor, Brill, 2005); and *Inequalities of the World* (editor, Verso, 2006).

Yang Der-Ruey received his MPhil and PhD in anthropology from the London School of Economics. He is currently working in the Department of Sociology, Nanjing University, China, as an Associate Professor. His recent research interests pertain to the relationship between religion, education and politics in different Chinese societies.

Acknowledgements

I would like to express my greatest appreciation for the financial support provided by the Faculty of Arts and Social Sciences, National University of Singapore, and the Asia Research Institute (ARI), National University of Singapore, which made possible the international workshop in July 2004 upon which this book is largely based. I would especially like to thank the then-head of the Department of Sociology, Hing Ai Yun, and the director of the Asia Research Institute, Anthony Reid, for their facilitation and encouragement of all the work that has led to this publication. My thanks also to Kevin Hewison, formerly of the Southeast Asia Research Institute, City University of Hong Kong (and now director of the Carolina Asia Center at the University of North Carolina), and Garry Rodan, director of the Asia Research Institute, Murdoch University, for the additional financial support they made possible and the part they played in putting the workshop and book together.

I would also like to express my gratitude to contributors to this book who have persevered from the initial workshop through all the obstacles and problems that inevitably accompany the publication of a collective endeavour such as this – including the various stages of editing and rewriting – which took up the better part of one year. I am grateful as well for the help of the discussants and other participants of the workshop in 2004 and to two anonymous referees for their comments and criticism of the manuscript at an earlier stage.

Christian Chua, my PhD student and assistant throughout most of the project, was a source of invaluable help from the very early planning phase and thus his vital role must be acknowledged. I would like to acknowledge as well the help provided by a number of students of the Department of Sociology, NUS, and administrative staff both at the Department and at ARI, especially in the preparation and holding of the workshop that led to this publication.

Madona Michael was a wonderful copy-editor and editorial assistant, whose work has greatly improved the final product, in spite of considerable time constraints. Thanks as well to Stephanie Rogers and others at Routledge for their usual splendid co-operation, to Toby Caroll for offering the cover photograph, and to Jun Aguilar for permission to use the chapter by Patricio Abinales that had appeared in a different version in *Philippine Studies*.

Vedi R. Hadiz
Singapore, January 2006

Introduction

Vedi R. Hadiz[1]

Central themes, questions and issues

The post-Cold-War era is primarily characterized by an international order dominated by one superpower, the USA. While US primacy has been unabashedly flaunted, particularly after 9/11, it had been apparent well before the promulgation of the US War on Terror. Not surprisingly, the unilateral pursuit of US economic, political and security interests became more possible than ever with the demise of the Soviet Union and the end of the Cold War.

The present collection is concerned with the overall effect of US primacy on social and political conflicts in Asia. In various chapters, the authors suggest that the USA's post-Cold-War agenda provides a more secure environment for illiberal and even anti-liberal interests in the region. This agenda tends to strengthen anti-democratic impulses in Asian societies, contrary to the claims of the supporters of Pax Americana, and may well exacerbate and complicate existing domestic social conflicts and struggles. Specifically, the War on Terror has affected the domestic balance of social power and interest in many Asian societies in ways that have pushed them in more illiberal or authoritarian directions. This collection as a whole also addresses how the requirements of the War on Terror intersect with and reinforce the requirements of neoliberal economic globalization, especially with regard to the interests of transnationalized sections of US capital. This, too, may find expression in the dynamics of social conflict and change in many parts of Asia.

It is significant, in our view, that unrivalled US power has lately been accompanied by the increasing drive to 'securitize' the US-led process of neoliberal economic globalization (see, for example, Higgott 2004). Moreover, events after 9/11 suggest that neoliberal economic globalization has now reached a distinct stage, one characterized by an increasing use of coercion, threat and violence as part of the process of 'disciplining' countries to meet the requirements of global markets (see Steinmetz 2003). Thus, economic neoliberalism, as a political project pushed by a succession of US administrations since the 1980s, has become increasingly illiberal – if not authoritarian – in its nature and consequences (see Robison 2004). Arguably, such developments are reflective of a 'structural' moment in the trajectory of neoliberal economic globalization rather than a mere passing, 'political' moment. Obviously, the securitization of the economic neoliberal agenda has profound implications around the globe, not least in Asia, particularly in relation to the terms under which individual societies become integrated into the global economy. Rodan and Hewison (2004: 397), for example, note that the USA firmly tied security to trade issues at the APEC conference in Bangkok in October 2003. On this occasion, it was made clear to Asian states that they were expected to meet US security demands, and that only those that co-operated fully in the War on Terror would enjoy unhindered access to the US market.

Given this background, there have been recent debates about the nature of US hegemony, with burgeoning critical literature on, especially, 'American Empire'. This body of literature includes major contributions by some of today's most eminent social scientists, including David Harvey (2003a; 2003b), Ellen Meiksins Wood (2003), Chalmers Johnson (2000) and Michael Mann (2003).[2] In different ways, these authors have attempted to decipher the origins, logic and future directions of a distinctly unipolar world order. Pieterse (2004: 59), for example, has pointed to specific strategies of what he calls the 'neoliberal Empire'. These include US 'experiments' in 'state-building' in Iraq and Afghanistan; 'fossil fuel imperialism' driven by the kind of logic discussed by Altvater (this volume); global and increasingly hi-tech militarization; and 'security assistance' in fighting terrorism. They also include the push for bilateral and free trade agreements; protection of US corporate interests; and economic conditionalities on foreign aid. Many of these 'strategies' of political and economic coercion and incentives, and some of the relationships between them, are explored in detail throughout this volume as they pertain to Asia.

Yet, how useful is 'empire' as a concept for understanding the dynamics and mechanics of the unipolar post-Cold-War order and its consequences for Asia? How consistent is 'empire' with the requirements of neoliberal economic globalization in its current phase? What are the consequences of 'empire' on unresolved, often violent, social conflicts in Asia, many of which are actually rooted in the bloody social conflicts that emerged in the context of the Cold War? In what ways do the legacies of the Cold War continue to linger, thus affecting the dynamics of social conflict in Asia in the present post-Cold-War environment? These are the central questions that this volume addresses, theoretically and through concrete case studies.

This volume concentrates then on the consequences of a unipolar world order centred on US power, with all of its inherent tensions and contradictions, for contemporary Asia. Many parts of this region have been and will likely continue to be major centres of capitalist accumulation and development. This volume examines the growing literature on American Empire in ways that are specifically relevant to the Asian region.[3] It highlights the intersections between the imperatives of maintaining global hegemony and the dynamics of social, political and economic conflict and change in various parts of Asia today, in an evermore economically neoliberal and globalized world. The authors of this edition also suggest that the current phase of neoliberal globalization in fact brings back many of the features of Cold War politics, and that these are manifest in the nature of domestic conflicts and struggles in the Asian societies discussed. In so far as neoliberal economic globalization is tied to post-Cold-War US primacy in the present stage, its political outcomes have been distinctively illiberal, if not anti-liberal.

Much of the recent theoretical literature on 'empire' has been a useful point of departure. Wood, for example, emphasizes the coercive aspects of a US-dominated 'empire of capital' that – in contradiction to theories of globalization that foresee their demise – require nation-states to safeguard the increasingly extensive global reach of internationally mobile capital, with the USA acting as the great imperial enforcer. Harvey, while paying much attention to the politics of oil in understanding the roots of many present-day conflicts, also discusses the tension between US foreign policy, which is purportedly geared towards spreading democracy and freedom around the world, and the requirements of a global market dominated by US 'capitalist imperialism'. The latter ultimately involves the employment of coercion and force vis-à-vis other countries. Michael Mann favours another explanation for the increasingly coercive character of American Empire: after the Cold War, the option of using force to achieve US policy aims became too enticing, particularly with the country's unrivalled military might. It is this military might that has allowed the USA the luxury of becoming increasingly intolerant of obstacles placed by others on the path of extending the mobility of transnational US capital, in particular. In this connection, authors like Gowan remind us of the peculiarities of US capitalism and the US state, the most distinctive feature being the degree to which the US capitalist class holds unchallenged sway over the formation of public policy (Gowan 2004a: 4). For Gowan, the key aspect of the problem is that the leading, transnationalized sections of this capitalist class have developed a stake in the preservation of US primacy for their own security and expansion, and that they have been able to instrumentally utilize the increasingly 'militarized' US state to further their interests. Interestingly, there is a rather long tradition of scholarship on US foreign policy towards Asia that explains the USA's first incursions into Asia and the Pacific in the nineteenth century and its later forays in the following century. These were made in relation to economic imperatives, and belie the traditional understanding of US 'isolationism' (see Iriye 1967; Williams 1972).

The relationship between many Asian countries and the USA has, in fact, been complex and contradictory. Many in Asia regard US hegemony as a condition for prosperity and development in the region. For example, US power is regarded by the former Singaporean Prime Minister, Lee Kuan Yew

(2004a; 2004b), as essentially benevolent in nature, both in terms of driving Asian economic growth and in staving off the threat of international terrorism.

Support for such a position is found, perhaps not surprisingly, from the conservative US political scientist Samuel Huntington. He was the proponent of the ultra-cultural essentialist 'Clash of Civilisations' thesis (Huntington 1993), which regained the attention of media pundits, academics and policy-makers around the world, including in the USA, immediately after 9/11. Huntington suggests that 'a world without US primacy' would be a world that is more chaotic, unstable and violent, and one in which there would be less democracy and economic prosperity (as quoted in Mann 2003: 7).[4] A similar view is put forward by Mallaby (2002), who argues that the USA must resolve to take up the burden of empire, for its own sake as well as for the benefit of world civilization, in a way that might be reminiscent of Kipling. Comparable ideas are expressed by Robert Kagan, who chides Europe for its unwillingness to shoulder part of the responsibility (Kagan 2003). Meanwhile, Deepak Lal's (2004) contribution to the debate is to argue that empire is a progressive historical force that ensures global order and prosperity, and to underline the threat of Islamic radicalism to an essentially benevolent American Empire. Interestingly, a major dissenting view in the USA is put forward by Francis Fukuyama, who fears that the 'end of history' he once predicted – marked by the triumph of and convergence in liberal democracy and free markets – may not actually take place (Appleyard 2004) as liberal ideals are subverted by the very actors who claim to promote them.

Nevertheless, there is hardly any agreement in Asia either as to the benevolence of US power in the region. From time to time, 'people's protest movements' against the USA or US interests have emerged in such places as South Korea, Indonesia and the Philippines. Essentially, these have been responses to the perceived repercussions of US presence in the region, whether physically in the form of military forces (as in South Korea and Japan) or in the sense of its capacity to intervene in the political or economic affairs of specific countries. In Indonesia, for example, anti-IMF sentiment after 1998 was broadly synonymous with growing anti-Americanism in various quarters – from secular NGO populists and intellectuals to sections of the increasingly vocal, though small, Muslim fundamentalist community. Anti-IMF sentiment also coalesced with anti-US sentiment in countries such as Thailand (Hewison 2000: 279–96).

In some instances, anti-US sentiment has been skilfully taken advantage of by a range of conservative interests in Asia. Southeast Asia provides some particularly good examples; witness the neo-populist rhetoric of Malaysia's former Prime Minister, Mahathir Mohamad, or those of a wide array of Indonesian politicians who try to outflank opponents by buttressing both their Muslim and nationalist credentials. In Malaysia, too, the policy of detention without trial under a draconian Internal Security Act has been defended by state officials, partly in reference to the corresponding US practice in Guantanamo Bay. At the same time, the War on Terror has given new legitimacy to authoritarian practices on the part of state elites who provide more unambiguous support for the USA's post-9/11 agenda, as are the cases of Thailand and Singapore (see Rodan and Hewison, this volume). For these and related reasons, the authors of the country case studies in this volume are particularly concerned with how US objectives in the Asian region intermingle with domestic power struggles and the multiple local sources of ongoing conflict and violence. As mentioned, a major point of interest is how a US-led process of neoliberal globalization is being accompanied by distinctly more illiberal and even authoritarian forms of politics, both globally and at the heart of empire itself.

This volume as a whole covers a very broad geographical area. It is concerned with societies that have very diverse histories and are internally complex in their own ways. It should be noted by the reader, however, that it is impossible to 'cover' all of the vast Asian continent.

It should be especially kept in mind that this book deliberately leaves out extended discussions of the Middle East. This is because the situation in that particularly volatile, violent and conflict-ridden part of the world is amply discussed elsewhere (see, for example, Khalidi 2004), above all, in relation to the Palestinian question and, more recently, the US quagmire in Iraq. By contrast, much less is written about the implications of empire – whether 'incoherent' or 'monolithic' – for Southeast or Northeast Asia, or the Indian sub-continent. Southeast Asia is now regarded as the 'second front', after the Middle East, in the US War on Terror, while Bangladesh is often being cast in the role of a new breeding ground for terrorists. Moreover, these are all regions in which the conflicts of the post-Cold-War era have, in many ways, emerged out of those rooted in the bygone decades of rivalry between capitalism and communism. It should be remembered that Asia was the site of two of the major 'open wars' of the otherwise 'cold' war, in the Korean Peninsula and Vietnam. It has also been the site of such pivotal and defining moments as the massacre of hundreds of thousands of Indonesian communists.

At the same time, the spectre of the Cold War continues to haunt the people of Northeast Asian countries such as Taiwan and the two Koreas in very tangible ways, as shown in chapters in this book. Japan remains an economic powerhouse in the region, in spite of an ongoing economic crisis that has dampened the enthusiasm of earlier decades about the country's potential to challenge US primacy. In so far as the War on Terror is concerned, the main effect on Japan has been the passing of legislation, with US encouragement, that has allowed Japanese soldiers to provide non-combat support for the US-led military operation in Afghanistan, and to be dispatched to Iraq. Given Japan's former history of militarism and imperial designs in Asia (Selden and So 2003), such developments have given rise to unease in Asian countries, which still harbour memories of the Second

World War, as well as a furore within Japan itself. Moreover, the presence of US troops, especially in Okinawa, sometimes elicits impassioned criticism in some quarters of Japanese society (Johnson 2000). These incidents, however, all seem unlikely to affect directly either the fundamental nature of social conflict in Japan or the trajectories of its economic and political regimes, until Japan is forced to dispense with its pacifist post-war constitution.

The implications of empire: conceptual considerations

First of all, does the USA qualify for empire 'status'? There is certainly little consensus on this question. As Judt (2004) notes, many Americans are uncomfortable with the idea of the USA as an imperial power, given the emphasis on 'American values', on such issues as individual freedom and liberty, and the country's own history of fighting for independence from an imperial power. Leading US neoconservative Robert Kagan, for example, states that the 'United States is neither an empire nor should it become one', and prefers the term 'successful global hegemon'.[5] Unlike 'traditional conservatives', 'neocons' like Kagan – as they have been dubbed – appeal for a strong and politically interventionist state. They want a USA that is capable of guaranteeing the political and security requirements of capitalism, as well as upholding the traditional values that all conservatives typically cherish. Interestingly, the idea of the USA as an empire – supported by authors such Lal (2004) and Ferguson (2004b), who both believe that the USA should stop denying its imperial 'status' for its own good – is also vehemently rejected by the US liberal Joseph Nye (2004a), a former US Assistant Secretary of Defense for International Security Affairs. Nye argues that there are clear limits to the USA's ability to get what it wants in the world. For him, this inability is quite unbefitting a supposed imperial power.

Nye certainly makes a valid point, as one could conceivably compile a long list of instances in which the USA has failed to achieve its objectives, say, on the diplomatic table, in relation to a number of diverse countries. Mann also rightly argues that the proponents of the idea of US imperialism might have over-exaggerated the omnipotence of US power, notwithstanding the country's unrivalled military might. He prefers, instead, to portray a much less coherent and even 'clumsy' American Empire that not only fails to get everything it wants, but unwittingly invites severe, sometimes surprising, repercussions for its actions. Mann thus supports Johnson's well-known notion of 'blowback', in which the 'cost' of empire includes being at the receiving end of unpleasant, unintended consequences of certain policies. Thus, US interests today are threatened by an Al Qaeda network that it helped create via support for the anti-Soviet mujahidin in Afghanistan – a form of 'blowback' that the empire has been unable to contain.[6]

It has been unnecessary for all the authors in this volume to adhere strictly to a single, all-embracing understanding of 'empire', for each deals with specific manifestations and consequences of this complex, multi-faceted phenomenon, whether theoretically or through concrete case studies. Indeed, Beeson prefers the more neutral 'hegemony' in his analysis of the rise of the 'neoconservatives' in the USA – the main proponents of a belligerently unilateralist US foreign policy. Jayasuriya criticizes the participants of the debates on new imperialism for overlooking important transformations in the nature of governance which are situated in the state, and that are crucial for the maintenance of neoliberalism as an economic and political project.

Robison, on the other hand, accepts the notion of a Pax Americana while dismissing the tendency of some analysts to exaggerate the conspiratorial and organizational capacity of the US elite. Therborn utilizes the notion of empire in part to emphasize the coercive and violent aspects of the maintenance of US global supremacy, in the context of broad-ranging social and economic changes in the world and in the USA itself. Altvater, meanwhile, makes strong connections between the growth of the USA's imperialist designs and the imperatives of a fossil-fuel-run global economy that is running out of time. In spite of these different points of emphases, the authors fundamentally recognize that post-Cold-War US primacy and the neoliberal economic agenda it advances have had globally illiberal political consequences; in many cases, they have stunted democratization projects and exacerbated violent conflict in many parts of the world, including in Asia.

Thus, the authors of the various case studies in this volume have all accommodated the factor of American Empire in their analyses of local, social and political dynamics. In particular, the War on Terror and its implications for the various countries is prominently analysed by several authors. Rodan and Hewison suggest that the current phase of the post-Cold-War international order is mainly characterized by dynamics similar to those of the Cold War, with US imperialism again supporting a range of 'friendly' authoritarian regimes while the objectives of human rights and democracy again take a back seat to security and economic considerations. Teltumbde, Sonn and others in this collection see strong associations between various areas of domestic conflict and the imperatives of imperial domination, both presently and historically. Indeed, the historical, Cold War and colonial era-rooted dimensions of present-day domestic conflicts and violence are examined in detail by Abinales and Khondker in relation to the Philippines and Bangladesh. Cui, writing on China, maintains that the Cold War never actually ended in East Asia, and suggests that contemporary rhetoric about 'democratic peace' can be perceived in that country as a means of justifying what is, instead, a new imperial project. Clearly, this has implications for China's own democracy movements. Hadiz looks at how the requirements of empire are affecting the balance of power in newly democratized Indonesia, commonly seen to be a major hotbed of Southeast Asian terrorism. Chaiwat provides a detailed look at how the violent conflict in Southern Thailand, which is also discussed by Rodan and Hewison, is linked to both the agenda of ascendant social forces at the national level and the requirements of US supremacy.

The complexity of domestic conflict within Asian societies, and the intersections between their internal and external sources, are amply displayed in the case studies. Lee and Yang, for example, show that competition for regional supremacy on the part of China and the USA has left an indelible imprint on the nature of ethnicized social conflict in Taiwan. Khoo provides a study of political Islam in Malaysia and examines its development in relation to changing relations between Islam and the state, the country's economic and social transformation, and the ideological issues grafted onto the War on Terror as it concerns Malaysia.

It is proposed here that 'empire' can be a useful tool through which to understand the dynamics of the post-Cold-War international order, in relation to the dynamics of change and conflicts in Asia today. The use of 'empire' here is multi-dimensional, indicating that the workings of empire manifest in various expressions of power: the push for US-led neoliberal economic globalization, US influence over domestic politics in individual countries, pre-emptive measures to secure US military and economic superiority, and the War on Terror itself. These actually do not contradict the understanding predominantly employed by the heartiest advocates of American Empire. The infamous US Defense Department internal document of 1992, for example, argues that the USA's post-Cold-War political and military aims should be to ensure, *by any means*, that no power emerges anywhere in the world, including Asia, that could rival the USA and 'overturn the established political and economic order' (Tyler 1992; Keller 2002). Lal (2004), moreover, links the War on Terror to the broader task of securing the economic liberties that are supposed to make continued economic globalization possible, and which he sees as being threatened today by Islamic radicalism.

Precautions, however, are necessary. It is very easy, for instance, to descend into the most un-nuanced versions of old-style dependency theory by placing the USA at the centre of an imperialist world order, and to which other states are unproblematically coerced into accepting a position of subordination. The crude centre–periphery metaphor does not need to make a comeback; elements of dependency theory can simply be harnessed to support the agenda of populist–authoritarian regimes, for which anti-Western xenophobia may be useful in mobilizing domestic political support. Thus, demonizing an external Other, in this case the USA, becomes only a means of diverting attention from domestic relations of subordination and exploitation. Such a conservative, even reactionary, dependency-inspired Third Worldism helps to prop up anti-democratic regimes that espouse anti-US rhetoric, even as they engage selectively with American Empire in the economic and security spheres (Hadiz 2004a).

But what kind of empire is so vulnerable that it cannot protect itself against terrorist attacks such as that which befell the World Trade Center in

New York? What kind of empire is so insecure about its own safety and security that it has to revert to all sorts of measures to defend itself against much weaker opponents, even at the cost of great discomfort to its own citizenry (Marable 2003)? There has been much debate, for example, about the rolling back of civil liberties and rights in the USA due to such innovations as the Patriot Act, a development that is being replicated in several other established Western democracies. Moreover, what kind of empire does not even seek direct jurisdictional control over the territory of others, notwithstanding the invasion of Iraq, and appears to be completely uninterested, unlike previous empires, in territorial annexation or colonization? Mann is essentially correct when he suggests that the 'new imperialists do not want to rule permanently over foreign lands', but prefer an 'indirect and informal Empire' through which they can threaten and coerce others (Mann 2003: 13–14). It should be noted, though, that earlier empires such as the Roman and British had combined forms of direct and indirect rule. Thus, Mann's characterization of the 'incoherent' empire might be the most apt – given its insecurities, vulnerabilities, internal contradictions and, not infrequently, ineptitude.

Thus, what we are considering in this book is a complex, somewhat incoherent and, admittedly, rather nebulous form of imperialism, but certainly not one that is quite as intangible and amorphous as suggested in the postmodernist account of Hardt and Negri (2000). 'Empire' underscores the coercive aspects of the current global economic and political order, in a way that directly contradicts the supposed social and political outcomes of economic globalization, as rather simplistically assumed by a range of neoliberals (see Friedman 2000); typically, these include the expansion of prosperity, development, freedom and peace around the globe. Adopting a position that underlines the coercive and violent nature of global economic and political order also contradicts the notion of US hegemony, which is mainly based on the deployment of mere 'soft power'. These include the appeal of the values, principles and way of life that the USA represents, as most famously advanced by Nye (2004b). This position is simply and demonstrably untenable. The world of empire is one that is violent and bloody, and this needs to be at the heart of any analysis of the present world order.

Yet, what is the purpose of imperial power in the present day? Here, it is useful to examine the constellation of power and interests at the heart of empire itself, as undertaken by Gowan (2004a) in his analysis of the power of transnationalized sections of the US capitalist class over the US state. This point is further discussed below.

If this notion of a world order based on a US capital-led advancement of the economic neoliberal agenda – facilitated by force when necessary – is accepted, the crucial issue that emerges is whether we are now at a structural moment in world historical time or at a mere political moment. The related question is whether American Empire is contingent on the continuing dominance of the neoconservatives and other assorted hawks in policy-making circles in Washington. Would a victory by John Kerry in the 2004 US Presidential election have reversed the imperial direction? Some would rightly argue, for example, that if Al Gore instead of George W. Bush had won the highly contentious election in 2000, it would have been highly unlikely that the USA would have invaded Iraq.

In considering these questions, it is useful to identify certain continuities at the heart of empire itself; primarily, the strong influence of leading, transnationalized sections of the US capitalist class on the US foreign-policy-making process, which is attributable to a host of structural and historical factors particular to the US trajectory. Of course, the US class structure is complex, and the composition of its capitalist class cannot be analysed perfunctorily given the many factions and competing interests involved, including that of C. Wright Mills' infamous 'industrial–military complex'. Recognizing these connections, however, has led Gowan to conclude that there has always been a general consensus since the end of the Cold War, among representatives of US business and US officialdom, regarding the requirement to 'rebuild the international capitalist political order as a community-under-American primacy' (Gowan 2004a: 24).

According to Gowan (2004a: 24), this imperative was only 'wrapped up in the language of cooperative security' during the Clinton administration. Significantly, the chief analyst in Clinton's National Security Council was Philip Bobbitt, who has lately envisioned the rise of a benevolent American Empire through which world peace would be guaranteed, but only after terrible periods of warfare among sovereign states (Bobbitt 2003). As Gowan also notes, both Madeleine Albright, Secretary of State under Bill Clinton, and her mentor, Carter-era adviser Zbigniew Brzezinski, have long been strongly supportive of the agenda of US primacy. Moreover, Clinton's National Security Adviser, Anthony Lake, has stressed that 'the fundamental feature of this era' is that of US dominance; thus, US 'interests and ideals compel us not only to be engaged, but to lead' (as quoted in Gowan 2004a: 24). The implication is that though the language of imperial domination has been most unabashedly on display since 9/11, its social and political under-pinnings have existed beforehand. Reinforcing these underpinnings is the ever-closer relationship between the security and economic aspects of the US agenda. Thus, even the US foreign aid policy has been provided a stronger element of coercion: in a programme announced by President Bush in 2002, seventy-nine of the poorest countries in the world would be eligible to receive assistance only if they fulfil criteria that involves 'days to start a business' as well as 'trade policy' (Soederberg 2004: 280).[7]

It is not surprising, therefore, that critics of the Bush foreign policy after 9/11 should feel that his administration has merely been realizing a 'script' written a decade earlier during the presidency of his immediate predecessor. This script was the product of strategic hawks personified by Paul Wolfowitz, Under Secretary of Defense in the Bush Junior administration, and arguably *the* leading proponent of neoconservative politics in present-day USA. As Beeson notes (in this volume), it was Wolfowitz, recently appointed to lead the World Bank, who penned the Defense Department document in 1992 that controversially proposed the following arguments (Keller 2002):

a) With the demise of the Soviet Union, the US doctrine should be to assure that no new superpower emerges to challenge the USA's benign domination of the globe.
b) The US would defend its position by being militarily powerful beyond challenge.
c) The US would act independently when collective action cannot be orchestrated through ad-hoc coalitions.
d) Pre-emptive attacks against states seeking to acquire nuclear, biological or chemical weapons were desirable.

Buried during the Clinton administration, these arguments now sound eminently familiar. Significantly, the document, innocuously entitled 'Defense Planning Guidance', was accompanied by scenarios of hypothetical wars, one of them being another one against Iraq. Though apparently softened after some of the content was published in the *New York Times*, Wolfowitz's ideas have now acquired 'official status' as the lynchpin of George W. Bush's *National Security Strategy* (Wood 2003: 160).

The ideological leanings of key operatives like Wolfowitz have clearly contributed to the distinctive 'muscular assertiveness' of the Bush administration. This assertiveness, however, has also been attributed to the influence exerted on the administration by such key interests as those of the domestic oil and military contractor industries (Tabb 2005).

From the Cold War to the War on Terror

Thus far, it has been suggested that contemporary domestic conflicts in Asia have been entangled in the political and economic imperatives of maintaining US supremacy following the end of the Cold War. It should be recognized as well, however, that the persisting legacies of the Cold War have been important in shaping the contours of domestic conflict in Asian societies today.

In Northeast Asia, for example, it is not hard to realize that the Cold War has never quite ended, that the same threat of open warfare that loomed in a previous era still persists and continuously colours the thoughts and actions of political actors. In places such as Indonesia – where the Cold War left a bloody legacy in the form of the massacre of hundreds of thousands of its citizens, perpetrated primarily by the country's own armed forces but also ordinary citizens – the growth of civil society was stunted by the three-decade-long rule of an iron-fisted dictator. The consequences of this are the many faults, contradictions and overall fragility of Indonesia's present-day new democracy.

Significantly, several of the societies under consideration in this collection were considered important 'bastions' against communism during the long Cold War era. In the context of the Cold War, countries such as South Korea and Taiwan were the recipients of huge amounts of material assistance, economic and military, for assuring the prosperity and security required to safeguard them against communist incursion. The 'success' of such societies was also taken as proof of the superiority of the capitalist way, for example the prosperous South in relation to the economic debacle of impoverished North Korea. A number of these were societies in which less than democratic regimes presided for considerable periods of time, and in alliance with the USA against domestic and international 'threats' of communism. Thus, their elites now consider themselves to be among the victors of the Cold War for having chosen the 'right' side to support.

In Indonesia, Malaysia, the Philippines, Thailand and Singapore – the 'dominoes' that were supposed to have fallen in case of a communist victory in Indochina – the triumph of anti-Left, pro-Western coalitions of interests in domestic struggles over power that took place from the 1950s to the 1970s have clearly left a lasting imprint on the social and political landscape. Except in the Philippines to some extent, the viability of the Left as a social and political force has long vanished. This made possible the rise of political regimes that have presided over capitalist development with only limited pressure from an organized working class or peasantry. In the Indian subcontinent, the effects of the three-way superpower competition throughout the Cold War (between the USA, the Soviet Union and China) have been profound in terms of the balance of power among an array of social forces that have been in competition with one another over the decades – from Maoists and Hindu fundamentalists in India (Teltumbde, this volume), to military dictators and Islamic zealots in Pakistan and Bangladesh – in a country whose very birth cannot be separated from the context of the Cold War (Khondker, this volume).

It was East and Southeast Asia, in particular, that produced models of successful capitalist development, especially as the export-oriented industrialization (EOI) strategies gathered steam in the 1970s and 1980s. By the next decade, the spread of finance capital around the globe had already further integrated the 'miracle' countries in this region to the world economy, though it was precisely such an integration via finance capital that proved calamitous in the late 1990s as the Asian economic crisis wreaked havoc (Beeson and Robison 2000; Wade 1998a). At the same time, an 'Asian' model of development, characterized by a strong developmental state that intervened pervasively in the market and the economy, came to pre-occupy many pages of the literature (see Weiss 1998). The success of countries like South Korea and Singapore seemed to epitomize this 'Asian' way, though Thailand, Malaysia and Indonesia were also regarded as success stories in spite of a more corruption-ridden variation of the model. It was only the Philippines that failed to ride fully the tide of East and Southeast Asian capitalist development success of these decades by usually lagging behind in terms of economic growth. Now (still officially communist) China is typically held up as the most robust representative of an Asian model of capitalist development.

It is significant that in many ways, the Asian paths of capitalist development stood in the way of the push towards the greater neoliberal economic globalization already being led by the USA and its appendages, the World Bank and the International Monetary Fund – both originally products of the now-deceased Bretton Woods system. Of course, countries in South Asia as well as Latin America, like those in East and Southeast Asia, have been subjected as well to pressure to 'open up' and liberalize their economies, with results that have often been contradictory and tenuous (Adams *et al.* 1999).

It was the Asian economic crisis of 1997–8 that finally made it possible for market neoliberals to proclaim the absence of alternatives. Though the Chinese economic giant was unscathed (Gore 2000) due to a closed capital account, the crisis took much of the lustre away from the 'Asian model'. It allowed economic neoliberals to fault the model's fundamental failings and 'irrationalities', and push for accelerated market reforms favourable to transnational capital mobility. Increasingly, these reforms were presented as conducive to the development of such virtues as good governance, civil society and democracy. As Hadiz argues in his chapter, some analysts virtually returned to a 1960s-style modernization theory when they envisaged a link between political liberalism and the advancement of market capitalism. This is in spite of overwhelming evidence from Asia and elsewhere that capitalism has been able to thrive under a variety of political regimes, and that there was no necessity for any functional convergence in political and economic liberalism (Hewison *et al.* 1993). Thus, the link that was made was always somewhat spurious; the real concern was with the construction of institutions of governance that would facilitate the operations of international capital and, at the same time, protect it from domestic predatory as well distributional coalitions.

The propensity for exclusionary forms of politics was only to be further emphasized with the watershed event of 9/11 and the declaration of the War on Terror, after which the intertwining of the US global economic and security agenda virtually became formalized. Thus, a major casualty of the War on Terror has undoubtedly been some of the basic values of democracy and human rights, as well as the notion of democracy itself as a worthwhile and viable domestic political project in some countries. Whether expressed as a particularly virulent form of secular nationalism or, increasingly, in a brand of populism infused with heavily moralistic, religious or anti-Western overtones, anti-Americanism is invariably combined with a degree of hostility to the values that the country purports to represent. In so far as the democratic project, rightly or wrongly, is associated in the collective global imagination as one that is supported by the US-led West, so will domestic pro-democracy actors find their political positions in peril. If the anti-Americanism of today, which is by no means confined to the Muslim world, is clearly a reaction to US global hegemony and its perceived aims, there is, beneath it, a strange process of mutual reinforcement in motion. The deployment of anti-US rhetoric in countries such as Indonesia, Malaysia, Pakistan or China requires the spectre of US power and dominance to disparage notions such as universal human rights as an imperialist sham. On the other hand, the no less moralistic US behemoth requires this belligerence to help validate its increasing militarism and security-oriented stance (Hadiz 2004a).

The contributions

The book is a compilation of papers, all but one of which were originally presented at an international workshop held at the National University of Singapore in July 2004, and subsequently revised for publication. A number of renowned social scientists from various disciplines, working both on the theoretical questions pertaining to the post-Cold-War international order and specialists on Asia or on individual Asian societies, attended this workshop. The interdisciplinary (as well as international) nature of this project reveals how the issue of American Empire and its consequences transcend artificial disciplinary (and national) boundaries.

This collection is intended to help fill a significant gap in the existing literature by specifically relating issues of empire, hegemony, neoliberal economic globalization and the international politics of violence and coercion to the processes of contemporary social, economic and political change in the broader Asian region. As mentioned earlier, a major objective of the book is to conceptualize continuing sources of domestic social and political conflict, tension and violence in Asia, in relation to the shifting imperatives of the world economic and political order that is dominated by one superpower. This book is unique in that it represents the collective effort of a range of scholars, from general theorists to area studies and country specialists, to produce a deeply reflective and critical compilation that is a result of intensive dialogue among them.

The structure of this volume is as follows: the first part largely consists of broader theoretical explorations of the nature and driving forces of American Empire/hegemony. These chapters provide a 'big picture' analysis that situates Asia within the broader international context. The second part consists of more detailed case studies, geared more specifically to examining the intersections between domestic conflict in Asia and the logic and mechanics of the US-dominated post-Cold-War international order.

Part I starts off with an overview of the 'configuration of world power' by Göran Therborn, which focuses on the 'pole' of US power and the 'triangle' of the Americas, Europe and Asia. The chapter provides a packed analysis of the complexities of post-Cold-War politics in various parts of the world. It links regional sociocultural, economic, political and demographic transformations, and the imperatives of a world order dominated by one super-power, which have produced a kind of 'Occidental despotism'. Therborn concludes that the 'future of democracy in Asia is likely to depend largely upon' the region finally overcoming 'the authoritarian rigidities and the manipulative clientelism of the long bygone Cold War era'.

Kanishka Jayasuriya follows with a chapter on the transformations of global governance in the context of neoliberal economic globalization, as expressed in transformations within the state. As he situates these global transformations firmly on the state itself, he examines the interest and insti-tutions that link together sections of the corps of state officials and managers across the capitalist world, thereby also rebuking theorists who have declared the redundancy of the state. For Jayasuriya, the emphasis on new imperialism, which focuses on the role and dominance of one super-state, obscures such developments and is circumscribed by an outdated 'Westphalian' view of the state. He revisits Kautsky's notion of ultra-imperialism to find new ways of making sense of the global transformation in governance and in the nature of power and conflict.

Jayasuriya's contribution is followed by Richard Robison's analysis of the emergence and contradictions of Pax Americana, and how Southeast Asia as a region fits into the post-Cold-War US agenda. Southeast Asia has, of course, been a focus of attention in recent years due to the emergence of radical Islamic terror networks with alleged links to Al Qaeda. Robison suggests that the requirements of consolidating US hegemony mean that the priority is now on cementing alliances with governments that can deliver loyalty and security in the region. The recent US neoconservative political turn, however, does not signal the end of the neoliberal epoch or its whole-sale replacement by a neoconservative era. Robison points out that global capital and financial markets remain the driving forces for institutional reform and change in the region's economies, as they have been in the last two decades.

Mark Beeson's chapter then examines the thinking and genealogy of the US 'neoconservatives', the term conferred on the policy-makers who have been shaping the direction of the Bush administration. Beeson suggests that the doctrinaire beliefs of the 'neocons' have not only resulted in an ill-judged transformation of US foreign policy, but, more generally, undermined the legitimacy of US authority. It is, of course, crucial to the concerns of this volume that the legitimacy of US authority has been undermined, given what it is *supposed* to represent. One highly possible consequence is the concomitant erosion of the legitimacy of domestic pro-democracy move-ments in Asia, and the strengthening of an anti-democratic impulse.

Elmar Altvater's chapter offers a critical analysis of one of the major driving forces of the logic of empire and of contemporary world conflicts – the politics of oil. Altvater argues firmly that the foreseeable exhaustion of fossil resources, thus the approaching end of the fossil energy regime, will result in the escalation of violent conflicts, globally and in Asia. Conflict for control over diminishing fossil fuel resources will increasingly shape the geopolitical considerations of the USA, with specific peace and security implications for various parts of the world. Central Asia, in which vast unexploited oil and natural gas reserves are believed to be located, is poised to grow in strategic importance as it will literally provide much of the fuel for future world growth, including in the emerging economies of China and India.

Part II of this collection kicks off with a comparative chapter by Garry Rodan and Kevin Hewison that deals with the Southeast Asian cases of Singapore and Thailand. The authors note that the end of the Cold War provided the USA with the opportunity to lead and support an accelerated neoliberal push, and that regimes that stood in the way were placed under scrutiny, especially if they were authoritarian. The securitization of US interests since 9/11, however, has seen a fundamental shift. On the basis of their case studies, Rodan and Hewison argue that the War on Terror is creating opportunities for the consolidation and promotion of authoritarian rule in Thailand, where Prime Minister Thaksin Shinawatra is undertaking a project for centralizing state power. In Singapore, the resultant state-of-siege environment has provided a new and important source of legitimacy for the long-ruling People's Action Party.

Vedi R. Hadiz follows with a chapter on Indonesia that focuses on struggles for Indonesian democratization and the interests of contending domestic social forces. This chapter also looks at the way these have become embedded within the mechanics and imperatives of a US-dominated world economic and political order. Hadiz assesses Indonesia's still tenuous new democracy, the often contradictory domestic impulses for rights and freedoms, and those for order and stability, especially in the context of terrorism and the apparent political resurgence of the Indonesian security forces. Hadiz argues that the War on Terror has strengthened the anti-democratic impulse in Indonesian state and society at this critical juncture for Indonesian democracy.

Militant, political Islam has recently emerged as the main political 'nemesis' of empire, and is placed at the core of the chapters that immediately follow. In his analysis of Islamic political groups in Malaysia, Khoo Boo Teik refutes many of the assumptions typically made about the nature of political Islam in this country, which cast it as a particularly archaic, reactionary and possibly destabilizing factor. Instead, Khoo presents a subtle analysis of 'political Islam' that places it against the background of the domestic Malaysian political economy and in the context of the War on Terror. In the process, he analyses the rivalry and ideological divisions within the Muslim–Malay community, conditioned by socio-economic inequalities arising out of a three-decade-long nationalist–capitalist project.

A critical history approach is applied by Patricio N. Abinales in his analysis of Mindanao in the Philippines. Mindanao, of course, has been the site of a long-standing 'Islamic' separatist movement; more recently, it has become enmeshed in the mechanizations of the War on Terror. Focusing on the changing nature of the triangular relationship among local Muslim elites, the central state based in Manila, and US imperialism, Abinales argues that a point of contention has always been the interest of local elites in maintaining political autonomy in relation to Manila. Conversely, US power has historically been viewed from within Mindanao as a relatively benign factor that has assisted some local agenda against those of the central state.

Thailand is brought into the equation again through an insightful chapter by Chaiwat Satha-Anand. He focuses on Muslim-dominated Southern Thailand, also the site of a long-standing separatist struggle. More recently, it has hosted escalating violence between Thai security forces and sections of the local majority-Muslim population. This violence has now also pitted sections of the local population – Buddhist and Muslim – against each other. Chaiwat links these conflicts with the imperatives of a growing authoritarian impulse emanating from Bangkok, suggestive of the rise of what he calls 'authoritarian democracy' and encouraged to a considerable extent by the overall climate induced by the War on Terror in the region.

The next chapters take the book to Northeast Asia. The astounding rise of China in recent decades has, of course, placed it as the main potential challenger to US primacy in the eyes of many observers, especially given Japan's now chronic economic problems. Zhiyuan Cui provides an insider look into the ways in which China's intellectuals and elites perceive the aims of US political neoconservatism and their possible impact on China's internal economic and political developments, as well as how these perceptions have come to be formed. His contribution shows a country that is increasingly confident of its international standing, in spite of the internal contradictions inherent in its rapid capitalist development. Yet, it is also a country suspicious of an imperial project that would entail the imposition of checks on its much anticipated emergence as a global power.

Sonn Hochul examines a nominal post-Cold-War South Korea, in which US troops are still stationed to help safeguard the country from an invasion by the communist North. The US presence in South Korea has been highly controversial, inducing the emergence of a nationalistic fervour that is largely directed at the USA, and which imbues various kinds of social movements. These social movements have targeted the economic neoliberal agenda, which is perceived as having reduced South Korea to virtual colony status, particularly in the wake of its near economic collapse during the recent Asian economic crisis. The resultant conflicts will, undoubtedly, influence the way in which the country seeks to reassert its status as a regional economic power.

Lee Wen-Chih and Yang Der-Ruey examine the intricacies of domestic social conflicts in Taiwan, expressed predominantly in the ethnicizing of political party competition in the island-state. Throughout the chapter, they stress how domestic conflicts in Taiwan are intrinsically entangled in the changing nature of the relationship and geopolitical considerations of the People's Republic of China and of the USA, over time. For them, issues of Taiwanese nationhood, identity and culture are inseparable from issues of superpower conflict. At the time of writing, the threat of open warfare between China and Taiwan over the latter's aspirations for independence was at near boiling point.

The final two chapters take this volume to still another part of the continent where the legacy of the Cold War is strongly felt – South Asia. In his chapter on Bangladesh, Habibul Haque Khondker traces that country's independence struggle in the early 1970s, which involved a war between Pakistan and India, and places it in the context of Cold-War-era superpower conflicts. For Khondker, the intermingling of domestic political conflicts in Bangladesh (after independence was attained) with superpower struggles resulted in the end of the possibility for a successful secular state. Thus, the legacy of the Cold War era still persists in Bangladesh as autocratic versions of Islam have now become a firm fixture in the political mainstream. This is an important observation given current US concerns about the growth of Islamic radicalism in Bangladesh, which is seen as fertile ground for developing anti-Western terror groups as a natural outgrowth.

The chapter on India by Anand Teltumbde tackles the thorny issue of the politics of Hindu fundamentalism and the strange alliance between Hindu fundamentalist forces and the proponents of economic neoliberalism. While the political practices and organization of radical Hindu fundamentalism are partly rooted, intriguingly, in European fascism, Teltumbde finds a growing affinity between the requirements of sectarian politics in India and the geostrategic and economic interests of the USA in South Asia. With the Cold-War-era conflict between India and Pakistan now relegated to the background, Anand argues that an alliance of convenience has emerged in the sub-continent between the USA and some of the most conservative and anti-democratic forces in India.

Preliminary conclusions

Taken together, all of the chapters reveal the complexities, at both macro and more micro levels, of the US-dominated post-Cold-War order, particularly where Asia is concerned. Rather than ushering in freedom, democracy and civility to the world – as imagined by the advocates of empire – the region is deeply embroiled in social conflicts, in which the position of anti-democratic and uncivil social forces are frequently bolstered. It is important to note, however, that criticism of the nature and consequences of US power as put forward by the authors of this book go well beyond those espoused in well-known populist, anti-globalization or neo-Third-Worldist circles. Together, they provide a nuanced and complex understanding of the links between economics and politics, of global transformations, international geo-strategic politics and domestic conflicts, and of the interests of contending social forces throughout Asia and in the USA. After all, the neocons certainly do not speak for all Americans, and obviously do not present an uncontested version of the US 'national interest'. Thus, hundreds of thousands marched on the streets of major US cities just before the invasion of Iraq. It is the values and interests of, especially, leading sections of the US capitalist class that tend to define this 'national interest' and shape national policy, in ways that are potentially and actually detrimental to the vast majority of the American people. Therefore, the future course of empire will be charted in many important ways on the basis of how these real and potential social conflicts within US society are played out and ultimately resolved.

As mentioned, many of the contributions underline as well that it is not possible to understand the nature of social conflict, and the sources of tensions and violence in individual Asian societies, without recourse to the historical legacies of the Cold War era. Indeed, in some societies, many aspects of the Cold War, and certainly its consequences, remain quite alive and well. Perhaps, most of all, they emphasize the near impossibility of understanding continuing domestic sources of conflict in a way that is dissociated from the unfolding imperatives of unrivalled US global hegemony over time. While this was clearly already the case during the long decades of the Cold War, such an assertion appears especially pertinent in the present context.

Finally, many of the authors voice concerns about the political consequences of the increasing securitization of the agenda of neoliberal economic globalization. The writing on the wall, so to speak, is really about no less than the advent of a world order that is becoming increasingly violent, coercive, illiberal and even authoritarian in its workings (Steinmetz 2003). In this case, the opportunities apparently presented by the end of the Cold War – in so far as such ideals of democracy, human rights and freedom were concerned – have likely passed us by, contrary to what is still imagined by well-known pseudo-prophets of only benign globalization (see Friedman 2000). The Brave New World we are all facing, in Asia and elsewhere, appears to be one that combines some of the most unsavoury aspects of rule by global markets with increasingly coercive forms of political illiberalism and authoritarianism – at the levels of both domestic and international governance.

Notes

1 The author would like to thank Chua Beng Huat, Kevin Hewison, Garry Rodan, Richard Robison and Anne Raffin, as well as two anonymous referees, for very useful comments on earlier versions of this chapter.

2 Of course, another famous – perhaps 'infamous' would be a better word – contribution to the literature has been Hardt and Negri's *Empire* (2000). This work is in many ways quite different from the other landmark works of recent years due to its distinctly post-modernist slant on issues of structures and agency, domination, and resistance.

3 Other recent books on American Empire include Odom and Dujarric (2004), Bacevich (2003), Boggs (2003) and Aronowitz and Gautney (2003).

4 It is notable that Huntington has been one of the most vociferous proponents of the idea of a US-led 'Western civilization', exalting the values of freedom and the like, in conflict with other 'civilizations', including 'Islam', which are supposedly culturally predisposed against such values.

5 See the short piece by Kagan (n.d.).

6 It is, perhaps, useful to recall that Rome – perhaps the ultimate 'model' of a successful empire – was sacked by 'barbarian' Germanic tribes and nearly overrun by the likes of the Huns under Attila. Its legions suffered numerous military defeats while its strongholds in the far reaches of its empire, in Britain for instance, had great difficulty overcoming local rebellions. Indeed, it is tempting to note some parallels in the devastation subjected on the New York Twin Towers and the successful military incursions into the heart of imperial Rome by lesser forces. The failings of Rome as the superpower of the ancient world do not nullify the fact that it was the greatest imperial force on earth at its zenith, much as the USA is today the world's unrivalled military and political power despite its vulnerabilities.

7 It must be remembered, though, that the USA, according to Mann, is the most miserly among the twenty-two wealthiest nations in the world in terms of providing foreign aid. US aid amounts only to half of its annual foreign arms sales, while the 2003 military budget, together with the State Department's security appropriations, was thirty times the size of foreign aid in the budget for the same year. Moreover, one-third of US foreign aid goes to one of the wealthiest countries in the world, Israel, while another one-fifth goes to Egypt, which is being effectively bribed not to invade Israel (Mann 2003: 53–4).

Part I

Theoretical issues and the international context

1 The pole and the triangle

US power and the triangle of the Americas, Asia and Europe

Göran Therborn

Analysing world power and its implications

This chapter is premised on three basic methodological tenets. First, world power is best grasped as a multilateral configuration. Studies should not be focused exclusively on the pole, or poles, of domination. Rather, they ought to pay some systematic attention to the network of global power relations. Second, world power is better understood as being multi-dimensional. It is not just or mainly economic, nor is it only or chiefly economic and military; it should be seen as being also demographic and cultural. Third, analyses should include the imbrication or interaction between the foreign and the domestic, between national and international politics and policy.

The Configuration of World Power

The outcome of the Second World War changed the world from a multi-polar to a bipolar one, pitting 'the free world' of the USA and its allies and satellites against 'the socialist camp' of the USSR and its own allies and satellites. There was, nevertheless, one attempt to make it a tripolar world, when the 'moment of Bandung' from its founding event in 1955 to the mid-1960s, till the escalation of the Vietnam War, the polarization of Latin America between guerrillas and (military) gorillas, the failures of African independence, and the eruption of paroxysmal Maosim- presented the 'Third World' as a seeming alternative. It too, however, came to be submerged in bipolarization, from Afghanistan to Angola, from Indonesia to Chile. Since the implosion of East European communism and the invitation of Milton Friedman as a state guest to Beijing, the world has become unipolar. The military superiority of the USA has recently become overwhelming, comparable only to the strength of the Mongols on the Eurasian continent in the thirteenth century. Crushing Saddam Hussein's Iraq in 1991 cost less than 300 American lives; in 2003, it cost less than 200 lives. US power is not uncontested, but it currently has no counterweight, which is a unique situation in world history. The great ancient empires – the Chinese, the Roman, the Baghdad Caliphate, the Mongol, the Inca – were, in fact, only regional powers. The modern British Empire, even at its late nineteenth-century peak, had to contend with serious rivals in various theatres of the world: with France and Germany in Europe, with France in Africa, with Russia and, increasingly, the USA and others in Asia.

At the current international exchange rates, the US economy accounts for almost a third of the world's production, a position that even industrial Britain never achieved. Today, it is more than twice the size of the second largest national economy in the world – Japan. Only in so far as the European Union can be treated as a single economic unit, which pertains mainly to international trade, can it be considered quite the equal of the US economy.

In terms of population, the USA is not outstanding, accommodating less than 5 per cent of the world's population. The USA, however, is the only significantly rich population in the world that is (almost) reproducing itself, with a fertility rate of about two children per woman, compared with 1.5 children per woman in the EU and 1.4 in Japan. By 2015, one out of four Japanese and one out of five Germans is likely to be above 65 years of age, but in the USA the projected figure is merely one out of seven.

Recent globalization has created a world culture, above all a global popular culture that was previously much more localized as compared to elite culture. Culturally, there is also an unrivalled US supremacy, particularly in science. The USA, for example, has accounted for 59 per cent of all Nobel Laureates in science and economics from 1946 to 2000 (calculated from data provided by the Nobel Foundation in Stockholm). In the area of mass consumption, the USA sells sixty-two of the world's most valued brands, including the top five, made up in part by Coca-Cola, Microsoft and IBM (*Business Week*, 4 August 2003). In the area of popular audio-visual culture, the USA is the only global net exporter of film, experiencing only regional competition from other net exporters in India and China.

Clearly, ours is a unipolar world. US world power, however, is nested in a complex global configuration in which the Americas, Asia and Europe may be seen to form a triangle, and in which the world economy and world politics have recently become more regionalized rather than globalized.

Regionalization is most visible and measurable in terms of trade. In Western Europe (including non-members of the EU), intra-regional (merchandise) trade made up 64 per cent of all exports in 1963 and 68 per cent in 2000. Intra-regional import shares grew from 56 per cent to 65 per cent. In North America, intra-NAFTA exports rose from 28 per cent to 50 per cent, while intra-regional imports remained at their previous level. The difference is the result of a surge in Asian imports and the US import surplus. Japanese trade in the same period became more Asian oriented. Chinese trade is also primarily Asian, in spite of its large export surplus to the USA (WTO 2001: Tables II.4, II.3 and II.5, respectively). The autumn 2004 free trade agreement between ASEAN and China underlines the regional impetus of current transnational economics (Payne 2004).

In politics, the EU stands as the vanguard of regionalization, recently extending geographically into Eastern Europe and policy-wise into security and foreign policy. The EU is also influential as a pole of attraction to the rest of Eastern Europe west of Russia, and to Turkey. The flawed Ukrainian presidential election of 2004 would hardly have been annulled but for the consistent democratic demands of the EU, and Turkey would not have embarked on a policy of reining in its formidable military and police apparatus without the attraction of the EU. The EU is the first interstate organization in world history to have made stringent demands of democratic conditions on each of its potential members. While not directly adhered to anywhere else, the regional politics of the EU has become an inspiring example to other parts of the world, most explicitly to Africa and its recent African Union, but much more cautiously to the Latin American Mercosur and to ASEAN.

There is also the important *de facto* regionalized context of international politics. Africa has become a hunting ground against potential US enemies, with detachments of 'quiet Americans' dispatched to the Sahel belt from Djibouti to Mauritania. The continent has some oil and mineral resources that are of interest, although on the whole, however, the impoverished continent has lost its geopolitical significance with the end of the Cold War. A languishing economy and, more so, the continuing misgovernment of Nigeria, are hampering South African efforts at regional leadership and a global voice. In a similar vein, Australia – for all its dogged loyalty to imperial wars overseas, from Gallipoli to Iraq – remains no more than a small imperial outpost.

The Americas make up the home turf of the USA. The Americas are where US imperialism began in the nineteenth century with devastating wars of aggression against Indians and Mexicans. After declining in importance during the USA's twentieth-century forays overseas, the Americas have recently become more important to the USA. Half of the latter's oil imports come from the Americas, while NAFTA has become a well-integrated trade bloc, absorbing half of the total exports of the three member countries and a good one-third of their imports. In the last two decades, Hispanic mass immigration has been significantly transforming US society, and it is the population of Hispanic women who are ensuring demographic vitality by making up almost all the fertility differential between the USA and Northwest Europe.

While remaining particularly bullying and brutal against perceived impertinence in its poor and weak Central American/Caribbean backyard, US imperialism has recently had to accommodate more autonomy among its neighbours. The foreign policies of NAFTA fellows Canada and Mexico are much more autonomous of the considerations of the White House and the Pentagon than those of many European states, while Brazil is now emerging as a hemispheric counterpart. Brazil under Lula has also emerged as a driving force of a new global South. Though sectors of the upper classes are prone to gringo adulation, there exists a strong Latin American cultural identity.

Hispanic immigration has substantially reinvigorated the weak US labour movement, supplying the experience of collective action and ethnic solidarity to the class struggles of janitors, cleaners and garment workers, of southern California in particular. The immigrant electoral weight is also likely to have a restraining influence on hemispheric imperialism, with the exception of policies against Cuba, where the old counter-revolutionary Miami immigrants still have the upper hand. In the 2004 US elections, Cuban immigrants delivered Florida to Bush.

The European alternative

The origins of the USA lie in Europe, which is the USA's main partner, economic competitor and, currently, its only significant alternative in terms of global governance. The historic links between the two were powerfully reforged during the two world wars and the Cold War. Europe is the world's major trader and international investor. About 40 per cent of world exports come from Europe (WTO 2001: Tables III.1, III.3, III.5), which holds about half the world's stock in transnational investment (UNCTAD 2002: 6ff.). Europe stands tall when it comes to its economic interests, as the recurrent WTO conflicts with the USA have demonstrated. The euro, moreover, is gradually becoming an alternative international reserve currency, although its recent appreciation against the dollar has been hurting European exports.

Europe is also a pioneer of international law, part of it medieval, and part of it early modern (seventeenth century). After the Second World War, Western Europe gradually developed a unique system of binding transnational law embodied both in a European Court of Human Rights – tied to the Council of Europe – and in the powerful EU Court of Justice. From this experience – and disastrous consequences of nationalism, though also a European invention – Europe has come to be the main supporter of the International Criminal Court, in spite of mounting US attacks on it (see Therborn 2002 for a further discussion).

European transnational integration has inspired similar, though much less ambitious, efforts in other parts of the world, as we have already noted. Europe offers an alternative model of global governance to the American Empire, one that is law bound, negotiating and peaceful. The lack of military clout, which is probably irremediable in a foreseeable future, renders this an impotent alternative in the face of unrestrained violence. Europe's attempts at pushing for a peaceful settlement in Palestine have been pathetically futile, while varying internal EU interests allowed the break-up of Yugoslavia to plunge into mass violence. On the other hand, the prospect of European integration has had clearly positive effects on democracy and human rights in the rest of Eastern Europe.

In the area of domestic political economy, Europe provides the most important alternative to US capitalism. It supports a welfare state with extensive social entitlements, comprising a GNP-weighted average of a quarter of Europe's national product compared to, in the mid-1990s, one-sixth of North America's and far less than a tenth of Asia's GDP (ILO 2000). There is pressure on the European welfare states, from (especially East European) international competition and from middle-class tax discontent. Furthermore, there is also growing demand from an ageing population. So far, the tendency has been to cut some income replacement rights while expanding social services (Castles 2004: Tables 2.1, 3.4). In the fifteen countries of the EU (till May 2004), social expenditure excluding education did not quite follow GDP growth for 1996–2000 and declined from 28.4 per cent to 27 per cent of GDP, while rising in real absolute terms by 6.9 per cent (European Commission 2003: Appendix II.)

Labour rights in Europe are constitutional and effective; even where trade union membership is low, as in France and Spain, most wages are set by collective bargaining. Europe, west of the former USSR and east of the British Isles, is also the least inegalitarian region of the world, with most Gini coefficients in the 25–28 range compared to above 35 in the USA and around 50 in China currently.[1] Yet, Europe is more a model of quality of life and social justice than of economic growth. European preferences for long holidays and short working weeks do not yield impressive figures of economic growth, which is also held back by European ageing. In the main parts of the world, economic growth remains the primary socio-economic objective.

Currently, Europe is politically tilting to the Right, after the leading social democracies failed to produce anything significantly positive from their incumbency around the millennium. Protest movements, on the other hand, have become larger in recent years but have faced great difficulties in translating protests into power and policy. German Christian Democracy, once a very important part of the European social model, has signalled its attraction to neoliberalism by electing the Director of the IMF as the new President of Germany. Blair and Berlusconi managed to make the right-wing Portuguese Premier Barroso the new President of the European Commission, whereupon he immediately took the opportunity to attack any policy of detached autonomy from the USA.

While in itself a manifestation of successful European integration, the enlargement of Eastern Europe is likely to weaken Europe in the short run, dividing it economically and politically, and complicating it institutionally. Even if their populations express public social concerns as readily as their counterparts in Western Europe, the politicians produced by the post-communist polities tend to be considerably more right wing than those in the West. Through its sizeable Muslim immigration, Western Europe is being affected by the current frustration and anger among those in the Muslim world.

The second Iraq War was very unpopular all over Europe, except in Britain and Poland, where about half the respective populations supported the war – until it became clear that there were no 'weapons of mass destruction', and that the occupation was widely resisted. 'Pre-emptive war' is morally repugnant to most people in post-war Europe; only in Britain, France and Poland does there still exist any significant nationalist military pride. Nevertheless, the external pressure on and the internal instincts of most European political leaders were to follow any US lead. The unexpected resistance from Schroeder and Chirac had different backgrounds. German post-war foreign policy has been slavishly loyal to any US argument, while public opinion has become largely pacifist after 1945. In the early 1980s, for instance, the non-governmental, social democratic Friedrich Ebert Foundation could cancel a seminar on Central America, where the USA was stoking up the Contras wars, at the slightest prodding from the US ambassador. The reunified 'Berlin Republic' gave Schroeder the courage to use opposition to the war successfully as a last-ditch attempt to prevent a looming electoral defeat.

The French case is different. As a recent colonial power, France has kept and cultivated the same imperial war instincts as the British. Initially, it looked as if the French government was prepared to participate in a UN-legitimized war against Iraq, but France has always kept a certain independence from the USA, and US/NATO arrogance is widely resented among the political elite. France also wants to see itself as having a particular rapport with the Arab world, and when French leaders realized that the Bush regime wanted to attack Iraq at all costs, they were appalled.

The Euro-American alliance has been fractured by the Iraq War, and Western Europe has seen an unprecedented level of critical opinions of the USA. On the other hand, all European leaders without exception, whether from a lack of moral stamina or from fear of economic consequences, are anxious to patch up their relationship with the USA and with the recently re-elected Bush. NATO is already part of the US war in Afghanistan, and it is gradually sliding into the Iraq War as well, as 'trainers' of Iraqi collaborators. Only Britain and a few East European clients will go along with a new US war against Iran or Syria, although resistance will be restrained and a mere token gesture. There is also no European government that is prepared to take on the USA for violations of the Geneva Convention with regard to prisoners of war and torture in the concentration camps at Guantanamo and Bagram, although even Blair and the Blairites are European enough to be discreetly critical of them.

Russia is mainly a European country; even plundered and impoverished, it remains a major player in Eurasian politics and economics. For the foreseeable future, its best chance of regaining international power seems to lie in forging an alliance with China, to which end some small steps are being taken. Yet, its imbroglio in Chechnya is inclining it in a US–Israeli direction vis-à-vis the house of Islam.

The five Asias

Asia is plural, and too large and heterogeneous to be treated as a single unit. There are at least five Asias: West, Central, South, Southeast and Northeast. West Asia is the prime conflict area in today's world, generated by an explosive combination of factors. The region is an old geopolitical hinge between Europe and Asia, with Turkey now trying to move into Europe, and sits on the world's largest known oil deposits. It is the birthplace of three militant religions that, contrary to conventional modernization theory, have recently become more, and not less, significant: Judaism, Christianity and Islam. At the centre of the conflict is the most recent colonial settler state, Israel, which for all its efforts has not managed to kill off or expel most of the natives living within its borders. Unconditional US support and subsidies have made Israel the most aggressive state in the world. A lavish oil rent and the militarized environment have strangled democratic popular politics and stifled the development of a productive economy in the Arab part of the region. This and the charged meaning of being at the centre of the Islamic world have made violent jihad a meaningful option for despairing and angry young Arab men.

To the USA, the region is important both strategically and ideologically: strategically, for the geopolitics of Eurasia and for control of – rather than a great dependence on – the oil that flows there; ideologically, the region is important for both Christian and Jewish religious reasons. A particularly heavy brew is the recent confluence of fundamentalist Christian Protestants and the most right wing of the US Jewish community, which regarded the embryonic Oslo land-for-peace compromise a betrayal of the Jewish claim to all of Palestine. This confluence provided the ideological avant-garde for the latest war on Iraq and it will be an important factor in any plans for future US wars in the region apparently planning for the next US wars in the region, against Iran and/or Syria, although continuing Iraqi insurgency is probably somewhat putting a damper on the administration's immediate enthusiasm for more wars.

Central Asia, so called, is not central but peripheral and economically negligible, at least until the full exploitation of recent oil and gas discoveries. Demographically, it is even more insignificant, with an off-centre position in contemporary geopolitics. Its historical–cultural roots are common to the Turkey and Iran of contemporary West Asia, but it has also been much affected by seventy years of Soviet rule of most parts of it and previous Russian influence. Through the contingency of the 1978 Revolution and the ensuing civil war, Afghanistan became to the Islamic Right what Spain had been to the Euro-American Left of the 1930s. The crucial difference is that the International Brigades and the domestic Left lost, whereas bin Laden and others won with the help of Saudi money, US weapons and the Pakistani secret services. From Afghanistan, the international jihadists then wreaked havoc on large parts of the world, from Chechnya to Algeria, before – and with true historical irony – taking on their former patrons in the Pentagon. The Americans have since transferred their support from the Islamists to secular right-wing authoritarian forces in Central Asia.

South Asia also remains economically marginal, responsible for only about 1 per cent of world merchandise export and 2 per cent of world production. It is, however, destined to become the world's most populous region in the near future, and South Asian economies have entered a fast lane of growth. The region's special niche of outsourced call centres, back-office electronic services and software development may give this economically expanding demography a particular edge. Socially and politi-cally, South Asia is the Asian region that is most similar to – or least different from – Europe and the Americas as a result of Indian class politics and social movements, command of the English language and well-developed experience in multilingual and multicultural communication. The January 2004 Mumbai Social Forum was, thus, a huge success, surpassing the largely monolingual and Latin regional Porto Alegre.

Yet, South Asia is also the world's largest poorhouse. It houses half the planet's 1 billion people living in abject poverty, and the largest number of undernourished children. In spite of its comparatively larger GDP per capita, India is in these respects worse off than Pakistan, but in a somewhat better position than Bangladesh (World Bank 2003: Table 2; UNDP 2003:199). On the other hand, as the 2004 election showed, complex Indian democracy keeps reminding politicians of pertinent social issues, even during periods of national economic growth and advances in foreign policy.

Musharraf's turning around of Pakistani foreign policy – from spon-soring the Taliban to aligning with the USA – has increased domestic tensions and violent conflicts, whereas the US-brokered rapprochement with India is a rare positive effect of the Bush government's policies that is bene-fiting both Pakistan and India. For the foreseeable future, however, South Asia will remain fundamentally divided. India's best chance of international significance, beyond being a destination for Euro-American outsourcing, lies in an Eastern turn towards ASEAN – a strategy China has already taken advantage of. Pakistan, on the other hand, has less to gain from becoming a paid policeman of the USA and more from developing into a modern Muslim country with linkages to West Asia and the Muslim Southeast.

Northeast Asia is the economic hub of Asia, and will probably become the economic centre of the world by the second half of the twenty-first century. Pursuing their own very specific blend of policies and networks, China and Northeast Asia, despite Japanese stagnation, have been the unex-pected winners of world economic development under the global auspices of neoliberal globalization. The not so distant days when ordinary Americans feared and some scholars were fascinated by 'Japan as No. 1' are rapidly being forgotten. There is now a broad consensus that China is fast becoming an economic world power. It overtook the USA in 2002–3 as the largest receiver of foreign investments (*Financial Times*, 23 September 2002; UNCTAD 2004: Ch.1). Only the USA, Japan and Germany have surpassed

China in export volume and overall economy (WTO 2004: Ch. 1). In terms of population, China is more than four times larger than the USA.

It might be true that China is still a country experiencing much poverty, and it has probably become the most unequal country in Asia, with a Gini coefficient of around 50, that is of Latin American proportions. In 2003, despite an economic growth rate of 9 per cent, the number of people living in abject misery actually increased from 28 to 29 million (Professor Li Qiang of Tsinghua University, personal communication, July 2004). The post-Maoist end to free primary education and health care is taking its toll on the rural poor. Nevertheless, the rest of the world has to recognize the colossal resurrection of China.

Regionalization of trade, investment and pop culture has not erased the deep political suspicion and irritation among Northeast Asian countries – between China and Japan, and between Korea and its two big neighbours. Successful US enlistment of Japan and South Korea into the occupation of Iraq is exacerbating friction with China. Japanese Premier Koizumi's continuing visits to the Yasakuni war shrine and closer military alignment with the USA appear to be long-term geopolitical errors, and are unlikely to do any good to Japanese capitalism. Growing Chinese power is likely to be mounted regionally rather than globally, in Southeast as well as Northeast Asia, and probably also in Central Asia. Continuing Japanese and South Korean subservience to the USA is likely to be costly, although accommodating the rising China is unlikely to be free of charge. Whether or not the Chinese will be wiser than were Japanese bullies in an earlier era remains to be seen, but anti-Chinese rioting or discrimination in Southeast Asian countries will certainly become dangerous.

Southeast Asia is, in some sense, the middle of Asia. Unlike 'Central Asia' or the 'Middle Kingdom', Southeast Asia is at the crossroads of cultures and religions with crucial inputs of Malay custom and Buddhism – which then produces a cultural mix that softens the stern patriarchies of West Asian Islam, South Asian Hinduism and East Asian Confucianism (see Therborn 2004: 123ff.). The revitalization of Islam is underlining this wide-ranging encounter on Malay soil, from Western Islam via South Asian cultures to Sinic civilization from the East. Politically, however, from its domestic politics to the setting up of ASEAN, the region is an ageing veteran of the Cold War despite some significant steps towards regional reconciliation, such as allowing the entry of Vietnam into ASEAN. A post-Cold-War integration of countries – ranging from the contentious democracy of the Philippines to the reclusive military junta of Myanmar and the Communist Party of Vietnam, together with managed, 'guided' or fragile and little institutionalized democracies in between – is no easy task. Yet it should be noted that all the governments of the region, even those of Thailand and the Philippines, have been very cautious in their reactions to recent US pressure, in distinguishing co-operation against terrorism from an all-out US war. With the surging of China, the rise of India and the uncertain recovery of the Indonesian economy, the economic future of the region seems to have many question marks.

Hopefully, this overview, brief and perhaps crude, has at least made clear that exercising world power and world hegemony is a complicated affair; it does not follow directly from the number of missiles one has or the size of one's wallet.

Occidental despotism and the nested politics of nations and the world

From the perspective of global governance, the world pursued by the Bushmen currently governing the USA may be summed up as 'Occidental despotism'. Perhaps 'enlightened' in intentions and certainly in rhetoric, but aiming at governing the world first of all through force and violence, unbound by any law or convention. The USA is unbound by the UN Charter against wars of aggression; in fact, it openly proclaims a doctrine of pre-emptive war, embroidered by the liberal *New York Times* editorialist Thomas Friedman into an ideology of war à la carte or 'wars of choice'. Thus, the USA is unfettered by international conventions on the treatment of prisoners of war and on torture; the US President–Commander-in-Chief is accountable only to himself. Unconcerned with the lives and properties of non-US civilians, who do not participate in US elections, the power grants US agents complete immunity from legal processes instigated by non-US victims.

These days, this lawless violence has even got its symbols: Guantanamo, Bagram and Abu Ghraib, and the explicit strategic goal of 'shock and awe'. The violence is actually deeply ingrained in mainstream US historical tradition, from the original combination of freedom and slavery by the 'Founding Fathers', to Jacksonian democracy and genocidal Indian wars. Also, the (American) West was won by violence, homestead settlers and large railway capital. The roles of gunmen, robbers and policemen were interchangeable, as embodied, among others, by the celebrated Western hero, Wyatt Earp. The experience of the Indian wars continued into the conquest of the Philippines, with the commanding order being 'I wish you to kill and burn' and to take no prisoners (Brigadier-General Jacob H. Smith to his troops, quoted by Ferguson 2004a: 49–50).

An intrinsic part of the story of modern Occidental despotism is that it is based on liberal democracy. Violence and brutality always run the risk of public exposure and public outrage; their contradiction of liberal tenets of freedom and democracy may be held up against them and their perpetrators, whose leaders are subjected to regular electoral challenges. The USA is a country in which it is difficult to keep state secrets hidden for very long. On the contrary, since the USA was constituted and developed through a peculiar and unique combination of freedom and slavery, of democracy and genocide, of courts and lynching parties, public outrage has never been able to settle the issue. Only sharp media scrutiny could, for a while at least, capture democratic attention.

The Iraqi children who were killed by a combination of the US/UN blockade and an inept and brutally careless regime have never entered into liberal opinion in the USA, neither have the tens of thousands of Iraqis killed in the current US/UK war nor, for that matter, the innumerable deaths in Russia after the reintroduction of capitalism (from 1992 to 1993, the reintroduction of capitalism and its concomitant social stresses caused an increase in Russian deaths by 526,000 persons; for sources and calculations, see Therborn 1995: 169). The combination of liberalism and deadly violence recurs, and liberal Democrats Woodrow Wilson, John Kennedy and Lyndon Johnson have been at least on par with right-wing Republicans Richard Nixon, Ronald Reagan and Baby Bush in their 'achievements'. Jolly Bill Clinton also made war, as well as love: first, by torpedoing the Vance/Owen peace plan for Bosnia and then stirring up armed combat, before going on to introduce 'humanitarian' bombing and ethnic cleansing in Kosovo while arguing that genocide was not taking place in Rwanda.

What is new today is the de-secularization or re-religionization of international and domestic politics. This is by no means a universal phenomenon; on the contrary, it is largely confined to two separate but crucial, interconnected and mutually sustaining areas – the USA and West Asia – although there has been a spillover into South and Southeast Asia. The USA remains the only religious *and* major developed country, flanked by the rather peripheral Ireland and Poland. Over the last decades, Christianity in the USA has developed a strong fundamentalist, nationalist and aggressively capitalist current, which now forms the base of right-wing Republicanism. In 2000, and even more so in 2004, it was fundamentalist Christianity that gave the presidency to George Bush. A holy 'war against terrorism' mobilized the well-insulated and protected small-town/suburban interior of the USA. This heartland of US patriotism has never experienced war, death and destruction in any other form than the waving of the flag and a few funerals of heroes.

It is an important aspect of contemporary USA that at the beginning of the twenty-first century, it remains the only developed country governed by nineteenth-century values. It is the only country that, in 2000, saw a majority (57 per cent) saying that religion was 'very important' in their lives; this is the same proportion as in India and much less than in Indonesia, but a contrast to 33 per cent in Ireland, 13 per cent in Britain, 9 per cent in Germany and 7 per cent in Japan. Together with Australia, the USA is the only developed country in which a large majority is 'very proud' of their nation. The figure in Britain is just about half, with 40 per cent in France and 23 per cent in Japan (Inglehart *et al.* 2004: Tables A6, G6).

The traditional anti-Semitism of right-wing US Christianity has largely been overcome, and replaced by a link-up with an extreme right-wing minority Jewish current. The far right-wing civilians in the Pentagon under

Rumsfeld were, in the mid-1990s, busy advising incoming Israeli Prime Minister Netanyahu on the best ways to halt the peace process in Palestine, which had been given a chance by the Oslo Accords and for which Prime Minister Rabin was assassinated. Much of the renewed brutality of the Bush regime seems to have been inspired by the Israeli example. Prominent Jewish American lawyers like Alan Dershowitz of Harvard brought the use of torture and collective reprisals into respectable US opinion with explicit reference to Israeli policy well before Bagram and Abu Ghraib. In Israel, the so-called revisionist tradition – long a minority voice against secular, social-izing Zionism and from which came the current governing Likud Party – has always taken Israel to be a genocidal project in the broad UN sense; that is, bent on making life impossible for a Palestinian people in Palestine. Israeli defeats and the self-inflicted failures of Arab secular nationalism have correspondingly made the sword of Islam the only remaining alterna-tive in much of Muslim West Asia. Once on the warpath, the clashing fundamentalisms of Judaism, Christianity and Islam sustain one another in a spiral of violence. To fundamentalist Jews and Christians, Muslims have no right to exist, at least not in Palestine. Fundamentalist Muslims feel the same way about Jews in Palestine (a substantial minority of Palestinians are Christian, so there is no Palestinian anti-Christianity). The attractions of Europe and anti-Arab sentiments have, on the other hand, made possible the emergence of a moderately conservative Muslim democracy in Turkey. The outcome of the still unstable post-dictatorial transition in Indonesia will be crucial to the prospects of political religion and democracy in Southeast Asia.

Recent globalization has had the unexpected effect of galvanizing indige-nous peoples into action, above all in India and Latin America. It has done so by simultaneously threatening these peoples' mode of existence, through dams and other large-scale 'development' projects, and through the push of subsidized high-productivity agricultural competition from abroad while, on the other hand, providing them with new political resources, a native intelli-gentsia, Internet connection, international contact conferences and rich-world NGO money. The result has been explosive protests in many places in Central India and America, in Mexican Chiapas and in the Andean region of South America. The extent to which recent peripheral rebellions in the countries of Southeast Asia, from Myanmar to the Philippines, are part of this pattern will have to be left to area studies experts.

The scare of terrorism has made life more difficult for international migrants everywhere, perhaps more so in Asia (and Africa), where migrant workers have yet to win any significant rights. The attempts by the Clinton administration, which owed considerable campaign funds to trade unions, to link free trade and labour rights failed to elicit significant support in the South, even from progressive Third Worldist organizations. Industrial devel-opment and economic growth, however, are spawning trade unionism in East Asia, perhaps most successfully in Taiwan, and even a new labour politics as with the Democratic Labour Party of South Korea; yet, class politics remain much weaker in Asia than in Europe.

Feminist politics also seem very underdeveloped in all of Asia, with rival religious fundamentalisms hindering their development. Nevertheless, the UN Decade for Women (1975–85) and the big UN Women's Conferences from Mexico (1975) to Beijing (1995) have left a lasting impact all over the world, reinforced by the rapid expansion of higher education of women that has reached even the Islamic republic of Iran and the Gulf states. Patriarchy has, at the least, become contestable everywhere, as has, it seems, its natural offspring – sexual trafficking in women.

Limits and prospects

US imperialism produces a very special variant of empire, which may be called Occidental despotism. With regard to world domination, the empire embodies the defining characteristics of despotism: unaccountability, freedom from any binding law, arbitrariness and violence. It is 'Occidental' in that its roots are in North Atlantic liberalism, while its current base is in a liberal democracy, together with uncontrolled public opinion and an inescapable electoral cycle. Since its foundation, US imperialism has also had a remarkable lack of attraction to the routine of rules and the responsible exercise of power. It resembles its Western film heroes who never shirk a lethal gunfight and ride away alone after all the bad guys have been killed. In its terms, killing is legitimate but ruling is not.

Since the mid-1980s, the USA has been, economically, the very opposite to an imperialist country in the classical twentieth-century sense of Hobson and Lenin as it is a capital importer. It runs a large trade deficit every year and is unable to pay for its own consumption. This is a structural weakness and a serious source of danger, though not necessarily fatal since East Asian creditors have no rational interest in calling in their debts, which finance East Asian exports.

There is hardly any convincing evidence to suggest imminent US decline or that it is already on the path to decline, unless one compares the US economy today with the extraordinary moment right after the Second World War when Japan, Germany and China were prostrate, the USSR was deeply wounded by horrendous casualties, and Britain was on the verge of bankruptcy. The USA is not just the largest economy in the world by far; more than twice the size of the second largest, it also leads the world in science, technology and popular culture. It has the most vibrant demography among the major economies and, at the present time, its military superiority is overwhelming. On the whole, the USA is more powerful than ever, save perhaps for the few years between Hiroshima and the Soviet nuclear bomb. Yet, it is also less popular and more disliked than ever before. For example, among South Koreans under the age of 40 years, the USA is now regarded as the main enemy of the country (*The Economist*, 19 April 2003: 11ff.), while Bush Junior is probably the most internationally detested president in US history. For all its attractive popular culture and opulent lifestyle, the USA is not politically hegemonic in the contemporary world. It is force and fear rather than admiration and respect that sustain its power. Although the game of liberal democracy promotes debates and wider options, imperial dissent is confined to a permanent minority. Only a major defeat, like that experienced with Vietnam, will call forth any serious opposition to imperialism.

This combination of power and a lack of trust and popularity presents a powerful threat to democracy all over the world. US pressure and local elite identification with the USA generate foreign and domestic policies in many countries that run against popular values, expectations and demands. To square the circle, then, local political elites have to devise ways of circumventing public opinion and democratic participation, and to do away with fair democratic procedures. Arab allies and clients of the USA have been doing this for a long time. The practice is now spreading, although it may occasionally backfire, as in the case of Spain.

China may soon become the world's largest economy and, by then, probably have the world's second largest population, but its lack of a culture of universalist ambition is more likely to make it the planet's main regional champion than a world hegemon. East Asia may return to what it had been for a millennium – a China-centred civilization.

Europe has long been the world's foremost trader and its leading lawyer. It is likely to continue in this role, but with a diminishing capital of past power and a fading demography. Hemispheric migration may, short of drastic US measures of closure, embed the US culturally and commercially in a multicultural US continent with a strong Hispanic–American, and correspondingly weaker Euro-American, accent.

The intercontinental triangle of power under US domination is held together by the USA, Britain and Japan, and two of these anchors are rather frail. As De Gaulle once said, Britain is an island, and it is not Europe. Britain is likely to keep on following the USA like a jolly boat after a big yacht, but not as a representative of Europe. Sooner rather than later, Japan will be overtaken by China in most respects, if not in wealth and age per capita. Sino-American relations will be at the centre of world politics and economics, with Europe acting as a significant economic bloc and a possible social model of some attraction. Impoverished and demographically declining but resource-rich Russia is historically a European country, but its best chance for the future probably is to use its Eurasian location for a 'special relationship' with China. Another triangle might emerge to challenge at least the weaker parts of the present one, one made up of Brazil, Africa (if South Africa and Nigeria can put their houses together) and India; this may play the USA, China and Europe as an alternative card. World politics not only are complicated but also offer plausible complex scenarios of the future.

Southeast Asia may have to develop its character as a multicultural cross-roads of Asia in order to find its best position in a world that is likely to become less unipolar and more triangular or, hopefully, even quadrangular if Africa gets its act together. The region's unique cultural strength lies in its natural cultural ties to all the other parts of Asia. In spite of the Arabian location of Mecca and the Kaaba, it is probable that the weight of Islamic culture will gradually tilt to the east, to Southeast and South Asia, with economic–cultural developments adding to their demographic weight. A vigorous reconstruction of ancient links with India is in the geopolitical interests of both sides. The future of democracy in the region is likely to depend largely on if and how countries will finally be able to overcome the authoritarian rigidities and manipulative clientelism of the bygone Cold War era.

However important US weapons of mass destruction are, the future of world society is most likely to be centred in Asia. Since neither Sinic nor Indic civilization have the missionary zeal of Euro-American Christianity (or of West Asian Islam), this Asian centrality is unlikely to be world domineering; instead, it will care less about, or become more tolerant of, other cultures and political systems. Half a millennium of European and, lately, Euro-American world domination will draw to a close, hopefully with a whimper rather than a bang.

Notes

1 The best comparative data on national income distributions are produced by the Luxemburg Income Study, which covers most of Europe, North America, Australia and Taiwan (www.lisproject.org/keyfigures). The Chinese figure derives from Professor Li Qiang at the Sociology Department of Tsinghua University, Beijing, personal communication, July 2004.

2 Beyond new imperialism

State and transnational regulatory governance in East Asia

Kanishka Jayasuriya

Introduction: towards a new transnational regulatory governance

The last decade in East Asia has been characterized by two key pivotal moments. One is a neoliberal moment that unravelled the policies, coalitions and state structures that underpinned the Asian economic miracle; the other is the post-9/11 War on Terror that led to a much more assertive and coercive role for the USA in East Asia. In each of these moments, of course, the role of the USA has been of central importance in pushing for more neoliberal economic reform and in seeking to reconfigure regional relations under the rubric of September 11. Most explanations of the role of the USA in East Asia are, however, resolutely focused on a 'realist' understanding of this relationship between the USA and East Asia. It is this realist 'state-centric' view of the USA in East Asia that can be framed either, in benevolent terms, as the country's exercise of a balancing and a restraining influence on an otherwise potentially dangerous region, or, more in terms of dependency, as the unequal relationship between a state with a preponderant economic and military capability and more marginal and peripheral states. In contrast to this 'outside-in' perspective, I argue in this chapter that we need to adopt an 'inside-out' analysis that focuses on the way the structures and modalities of governance are exercised within the state rather than on how they are imposed from the outside. In this context, I argue that the relationship between the USA and East Asia be analysed in terms of a new space of regulatory governance that – and this is really the nub of the argument – domesticates US influence within the very structures of East Asian states.

This inside-out approach needs to be clearly distinguished from those which suggest that recent US foreign policy marks a shift from a so-called 'benevolent' hegemony, typified by its posture in the post-war period, to a more militaristic and coercive stance. For Perry Anderson (2002), the end of the Cold War and the advance of economic globalization changed the equilibrium between the force and consent that drove US policy in the period after the Second World War. Instead, in the aftermath of the Cold War, the balance tilted towards a more coercive hegemony, as:

with the erasure of the USSR, there was no longer any countervailing force capable of withstanding US military might. The days when it could be checkmated in Vietnam, or suffer proxy defeat in Southern Africa were over. These interrelated changes were eventually bound to alter the role of the United States in the World. The chemical formula of power was in solution.

(Anderson 2002: 7)

This is not an isolated example. The recently fashionable terms of 'empire' or 'new imperialism' are replete with the assumption that hegemony is, in some sense, exercised in direct fashion over a subordinate state (Ignatieff 2003; Harvey 2003a).[1] The problem with this line of reasoning is that it elides the significant transformation in the nature of the state as well as the broader global environment in which it operates. Most accounts of hegemony seem to have missed the decisive way in which recent changes in the global order reflect a far deeper mutation in the modes and mechanisms of political rule that are embodied in the arrangement of transnational regulatory governance. In fact, as Woods (2003) has persuasively argued, the USA in the post-war period has mostly exercised control through indirect rather than direct means. As Woods notes:

a distinctive and essential characteristic of capitalist imperialism [is] that its economic reach far exceeds its direct political and military grasp. It can only rely on the economic imperatives of 'the market' to do much of its imperial work. This sharply differentiates it from earlier forms of economic imperialism, which depended directly on such extra economic powers – whether territorial empires which could reach only as far as the capacity of their direct coercive powers to impose their rule, or commercial empires whose advantage depended on domination of the seas or other trade routes.

(Woods 2003: 153)

Persuasive as Woods is in emphasizing the fact that the state is as crucial as ever in ensuring the maintenance and stability of markets, her account leaves out the way in which the state is being transformed through the operation of global economic imperatives. It is this transformation that we have tried to grasp through the notion of transnational regulatory governance. Further, it is this transnational regulatory governance – and here I part company with writers such as Woods (2003) and Harvey (2003a) – that has enmeshed all the major capitalist economies in a manner that Kautsky (1970) described as 'ultra imperialism'. Ultra imperialism refers to what Kautsky thought to be the deepening engagement among core capitalist countries, an engagement driven by the imperatives of global as opposed to national capitalism. Tempting as it may be in the aftermath of 9/11 to resuscitate various notions of hegemony or new imperialism, the fact remains that these notions of hegemony or new imperialism are trapped within the Westphalian framework. In contrast, my argument is that the intensification of global capitalism creates the conditions for the emergence of new webs of regulatory governance, which link capitalist states together in what may be called a globalized form of ultra imperialism.

The idea of globality[2] proposed by Shaw (2000) is useful in this context. Shaw suggests that globality may be found 'in the dominance of a single set of new norms and institutions, which more or less governs the various state centres'. In turn, Shaw's notion of globality bears resemblance to the early work of Keohane and Nye (1977) on complex interdependence, and presents a very different perspective to Kautsky's (1970) notion of ultra imperialism. Working within a similar transnational state framework, Robinson (2004) has used the notion of transnational state apparatus, which is defined as 'an emerging network that comprises transformed and externally integrated national states, *together with* the supranational economic and political forums, and has not yet acquired any centralised institutional form' (Robinson 2004: 88). Supplementing Robinson's claim for a transnational state is the claim that economic globalization has produced a new transnational capitalist class whose political counterpart is the emergence of a new transnational state apparatus. Rather than construing this entity as a new form of globality or as a transnational state apparatus, however, it is much more useful to see the emergence of this new ultra imperialism as the creation of often multiple regulatory spaces that cut across the boundaries of the national and the transnational.[3] This chapter is a first cut at seeking to situate the role of East Asia within this broader framework of transnational regulatory governance.

The argument then is that it is the constitution of these new regulatory spaces, rather than the role of the USA, that defines the post-Cold-War order. Of course, this is not to suggest that there is some kind of supranational state that supplants the role of the national state apparatus, but rather that the national *state itself becomes the site* of transnational governance. This allows us to move beyond the somewhat sterile debate between multilateralism and unipolarity. What this debate overlooks, I think, is the fact that recent changes in the global order have reconstituted systems of internal governance. While unipolarity suggests a reinforced hegemony within the international system, it obscures the more important reality – that new and innovative forms of governance are being constituted to manage the global economic and political order.

What this compels us to examine is not so much the role of empire but the ways in which different forms of political rule are instantiated within the state apparatus. These new forms of political rule transform the state in a way that ruptures those notions of Westphalian statehood that have been central to international relations theory. Payne, in writing about US–Caribbean relations, makes the more general point that:

The symbolic rhetoric and behaviour of state to state world still goes on, and is certainly not yet irrelevant, but it does not catch the essence of the contemporary US–Caribbean and transgovernmental policy communities (here, using Keohane and Nye's language) in with different actors within the US state/society complex and within the various Caribbean state/society complexes (here using Cox's language) engage each other in different policy arenas where there are no automatic priorities.

(Payne 2000: 82)

What Payne well points out here is the fact that it is not state-to-state relations that matter, but the way that new spaces of governance are being constituted, through which new forms of political rule are being exercised.

From this inside-out perspective, Panitch (2000) in his excellent paper – building on the earlier work of Poulantzas (1978a; 1978b) – has recognized that the crucial point is that the dynamics of imperialism need to be approached through the internal byways of the capitalist state rather than the superhighway of US hegemony.[4] As this indicates, what really marks out the notion of transnational regulatory governance is the fact that the compulsive pressure of economic globalization, or indeed militarization, is located not outside the state but within its internal structures. Most proponents of new imperialism or renewed hegemony adopt an outside-in approach to globalization, where the compulsive pressures of globalization are located outside the state. Instead, I argue in this chapter that these pressures of globalization are located within the institutions of the state itself. This was, of course, a point that was central to Poulantzas's (1978a; 1978b) analysis of the state nearly three decades ago. He argues that international functions of the state are no longer simply added on to the state but are the 'expressions of their internalised transformations' (Poulantzas 1978a: 82). Panitch,[5] in contrast, argues that:

> the 'regime' theories dominant in the field of international relations are manifestly unhelpful in understanding this development, misrepresenting as cooperative understandings what were in reality structural manifestations of a hierarchically organized international political economy.
>
> (Panitch 2002: 13)

This really is the core of my argument: the internal transformation of the state and the consequent interlocking web of regulatory governance within advanced capitalist countries together make up the most distinctive property of the new transnational regulatory governance.

This regulatory framework allows us to transcend the very distinction between the 'external' and the 'internal' that so defines the realist understating of global political economy of a realist bent, be it in the form of new hegemony or a new imperialism. Adopting such an approach has a two-fold advantage. First, it views the process of neoliberalism as a political rather than an economic process, and this enables us to see neoliberalism as a constantly moving set of political projects within the state. Second, it brings back, as Panitch (2000) well argues, the state as the central site through which new programmes of governance are being implemented and resisted. Panitch and Gindin (2004) note that:

> these contradictions and conflicts are located not so much in the relationship between the advanced capitalist states as within these states, as they try to manage their internal processes of accumulation, legitimation and class struggle. This is no less true of the American state as it tries to manage and cope with complexities of neo-imperial globalisation.
>
> (Panitch and Gindin 2004: 24)

It needs to be pointed out that there is often conflict and resistance to these new governance arrangements, reflected in conflicts within the state.

The emergence of this transnational regulatory governance signals a dramatic change from Westphalian models of sovereignty. What we have, instead, is the embryonic form of a set of transnational state structures that cut across traditionally defined national boundaries thereby creating, in effect, a new post-Westphalian state and international order. There is no single sovereign centre within the global order, and neither can the global order be reducible to our usual Westphalian order of a multiple and pluralist sovereign centre within the global order. It is sovereignty itself that is being rapidly reconfigured in the direction of what I call 'complex sovereignty'. Indeed, Hardt and Negri (2000), in their much discussed book on empire, make this a central focus of their analysis, but the almost mystical nature of what they assume to be a new decentralized sovereignty obscures the transformation not just in the regulation of the global economic order but in its increasingly coercive nature, which Higgott (2003a) calls the 'securitisation of globalisation'.

East Asia and the spaces of transnational regulatory governance

The new transnational regulatory governance

The advantage of this analysis is in situating USA–East Asia relations within a broader framework of regulatory space that understands that neoliberalism is not just a set of economic practices or policies but a political project that seeks to reshape the internal architecture of the state. It is the internal transformation of the state, not the relationship between states and the US hegemony or empire, that lies at the core of the new transnational regulatory governance and the emerging global order. It is undeniable that the political frame of transnational regulatory governance must be broad and flexible enough to encompass different political projects within this transnational entity. Nevertheless, it does enable us to explore how emerging global capitalism can be framed in terms of these new transnational political structures, which are beyond the conventional boundaries of the national and the international.

Breslin, in an analysis of China and the new global political economy, notes the emergence of a group of globalized bureaucrats, pointing out that:

> This group, epitomised by the policies of Zhu Rongji, is engaged in a process of making the investment regime within China more and more liberalised and 'attractive' to international capital, and reforming the domestic economic structure to reduce domestic protectionism, and institute a more neo-liberal economic paradigm.
>
> (Breslin: 2002: 25)

It is these 'globalizing bureaucrats' that play a key role in the management of new systems of transnational regulatory governance. Hence, it is the enrolment of these state actors in regulatory governance, the modes of governance within these new regulatory practices, and the unequal relationship among various sets of globalizing bureaucrats that define the manner in which the new regulatory state is incorporated into the global order. One of the main changes after September 11 is the emergence of new, more security-oriented globalizing bureaucrats who exert much more influence at both the national and transnational levels of governance.

For example, in the growing area of military and security co-operation, we see not only merely close interstate collaboration, but also a more profound process of the incorporation of these state actors within a new security-oriented transnational regulatory governance. These new spaces of transnational regulatory governance increasingly encompass security and military co-operation. For example, Ganesan (2004) argues:

> The U.S. has extended the participation of its annual bilateral military exercise with Thailand, Cobra Gold, to include 'friendly' regional countries like Malaysia, the Philippines and Singapore. Finally, Thaksin, in contrast to his predecessors, has opened the former U.S. airbase in U Tapao and naval base in Sattahip to allow for the stationing of military hardware and munitions for forward deployment and operations and the U.S., in a seemingly reciprocal gesture, has granted Thailand 'Non-NATO' ally status.
>
> (Ganesan 2004: 36–7)

Granting Thailand the status of major non-NATO ally is more than a symbolic pat on the back for a loyal soldier in the War on Terror; rather, it serves to enmesh Thailand in a complex security web across Southeast Asia that now imperially weaves itself through US allies such as Australia, Singapore and the Philippines.

At the same time, these new 'globalizing bureaucrats', to use Breslin's terms, form a larger pattern of network governance that brings together various globalizing actors, especially at the regional level. These networks now underpin the creation of various regional regulatory frameworks. This process has been extensively documented in the EU; a similar dynamic that is discernible in the evolving process of regionalization in East Asia is the mesh between emerging regulatory states and new patterns of regional governance. A crucial dimension of this regional governance is the way it manages to locate the *regional* within the *domestic*. This new form of regulatory region-alism reflects the recognition that region-wide regulatory frameworks, such as monetary co-ordination and macroeconomic policies, can be implemented and policed at a local level (Jayasuriya 2004). One nascent illustration of the emergence of this system of regional multi-level regulation is the ASEAN regional surveillance process (ASP), which was endorsed by ASEAN finan-cial ministers in December 1998 (Manupipatpong 2002). What is clearly discernible with this ASP process is that it links national and international regulatory governance through the internationalization of various state agencies and actors. From this perspective, the regulatory state is not a state form that is confined to the territorial boundaries of the national state. Rather, it should be seen as a system of multi-level governance that connects international organizations, such as the IMF, with regional entities such as the Asian Development Bank (ADB) and various national, sub-national and local entities.

Methods and modalities of regulatory governance

The emergence of these new spaces of transnational regulatory governance permits the articulation of new methods and modalities of governance. It is within this context that we need to locate the recent emergence of the so-called new bilateralism. Perhaps the most interesting development of these new regulatory mechanisms has been through what has been termed the new bilateralism: that is, the increasing propensity of governments to enter into preferential trading agreements on a bilateral rather than a multilateral or regional basis. In fact, bilateralism is 'arguably the most dramatic develop-ment in intergovernmental relations in the western Pacific since the financial crises of 1997–98' (Ravenhill 2004: 61).

There are three important dimensions to this new bilateralism. First and most important, a bilateral arrangement is much more than a set of agree-ments about trade; it involves fundamental changes in the internal governance within the state. For example, it may involve requirements on corporate transparency that necessitate significant changes in national regimes of corporate governance. Similarly, most trade agreements with less developed countries place a stronger emphasis on the imposition of market disciplines than on trade liberalization itself (Phillips 2004). Therefore, these bilateral agreements should be seen as part of a broader regulatory project that reshapes the state by imposing economic disciplines.

Second, the shift towards bilateralism permits what may be called those 'pivotal states' at the centre of the regional geopolitical economy to establish deeper integration among themselves and be entrenched in the broader strategies of transnational governance. Within Southeast Asia, Singapore clearly performs such a role. It has FTA agreements with Australia, Japan, New Zealand and the USA, and also has a number of other agreements in active negotiation (Dent 2004). In this case, we see how Singapore becomes a bilateral hub through which the new bilateralism reconfigures the regional order. Yet another example of this process of deep integration is the emerging Singapore–Thailand economic and political partnership that has been formalized as the Singapore–Thailand Enhanced Economic Relationship (STEER) framework. As Dent notes:

> This is institutionally anchored in the STEER framework, first announced in February 2002 and formally established by an inaugural summit convened in August 2003. At this meeting, Singapore and Thailand announced their intention to create a bilateral foundation for greater economic integration within the ASEAN based on a 'one economy, two countries'.
>
> (Dent 2004: 7–8)

STEER itself is part of a broader partnership between Thailand and Singapore. Once again, the point is that these framework agreements are not so much about trade liberalization as they are about the increasing integration of these states through such bilateral agreements, with the broader framework of transnational governance. There is also, within this framework, a strong geopolitical element: both Thailand and Singapore have close security links with the USA and have been crucial to the so-called War on Terror. It is these geopolitical hubs that are crucial in the emerging system of transnational regulatory governance. True enough, the USA is weaving a complex hub-and-spoke architecture within the region that is strongly reminiscent of Cold War strategies; yet, at the same time, this hub-and-spoke arrangement depends to a great extent on the creation of 'regional nodes' such as Singapore, which are used to integrate other states in the region to new regulatory forms of governance.

Finally, one of the hidden aspects of bilateralism is the fact that it allows for the negotiation of the complex interests of domestic capital within the global political economy. As we move from an international to a global economy, it becomes impossible to counterpoise the interests of domestic capital to foreign capital. Domestic capital itself is fractured and connected to the global economy and global capital. From this perspective, it is impossible to draw a simplistic typology of protectionist and internationalist interest within the capitalist class because capital (both foreign and domestic) has contradictory and mixed interests in various foreign economic policies. More to the point, these contradictory interests are played out within the state, and bilateralism provides a means of accommodating this complex play of interests. Again, at the heart of this new transnational regulatory governance is the fact that the tensions and contradictions of global capitalism are mirrored in conflicts inside the state as foreign economic policy is effectively nationalized. Ravenhill notes that one of the major reasons for FTAs within the Asia–Pacific has been due to the fact that the:

> increased interest of business groups in preferential trade agreements was stimulated by the growth of such arrangements elsewhere and the start of schedules for their implementation. Domestic business interests found themselves disadvantaged in markets where their competitors enjoyed preferential access.
>
> (Ravenhill 2004: 65)

At the same time, the wide range of exclusions allowed by the FTA has enabled sections of domestic capital to protect certain key interests. The point, then, is that global economy means that the 'concept of the domestic bourgeoisie is related to the process of internationalization, and does not refer to a bourgeoisie "enclosed" within a "national" space' (Poulantzas 1978a: 74). It is this complex interplay between domestic and foreign capital that is accommodated in the growth of the new bilateralism. Perhaps the most interesting dimension of this new bilateralism is the means through which it provides for management and imposition of the economic disciplines within the new framework of transnational regulatory governance.

Understood in this light, bilateralism can be viewed as evidence of the emergence of a new space of transnational regulatory space. In this sense, bilateralism is not really about the decline of the multilateral trading as it is about the constitution of a new space of regulatory governance that is located within the domestic state apparatus. For the USA, this provides an effective and flexible means of managing regional economic issues within an increasingly complex global capitalism.

What the analysis starkly demonstrates is that neoliberalism is not merely a set of economic prescriptions but a political project that seeks to transform the internal governance of the state. More importantly, such an approach allows us to move beyond the somewhat sterile debate between multilateralism and unilateralism. What this debate on unilateralism overlooks, I think, is the fact that recent changes in the global order are manifest in the transformation and reconstitution of the state within new forms of internal governance.

While unilateralism or unipolarity suggests a reinforced hegemony within the international system, it obscures the more important reality that new and innovative forms of governance are being constituted to manage the global economic and political order. Unipolarity or new imperialism remains stuck within the outdated categories of Westphalian statehood. For example, to the extent that multilateralism at both levels – regional and national – was chiefly concerned with trade liberalization in the area of foreign economic policy, it is now clear that this trade liberalization agenda has run out of steam. Indeed, the pressing issues in the global economic environment are not so much trade liberalization between 'national economic entities' as they are about the imposition of new forms of regulatory governance within the state. This regional governance is distinguished by an emphasis on the development of policy co-ordination and harmonization. This is a form of regulatory governance that should not be viewed as a departure from the disciplines of the global economy, but as an attempt to instantiate the disciplines of neoliberalism within the broader ensemble of regional governance.

Governing the new transnational regulatory space: an authoritarian governance?

To what extent is the militarization of the global order since the events of 9/11 a continuation of the regulatory governance that has advanced since the 1990s; or is it something qualitatively different? Indeed, some writers have suggested that the events of 9/11 reflect a move away from the dominant themes of economic globalization towards more security-oriented issues. In an incisive argument, Lipschutz (2002) has suggested that this reorientation is from what he calls 'disciplinary neo-liberalism' to one based much more on the military might of the USA. There is no doubt that this is a powerful argument that delineates the way in which the regulation of the global order has shifted from a predominately 'soft', decentralized and diffused system of regulation to a more military-dominated, US-based order. Indeed, Higgott has advanced a parallel argument that economic globalization 'is now seen not simply in neo-liberal economic terms, but also through the lenses of the national security agenda of the United States' (Higgott 2003a: 5). Arguing along these lines, he suggests that US foreign economic policy is becoming increasingly securitized, and that this marks a significant change from the US foreign economic policy of the 1990s, which sought to subordinate security to economic concerns. In effect, the greater militarization of the global economy in the aftermath of the War on Terror constrains the unbridled economic globalization of the 1990s. Hence:

> policies geared to towards controlling globalization, unlike in the more laissez faire period of the last decades of the 20th century when the market alone was meant to drive it, have a much stronger place in US policy under the Bush Administration.
>
> (Higgott 2003a: 20)

In the early decades of the twenty-first century, both Lipschutz and Higgott seem to suggest that economic globalization will be subordinated to an increasingly securitized global agenda.

While these arguments are persuasive in terms of the changed dynamics of economic globalization in the post-9/11 era, we need to be careful in making the distinction between the securitization of globalization and the state of exception; the political shell and economics of this new global order are still tethered to a form of economic globalization. Securitization of the global political order and a system of economic constitutionalism are not mutually exclusive. It is more useful to see the unfolding of the process of neoliberal globalization as having given rise to a variegated series of governance projects in the last decade and a half. These have sought to recalibrate the engine of post-war multilateralism – the 'UN Republic', in Lipschutz's terms. In the 1990s, this system of economic constitutionalism, as Lipschutz and Higgott observe, was configured to a decentralized system of multilateralism that is now being replaced by a more coercive US-based system of global governance. The events of 9/11, however, gave way not only to a new governance project but to one that sought to establish the foundations of a new global constitutional order; this is not just a recalibration, but a reconstitution of the post-war engine of international liberalism. Therefore, what is significant about the post-9/11 economic order is the fact that economic constitutionalism is contained within a political core that operates outside of the normal process of international legality. As Steinmetz (2003) aptly comments, global economic openness remains central to US foreign policy objectives, but economic constitutionalism now functions within the more authoritarian frame of a global state of exception. None of this should be surprising, however, as the experience of capitalist industrialization in East Asia and elsewhere has shown that markets are compatible with a diverse array of political forms. Likewise, global capitalism is compatible with a diverse array of political forms, and the events of 9/11 signal a shift towards a more authoritarian political form. What is central to both the economic and more security-oriented regulatory project is not the shift towards a more coercive policy by the USA, but the increasing transnationalization of regulatory governance.

In fact, rather than counterpoising economic to military globalization, the new transnational regulatory governance reorganizes the spaces of the global polity into zones of normality or exception, or it creates different spaces of regulatory governance. In other words, to use Ong's (2002) rather revealing terminology, it suggests a 'new spatiality' that points to anthropological texturing of spaces of order and disorder. In an earlier analysis of sovereignty, Ong (1999) – with her notion of 'graduated sovereignty' – presents a perspective on the transformation of sovereignty. Graduated sovereignty, which has broader applicability than the Southeast Asian focus of study, refers to the way in which 'the state flexibly manages different population segments located in various zones of sovereignty, or a system of graduated sovereignty that is superimposed on the conventional arrangements of national states in Southeast Asia' (Ong 1999: 224).

One of the main effects of this new sovereignty is the development of what Ong calls 'zoning technologies': that is, the use of various forms of political technologies to demarcate zones of governance. This serves to:

> identify recent state strategies in Southeast Asia that focus not on an overall developmental project but rather on the management of spaces and populations in order to achieve developmental ends. In Malaysia, for instance, post developmental strategies in the 1980s regulate spaces and populations according to their relationship to modes of global production.
>
> (Ong 2004: 7)

Good examples can be taken from a wide variety of areas ranging from the special economic zones of greater China, which are the subject of Ong's analysis, to the ways in which Southeast Asian governments such as that of the Philippines have managed to declare zones of emergency, which are now thought to be more prone to 'terrorist' action. The operation of zoning technologies is most evident in the various counter terrorism operations aimed at disrupting what are termed the 'functional spaces' of terrorism. Functional space is defined as the ability to carry out various activities in support of various organizations (Ramakrishna 2004). Of course, defining functional space in this way serves to criminalize all manner of activity from finance to the ability to travel. More to the point, these functional spaces all extend to the ideological and political spaces that allow these organizations to flourish. From this perspective, 'a counter terrorism thrust is needed to close the network's all important political space' (Ramakrishna 2004: 325). In all these examples, we can see the operation of the kinds of 'zoning technologies' used to distinguish normal political space from those spaces that are subject to police action and monitoring. In short, in distinguishing between 'good' and 'bad' political spaces, one sees the operation of an important zoning technology. This is the issue: these spaces of exception are subject to exceptional and emergency measures that operate outside normal legal and constitutional processes. It is these zoning technologies that help to demarcate the multiple spaces of regulatory governance in East Asia.

Conclusion

The transnational regulatory space framework allows us to move beyond the somewhat sterile debate as to whether the post-9/11 world order represents the assertion of a hard-edged unilateralism. Some have suggested that the events of 9/11 have led to a new imperialism or a more militarily assertive role for the USA in Southeast Asia. The problem with this approach to USA–Southeast Asia relations is that it assumes a broadly 'outside-in' perspective on external pressure from the USA. In these accounts, the state is conceptualized very much in a state-centric view of external subordination. While this might have some radical and even 'Third Worldish' overtones, it remains very much a realist understanding of the global political economy. What this approach overlooks, I think, is the fact that recent changes in the global order reconstitute systems of internal governance. In contrast, I suggest in this chapter that the dynamics of these undoubtedly important external influences are to be found within the internal transformation of the state. Approaching this from the 'inside-out' perspective allows us to locate the dynamics of the new global order in the internal transformation of the state. New imperialism, while suggesting a reinforced hegemony within the international system, obscures the more important reality that new and innovative forms of governance are being constituted to manage the global economic and political order.

My basic argument, then, is that we need to identify changing forms of internal governance within the broader space of transnational regulatory governance. In terms of this analysis, the events of 9/11 do not so much reflect the growth of a new imperialism as they are a consolidation of new forms of transnational structures and regulatory forms that remain – even while they may be dominated by the USA – much more than a simple assertion of US political power. It is here that Kautsky's notion of ultra imperialism helps us to understand this new global order as a form of transnational regulatory governance that works through the instantiation of regulatory disciplines within the state.

As globalization is a microeconomic process, the emergent global economy requires the regulation of areas previously considered to be in the domestic domain. Globalization brings with it a new ensemble of governance institutions; it is these new structures that shape and influence the architecture of the state. A central feature of this new transnational regulatory governance is that the distinction between external and internal – one of the founding binaries of the Westphalian state – becomes increasingly problematic as domestic regulatory agencies develop connections with their foreign counterparts as well as with transnational regulatory bodies, thereby taking on a 'global' function. New forms of governance are being constituted within these regulatory spaces. It is important to understand that these regulatory webs often do not depend on formal international treaties or on international organizations for their enforcement. Rather, these emerging transnational regulatory spaces depend on – and, in fact, require – the active participation of agencies within the state. At the same time, we need to be careful in analysing these new transnational regulatory spaces not simply as a functionalist response to the global political economy but as a political arena that can be a site of resistance and contestation to new forms of internal governance.

The emergence of these forms of transnational regulatory spaces demonstrates the reconstitution of statehood in these new systems of global regulation. In short, the new transnational regulatory framework creates new forms of complex sovereignty that create new institutions and spaces that cut across national and transnational boundaries. This chapter, then, is a first-cut framework for the analysis of the insertion of East Asia within a system of transnational forms of regulation. It allows us to understand how new mechanisms of governance that are being constituted operate indirectly through the changing architecture of state rather than through the direct exercise of hegemony, imperial or otherwise.

Notes

1 See Bowden (2002) for a good overview of the conservative literature on Empire.
2 For similar versions of this notion of a set of interconnected executive structures, see Jayasuriya (1999) and Agnew and Corbridge (1995).
3 In this sense, our notion of transnational regulatory space has some similarities to Keohane and Nye's (1977) notion of transnational governmental policy communities. Useful as this framework is, it remains trapped within a state-centric notion of intra-governmentalism, whereas the transnational regulatory governance framework I seek to emphasize here is the way in which these new regulatory spaces are transforming the nature and character of the state. At the same time these new spaces reproduce – through various modalities and forms of governance – forms of inequality and subordination within the global political economy.
4 Panitch and Gindin (2004) do note that Kautsky's framework remains far too economistic and fails to theorize adequately the role of the state as such in the new constitution of the global order.
5 See also Panitch and Gindin (2004).

3 The reordering of Pax Americana
How does Southeast Asia fit in?

Richard Robison

Since the end of the colonial era, the evolution of Southeast Asia's place in the global system has been defined in two main phases. Throughout the 1950s and 1960s, and until the final retreat from Vietnam, it was the Cold War that dictated an engagement that was almost entirely geopolitical in nature and focused upon the consolidation of powerful anti-communist governments within a broad US-led alliance aimed at defeating various revolutionary political movements. As the Cold War waned, the logic of engagement shifted into the sphere of economics as the major Western economies, notably the USA, liquidated their decaying manufacturing bases to reorganize their ascendancy within in a system of global (especially financial) markets. Thus, Southeast Asia was drawn into a larger global project that was aimed at dismantling protected state-led capitalist systems by forcing open markets and deregulating financial regimes. This was a period in which neoliberal ideas took centre stage.[1] The IMF, the World Bank as well as economic technocrats within economic ministries across the region became key players as they attempted to force market-oriented programmes of structural adjustment on interventionist states. This was also an era defined by the ascendance of institutions of global governance such as the World Trade Organization (WTO) and the Asia–Pacific Economic Cooperation (APEC).

As the century drew to a close, however, it became increasingly apparent that this seemingly inexorable drive towards a neoliberal global agenda was stalling in several important respects. On the one hand, the governments of Malaysia, Thailand, Indonesia and Singapore had created various hybrid market economies that challenged some of the very fundamentals of neoliberalism, not least in terms of the political and social governance systems within which markets were organized. At the same time, the advocates of neoliberal orthodoxy in the USA itself were forced to give way to a new alliance of conservative and neoconservative forces; for them, the protection of US primacy lay in the direct extension of US power and political institutions. The USA, thus, moved to reorganize the basis of its hegemony, increasingly within bilateral alliances in which security was a central concern, rather than through the general globalization of market relations and rules. Thus, a third stage in the evolution of Southeast Asia's global relationships is now defined within what we might term a new Pax Americana.

There are two main questions at the heart of this chapter. What is different about the new Pax Americana compared to the previous period of neoliberal hegemony, and does it really represent the end of an epoch? Are we witnessing a new structural watershed in the global economy, the functional imperatives of which are forcing the USA into new ways of maintaining its primacy? Is it, more simply, a watershed in the configuration of power within the USA as a new coalition of conservative and corporate interests stamp their authority on the White House?[2] A second question concerns the impact of this realignment in Southeast Asia and what it means for the various state–market hybrids that emerged in the region during the neoliberal period and were so shaken by the Asian economic crisis. Are the different cocktails of state and market power generated in the neoliberal era and embedded in variants of social contract populism, oligarchy and authoritarian power that are essentially inimical to the new Pax Americana? Are they, instead, embraced and strengthened within it?

Explaining the watershed

The confused realignments now taking place in the region are understood in fundamentally diverging ways. Within the neoliberal perspective, it is a period characterized primarily by reorganization in the wake of the economic crisis of 1997–8, which is ultimately propelling the region in a fitful but inevitable path towards markets. This view contrasts with the various perceptions of a period defined by increasing conflict between the various illiberal and populist forms of market capitalism that have developed within the region, and both neoliberalism in general and US global primacy in particular. A third approach sees events becoming increasingly defined within the evolution of a new Pax Americana that is establishing a strategic accommodation between the USA and the illiberal market systems of the region.

Neoliberal responses: the fitful path to convergence

Events in Southeast Asia before and after the Asian economic crisis appear to contradict many of the central assumptions of liberals – that the world was caught in an inexorable and abstracted process of convergence towards the end of history, either as a triumph of democracy (Fukuyama 1992) or through the embrace of the universal rationality of markets (Friedman 1997). After all, many of the economies that had enjoyed rapid growth and were regarded by the World Bank as models of responsible economic management were, in fact, defined by pervasive cronyism and state intervention in the free operation of the market.

For some neoliberals, this seeming paradox was resolved by the shock of a crisis that demonstrated the real costs of failing to embrace the natural efficiencies of the market. The crisis was widely viewed, particularly in the IMF, as a blessing in disguise and a lesson that one could not accept the benefits of global financial markets without also accepting its disciplines (see Camdessus, cited in *Asian Wall Street Journal*, 3 December 1997: 1). Further, as Thomas Friedman (1997) argued, the crisis has made it clearer to the political leaders and officials of Southeast Asia and elsewhere the ultimate political and economic costs of cronyism and rent seeking. These stand in contrast against the collective social rewards of prosperity and mutual benefits that come from putting on the 'golden straitjacket' and accepting the various rules of fiscal, monetary and institutional order that will attract investment. Thus, the watershed represents, in this view, a return to the neoliberal fold rather than a shift into a new paradigm, a view demonstrated by the strict adjustment programmes enforced by the IMF to reform in an unprecedented way the policy and institutional frameworks in many countries of the region.

This belief that the basic dynamic now at work in Southeast Asia was a renewed embrace of the natural efficiency of markets was countered by more pessimistic views within other sectors of the neoliberal camp. These views suggested that the crisis had taken place despite the extensive market reforms already in place, thus indicating deeper problems of weak institutions, lack of state capacity and an absence of civil society or inadequate social capital. For a Southeast Asia that had collapsed and proved itself, for the most part, unable to be a serious player in the global market, the immediate future was one of rehabilitation. The task had shifted from market reform to enforcing the prerequisite institutional changes for the efficient operation of markets, while the new mantras became those of capacity building, good governance, empowerment and ownership (Stiglitz 1998; World Bank 1997; 2000/01).

For neoliberals, therefore, the focus remained on the undoubted and pervasive extension of the values and relationships of the markets throughout the region. It was a contest that pitted, on the one hand, the rational technocrats within governments and international institutions that sought to impose the general public welfare through market reforms against various vested interests and predatory coalitions, the latter influential within the political systems of the region (McLeod 2002; 2004). In other words, there was really no fundamental shift in the circumstances within which contending positions were defined or resolved. Others, however, were to see events as being increasingly defined by the attempts of various developmental or populist market states to carve a different path towards economic and social change, and breaking the grip of the neoliberal West.

The collision of East and West or North and South

The idea that the evolution of the region might be understood in terms of a bitter struggle among different models of capitalism reflects Samuel

Huntington's (1993) view that we are caught within a grand clash of civilizations for which there is no resolution. While I do not wish to spend much time on this over-discussed perspective, variants of this idea have made up a persistent theme within political debates across the Southeast Asian region. Not least are the sort of 'Asian Values' ideas put around in the 1990s by various Asian leaders, including Lee Kuan Yew and Mahathir Mohamad. Here, Huntington's clash of civilizations was replaced with a clash of culturally determined models of social and political organization that pit the individualism of Anglo-Saxon liberalism against Asian systems, as defined by social discipline and strong leadership. Attempts to enforce liberal market and democratic reforms, thus, become not only cultural warfare but also attempts to stifle successful Asian economic and social models (Zakaria 1994; 1997; Mahbubani 1993). For Malaysia's Prime Minister at the time, Mahathir Mohamad, and for some other regional leaders, the Asian economic crisis was little more than a device of governments and speculators in the West to destroy healthy Asian economies and buy up assets (see, for example, Mahathir Mohamad 1998).

Such arguments often descended into crude conspiracy theories supported by ideas of cultural relativism that were intended to whitewash various predatory and authoritarian modes of rule and insulate them from pressures for political and social reform (Robison 1996; Rodan 1996b). Nevertheless, the idea of a collision also found some resonance among a wide range of Western scholars, for whom the origins of the Asian economic crisis and the role of the IMF and World Bank in its resolution – specifically in relation to the opening of capital accounts – were clearly more than just a matter of imposing market fundamentals. More radically, they were seen as opportunistic interventions by the USA and other powerful nations to take advantage of periodic structural crises in order to bring down state-led economic systems. They were also seen as opportunities for imposing Anglo-Saxon market agenda or even to enable global corporations to seize assets burdened by debt at cut-rate prices (Wade and Veneroso 1998; Winters 2000).

More recently, however, the global struggle for power has been seen as far more than opportunist interventions to seize advantages in the market or impose or reject neoliberal agendas. In this view, there really is a transition from the neoliberal epoch, as the game itself changed towards a cruder reassertion of global political empire as defined by new political alliances in the core economies. These potentially opened the door for the embrace of various illiberal or predatory regimes on the basis of a shared conservative social and political perspective, and interest in the primacy of security.

The new empire

The idea of a global system defined by hegemony and empire has long been an important theme in ideas about globalization, not least within the dependency theories of the 1970s. A recent resurgence of writings about the idea of an American Empire has emerged, although it is more ambivalent than the dependency theory about whether global economic relationships necessarily constitute a zero sum game or may also have specific benefits for other players. This growing interest in empire is fuelled by the emergence within the USA of a powerful and influential neoconservative thesis that sees the main threat to the USA's global primacy in spiralling political threats, chaos and violence.[3] In this view, the task becomes more than just one of waiting for the discipline of global markets to take effect or for effective institutions to emerge in response to problems of inefficiency. There is now a responsibility for the USA directly to tackle rogue or failed states, and to impose its values and institutions in the context of a new imperial venture (Kagan 1998; Cooper 2002; Mallaby 2002).

Two central issues are embedded in the notion of empire. Is the re-emergence of empire defined by structural shifts in the global economy that impose an almost functional requirement that the USA must intervene increasingly and directly to shape political regimes so as to protect its hegemony? Or is it the consequence of a decisive shift in the configuration of political and social power in the USA towards an alliance of social conservatism and big business assembled around the presidency of George Bush (Micklethwaite and Wooldridge 2004; Harvey 2003a; Tabb 2002; Mann 2001; Gowan 2004a; 2004b)? While the emergence of a reconstituted Pax Americana has had dramatic consequences for people like Saddam Hussein, the implications for regimes in Southeast Asia may be more benign, where a common interest in protecting themselves from various forms of insurrection may take precedence over disputes about markets, human rights and democracy.

The Pax Americana, crisis and the reorganization of the global order

Here is a brief argument about a world defined by Pax Americana. From the Second World War until the 1970s, the USA established a position of political hegemony based on its leadership of an anti-communist coalition in the Cold War. Its own economic ascendancy was largely based on a protected manufacturing base that was designed to serve its own booming domestic markets and a global economic stability guaranteed by the Bretton Woods arrangements. Such a system began to develop its own contradictions as important elements of the established industrial sector in the USA and Europe became unable to compete with newer, low-cost centres of manufacturing, mainly in Asia. As the costs of protecting and subsidizing this decaying manufacturing base imposed increasing fiscal and balance-of-payment pressures on Western governments, they were forced to abandon uncompetitive manufacturing sectors. They refocused on the creation of a new economic basis of global economic ascendancy located primarily in the financial sector, but also in technology, global corporate and legal services.

Domestic manufacturers and organized labour were abandoned as the balance of power within the USA itself shifted to an alliance of governments with globalized elements of domestic capital (Harvey 2003a; Gowan 2004a; Gowan 2004b).

Thus, the tasks for the US government became not those of maintaining protected domestic manufacturing bases but those of ensuring that the global restrictions on the free movement of banking and finance capital were removed. They also had to make sure that policy settings, property rights, and governance and regulation systems permitted the free operation of global investors. By establishing the US currency as the global reserve currency, there was no limit on trade deficits; these could be handled by creating currency at will and by the pressure for other governments to hold more US currency. The continuing inflow of cheap imports fuelled consumer-driven growth within the USA. To back up this system, there were a range of international governance mechanisms such as the WTO and the IMF. The latter, in this view, operated as the mechanism for bailing out creditors and shifting losses that might provoke periodic panic among creditors onto the citizens of debtor countries. Combined with an agenda for privatization, a general agreement on trade and services concluded by the WTO has facilitated a global private market in the health industry, and in education, public utilities and pensions (Wade 2002).

Is this, as Wade suggests, 'A Machiavellian interpretation of the U.S. role in the world economy since the end of the Bretton Woods regime around 1970?' The answer, as Wade himself notes, is 'Yes'. This is not to deny, however, the calculated focus on achieving and protecting US hegemony, which has been behind the actions of successive US governments. As Wade also observes, we cannot say that the USA's engineering of its own dominance has not been performed, at times, for the general good and that others have not benefited. 'But, often its clout has been used solely in the interests of its richest citizens and most powerful corporations. This latter tendency has been dominant lately' (Wade 2002). All this leads to the question of where things began to go wrong, and what new crises have meant for this strategy to be no longer fully appropriate.

The problems emerged at three levels. The USA's economic growth was fuelled by a vigorous inflow of low-priced goods, and public expenditure on the military and other sectors that, paradoxically, stimulated growth in a perverse Keynesian package; the USA enjoyed a resurgence of boom growth in the 1990s that exacerbated growing budget and current account deficits. Even though many orthodox economists have expressed some alarm at the extent of the USA's growing debt, this was not an immediate problem so long as the, mainly, Asian central banks decided to keep large amounts of their currency in dollar-denominated bonds in the USA. The fear of a collapse of the US consumer market – the engine that drove growth in China and other Asian countries – provided the basis for a mutually dependent embrace (Wolf 2003; Hale 2003; Harvey 2003a: 203). More urgent were the episodes of asset deflation that occurred in the late 1990s at the end of the dot.com boom, and after the revelations of corporate fraud and dishonesty that led to the collapse of such giants as Enron and WorldCom. The edifice of shareholder value, mergers and acquisitions that had defined corporate America (not to mention Britain, Australia and, increasingly, Europe) clearly required some rethinking.

The neoliberal models also began to confront difficulties as they were exported. It became increasingly recognized, even within the neoliberal camp, that the harsh structural adjustment policies often imposed were not producing the predicted economic growth, employment and general development. Of course, one might ask whether the failure of a broader and constructive economic and social transformation was of consequence so long as markets were forced open, and property rights for international investors and financiers established. The point is that the persisting poverty and state–market hybrids that were often the result of shock therapy and structural transition were also to become the hothouses of the social and political disintegration, social conflict and resentment that have characterized much of Africa, Colombia and Peru in Latin America and some Eastern European countries.

On the other side of the coin, the global spread of neoliberal agendas has also been accompanied by the rise of powerful states that were able to impose political order and organize the orderly operation of economic life. At one end of the scale, a highly centralized system of state control provided the framework for rapid economic growth and effective governance of markets in Singapore (Rodan 2001). At the other extreme, various programmes of privatization and deregulation were to usher in a shift from public to private wealth, and the rise of states that became the possession of powerful individuals or oligarchies. Russia and Indonesia represent, perhaps, the most dramatic examples of this pattern (Robison and Hadiz 2004; Holstrom and Smith 2000).[4] Various market hybrids have harboured unconstrained systems of capitalism, in which new private interests have become the backbone of the illicit trade in drugs, human beings and endangered species, and where criminal activities and unchecked migration flowed into the global economy.

Once again, the question might be asked: so what if pristine market objectives or democratic agenda are sacrificed to the deeper objectives of consolidating the grip of global *rentier* capitalism? After all, it might be argued that this is the real objective. The answer is that in some cases, the sort of authoritarian or populist rule established for short-term strategic gain or to head off left-wing or social democrat governments often became incubators for other, more atavistic and populist movements hostile to liberalism. This was the case when the USA engineered the overthrow of Iranian Prime Minister Mossadegh in the 1950s to make way for the Palavi regime, thereby providing the incubator for the present system of reactionary clericalism. In other examples, such as in Saudi Arabia, highly volatile political pressure cookers are preserved in the face of growing social unrest and disenchantment by deepening engagement with global markets as suppliers of oil and as major international investors. In Southeast Asia, the sort of political capitalism that often accompanied and was consolidated in the rise of markets entrenched predatory and clientist relationships that proved extremely vulnerable to global financial instability and crisis; Indonesia and Thailand make good examples (Robison and Rosser 1998; Hewison 2000).

At the global level, too, the neoliberal epoch resulted in important geopolitical dilemmas for the Pax Americana, as the spread of market capitalism began to produce incipient centres of power and influence – such as Russia and China – outside the immediate ambit of US hegemony. Moves towards the establishment of various regional financial, trade and strategic arrangements to balance US ascendancy began to emerge. Europe, with its internal market and security co-operation, constituted a major focal point for a growing monetary and strategic alternative, but the prospect of a new regional power in Asia under Chinese leadership also enters into the equation, as we shall see later.

What now? New tasks for Pax Americana

As we have seen, many of these problems were recognized within the neoliberal camp and by governments and businesses in the West. The remedies for the difficulties now confronting the USA might be seen, ironically, as calling for a good dose of structural adjustment and IMF austerity policies, as noted by Harvey (2003b: 75–6). This, however, was never going to happen. The US government opted for programmes of sustained currency devaluation aimed at exporting some of the costs of asset deflation. They were also attempts at containing some of the larger corporate excesses that had been, in some degree, set loose by the policies of the Bush administration itself. As we have seen, other problems that emerged in the process of exporting market capitalism would be addressed by retreating from some of the excesses of what Stiglitz and others call 'market fundamentalism', and by concentrating on building institutional capacity, improving the effectiveness of states by insulating them from the predatory raids of rent-seekers, and disciplining civil society.[5]

Yet, all these seem to be have been somewhat overtaken in the wake of the attack on the Twin Towers in September 2001 and terrorist raids that preceded and followed it in Yemen, East Africa, Bali, Madrid and elsewhere. The neoconservative ascendancy over neoliberals and traditional conservatives in determining the US policy agenda brought with it a new interpretation of the problem. In this view, the USA faced a hostile world. It confronted a world of failed states that were incubating resentment and terror, and a global order in which the USA was constrained by the demands of multilateral collaboration and the dead weight of bodies like the UN. The answers lay in pre-emptive and unilateral action to promote regime change where necessary and to rebuild states (Mallaby 2002; Cooper 2002; Fidler and Baker 2003). This may be understood as a fundamental sea change in the balance of power and ideology within the USA, and a challenge to both conservative isolationism and neoliberal market agendas that are under increasing pressure after the debacle in Iraq (Leonard 2004).

There is certainly much to support the view of neoconservatism as being inimical to previously ascendant neoliberalism. Neoliberals within such organizations as the Cato Institute, and those writing in such organs as *The Economist* (3–9 April 2004: 11, 24–6, 49), have been strident in their attacks on the Bush administration's retreat from market principles and political libertarian ideals. The role of the IMF as a guarantor for US banks making imprudent and risky investments in Asia came under special attack (*AWSJ*, 18 December 1997; 5 February 1998). So, too, has the apparent retreat from generalized free trade agenda under the WTO as the US government began aggressive moves towards the establishment of bilateral trade agreements that tied security and economic interests together more closely (Bhagwati and Panagariya 2003; Higgott 2004). Neoliberals have also been highly critical of the harsh security measures introduced to enforce the new security agenda, and the undermining of market policies by powerful business interests close to the Bush administration (Zingales and McCormack 2003).

On the other hand, for analysts such as Gowan and Harvey, the neoconservative focus on empire is integral to, and not separate from, the long-term task of ensuring the selective opening of global markets and enforcement of property rights as required by the USA. While neoliberals had focused on institution building and the creation of social capital to prop up their agenda as it flagged, the problem for Gowan and Harvey is nothing less than the political task of reorganizing and rebuilding the global capitalist political order as a community under US primacy. In other words, it is argued that US economic ascendancy ultimately rests on its political and military primacy, just as the British Empire did.[6] As the old system of primacy constructed in the Cold War decayed with the collapse of the Soviet Union, a new form of global political primacy, a new Pax Americana, was needed. Thus, the rise of the neoconservatives to push aside neoliberals and conservatives in the US policy community since the beginning of this century is not seen simply as a response to a changed national mood; it is a new and necessary means of enforcing the same agenda.

Such a rebuilding, argues Gowan, embodies several new problems. Not least of these is how to incorporate into the system of primacy such potential superpowers as China, Russia and, indeed, an increasingly unified Europe that is now competing for global markets and resources, particularly in the sensitive Central Asian and Middle Eastern theatres. A second problem is the risk of a retreat to isolationism within the USA as the costs of active global hegemony become increasingly apparent. A third difficulty is in maintaining co-operative alliances with increasingly suspicious domestic bourgeoisie in Europe and East Asia. This is especially so within East Asia, where it is suggested that US Treasury activity before and after the crisis has raised suspicions that financial volatility may have been manipulated to ensure the collapse of new economic challengers and to open the door for new buyouts by US investors at bargain basement prices (Gowan 2004a).

Thus, the Bush policies are understood as a plan for regaining political and security primacy, of which its hegemony in global markets was an essential component. A dramatic forward push into the Eastern Mediterranean, Central Asia and the Middle East was designed, in this view, to secure strategic control over oil resources and to break up potential collaborative control over reserves by Europe, China and Russia. In the meantime, it has been argued that the prospect of terror offers the opportunity – or the excuse – to reconstruct geopolitical primacy under US leadership around the issue of common defence against rogue and failed states, and oppressive regimes. Legitimized as a US plan to bring democracy to the region, it was argued that Bush was able to engage in the deliberate baiting of Islam and terrorism through the USA's Palestine policy and invasion of Iraq. In China, which is potentially the greatest threat, Gowan proposes that:

> The task of US strategy is to prevent China from becoming the centre of a cohesive regional political economy while simultaneously attempting to transform China in ways that will make it structurally dependent upon the USA. All the resources of the American state – economic statecraft, military statecraft – and ideological instruments, will be mobilised for this battle in the coming years.

Thus, Gowan argued, the USA will focus on opening Chinese agriculture to foreign imports, dismantling the state-owned sector and opening its capital markets in the knowledge that the impact on the Chinese peasantry, its workers and its currency are potentially highly destabilizing (Gowan 2004a: 312, 313).

Whether things are really as conspiratorial as this is not the central question. Rather, it is whether the new Pax Americana is the product of a structural imperative or a political one. While it is true that US hegemony is becoming increasingly shaky, there are several possible ways of dealing with this. In any case, the links between geopolitical primacy and economic hegemony are not so clear. Even Japan, Taiwan and South Korea – countries that may have been most dependent on US military protection over the past decades – were precisely the ones that could get under the economic skin of the USA, not only to challenge it in its own backyard and in global markets, but to keep it largely out of their own markets to insulate themselves against US investors. These were the very countries that, in the view of Gowan and Harvey, became such a threat that the USA was forced to engineer a financial crisis in order to bring them to heel.

Other strategies have equally powerful claims. One is to maintain the sort of military intervention that has always been part of the US armoury in the enforcement of its global economic hegemony (Friedman 1997: 373). These were quite different from the ambitious plans to impose whole systems of markets and democracy,[7] limited usually to propping up or dismissing dictators or protecting US investors. Also, the economic instruments the USA may wield to impose its will are extensive and varied. They include privileged access to US consumer markets, access to US aid and loans, and, more recently, the benefits of bilateral trade deals. International agencies also bring considerable leverage to bear on debt-ridden governments and individuals, while organizations such as the IMF and private ratings agencies are decisive in setting the borrowing costs in debtor nations. Most of all, though, many of the countries that might want to undermine US hegemony have been impelled to support both it and the dollarized global financial system simply to protect the huge consumer market that has been the primary driver of the world economy (Wolf 2003).

The point is that the move towards a neoconservative agenda for global policy tells us more about the important shifts of power in the USA that have transformed the Republican Party into the party of conservative and Christian values in the South and West, and reflect its capture of much of the conservative blue-collar vote (Micklethwaite and Wooldridge 2004). It tells us more about the triumph of a crude alliance of social conservatism and global *rentier* capital under the Bush administration than it does about global economic imperatives. Perhaps, the global factors most important were the terrorist attacks on the USA itself, specifically 9/11. These opened the door for those who had been advocating an imperial agenda of pre-emptive intervention, unilateral action, the primacy of security over agenda of market fundamentalism in international policy, and the direct enforcement of regime change.

The point is that we must evaluate the new Pax Americana in terms of the agenda and ideologies of those new coalitions of conservative and neoconservative interests that now prevail, and for which US ascendancy is to be found in the construction of a new geopolitical ascendancy rather than the rolling out of global markets. What is the future for the post-crisis regimes of Southeast Asia within this new era? Will they be seen as potential rivals in a new China-led alliance, or the sort of rogue or failed states that need a good dose of pre-emptive intervention to impose markets? Or will the common fear of terror and insurgency constitute a new basis for new trade, and strategic and political alliances between the USA and these various illiberal systems of market capitalism?

Implications for Southeast Asia

Southeast Asia had loomed large in US global calculations in the 1960s and 1970s as the Cold War raged and Vietnam was a pre-occupation. So long as communist movements flourished in Indonesia, Thailand and the Philippines, the USA had been prepared to engage directly in wars and regime change across the region. In the years since, however, Southeast Asia has faded from the radar screens of the USA as it has not been central to the new agenda of neoliberal globalization. Apart from oil and mineral exploration and, more recently, public infrastructure, US investment there has been relatively small, particularly in comparison to Northeast Asian investment. The boom that occurred in the region, in the low-wage export manufacture of the late 1980s, was mainly fuelled by Northeast Asian investment.

To some extent, the Asian economic crisis changed things. Through the IMF in particular, the USA found a new focus in the region aimed specifically at enforcing neoliberal policy and institutional reforms. In this process, governments in Thailand, Indonesia, Malaysia and Singapore have, in their various ways, collided with the neoliberal orthodoxy. Apart from the well-publicized assaults on neoliberal prescriptions for open capital accounts by Malaysia's Prime Minister, Mahathir Mohamad, and his enthusiasm for regional alliances to counter US influence, the IMF ran into trouble in Indonesia when recalcitrant politicians and businessmen resisted and frustrated reforms. In Thailand, Prime Minister Thaksin has increasingly embedded his political authority in populist social contracts. In other words, there were all the makings of a stand-off between the USA and the region. This was not simply a case of national interest coming under threat from neoliberalism. The very configurations of state and social power were at stake, where regimes relied upon extensive control of the economy or clientist networks for their authority. The question is whether the new circumstances of terrorist threat and the shift of power in the USA would defuse or focus this collision.

A regional challenge to Pax Americana?

As we have seen, several theorists of the new imperialism argued that the USA faced the prospect of Asia emerging as a regional threat to its hegemony under the leadership of China. There is no doubt of China's dramatic growth as a new economic superpower (see Cui, this volume), or of its becoming an increasingly important investor in Southeast Asia, especially in the resources and energy sectors. There is a real prospect of a China-led regional sphere that would include Southeast Asia. If so, will Southeast Asia become part of a new battleground between the USA and China?

The idea that Southeast Asia might consolidate itself within regional organizations and alliances rather than under US hegemony is not new. Former Malaysian Prime Minister Mahathir Mohamad had long been a champion of a so-called 'look East' strategy that offered vague calls to follow Japanese models of economic organization. Later, he was to propose the formation of an East Asian Economic Caucus (EAEC) that would exclude US membership and promote a challenge to the US-led APEC (Asia–Pacific Economic Committee) (Higgott and Stubbs 1995). More recently, after the crisis, an expanded Association of Southeast Asian Nations (ASEAN) has been established to encompass China, South Korea and Japan (ASEAN plus 3), and there have also been the first moves towards an Asian version of the IMF, namely the AMF or the Asian Monetary Fund.

There is no great likelihood that a regional bloc might emerge in the medium-term future to include Southeast Asia in some sort of challenge to US hegemony. The countries of the region are linked in dense networks of global economic relationships and within established international economic institutions, notably the WTO (Hund 2003). Nevertheless, the risk of yielding regional leadership to China is a real one for the USA. The way it tackles the problem has real implications for Southeast Asia. As we have seen, Gowan suggested that the USA would be forced to derail the Chinese challenge by destabilizing the process of growth in China, including, among other things, forcing China into an expensive arms race through brinkmanship with Taiwan. The options, however, are likely to be less dramatic.

A first option is for the USA to throw its weight behind the rehabilitation of the ailing APEC in an effort to construct a much larger arena within which trade and other forms of economic co-operation might be undertaken; thus, this could diffuse the push to regionalism within East Asia and China's potential influence. A second option – ironically, the converse of the neoliberal agenda of APEC – is to counter China and Northeast Asia's vigorous efforts to construct networks of bilateral trade agreements (BTAs) that link them with Southeast Asian countries (Goodman 2004). This means a race to construct a counter-set of bilateral arrangements. This race is already underway as a raft of new BTAs is being developed (Ravenhill 2004). These are less free trade agreements than they are negotiated trade preference deals made partly on the grounds of security and geopolitical considerations.

Pax Americana, illiberalism and oligarchy

US global interests become entangled with the evolution of domestic political and social interests in conflict over the rules of global markets, institutions and property rights. In these, the central issue is no longer the opening of markets but, increasingly, the enforcement of specific systems of governance. The Asian economic crisis created an apparent breakthrough against the redoubts of nationalist and predatory systems of 'political' capitalism, particularly in Thailand and Indonesia where the IMF was able to enforce a range of far-reaching market and institutional reforms as conditions of large rescue packages (Robison and Rosser, 1998; Lauridson 1998; Hewison 2004). Yet, in both countries, the drive to deepening neoliberal reforms soon stalled.

Resistance to market and institutional reforms is most accurately understood as moves to protect the social ascendancy of various alliances of state and class power generated in the neoliberal period, rather than simply as reactions to the liberal market reforms that opened the door to so much damage in 1997. As Hewison (2004) points out, Prime Minister Thaksin saw the post-crisis period as an opportunity to establish the political dominance of specific business interests through a new social contract, which included measures to provide selective protection from foreign ownership and allocate welfare benefits and business opportunities. In Indonesia, former President Megawati found that trying to keep together a vastly expanded new alliance of state and business oligarchies within the new democratic and decentralized political arrangements also required populist and nationalist agenda. Officials, parliamentarians and business interests resisted demands for institutional reform and the effective prosecution of corruptors, as well as demands for repayment of corporate debt; the institution of effective bankruptcy laws; and reform of the judiciary (Robison and Hadiz 2004).

The USA thus now finds itself dealing with governments that are highly ambivalent about market and political reform, and which have had their fingers burnt by the volatility of global capital markets. Creditors have found difficulty in securing debt repayment following the collapse of businesses after the crisis in Thailand and Indonesia, where the legal mechanisms for redress are weak. Investors now find the opaque and overlapping authority of officials and cliques of business interests so pervasive that resource investment in the mining sector has been badly damaged. Regulatory controls have proven so fluid in many instances, particularly in Indonesia, that many foreign investors have come to grief at the hands of local partners operating in tandem with officials and judges.[8]

Thus, the task of forcing the region's economies open and enforcing the guarantee of property rights collides, in specific but critical situations, with the vested interests of the most powerful alliances of state and social power. Yet, this may not matter so much in the long term. While Northeast Asian investors have been able to entrench themselves in low-wage export manufacture where the oligarchies are not present, US and other foreign investors have focused on the energy and resources sectors. In strategic instances, they have been able to take advantage of politico-business alliances operating within the murky world of collusion and corruption. As we saw in the 1990s, global financial markets were eager to flood the region with dollars even though it was well known that the regulatory underpinnings of business were, for the most part, extremely weak and dependent upon political guarantees.

In the years leading up to the economic crisis, investors were also willing to plunge into shady alliances where the rewards were high and where success might be contingent on political guarantees rather than commercial factors.[9] After the crisis, despite a general retreat of investment from Indonesia, we find that the public offering of newly recapitalized banks has attracted very substantial interest. It has also provided a boost to the capital market in Indonesia because the perceived rewards are considered to outweigh the risks.

There is a further and more compelling reason why the tensions between market agenda and ruling coalitions in the region will not become a focus of ongoing conflict. The spectre of failed states has placed the neoliberal agenda of market reform, administrative decentralization and democratization into an ambiguous holding pattern. Enthusiasm for decentralization in Indonesia and Thailand has become more qualified, even within the World Bank and USAID, as the implications for economic governance, political uncertainty and even lawlessness have become apparent for economic investment. Indonesia gives particular concern to spreading fiscal irresponsibility; manipulating budgets by vested interests; and replicating various tolls, royalties and other types of rent on the part of various overlapping regional and provincial governments and their supporters (Hadiz 2004b). These factors are not inconsequential in the recent decline in investment and exploration in the resource sector by foreign miners.

At the same time, the USA's security and strategic interests in the region increasingly counterbalance its market objectives and, currently, overwhelm them. The threat to the USA from organized global terror, and political disorder that enables growing civil conflict to spill over into unchecked population movements, and the enhancement of global criminal activity is not absent in Southeast Asia. Indeed, the region has been witness to several dramatic incidents of terrorist activity, and has been home to organizations with connections to global Islamic fundamentalist movements. The Bali and Jakarta bombings, violence in Southern Philippines and Southern Thailand, and unrest in Aceh and Ambon all add weight to US concerns (International Crisis Group 2001; 2002).

In such circumstances, the neoconservative agenda for breaking open regimes to impose the markets and democracies that have proven so elusive, and to deal with the threat of terror, appears to be, in their own words, 'mugged by reality'. As we have seen elsewhere, especially in Pakistan, the requirements for consolidating US hegemony mean that the priority is on cementing alliances with governments that can deliver order, loyalty and security. Both the USA and Australia have revised their attitude towards the discredited Indonesian security forces, for example, and now provide assistance towards their consolidation through training programmes. This well suits governments in the region that are increasingly nervous about popular unrest and the threat of militant Islam. A new accord has been struck that is profoundly conservative in its nature, and it winds back the neoliberal advance.

Conclusion

It is an exaggeration to say that the epoch of neoliberalism has been replaced by one of neoconservatism in the relations between Southeast Asia and the USA. Global capital and financial markets are still the main drivers of institutional reform and change in the region's economies, and pressure to operate in global markets is forcing a transformation of the region's corporations and banks. These events will continue to influence the politics of the region and transform the social interests that make up the political arena. A shift of power in the USA, however, and panic about threats to US global hegemony, combine to enforce a neoconservative accommodation with governments to sustain, at the present conjuncture, various illiberal and populist forms of market regimes.

Notes

1 Neoliberalism is understood and used in this chapter as constituting two levels. First, it is firmly based on neoclassical economics, with its idea that the most efficient allocation of resources is achieved by a natural and self-regulating market driven by its own internal laws. The policy implications of this are, among others, privatization, outsourcing, fiscal austerity and the retreat of the state – factors embedded in the so-called Washington Consensus. Neoliberalism, however, might be seen to extend beyond neoclassical economics through its more ambitious programme of extending the values and relationships of the market to all spheres of political and social life. This involves attention to the construction of systems of political and social governance within which markets may be protected from politics. Thus, a central feature of neoliberalism is not the dismantling of the state but its reorganization as an instrument that is insulated from vested interests of distributional coalitions, and concerned with the effective regulation of the market (see Cerny 2004; Treanor 2004; Peters 2004).

2 It should be noted that conservatism has important differences with neoconservatism (discussed below). Briefly, while conservatism is generally associated with the defence and preservation of entrenched structures of social and political hierarchy and privilege, neoconservatives are closer to the neoliberal view that the market can sort out the configuration of power and privilege, and that this may be a volatile process. In terms of foreign policy, conservatives are realists in their belief that global order is achieved in struggles among nations over national interest. Conservatives might support intervention to protect US interests, supporting or bringing down rulers where necessary. Neoconservatives see nothing less than the export of US political and social values and institutions as being necessary for the establishment of a global order in which US interests are safe.

3 There is huge and growing literature on neoconservatism. Its basic principles are increasingly embedded in the National Security Strategy Documents of the United States. Max Boot (2004), a prominent neoconservative, provides an interesting response to various criticisms and provides a good bibliography of works on neoconservatism and by neoconservatives themselves.

4 At various times, the USA has given its political support to more sinister regimes such as Mobutu in Zaire, the Sauds in Saudi Arabia and even Saddam Hussein in Iraq, to achieve either economic change or the strategic ends considered necessary for sustaining its position of global hegemony.

5 See here the extensive literature on the so-called post-Washington Consensus (Harriss 2002; Fine *et al.* 2001; Rodan *et al.* 2001).

6 Gowan describes primacy as constituting (a) a basic security dependency upon the USA by other states; (b) US management of the geopolitical and accumulation strategies of other major capitalist states; and (c) a US claim of special rights and privileges outside stable rules and institutions (Gowan 2004a).

7 See, for example, Bush's plans to transform the Middle East through the direct use of trade agreements as leverage to enforce social, democratic and economic reform (Alden and Khalaf 2003).

8 See, for example, the case of Manulife, the Canadian insurer that became the victim of a bizarre scam by its Indonesian partner shortly after the economic crisis. Such incidents continue to occur (*Tempo*, 25 June–1 July 2002).

9 The entry of foreign investors into the Indonesian power generation industry is just one example of this. Here, consortia formed around Soeharto's family members with licences to construct power generation plants and sell electricity in circumstances where the Indonesian state was to be saddled with both massive over-invoicing and over-pricing. Ironically, US and other foreign investors in this sector, backed by their governments that had supplied over US$4 billion in finance through export credit banks, were to clash with Indonesian reformers seeking to rescind or renegotiate many of these deals. For them, it was a case of property rights (Robison 2001).

4 The rise of the 'neocons' and the evolution of US foreign policy

Mark Beeson

Introduction

Powerful countries have always had the capacity and the desire to influence the international system of which they are a part (Watson 1992). What is remarkable about the contemporary era is that one country, the USA, is far more influential than any other in this regard. The USA has a unique potential to shape both the rules and regulations that govern the increasingly interconnected international system, and the behaviour of the other states and non-state actors that effectively constitute it. Consequently, in an era of 'unipolarity', the USA's foreign and domestic policies have assumed unprecedented prominence in the affairs of other nations and regions as they seek to accommodate, and where possible benefit from, the evolution of US hegemony. This is an especially challenging development at a time when neoconservative thinking has exerted a powerful influence on US foreign policy, making it both more unilateral and difficult to accommodate.

To make sense of the extent and impact of US power, we need to place the development of US hegemony in its specific historical context. Consequently, the first part of this chapter briefly traces the evolution of US power over the last fifty years or so. This analysis reveals not only the evolving nature of US power, but also the different ways in which it has affected Western Europe and East Asia. This provides the basis for a more detailed examination of the contemporary period and the rise of the so-called 'neocons', some of whom have plainly exerted a powerful influence over recent US foreign policy. A historically informed analysis also has the merit of highlighting some important continuities in US policy that have structural, rather than contingent or ideological, bases. As we shall see, however, agency continues to matter in international affairs, and the neocons have been able to influence profoundly the course and content of contemporary US foreign policy, initially through proselytizing and, more recently, by the accession to power of key neocon thinkers and activists. The central conclusion of this chapter is that the USA's remarkable military, economic and political power provided it with the opportunity to influence profoundly the development of the international system, yet the precise way this has happened owes a great deal to the efforts and ideas of a surprisingly small coterie of intellectuals, the inauguration of a political regime in Washington that was sympathetic to their ideas, and the paradoxical impact of a significantly reconfigured security and geopolitical environment.

The ancien régime

The post-war order created under the auspices of US hegemony had a number of distinctive features. Significantly, some of the institutional structures, ideas and practices that are synonymous with the early phase of US dominance generally, and the establishment of the Bretton Woods regime in particular, either have already evolved into something quite different from what their original architects intended, or are likely to be transformed by recent policy initiatives from the current Bush administration. Having said this, it is also important to recognize that economic and security issues have different logics or dynamics, despite the fact that they have – until fairly recently, at least – been a relatively integrated part of the USA's overarching geopolitical orientation to the rest of the world (Mastanduno 1998). To make sense of recent policy innovations associated with the George W. Bush administration, it is necessary to disentangle the broadly economic and strategic aspects of US policy.

The Bretton Woods institutions – the World Bank, the International Monetary Fund and the General Agreement on Tariffs and Trade (GATT) – are the most important expressions of the USA's post-war dominance and its desire to create an institutionalized international order that embodied its norms and values, and one that was explicitly designed to avoid the 'mistakes' of the interwar period when the world's economies collapsed into depression and autarky (Latham 1997; Leffler 1992). Even if the USA has arguably been the principal beneficiary of the liberal economic order it helped create, there is no doubt that others, too, have benefited. Indeed, the period in which the USA provided the aid and investment that facilitated post-war reconstruction in Western Europe and Japan is rightly regarded as the high-water mark of enlightened US diplomacy (Kunz 1997), and provides a telling counterpoint to contemporary policy. By contrast with current policy, the architects of the USA's post-war policies were keen to ensure that the new international order should be multilateral, and that the sort of bilateralism that was associated with the interwar period should be actively discouraged (Pollard 1985: 65). Significantly, the design of Europe's nascent security architecture also had a multilateral basis (Weber 1993). This has, subsequently, facilitated European integration and, as a consequence, has given a degree of equality to US–European relations. The situation in East Asia has been very different – US perceptions of the region and its capacity to participate effectively in the emerging transnational institutional architecture led it to develop a distinctive bilateral security framework across the region that persists to this day (Hemmer and Katzenstein 2002).

Although US policy towards East Asia has been and remains different to its European-oriented position, it provided a permissive environment within which many of East Asia's export-oriented, frequently mercantilist regimes were able to prosper. The USA provided the crucial markets that underpinned much of East Asia's post-war industrialization and turned a blind eye to political practices and economic structures that it might have otherwise disapproved (Beeson 2004). The USA also provided, either directly through aid and investment or indirectly through the stimulatory impact of the Korean and Vietnam Wars, the critical catalyst to underpin development in the non-communist parts of East Asia (Stubbs 1999).

A number of points are worth highlighting about the nature of US hegemony and its differential impact in East Asia. First, US hegemony has always been shaped by the complex interplay of structure and agency, economic and strategic factors, and the contingent and the universal. Consequently, its impact has been quite different in different parts of the world. The political economies of Western Europe were historically more developed and closely aligned to the US model than were the emerging economies of East Asia, thus significantly altering the trajectory of post-war development. Crucially, Western Europe has been less reliant than East Asia on US markets to underpin its development. Similarly, while the Cold War may have provided the universal geopolitical backdrop against which development everywhere unfolded, the predilection for bilateral security relations in East Asia meant that the prospects for a process of Western-European-style economic, political and – especially – strategic integration were always much more remote. The second point to make, therefore, is that US hegemony has a pronounced regional accent that continues to influence the distinctive course of development in East Asia to this day (Beeson 2003).

The third aspect of US hegemony that emerges from this highly truncated consideration of the post-war international order is that the USA's relationship with the world is a two-way street; the fact that the USA took upon itself the leadership of the 'free world' in the aftermath of the Second World War, when its pre-eminent position was increasingly apparent, not only had a powerful impact on the rest of the world but also profoundly affected and reflected the USA's domestic position. The development of a US 'security state', and the concomitant influence of what Eisenhower famously described as the 'military–industrial complex', remains a powerful force in US policy making. It has also come to influence the development and relative strength of the USA's own domestic political institutions and relationships (Hogan 1998). The emergence of the War on Terror has already had a similarly transformative impact on the structure of domestic institutions in the USA (Eccleston 2002). The relative importance of strategic issues and the domestic lobbies that attempt to shape public policy in this area will clearly be a function of the wider geopolitical context.

It is no coincidence, for example, that the USA began to behave more like a 'normal' state as far as foreign policy, generally, and trade policy in particular were concerned in the aftermath of the Cold War and the waning importance of geo-strategic issues. The USA's relationship with Japan epitomizes the shifting priorities of various US administrations as they sought to reconfigure critical bilateral economic relationships through direct political leverage (Pempel 2004; Schoppa 1997). Despite the ending of the Cold War and a dramatically reconfigured geopolitical environment, the USA is still able to exploit its strategic dominance and Japan's continuing subordinate role. Japan has embarked on a major reassessment of its defence policies to allow it to play both a supporting role in the 'coalition of the willing' in Iraq, and an active role in the USA's proposed ballistic missile defence programme. Significantly, Japanese defence planners now talk of 'common' strategic interests and seem prepared to play a much more active and prominent role in a globally oriented strategic posture that reflects US priorities.

The geo-strategic context in which particular relationships are embedded is a potentially critical determinant of the nature of that relationship – whether bilateral, multilateral or even unilateral – and of the nature and relative importance of the accompanying ideological or ideational discourse. To understand the nature of contemporary hegemony, therefore, when strategic issues are back at the top of the policy-making agenda, we need not only to consider the role of ideas, institutions and interests, but also to recognize the continuing importance of strategic factors. US power, in other words, is a complex of – and realized within – an amalgam of institutionalized power, dominant ideas and the wider geo-strategic context. Different hegemonic periods will be shaped by the interplay of these factors, none of which is determinant but all of which are constraining. To understand US hegemony under George W. Bush and the prospects for this administration's distinctive vision, we need to look more closely at the continuities and departures that have distinguished US foreign policy.

American exceptionalism and the legacy of history

A historically informed analysis of contemporary US foreign policy reveals a number of important continuities with earlier periods, as well as some surprising differences that set apart the administration of George W. Bush. Before we can make sense of the latter, however, and recognize how much of a departure *some* aspects of recent policy are, it is helpful to sketch briefly some of the more general historical influences on US foreign policy making.

The USA's unique historical developments, especially the distinctive social traditions and conditions that emerged from its revolutionary origins, have underpinned the idea of 'American exceptionalism'. While outsiders may regard the US attachment to liberty, egalitarianism, individualism, populism and laissez-faire economics – which Lipset claims embody the 'American creed' – we, with varying degrees of admiration or incredulity, should not underestimate how powerful a force such ideas have been in defining a sense of national identity and, by extension, US foreign policy. Indeed, unless we recognize how important the moral dimension of both the USA's domestic life and its foreign policy *is*, we shall not be able to understand why the characterization of the Bush regime's post-9/11 policy stance as a 'war against evil' resonated so powerfully with so many Americans. As Lipset (1996: 20) points out:

> To endorse a war and call on people to kill others and die for the country, Americans must define their role in a conflict as being on God's side against Satan–for morality against evil, not, in its self-perception, to defend national interests.

Critical theorists and the temperamentally cynical may regard the legitimating discourse that emerged around the War on Terror with a good deal of scepticism. Yet, in a country where well over 90 per cent of the population profess a belief in God, it is difficult to overestimate the continuing importance of religion in general and Christianity in particular as a source of identity, belief and political mobilization. Indeed, so powerful does religion remain in American life that some observers question whether the USA is a secular state at all (Gray 1998).

Unsurprisingly, therefore, this sense of exceptionalism, and the belief that the USA is a unique country with a possibly God-given historical mission, has shaped US foreign policy and given rise to the idea that the USA and its values must provide a beacon for the world (McDougall 1997). Crucially, however, this is a vision that needs to be actively exported; assumptions about the presumed superiority, universality and desirability of American values – in combination with a growing economic, political and strategic power to impose such a morally informed model on other countries – means that the USA's increasing engagement with the world would be overlaid with distinctive American norms on the one hand, and inescapable structural dominance on the other. Consequently, the key question has always been about how, rather than if, such an engagement would occur. As Lake (1999) points out, the central story of US foreign policy in the twentieth century, during which the USA became hegemonic, was not about a conflict between isolationists and internationalists, but between unilateralists and multilateralists. The experience of the catastrophic, unilateralist interwar period, and the contrast with the decisive role the USA played in creating the post-war order, appeared to have permanently resolved this tension in favour of the multilateralists. But recent events serve as a reminder that policy is not structurally determined or inescapably path dependent, but is susceptible to reconstruction by those with an alternative vision, ideology or grand strategy. In other words, what Susan Strange (1994) described as the USA's 'structural power' in the international system may inevitably make it the dominant power of the era, but this does not determine either the content of its foreign policy or the precise nature of its engagement with the world.

While the specific content of US foreign policy at any given moment may reflect agency more than structure, foreign policy itself has provided an important domestic ideological coherence and underpinned a sense of national identity for an increasingly diverse population (Hunt 1987). National identity and foreign policy exist in a mutually constitutive, dialectical relationship in which – in the USA, at least – the discursive privileging of democracy occupies a central place (Smith 1994). This helps to account for the powerful continuities in US foreign policy from the Truman policy of containment to the Bush doctrine of pre-emption. Although the means by which US goals are achieved are contingently determined, and the 'other' in opposition to which an American identity is defined may vary, key elements of the USA's sense of itself and the role of its foreign policy display remarkable continuity. Making the world a better place by defending and, where possible, exporting democratic ideals and liberal capitalism have been the recurring leitmotifs of US foreign policy. The current generations of neocon thinkers, however, differ from earlier Wilsonian idealists because 'their promotion of democracy is not for the sake of democracy and human rights in and of themselves. Rather, democracy promotion is meant to bolster America's security and to further world pre-eminence' (Wolfson 2004: 46). This creates a potential contradiction and tension at the heart of US foreign policy, because there is a presumption about the superiority of the USA's domestic values and political practices, and a concomitant assumption about the need for its foreign policy to be legitimate (Nau 2002). It is precisely this domestically legitimated aspect of US power that is being eroded by current policy; the USA's image of itself as a champion of freedom and democracy, and the powerful tradition of anti-imperialism in US foreign policy (Smith 1994: 143) is profoundly undercut by the current conflict in Iraq, the rising tide of anti-Americanism worldwide, and the alienation of formerly stalwart democratic allies.

This is arguably the most distinctive and misconceived aspect of contemporary US policy. Not only is the war in Iraq, like the war in Vietnam before it, likely to prove divisive in the USA itself, but it will undermine the country's claims to legitimately lead the post-Cold-War world and embody its putative moral order. As a number of scholars have observed (Smith 2000; Ikenberry 2001), American values and the very structures of the US economy and polity seem uniquely in accord with long-run transformations in the international system, structural changes that ought to confirm the centrality and legitimacy of US power. Yet, it is precisely these aspects of US primacy that are presently being eroded by the influence of that tight coterie of advisers and ideologues who have come to be known as the neocons. Despite their rapid recent rise to prominence under Bush Jr, as with the USA's overall foreign policy tradition, there are surprising continuities and contradictions hidden beneath the neocon label.

The evolution of neo-conservative strategic thinking

To describe the group of advisers who currently exert such an influence over both George W. Bush and, more generally, US foreign policy as neoconservative would be something of a misnomer. The label was originally applied to a group of largely Jewish left-wing intellectuals who became increasingly disenchanted with socialism, and who ultimately became prominent opponents of communism. This grounding in the ideological struggles of the 1950s and 1960s helps to explain the importance attached to influencing the ideational milieu within which policy is shaped, and the prominent role played in US policy debates by journals such as *Commentary*, *The Public Interest*, *The National Interest* and, more recently, *The Weekly Standard*. Although elements of 'neoconservative' thought can be traced back to seminal policy interventions by George Keenan and Paul Nitze[1] – figures who did more than anyone else to shape the overall parameters of US grand strategy in the postwar period (Gaddis 1982) – in the late 1940s and early 1950s, neoconservatism's 'first main faction' was led by Irving Kristol and Jeanne Kirkpatrick, former Reagan Cabinet member and US representative to the UN (Dorrien 1993: 124).

Kristol is frequently considered the 'godfather' of contemporary neoconservatism, having played a crucial role in promulgating neoconservative ideas through key outlets such as *The Public Interest*. This tradition was continued by his son William, the current editor of the highly influential *Weekly Standard* and chairman of the Project for the New American Century. The elder Kristol argues that neoconservatism is a 'persuasion' rather than a movement, and one grounded in 'attitudes derived from historical experience'. It is their particularly Manichean reading of history that underpins the neoconservatives' distinctive attitude to state power, an attitude that is fundamentally at odds with the USA's more liberal traditions. As Kristol (2003: 24) puts it:

> Neocons do not feel that [Hayekian] kind of alarm or anxiety about the growth of the state in the past century, seeing it as natural, indeed inevitable . . . People have always preferred strong government to weak government. . . . Neocons feel at home in today's America to a degree that more traditional conservatives do not.

It is this recognition of the potential importance of US power and the – overstated, as we now know – prospect of its relative diminution that concerned the likes of Kristol and other prominent neoconservatives such as Norman Podhoretz (1980), a former editor of *Commentary*. Significantly, it is precisely this aspect of US foreign policy – the nature of US power and the purposes to which it ought to be employed – that has so exercised the minds of the current generation of neocons who are presently shaping US foreign policy.

Charles Krauthammer has been one of the key influences on contemporary neocons as well as a powerful advocate of a more assertive US foreign policy. The pivotal events for Krauthammer were the Presidency of Ronald Reagan during the 1980s, the 'defeat' of the Soviet Union during this period, and the emergence of the USA as the sole superpower as a consequence at the beginning of the 1990s (Winik 1996).

Krauthammer (1991: 25) was among the first to recognize that the end of the Cold War had created a new era of unipolarity, in which the old multilateral order was being replaced by a form of 'pseudo-multilateralism', and in which the USA would pay lip service to collective security while acting 'essentially alone'. In a world of new, emerging threats to stability, there was only one answer:

> Our best hope for safety in such times, as in difficult times past, is in American strength and will – the strength and will to lead a unipolar world, unashamedly laying down the rules of world order and being prepared to enforce them.
>
> (Krauthammer 1991: 33)

The presumptions that multilateralism is ineffective and unworkable, that 'for all the bleating about hegemony, no nation wants genuine multipolarity', and that the 'benevolent hegemony exercised by the United States is good for a vast portion of the world's population'(Kagan 1998: 26, 31), underpin the sense of 'realism', moral righteousness and certitude that inform neocon policy prescriptions. While the neocons may not be the first political clique to fall under the spell of its own rhetoric, what really distinguishes the neocons is the way these ideas crystallized in specific policy proposals and, ultimately, shaped foreign policy itself.

Like the earlier generation of right-wing activists in Britain who underpinned Margaret Thatcher's rise to power and her conversion to neoliberal ideas (see Cockett 1994), neocons in the USA continue to promulgate their ideas through influential journals and key think tanks like the aforementioned PNAC,[2] the American Enterprise Institute, the Jewish Institute for National Security Affairs, the Hudson Institute, the Heritage Foundation and the Center for Security Policy. What is distinctive about the American movement, however, is the current prominence of neocon intellectuals and policy activists within the ranks of the current Bush administration. It is, however, important to recognize that neocons were influencing the course of US foreign policy even before their recent accession to power. Ex- Deputy Defense Secretary Paul Wolfowitz, for example, is widely considered to be the intellectual driving force behind the more unilateral, pre-emptive policy orientation of the current Bush administration. Wolfowitz achieved a degree of notoriety as the author of the 1992 Defense Planning Guidance.[3] Although the report was deemed too shocking for widespread consumption at the time and was subsequently rewritten, Wolfowitz, then Under Secretary of Defense Policy, outlined a number of the ideas, especially the active pursuit of US military dominance and the unilateral application of power. These policies have become the centrepiece of foreign policy under George W. Bush and are now widely regarded as mainstream policy positions. This discursive transformation is indicative of just how much the debate has shifted, and just how influential neocon ideas have become. Indeed, the fact that Wolfowitz has become President of the World Bank is indicative of both the continuing prominence of neocon figures and the ability of the USA to fill such key vacancies with its preferred candidates, despite widespread opposition to Wolfowitz's candidature.

It is also important to recognize that Wolfowitz advocates a more aggressive approach to China (Mann 2004: 114), the USA's principal strategic competitor in East Asia; this is a view that is entirely in keeping with long-standing neocon thinking about Asia and the application of US power (Kagan and Kristol 2000a: 64). Indeed, it is striking that in comparison to the USA, China's recent diplomacy looks increasingly far-sighted, sophisticated and reassuring – at least, as far as its neighbours in East Asia are concerned (Shambaugh 2004/5). Yet, the US position towards China remains predicated on pointed attempts to discourage any military expansionism part (Shanker 2005), despite major growth in the USA's own defence spending under the current Bush administration. While there is a degree of hypocrisy here on the part of the USA, perhaps it is, more importantly, indicative of the possible limits of its hegemonic influence. China's rapid economic growth makes it both an economic rival and a critical source of capital inflows to underpin the USA's own spending (Ravenhill 2006), of which military expenditure is an increasingly prominent part. Clearly, there are limits to the USA's capacity to fund its global ambitions (Ferguson and Kotlikoff 2003) and potential constraints on its economic and, by extension, foreign policy autonomy. Such complexities, however, are remarkably absent from neocon thinking.

Richard Perle, former Assistant Secretary of Defense during the Reagan era, founder of the Center for Security Policy, Fellow of the American Enterprise Institute and advocate of the forceful reordering of the Middle East, has been another prominent neocon intellectual who has helped redefine US foreign policy. Like Wolfowitz, Perle is Jewish, and while this should not matter, it may. It is hardly anti-Semitic to observe that Perle has close links to Israel's right-wing Likud Party and was the architect of a commissioned report, *A Clean Break: A New Strategy for Securing the Realm.*[4] This report called for abandoning the negotiations for land for peace with the Palestinians and advocated Israel's right to use pre-emptive force where necessary. Similarly, Wolfowitz was widely considered to have been Israel's strongest supporter in the Reagan administration (Mann 2004). The point to make is that the long-standing pro-Israeli stance in the USA, which has become such an apparently non-negotiable part of US foreign policy, can be traced – in part at least – to neocon influences and thinking. Indeed, this pro-Israeli bias has been consolidated by the appointment of Elliott Abrams to head the National Security Council. Abrams is a prominent advocate of 'regime change' in the Middle East and, despite having been indicted for lying to Congress about his role in the Iran–Contra scandal, exerts a powerful influence over current policy (Lobe 2002: online version).

There is, then, a decades-long tradition of neoconservative thinking that has advocated a more forceful utilization of US power; a less inhibited championing of 'American values'; and a concomitant recalibration of US foreign policy priorities, of which support of Israel has become a crucial, non-negotiable component. The ending of the Cold War, the increased concern with radical Islam, and the election of a foreign policy ingénue like Bush Jr created the preconditions within which the neocon agenda could be unambiguously realized.

Grand strategy, Bush Jr and the War On Terror

If US foreign policy is informed by a grand strategy in the present era, it is clearly one based on the development and application of US primacy (Posen and Ross 1996–97). The pursuit of 'full spectrum dominance' or permanent, overwhelming military superiority in every sphere (see Klare 2002); the repudiation or selective use of multilateralism (Martin 2003); and the desire to contain challenges to US hegemony are not simply characteristics of contemporary policy under George W. Bush. As we have seen, such ideas have been in circulation for more than a decade. What they required to become the basis of policy was a favourable conjuncture of international and domestic circumstances. The installation of influential neocon thinkers and activists in the Bush administration was the key domestic precondition for the recalibration of US foreign policy. In addition to Wolfowitz, Perle and Abrams, other key neocon figures to obtain powerful positions include Michael Ledeen[5] (Principal Advisor to Karl Rove, Bush's own key adviser); Lewis 'Scooter' Libby, Chief of Staff and National Security Advisor to Vice-President Dick Cheney; and John Bolton, Under Secretary of State for Arms Control and International Security and former Vice-President of the American Enterprise Institute.[6] The critical international factor that allowed the neocons to consolidate their influence on US foreign policy was, paradoxically enough, 9/11.

Despite the furore currently swirling around the question of what the Bush administration could or should have known or done before 9/11 (Clarke 2004; Woodward 2004), it is important to recognize that in the immediate aftermath of the original attacks, 9/11 was seen by key Bush administration figures like Secretary of Defense Donald Rumsfeld as an opportunity to expand US hegemony more aggressively and pursue long-term goals that might have been difficult to justify otherwise (Bacevich 2002: 227; Daadler and Lindsay 2003: 13). In this context, it is useful to distinguish between long-term strategic goals like regime change in Iraq and the desire to use US power to reshape the Middle East (Gordon 2003), from the ad hoc and occasionally inept tactical conduct of the War on Terror (Woodward 2003; Clarke 2004). Consequently, the major significance of the War on Terror was to give a strategic rationale and ideological gloss to both a major shift in the USA's own strategic doctrine, and to a profound change in the status and operation of the multilateral order that had prevailed for the preceding fifty years or so (Martin 2003). The new order was captured in the so-called doctrine of pre-emption, in which the USA claimed the right to act unilaterally and pre-emptively – in defiance of international law and principle – to counter perceived threats to its own security (Bush 2002; White House 2002).

In part, then, recent US policy is an extension of an older tradition of US exceptionalism and a desire to export the democratic and liberal values that accompany it. The linking of US foreign policy to such lofty objectives may provide a convenient ideological smoke screen for, and consolidate the grip of, an economic order that disproportionately benefits the USA (Robinson 1996). Yet, it is also true that such expansive ideals are taken seriously in a nation that remains ideologically, culturally and temperamentally different from even its closest allies (Kagan 2003). In short, there are powerful ideational influences that help explain the shape of current US policy.

There are also more prosaic and tangible forces. As the *National Energy Policy* (NEPDG 2001) report (which Vice-President Cheney chaired) made clear, US dependence on foreign oil increased from 35 to over 50 per cent between 1973 and 2000. This is a situation that will inevitably get worse, with the USA becoming increasingly dependent on the Middle East for future oil supplies. It is not necessary to be a conspiracy theorist or argue that the Iraq invasion was 'all about oil' to recognize that the stability of the Middle East has a far greater importance for the USA's long-term strategic, economic and domestic political position than, say, Africa, whose citizens might have equally compelling claims to US attention on the grounds of human rights abuses and predatory despotism. Certainly, the Middle East's strategic importance was clear to an ex-oil company executive like Cheney, who argued that Iraq's unpredictability and potential hostility meant that there might be a 'need for military intervention' (quoted in Mann 2003: 208). The increased importance of Central Asia – and the USA's willingness to tolerate Iraq-like human rights abuses by the leaders of a number of Central Asian republics (see Johnson 2004) – is further evidence of the strategic importance of oil, the increasingly global reach of the US grand strategy, and the selective nature of the Bush administration's moral outrage.

While the USA's more assertive, unilateral, pre-emptive and militaristic grand strategy may have been decades in the making and owes a great deal to the influence of successive generations of broadly neoconservative thinkers and policy activists, it is unlikely to survive for long in its current form. Nation building and the establishment of stability is plainly a far more challenging, longer and more expensive process than wining military victories against vastly inferior foes (Rhodes 2003). Empires are expensive, and it is as much this as any other factor that is likely to undermine the hopes of the neo-imperialists. The rapidly deteriorating budgetary position in the USA means that it simply cannot afford such foreign adventures despite the scale of the US economy (Ferguson and Kotlikoff 2003). More fundamentally, perhaps, not only is US imperialism especially difficult for Americans to justify normatively, but it also does not have a good track record. As Schwenninger (2003: 36) points out, those areas in which the USA has intervened most directly and enjoyed the greatest dominance – the Middle East, and Central and South America – have also been the most troubled and unstable. It is becoming painfully clear that utilizing the USA's undoubted power is a good deal more complex than the ideologically driven views of the neocons would have us believe. It will be interesting to see if a group that prides itself on its hard-headedness and realism can address the problems of mundane reality that are becoming so apparent in the Middle East.

Concluding remarks

Security issues look set to dominate the foreign policy agenda of the Bush regime for the foreseeable future. Yet containing, let alone defeating, terrorism would seem to require a multi-faceted effort that encompasses long-term economic and political reform, together with a major rethinking of the way the USA's international relations are conducted (Cronin 2002). It is increasingly uncontroversial to suggest that the USA's coercive, militaristic strategy since 9/11 is actually more likely to generate resentment, opposition and terrorist actions than to eliminate them (Mann 2001). Even if we put aside the fact that the entire rationale for the attack on Iraq was debatable at best and fraudulent at worst, recent events have highlighted just how ill-conceived the strategy was and how open-ended the commitment remains. My intention in this chapter has not been to assess the efficacy of the USA's response to terrorism or perceived threats to domestic security. Rather, I have attempted to describe the way an influential coterie of ideologues came to exert such a powerful influence over the construction of US foreign policy. By way of conclusion, therefore, I want to highlight a number of implications that flow from the rise of the neocons and the reconfiguration of US foreign policy.

First, it does make a difference who runs the USA. The major part of US power is undoubtedly structural and based on its overwhelming strategic dominance, economic weight and political leverage. The actions of the Bush administration and its preconceived determination to implement regime change in the Middle East, pursue even greater military dominance, and overturn the existent multilateral order, however, serve as powerful reminders that agency continues to matter. The contrast with the Clinton administration, which showed a greater willingness to cultivate allies, act multilaterally and avoid foreign entanglements where possible, is a telling one, as is the disdainful view of the neocons, which characterizes such earlier policies as vacillation. Yet, as Chalmers Johnson (2004: 255) perceptively points out, in many ways, 'Clinton was actually a much more effective imperialist than George W. Bush'. The reason: US power was less coercive and operated more indirectly through the international institutional architecture that the USA was instrumental in creating, and over which it continues to exert a dominant influence (Woods 2003). Thus, it was able to achieve its goals at a lower cost and with less resistance. The situation now could hardly be more different, as formerly stalwart allies like Germany and France have distanced themselves from the policies of the Bush regime, and as global hostility to the USA grows rapidly (PRC 2004).

Consequently, the second point to make is both practical and theoretical: 'American interests' may be rather more diverse than this label implies, but they are likely to be better served when US power is institutionalized and perceived as being legitimate. In other words, those models of hegemony that take the ideational aspect of US power seriously and recognize the USA's historical capacity legitimately to play a dominant role in creating the rules, regulations and institutions that pass for global governance not only provide a more complete understanding of the way US power has operated over the last fifty years or so, but also may provide a more durable blueprint for its continuing application and rehabilitation. For a group of intellectuals that were initially so alive to the importance of ideas in winning policy debates and reshaping the conventional wisdom in the USA, it is striking and revealing that this insight seems to have been forgotten or, more accurately, not applied widely enough. Recent events remind us that to be effective and durable, ideas, policies and even grand strategies need to have a purchase beyond the political elites who shape policy in Washington; they must also be embedded in some sort of wider national and even transnational institutional and societal contexts.

The third point that emerges from a consideration of contemporary foreign policy is that for all the attention paid to the USA's 'soft power' and the undoubted attraction of many aspects of American lifestyles and living standards (Nye 2002), the legitimacy of US ideas and policies is being systematically eroded by a highly doctrinaire, ideologically driven and nationalistic administration. This is an especially egregious failing given that at the beginning of the twenty-first century, with the Cold War ended and with no rivals for global leadership, the USA found itself in a unique, unipolar position. As David Armstrong (2002: 78) perceptively points out:

> With the Soviet Union gone, the United States had a choice. It could capitalize on the euphoria of the moment by nurturing cooperative relations and developing multilateral structures to help guide the global realignment taking place; or it could consolidate its power and pursue a strategy of unilateralism and global dominance. It chose the latter course.

Given the USA's unprecedented global dominance, we must all live with the consequences of that choice; if nothing else, it is a reminder that agency matters at moments of historical fluidity. Unlike an earlier generation of US policy-makers in the aftermath of the Second World War (Beeson 2005), however, the USA has used its hegemonic position to pursue, unilaterally and militarily, narrowly and nationally conceived goals. The latter are not only generally misconceived and corrosive of the established international order, they also – unlike in the previous era – offer little to the majority of the world's population. It may be that some testing of the limits of, and possibilities inherent in, US unipolarity was an inevitable consequence of the unique geopolitical circumstances that became more apparent as the 1990s wore on. The USA's remarkable structurally embedded dominance means that whoever is in power in the USA will inevitably exercise a profound impact on the rest of the world. What the rise of the neocons demonstrates is that this latent potential can be bent to ideological ends that may undermine the existing international system and the complex relationships, political structures and normative values that have underpinned it for some fifty years. Thus, one of the great ironies of the rise of the neocons is that they have proven to be anything but conservative, and may yet have a more destructive impact on the old order than the likes of Osama bin Laden could ever hope to have.

Notes

1 It is worth noting that Nitze in particular was a mentor for both Wolfowitz and Perle in the early stages of their respective careers (see Mann 2004).
2 The Project for the New American Century has been an especially influential institution, not least for publishing Kagan and Kristol's (2000b) edited collection *Present Dangers*, which includes works by many of the leading neocon strategists such as Perle, Wolfowitz and Abrams. It has also provided a blueprint for the Bush administration's foreign policy.
3 While this document was initially highly restricted and actively suppressed before being substantially rewritten, it is now available in edited form. See *Frontline* at: http://www.pbs.org/wgbh/pages/frontline/shows/iraq/etc/wolf.html.
4 A copy of this report may be read at: http://www.israeleconomy.org/strat1.htm.
5 Ledeen is especially notorious for his views about the supposed basis of relations among nations, his strong support for Israel, and his contempt for the Oslo peace process as a consequence. He is quoted as saying, 'I don't know of a case in history where peace has been accomplished in any way other than one side winning a war and imposing terms on the other side' (cited in Lobe 2002).
6 The fact that the Bush Administration was able to appoint Bolton as its US Ambassador is indicative of America's continuing ability to achieve its goals in the face of significant opposition.

5 International conflicts and Asia at the end of the fossil energy regime

Elmar Altvater

Introduction: from 'grand chessboard' to the great quagmire

After the demise of the 'socialist system' at the end of the 1980s, the discourse on 'globalization' became dominant in the social sciences. The volume of literature on the subject that has since been published is immeasurably vast. For E. Luttwak (1994) and K. Ohmae (1990), the most prominent proponents of the idea of a new era of 'geo-economics', the main characteristics of globalization are: economic competition on global markets in place of political conflicts in international relations, and the transformation of the binary logics of political enemies and hostile nation-states into the peaceful rules of (by definition) an era of multilateral systems and of free trade. In the meantime, however, and especially after 11 September 2001, the binary interpretation of the world as divided into accepted friends and hostile foes has returned into favour. This notion has been forcefully pushed for, particularly by the Bush administration and the neoconservative think tanks and media that are backing it ideologically.

But is it only ideology that guides the USA in following the path made possible by the 'unipolar moment' (announced by Charles Krauthammer immediately after the end of the Soviet bloc and incessantly repeated since) signaled by the collapse of the Soviet Union (Brzezinski 1997)? Is it instead being led towards the unilateralist path of a superpower by powerful domestic economic interests? How important is it for the geopolitical stance of the USA that leading figures such as Cheney, Rice, Rumsfeld and many others, including Bush himself, have strong ties to the California–Texas oil industry? Is the Bush administration driven by a Wall Street–military–CalTex complex?

I will try to give an answer to these questions by, first, analysing the implications of the predominant fossil energy regime and the dependence of modern capitalist countries on the secure supply of petroleum and, second, by dealing with the relationship between the development of financial markets and the foreseeable exhaustion of fossil resources – a subject disregarded in most analyses of geopolitics. Third, it is necessary to analyse the socio-economic and political dynamics arising from a harsher conflict over oil supplies at the end of the fossil energy regime. Is a period of new 'oil imperialism' returning, and what are the consequences of the greenhouse effect on world peace? Is humankind becoming engulfed in a grand 'quagmire', one that US Defense Secretary Rumsfeld spoke about during a press conference after the provisional end of the war against Afghanistan on 27 November 2001 (Giesenfeld 2004)? Is the quagmire of the Afghanistan and Iraq Wars and of potential 'conflicts among the great powers, arising from their competitive pursuit of strategic advantage' (Klare 2004: 181) in the Gulf and Caspian Sea areas an outcome of the so-called 'strategy of maximum extraction' (Klare 2004: 82 *passim*) of oil for capitalist accumulation and valorization? These questions have to be addressed by taking the dynamics of modern capitalism into consideration. Fourth, in my concluding remarks, I provide a brief overview on the necessary future transition to a renewable energy regime, to a 'postpetroleum economy' (Klare 2004: 197 *passim*), because 'a bold policy to end the nefarious addiction to oil would . . . be the best strategy to win the epic struggle against terrorism – and may be the only one that works' (Kleveman 2004: xx).

Generally, the dynamics of capitalism are the outcome of science and technology, of the social form of surplus-value production (capitalist mode of production) and, last but not least, of the massive use of fossil fuels (energy regime).[1] Access to energy resources has always been a major cause of conflict and violence (Clark 1991). As we approach the end of the fossil energy regime, we are witnessing increasingly sharp conflicts about access to resources, as well as conflicts resulting from the ecological degradation of large territories as a major consequence of the extraction and combustion of oil. The dimensions of these conflicts take the form of disputes over trade, or they appear as diplomatic pressure, or as economic blackmailing. Conflicts about oil have also led to open wars, waged by the 'only super-power' against Afghanistan and Iraq,[2] or among informal warlords and formal governments with regard to access to oil fields and extraction of oil in Africa (Sudan, Angola, Nigeria) or Latin America (Colombia). The fossil energy regime is highly conflict-prone; the 'Grand Chessboard' (Brzezinski 1997) has become a great quagmire that covers large parts of the world, but with its deepest pools in the Gulf, the Caucasus and in Central Asian regions.

The congruence of capitalism and the fossil energy regime

We must first discuss the reasons for the dependence of modern societies on oil. Without a continuous supply and massive use of fossil energies, modern capitalism would be locked within the boundaries of biotic energies such as wind, water and biomasses. In ancient societies (in Europe as well as in Latin America and Asia), although capitalist social forms had already put down some weak roots, these could not flourish because of an insufficient technological basis and the lack of fossil energy. The economy was restricted by a reliance on 'slow' biotic energies that did not allow a capitalist acceleration of production, that is a decisive increase in productivity. Conversely, fossil energy would not have played its decisive role without the social formation of capitalism and its all-encompassing dynamics. Three forces drove that development: (1) the 'European rationality of world domination' (as termed by Max Weber), (2) the dynamics of money in the form of capital (as analysed by Marx), and (3) the comprehensive use of fossil energies in the course of a 'Promethean Revolution' (Georgescu-Roegen 1971). This combination was the main cause for the take-off of modern societies into an era of accelerated growth. Consequently, the Industrial Revolution marks no less than a transition from an *open* energy system (virtually unlimited solar radiation) to a *closed* energy system (based on limited stocks of fossil resources).

One caveat is necessary: although the capitalist 'growth machine' is almost entirely powered by fossil energy (and, thus, stuck in a closed system), human and natural life in general is almost entirely dependent on solar radiation (that is, on an open system). Daylight; the warming of the atmosphere, the water and the soil; the growth of living things; the provision of food and such result from solar radiation and depend on fossil energy consumption only to a small extent. Primary human needs are satisfied only by using energy in the form of organic food (containing proteins, fats, carbohydrates, vitamins, minerals and water) and – in a transformed manner – as clothing and shelter, not to mention the availability of oxygen.

This contradiction between life conditions in an open system and economic conditions that rely on a closed system is of the utmost importance. Capitalism has constructed something like a 'Berlin Wall' between the open system that modulates entropy and the closed system, which is characterized by increasing entropy. Today, and possibly forever, it is impossible to power the machine of capitalist accumulation with solar radiation; it simply does not have the advantages that fossil energies have, namely the potential of time and space compression. On the other hand, the fossil energy regime of the capitalist economy has a highly destructive effect on life on Earth, which is 'powered' almost completely by solar radiation. The degradation of nature – the greenhouse effect, ozone-layer depletion, the loss of biodiversity, desertification, the disappearance of tropical rain forests – and the deterioration of the systems of transforming solar radiation into useful energy for the evolution of nature, are due in great measure to the working of the fossil energy system. Thus, the capitalist socio-economic formation is deeply based on a system that reproduces 'energy apartheid'.

Although nature contains all the resources necessary for humankind to survive, fossil resources allow an increase in 'the wealth of nations'. The latter, since Adam Smith, has been attributed to the historical mission of capitalism – a belief that was shared by Marx and Engels, as is evident in the *Communist Manifesto* of 1848. The undeniable advantage of fossil (and nuclear) energies over solar energy is the congruence of their physical properties with the socio-economic and political logics of capitalist development:

- First, they can be used without consideration of space and place. Industries no longer need to be located in proximity to energy resources, as it has become simple to transport energy resources to any place in the world. The fossil energy system spreads itself far and wide by creating logistical networks that cover the globe. It is, so to speak, 'autopoetic' as it allows the transport of energy to remote places, thus drawing these locations into the fossil system and, then, into the world of capitalist value- and surplus-value production. Energy supply, therefore, is only one factor among many others in decisions about where production is to take place. The availability of local sources of energy has only a minor impact on competition for locations in the global space.

- Second, fossil energies can be used twenty-four hours a day, 365 days a year, with constant intensity. They allow production processes to be organized independently of social time schedules, and biological and other natural rhythms. The time regime of modernity follows the logics of profitability and shareholder value, the reason being that fossil energies can be stored and consumed without reference to natural time patterns and need to agree with the timetable that will maximize profits.

- Third, fossil energies enable the extreme *acceleration* of processes, that is the 'compression of time and space' (Harvey 1996; Altvater and Mahnkopf 2004). Their use promotes an increase in productivity that allows the production of more commodities within a given time span, or the reduction of the time needed to produce a given quantity of products. Since time and space are the co-ordinates of the natural world in which we live, their compression implies a serious disregard for the natural conditions of work and life.

- Fourth, fossil energies can be used very flexibly with regard to the quantities of energy consumed or the temporal distribution and spatial location of consumption. The development of electricity networks and the electric motor, the illumination of whole cities at night, and the gasoline and diesel engines are decisive indications of an increasingly flexible use of energy inputs, of the mobilization and acceleration of economic processes, and of an individualization of social life that had never before existed in human history. Managerial decisions in capitalist firms can now follow the logics of profitability without having to take into account energy restrictions or spatial and temporal constraints. Therefore, accumulation and growth must be understood as being increasingly independent of natural conditions and their limitations.

This congruence is the major cause of high rates of economic growth. Since the emergence of modern capitalism, world population has increased faster than ever before. Moreover, economic growth became independent of population growth because of the enormous increase in productivity. Therefore, contrary to Malthus's predictions, per capita incomes have also increased.

In an OECD study, Angus Maddison shows that in the first millennium of the Common Era, world population grew at an average annual rate of 0.02 per cent, from 230.8 million to 268.3 million. From 1000 to 1820 CE, the number increased to 1041.1 million. GDP per capita followed a similar trend: in the first millennium CE, there was a slight decrease from an average of US$444 to US$435 per person per year (in the 1990 equivalent dollar standard that Maddison used).[3] Between 1000 and 1820 CE, however, there was an increase to $667 per capita.

It is interesting to note that in the first millennium, the income divergences of calculated monetary income in Western Europe, Japan, Latin America, Eastern Europe, Africa and Asia were very small (see Table 5.1). In the second millennium, however, the divergence of per capita incomes increased remarkably. The average world per capita income increased from 1820 to 1998; in the mere span of 178 years, it grew from US$667 to US$5709 (in Maddison's international dollar standard of 1990). Income distribution in the same period became more uneven: 1998 average per capita income was US$17,921 in Western Europe, $26,146 in North America (the USA and Canada), US$2,936 in Asia (excluding Japan) and US$1,368 in Africa (Maddison 2001: 28).

Table 5.1: Level and growth rates of per capita GNP in different world regions from the years 0 to 1998

Year/period	0	1000	1820	1998	0–1000	1000–1820	1820–1998
Region	In international dollars of 1990				Average annual growth rates		
Western Europe	450	400	1,232	17,921	-0.01	0.14	1.51
Western settlers, colonies	400	400	1,201	26,146	0.00	0.13	1.75
Japan	400	425	669	20,143	0.01	0.06	1.93
Latin America	400	400	665	5,795	0.00	0.06	1.22
Eastern Europe and former Soviet Union	400	400	667	4,354	0.00	0.06	1.06
Asia (except Japan)	450	450	575	2,936	0.00	0.03	0.92
Africa	425	416	418	1,368	0.00	0.00	0.67
World	444	435	667	5,709	0.00	0.05	1.21

Source: Maddison, Angus (2001): The World Economy – A Millennial Perspective, OECD, Development Centre Studies, Paris, Table 1-2, p. 28.

Economic growth has become a fetish worldwide. By the twentieth century economic growth came to be seen as the most important goal of economic activity. Growth and growth theory first became central concerns in the planning processes of the socialist Soviet Union, for example. They then made up the dominant economic discourse in the course of competition between the capitalist and Soviet–socialist systems, together with the development of Keynesian economics. Today, growth is the most unchallenged concept of economic theory and policy – from the World Bank to local governments – regardless of the paradigmatic approach that is chosen. Growth is advocated as the main remedy for the problems of the world – from unemployment, poverty and underdevelopment, to the fiscal crisis of the state and so on. Of course, real income growth does enlarge the funds to be distributed, thus facilitating political processes. The question, however, is this: is growth possible for ever, is growth 'triumphant' (Easterlin 1998)? It clearly is not. In a closed system (such as the fossil energy regime), resource stocks – in our case, oil – are limited and exploration for these and their extraction over time become more and more difficult, expensive and conflict-prone.

'Valorization' of resources and 'financialization' of capitalism

The problems arising from the limitedness of fossil fuel supplies are accentuated when we consider the tendency for valorization[4] of natural and social resources, and the modern 'financialization' of capitalism. Valorization is the general subordination of labour and nature under the regime of capitalist surplus-value production and accumulation, which drags them from the open solar energy system into the closed fossil energy system. This general tendency appears in varying historical forms and allows us to distinguish among the historical stages of capitalist development, and among modes of regulation and regimes of accumulation.

I will build on a rather recent debate that stresses anew the exploitative character of 'accumulation by dispossession' (Harvey 2003b). Modern capitalism – comparable to pre-industrial capitalism and to the forms of original or primary accumulation – relies on 'unequal exchange', where profits are appropriated by expropriating third parties, both peoples and classes. 'Enclosures' are not restricted to early capitalism, as in the England of the sixteenth to eighteenth centuries, as is required for so-called 'primary accumulation'; instead, they remain a common feature of capitalism until now (De Angelis 2004). 'Enclosure' establishes private property rights, and involves the predatory seizure and private appropriation of former natural and cultural commons and produced public goods, such as infrastructure. This is not an outdated form of depredation practised by ruling elites in less developed countries but is a highly sophisticated strategy, comparable to 'rent-seeking', for increasing 'shareholder value' without productively creating it. It includes methods of 'creative book keeping', and grand corruption and fraud, as recently demonstrated in the Enron and Parmalat cases and in numerous similar scandals. It also relies on wage reductions, cutbacks in social expenditure or a considerable prolonging of working hours in countries that, in the past decades, have built up a comprehensive welfare system. The all-encompassing privatization of public goods and services is also an expropriation of people for the benefit of financial investors. Last but not least, dispossession has been organized on a large scale by the Bretton Woods institutions, by means of structural adjustment plans that allow TNCs to buy out state-owned industries of indebted countries from Argentina to South Korea.

With regard to accumulation by dispossession, it makes sense to use the Marxian distinction between absolute and relative surplus-value production (Marx 1970: 3rd–5th parts). The first method is geared towards an increase

Table 5.2: Real growth rates and real interest rates

	GDP (real growth rate; nominal growth rate less inflation)				Real interest rates (%) (interest rates on ten - year government bonds less inflation rate)	
	World	G7	Developing countries	Western hemisphere	USA	Euro region
1980–9 (annual average)	3.41	3.01	4.2	2.11	4.94	–
1990	2.8	2.8	3.6	0.6	3.15	–
1991	1.6	1.0	5.0	4.0	3.63	–
1992	2.2	2.0	6.2	3.6	4.02	–
1993	2.4	1.3	6.3	4.0	2.92	–
1994	3.7	3.1	6.7	5.0	4.47	–
1995	3.7	2.4	6.1	1.8	3.77	–
1996	4.0	2.7	6.6	3.6	3.51	5.08
1997	4.2	3.2	5.9	5.2	4.01	4.38
1998	2.8	2.8	3.5	2.3	3.71	3.61
1999	3.6	3.0	3.9	0.2	3.35	3.58
2000	4.8	3.5	5.7	4.0	2.65	3.06
2001	2.4	0.8	4.1	0.7	2.19	2.92

Source: IMF, World Economic Outlook, Database, http://www.imf.org/external/pubs/ft/weo/ 2003/02/data/index.htm (1 February 2004), author's own calculations; more elaborated: Altvater (2004)

in working hours while reducing wage costs, in order to increase surplus value or profits; it is only a 'formal subsumption of labour under capital'. The latter is the appropriate method in modern capitalism – the 'real subsumption of labour under capital' (Marx 1970: 14th chapter) – by increasing surplus value and profits through increasing productivity in the production of wage goods. The production of *absolute* surplus value has again come to be of decisive importance because profits gained with the methods of *relative* surplus production, that is by means of increasing productivity,[5] do not sufficiently meet the claims of capitalist firms and monetary wealth owners. Under the conditions of globalization, interest rates are set on global financial markets to be used by globally operating rating agencies as benchmarks of profitability. Therefore, profit rates or 'shareholder value' produced in the 'real economy' have to be pushed to the level of interest yields on global markets.

Real interest rates (the benchmarks of profitability) since the end of the 1970s, however, have become much higher than real growth rates (see Table 5.2). This difference is an indication that interest rates exceeded the profits produced by means of relative surplus-value production. The 'hard budget constraint' exerted by high interest rates on investors now works as a profit squeeze. Table 5.2 sheds some light on the relationship between real interest rates and real growth rates in the last two decades. The data indicate a level of real interest rates that is consistently higher than the level of real growth rates.

In Asia, too, real interest rates have been extremely high. A Central Bank of the Philippines publication on real interest rates (difference between prime rate and inflation rate) in Southeast Asian countries in late summer 1999, which reviewed the period after the Asian crisis, reveals real interest rates of 5.34 per cent in the Philippines, 17.23 per cent in Indonesia, 14.6 per cent in Hong Kong, 9.3 per cent in Thailand, 8.95 per cent in South Korea, 7.25 per cent in Taiwan, 5.28 per cent in Singapore and 4.6 per cent in Malaysia (Central Bank of the Philippines, News Release, 22 October 1999). In Brazil, real interest rates reached more than 10 per cent in 2002 and 2003 (Folha de Sao Paulo, 18 December 2003).

The 'monetary economy' – in particular, stock markets and institutional investors – exerts 'financial repression' over the 'real economy'[6] because it is highly unlikely that real interest rates of 7 per cent to 17 per cent can be surpassed by real growth rates. This situation, where revenues on financial investment are higher than those on real investment, has been called the 'financialization' of modern 'post-Fordist' capitalism (Aglietta 2000; Chesnais and Serfati 2003). The financial sectors of the global economy are rapidly expanding, whereas the real economy is growing only slowly, hamstrung by economic, social and ecological factors that limit growth (Altvater and Mahnkopf 2004; Altvater 2004; Felix 2002). This is a major reason for the current application of methods of absolute surplus-value production for the purpose of boosting accumulation.

Other consequences of the prohibitive burden of debt service resulting from high interest rates are the financial crises that have hit most of the world's indebted countries since the early 1980s. The Asian crisis of 1997 is a telling example of the destructive effects of financial markets and their inherent instability on the real wealth and living conditions of ordinary people. After the crisis of 1997, Indonesia had to divert about 40 per cent of its GDP to the collapsing banking industry in order to bail out creditors and investors. In 1995, Mexico lost about 20 per cent of its GDP; in 1994, the Czech Republic lost 15 per cent; Russia about 40 per cent in the period 1994–8; South Korea and Thailand lost 25 per cent and 22 per cent, respectively; and 1994–7 saw Argentina lose about 30 per cent and then, after 2001, a large chunk of its GDP (World Bank 2000: 8; de Luna Martínez 2002: 77). High real interest rates require high real growth rates in order to fulfil the necessities of debt service; otherwise, a financial crisis inevitably occurs. In such cases, monetary wealth owners simply satisfy their claims by milking the economic substance of unfortunate countries, with the result that large parts of the population sink into poverty.

This is where the 'financialization' of modern capitalism is linked to the growing demand for oil; hence, the valorization of fossil resources comes into play. High real interest rates demand high GNP growth rates, and under the prevailing patterns of technological deployment, growth can only be achieved by an intensive use of fossil energy. Thus, the operation of global financial markets has an impact on oil extraction and oil markets.[7] Moreover, the globalization of Western production and consumption patterns has resulted in a growing demand for oil. Newly industrializing countries crowd into the oil markets and add to the already insatiable demands of the OECD countries.

The financial claims and the demand arising from the spread of Western lifestyle patterns can grow without acknowledging any social or natural limits, as financial claims follow the auto-referential logic of money and capital. The availability of oil – the fuel of the growth machine – is, on the other hand, subject to natural limitations.

The crisis of the fossil energy regime

Generally, in capitalist calculations, ecological limits are recognized only when they increase the cost of economic processes,[8] either on the input or output side of production. This is because oil stocks are limited and will inevitably run out in the coming decades. Oil production has now probably reached its peak; that is, oil production is greater than the amount of new reserves being found. Moreover, the exploitation of known reserves has become more and more expensive – the last 10 per cent of oil in a field is much more difficult and expensive to extract than the first 10 per cent. On the side of output, limits to the combustion of fossil fuel have become ever more evident because of the deleterious effects on the climate, as well as the social, economic and political consequences.

Possible climate conflicts

One major result of fossil fuel combustion is the enormous increase in greenhouse gas emissions, hence the warming of the atmosphere. According to the Intergovernmental Panel on Climate Change (IPCC 2001), the average global temperature has risen by approximately 0.6°C in the twentieth century. The average surface air temperature is expected to rise by 0.4°C to 5.8°C by 2100, and sea level is projected to rise by 0.09 m to 0.88 m by that same year.

In recent years, there has been much scientific progress in realistically assessing the effects of world temperature increases on sea levels, coastal areas, small and low-lying islands, desertification, agricultural climate zones and biodiversity, although the total climate effects resulting from fossil fuel combustion are still uncertain. Nevertheless, only a few studies flatly dismiss any negative effects of climate change; most studies present serious scenarios of dramatic effects on future living conditions on Earth. The greenhouse effect is expensive, its annual cost has been calculated to reach US$2,000 billion by the middle of this century. According to these calculations, Asia will have to bear US$840 billion, the USA US$325 billion and Europe US$280 billion (Kemfert 2004).

Paradoxically, one of the most pessimistic worst-case scenarios of climate change has been presented in a study commissioned by the Pentagon, carried out by Doug Randall and Peter Schwartz (2003) of the Global Business Network. Since the effects of global warming are not (or will not be) felt equally everywhere, the various regions of the world may exhibit different patterns of climate change. Some regions will suffer a rising sea level, while others will be hit by severe drought (Southern China and Northern Europe). Some regions may even be confronted by a colder climate in the near future because of the changing global air and water circulation. The study was based on the maximum assumption of the IPCC that the average global temperature is likely to increase by up to 5.8°C by 2100. Once this rise in temperature causes the Greenland ice sheet to melt, the Gulf Stream may change direction as a result of the lower density and salination of the North Atlantic Ocean. The resulting collapse of thermohaline circulation is 'disrupting the temperate climate of Europe . . . Ocean circulation patterns change, bringing less warm water north and causing an immediate shift in the weather in Northern Europe and eastern North America. . . . ' (Randall and Schwartz 2003: 9). Europe would be heavily affected in the event of an abrupt change in climate:

> it's likely that food, water, and energy resource constraints will first be managed through economic, political, and diplomatic means such as

treaties and trade embargoes. Over time though, conflicts over land and water use are likely to become more severe – and more violent. As states become increasingly desperate, the pressure for action will grow.

(ibid.: 16)

Even if the climate change is neither dramatic nor as sudden as assumed in the Pentagon scenario (this is the opinion of the majority of climate researchers), it is obvious how conflict-prone and costly – in resources and in human terms – the use of fossil energies actually is. Greenhouse gas emissions and their impact will be felt on both sides of the production process: the 'input side' and the 'output side'.

'Peakoil'

Since the 1990s, there has been a peak in fossil energy production in many oil regions; the number of barrels explored for and found in new reserves is lower than the annual increase in oil production, which means that there is an obvious decline in oil stocks (Global Challenge Network 2002). Although we cannot tell exactly when oil and gas fields will be depleted, we do have convincing evidence that the peak in oil production in some areas has already passed, and that the peak in global oil extraction and production will arrive fairly soon.

In the case of the USA, oil production since the 1970s has been declining, whereas consumption still grows exponentially. This means that the gap between the supply from domestic production and domestic consumption has to be filled by increasing oil imports (Klare 2004: 14–17). For the USA, the 'peakoil problem' can be temporarily resolved by tapping foreign reserves,

Table 5.3: Reserves and annual production of mineral oil and gas

	Reserves		Share of global reserves (%)		Reserves, production in years	
	Oil (million barrels)	Gas (1,000 billion m³)	Oil (million barrels)	Gas (1,000 billion m³)	Oil	Gas
Middle East	686	56.1	65.0	36	92	>200
Latin America	111	7.3	11.0	5	30	53
Africa	77	11.8	7.4	8	27	89
Russia	60	47.6	5.7	31	22	81
Asia–Pacific	39	12.6	3.7	8	14	42
USA, Canada	37	6.9	3.6	4	10	9
Europe	19	5.8	1.8	4	8	20
Caspian region	17	6.6	1.6	4	28	57
World	1,048	155.8	100.0	100	41	61
OPEC	819	–	78.0	–	82	–

Source: Müller, Friedemann (2004) *Klimapolitik und Energieversorgungssicherheit*, SWP-Studie, Berlin, April 2004, p. 17.

yet growing US oil imports mean that the 'peakoil problem' will more quickly become relevant in other oil regions. In the summer of 2004, the Organization of Petroleum Exporting Countries revealed that its members drilled 6.5 per cent fewer wells in 2003 than in the previous year (*Financial Times*, 25 August 2004). Unless this decline is just a one-time occurrence, it is an unerring sign that the peak of oil extraction will soon be reached. Table 5.3 shows the static extent of oil reserves, assuming present reserves and production and excluding increases in demand for oil.

Table 5.3 presents a much more optimistic view on oil reserves than 'peakoil' calculations, the reason being that it does not take into account the greater difficulties and costs of extraction in the course of exploiting and exhausting oil fields. Oil production is dependent on extraction technologies and on the evaluation of reserves in relation to the demand for oil. The first factor is emphasized by neoclassical economists, who recommend capital investment in the exploration of oil fields and oil extraction logistics to increase oil supplies and keep them in pace with growing demand. Natural scarcity, interpreted as a lack of 'nature capital', can be compensated by inputs of money capital. The second factor, evaluating the reserves, is highly dependent on the interests of all parties involved in oil markets – producers, consumers, dealers and, last but not least, politicians. Thus, the estimates of world reserves vary substantially, ranging from 1149 billion barrels (BP) to 780 billion barrels (ASPO) in 2003.

The data published by BP are based on information provided by private oil companies; hence, they are naturally biased.[9] For their part, OPEC countries are interested in high reserve figures for two reasons. First, oil producers increase their reserve estimates in order to get a higher OPEC oil production quota. Typically, in the late 1980s, 'six of the 11 OPEC nations increased their reserve figures by colossal amounts, ranging from 42 to 197 percent, they did so only to boost their export quotas' (Campbell and Laherrère 1998; available at http://www.dieoff.org/page140.htm). In 1983, during the war against Iran, Iraq reported an increase in its reserves of 11 billion barrels even though no new fields had been discovered. In 1985, Kuwait announced an increase in reserves by 50 per cent without offering any proof.

The second reason for reporting high reserves is to reassure oil consumers. High reserves signal that there will be no shortage of oil in the future, therefore, there is no need to search for alternative energy sources. On the other hand, reserves may be deliberately underestimated in order to increase the hidden reserves of an oil company or to inflate oil prices so that it seems profitable to explore unconventional oil (such as deep-sea oil, oil sand, polar oil and heavy oil) and warrant high investment in new infrastructure (pipelines, tankers, refineries, etc.).

Oil price increases will especially affect oil-importing countries; however, the import burden is not equally distributed throughout the world (Table 5.4). Countries with a low income per capita have relatively higher import

Table 5.4: Imports of fuels and export revenues of selected countries, 2002 (in US$million)

Country	Imports of fuels	Total export revenues	Share of fuel imports in total imports (%)	Share of fuel imports in export revenues
Argentina[a]	798	26,610	3.9	2.9
Brazil	7,549	60,362	15.2	12.5
Peru	1,034	7,688	13.7	13.4
Mexico	4,455	160,682	2.3	2.7
Pakistan	3,004	9,913	26.7	30.3
South Africa	3,269	29,723	13.0	11.0
China	19,285	325,565	6.5	5.9
India[a]	15,935	49,251	31.7	32.4
USA	121,927	693,860	10.1	17.6
EU[b]	129,868	939,804	13.9	13.8

[a] 2001.
[b] Imports and exports from or to third countries.
Source: Author's own calculations; data from WTO, Trade Statistics 2003.

expenses than those with a high GNP per capita. Countries with currencies subject to revaluation vis-à-vis the US dollar suffer less from an increase in oil prices than those that need devaluation vis-à-vis the US dollar. The 'oil-seigniorage' position, however, will continue to be held by the USA as long as the oil price is invoiced in US dollars.

These figures were calculated before the dramatic oil price increases in 2004. Thus, many oil-importing countries now face more serious difficulty in paying the oil bill.

Whereas oil-producing countries in the Middle East, Russia and North Africa benefit from very high oil revenues, oil-importing countries, especially the poor Sub-Saharan economies, suffer the burden of large oil bills. Thus, high oil prices help to exacerbate already existing global inequalities. Oil importers such as China are projected to import more than five times more oil in 2025 than in 2001, under the premise that there will be continued economic growth (Klare 2004: 165). China is not a unique case; many countries will increase their demand for oil in the course of further industrialization, and declining reserves may deepen conflicts about access to oil reserves.

Oil imperialism

Access to oil, even in the hands of individual countries and private corporations, can be understood as the provision of a (global) public good, since oil is of decisive importance in energy security under the premises of the fossil energy regime. Oil distribution can be left to market forces and the processes of price formation, such that oil consumers that cannot afford to pay the oil invoices are barred from accessing it. On the other hand, oil distribution could be organized as a democratic, just rationing of oil reserves, a prospect that appears unrealistic at the moment. The third mode of distributing oil reserves concerns the exercise of political power and military violence.

The battle now is over the control of scarce oil resources, producing a new 'petrostrategy', which combines geo-economics and geopolitics. All 'powers have a vital stake in the global flow of oil, and all . . . seek some degree of control over the political dynamics of the most important oil-producing regions' (Klare 2004: 147). From the standpoint of individual nations, control of remote oil regions is part of an oil security strategy; as a result, the USA, the EU, NATO, Russia, China and many other nations have set up national strategies of energy security. The proposed Constitution of the EU provides a common European military force for intervention in all parts of the world in order to strengthen European security. The new concept of security also includes energy security, and as long as this is identical to the secure supply of oil and gas, the dependence on fossil energy will remain conflict-prone.

Table 5.5 gives an indication of the regional dependency of oil-importing countries. Europe is heavily dependent on the countries of the former Soviet Union, whereas the USA imports the largest part of its oil from Latin America and the Gulf–OPEC countries.

In the USA, too, energy security is one of the priorities of US foreign policy (Cheney Report 2001; Klare 2004: 56 *passim*). An energy–security

Table 5.5: Flows of oil, 2002 (million barrels per day)

To From	USA	Europe	East and Southeast Asia	Rest of the world	Total
Gulf-OPEC	2.31	3.24	11.29	1.22	18.06
Former Soviet Union	0.20	4.35	0.40	0.42	5.37
North Africa	0.28	1.77	0.20	0.37	2.62
West Africa	1.12	0.71	1.04	0.26	3.13
Latin America	3.95	0.47	0.19	0.32	4.93
Canada	1.94	0.01	0.001	0.00	1.96
Rest of the world	1.56	1.35	3.21	1.44	7.56
Total	11.36	11.90	16.34	4.03	43.63

Source: Müller, Friedemann (2004) *Klimapolitik und Energieversorgungssicherheit*, SWP-Studie, Berlin, April 2004, p. 16.

policy refers to several dimensions: first, to strategic control of oil territo-ries; second, to the strategic control of oil logistics (pipelines, oil tanker routes, secure refineries and storage); third, to influencing price levels by controlling supply and demand; and fourth, it aims to determine currency in which the price of oil is invoiced. When we consider the many complex strands in a strategy of oil security or 'oil imperialism', the formula of 'blood for oil' seems too simple, yet it is essentially correct. More countries are explicitly trying to secure access to oil fields that have already passed their peak. The means of distribution of oil are either co-operative or competitive, such that conflicts between oil-importing and oil-producing countries are ever threatening to break out.

The combination of market forces and military power is a core element in the ideologies of US neoconservatives, for whom the invisible hand of the market must be assisted by the visible fist of the US Army. This a contradic-tory position only at first glance; considered more closely, it refers to a long 'oil-empire' tradition. US wealth, power and supremacy are founded on 'cheap and abundant oil flows' (Klare 2004) from the Rockefeller–Baku connection in the nineteenth century to the war against Iraq and the grip on the Central Asian and African oil reserves.

First, the US government aims to secure strategic control over oil regions whether by means of diplomacy and friendly relations, or through pressure and subversion, as in some Latin American and African countries, or by using massive military power as in Iraq and, to a lesser extent, Central Asia. The Iraq War and the attempt to gain control over a country with estimated reserves of more than 100 billion barrels, however, does seem irrational – the military occupation of a country with a hostile population that puts up resistance is extremely expensive. Further, in ways that are difficult to assess, the exercise may well have a demoralizing impact on the hegemony and often-cited 'imperial overstretch' of the global superpower,[10] not to mention the many victims among the civilian population. The conclusion that follows is that militarily enforced access to oil territories is, at best, a 'second-best' solution compared to other means of exerting pressure on governments.

Second, the strategic control of oil logistics is also expensive, albeit to a lesser extent. The exercise requires the collaboration of governments in countries transversed by pipelines, and in countries traversed by tankers. The waters around the Horn of Africa at the entrance to the Red Sea are protected against 'terrorist attacks' by the German Navy in collaboration with the navies of other NATO members. The Straits of Malacca are protected against pirates and supposed terrorists by the Indonesian, Singaporean and Malaysian Navies. In Central Asia, the USA has created what is sometimes designated a 'Pipelineistan', which encompasses transit territories for pipelines, much like the one under construction from Baku via Tbilisi to the Turkish port of Ceyhan (BTC-pipeline), which avoids transit through Russia, or the projected transCaspian-pipeline from the Tengis oil field in Western Kazakhstan to Baku and along the eastern shores of the

Caspian Sea via Afghanistan to Pakistan. Conflicting interests, however, are at play. The USA has created major military bases in Central Asia and there are US oil firms present. Relying as it does on corrupt, authoritarian regimes, US dominance here is precarious and faces challenges – not only from 'terrorists' but also from considerable parts of the population.

The presence of other players in the 'Great Game' cannot be overlooked. China needs Central Asian oil to fuel its domestic economy, while Iran is a regional power with close ties to China. Russia, too, has an important stake in the region, which until 1991 was part of the Soviet Union.

Third, the influence on oil supplies is only possible by influencing OPEC or by putting diplomatic pressure on individual oil producers, or by carrying out oil exploration (that is, a valorization of resources) in parts of the world that, up to now, have not been fully included in the 'oil empire'. The occupation of Iraq and the establishment of a US-dependent government – only formally sovereign – has enabled the USA to exert some influence on OPEC decisions, since Iraq is a member country. Placing diplomatic pressure on oil producers to increase exports is a measure that is quite commonly practised by other rich oil-consuming countries besides the USA. It is doubtful if the global supply will be significantly enlarged by newly discovered oil reserves, as it is unlikely that even these new reserves can keep apace with the growing demand for oil.

Is it possible to influence the demand? The answer is both positive and negative. On the one hand, the USA is still the most important oil consumer; it is also the most inflexible because of its inability or unwillingness to reduce oil consumption. On the other hand, new oil consumers such as China, India and other newly industrializing countries are crowding the market. China and India alone are responsible for three-quarters of the additional oil demand in 2004.

Fourth, the last aspect of an energy–security policy concerns the currency of the oil bill. In the 1970s, the US dollar fell sharply against other currencies and there was increased inflation in the USA. Faced with this situation, the oil-exporting countries managed to exploit the opportunity of the Israeli–Arab Yom Kippur War of October 1973 to increase the oil price, a move that was experienced as a severe 'shock' by oil-importing countries. Thirty years later, however, the situation has changed because there is now an alternative currency to the US dollar, namely the euro. In June 2003, however, OPEC decided to continue invoicing in US dollars although some governments, above all Venezuela and (pre-invasion) Iraq, had been planning on switching to the euro.

US domination of all the other dimensions of 'oil governance' and oil security ensures that there will be no change in the oil currency, although it is uncertain if this situation will last for ever. The loss in value of the US dollar vis-à-vis the euro, and the huge twin deficits in the current account and federal budget that are being borne by the US economy, present the euro as a more attractive oil currency for oil exporters.

This option could also become attractive for other countries, particularly Japan, China and Russia, whose huge official reserves consist of US financial assets. According to *The Economist* (10 January 2004), at the end of 2003, Japan held reserves totalling US$673.5 billion, China had US$406 billion, Hong Kong had US$114.1 billion, South Korea US$150.3 billion and Taiwan US$206.3 billion. Russia is estimated to have more than US$100 billion. There is the distressing possibility that these reserves would lose part of their value in the event that the US dollar suffers devaluation, a phenomenon already underway in late 2004. These countries may be able to switch their reserves to alternative currencies, most notably the euro, but may do so slowly to avoid creating turbulence in currency markets. Senior officials of the People's Bank of China have, in fact, declared their intention to increase the share of the euro in its reserves. The euro share of the reserves of Asian central banks presently, however, stands at just 6 per cent, so the degree of movement towards the euro should not be overstated (Solans 2004: 12). Yet, there is a greater likelihood for such a switch to the extent that there are further increases in the twin deficits in the US budget and the current account. Again, we have to take into account the intertwined structures of global oil and global finance, such that a strategy that aims to prevent conflicts must include regulation of both the oil market and the global financial markets. The switch of oil currency from the US dollar to the euro would have a major negative effect on the US economy, thus on the world economy as a whole.

Transition to a renewable energy regime

Looming on the horizon of disputes on energy security is a serious conflict between the US dollar and the euro, between North America and Europe. Oil imperialism obviously brings with it conflict dimensions that have the potential to jeopardize the peaceful co-existence of peoples throughout the world. Thus, the persistent dependence on fossil energy combustion beyond the 'peakoil' point to the brink of exhausting reserves has not only further deleterious consequences for the global environment, but also an increasingly negative impact on the global public good of world peace and ecological sustainability. Therefore, the transition to a 'post-petroleum economy' (Klare 2004: 197 *passim*) is a necessity that entails improvements in energy efficiency, more reliance on domestic energy sources and a reduction in dependency on imported fuels. Moreover, every effort should be made to develop an alternative energy regime based on renewable resources, namely solar energy and photovoltaic, wind, water and biotic energies, among other sources. The necessary technologies and appropriate social institutions are already available, although research, political support and economic subsidies in the industrialized world are still largely siphoned into traditional fossil and nuclear energy production instead of renewable energies.

In the long run, however, the 'energy apartheid' system must be overcome by a transition from the closed fossil energy system with its increasing entropy to the open solar energy system with constant entropy. Such a transition is possible and the 'window of opportunity' is still open, for:

> renewable energies are becoming constantly cheaper, through the mass production of the plants and technical optimizations. Atomic and fossil energy in contrast are becoming more expensive, through increasing extraction costs and environmental damages as well as the increasing technical and military safety measures.
> (World Council for Renewable Energies: Renewable Energies instead of Nuclear Power http://www.eurosolar.org/new/en/downloads/ Anzeigenkampagne_Englisch.pdf)

The transformation of the energy system will only succeed through a transformation of the social system, since the energy system does not exist independently of production, reproduction, politics and culture. It is necessary to surmount the above-mentioned 'Berlin Wall' and its related 'ideological mindset' that separates the fossil fuel regime from the life energies from the Sun. This is a long-term project that will need deep changes in daily life patterns, technologies, the built environment, political participation and global financial architecture, to name but a few aspects.

Notes

1 I am fully aware that the political revolution and creation of a modern bourgeois system are of utmost importance for the further development of capitalist societies, but these topics are not within the scope of this chapter.
2 The war against Yugoslavia of 1999 can be interpreted as part of the geopolitical 'Great Game' about resources, too. It helped to establish military bases in the Balkans and bridge the territorial gap between Central European NATO members (Hungary) on the one side and Greece and Turkey on the other. Moreover, it became possible to lock up Russia and other competing powers in a geo-strategic line-up of Eastern European (Georgia, Ukraine) and Caspian states (Azerbaijan, Uzbekistan, Kyrgyzstan, Afghanistan).
3 Maddison, of course, is aware of the problems arising from measuring monetary flows over 2,000 years in the dollar denominations of 1990. Interpreting these figures, therefore, requires extreme caution. Nevertheless, the data are plausible even though their precision is legitimately doubtful.
4 'Valorization' is both surplus-value production and the initial stage of a transfer of resources (which, until then, were not values) into the world of values, where they are subject to the conditions of value and surplus-value production. The French and German terms are clearer than the English term: *mise-en-valeur* and *Inwertsetzung*.
5 Increasing productivity under the 'Fordist regime' was accompanied by wage increases and a reduction of labour time, thus creating a growing demand for a growing supply of goods and services. Since the 1970s, however, this 'Fordist equation' has lost its historical validity.
6 In the economic literature, 'financial repression' is understood as the regulation and control of financial markets by government: 'In this view financial repression

refers to a set of policies, laws, formal regulations, and informal controls, imposed by governments on the financial sector, that distort financial prices – interest rates and foreign exchange rates – and inhibit the operation of financial intermediaries at their full potential . . . Successful financial repression increases the demand for credit, and at the same time, creates disincentives to save' (Denizer *et al.* 1998). Here, contrary to the neoclassical concept, the term is used to make more lucid the pressures exerted by financial claims on the real economy.

7 It can only be mentioned in passing here that two other pressures are also exerted by the financial system on the quantities and prices of supplies offered on the world's oil markets. One arises from speculation in the futures markets. The other results from the heavy 'petrodollar' and 'petro-euro' investments of rich Gulf oil producers in financial assets, which has led to their incomes being just as dependent on interest flows as on oil revenues.

8 Gold is a telling example. Notwithstanding its very nature as a limited resource, gold functions socially and economically as money. Since capitalist accumulation ignores natural boundaries and money is a social construct, the function of money has been decoupled from the natural form of limited gold and assigned to paper money or electronic bits and bytes. The natural form of money has completely disappeared. Attempts to revive gold as the natural form of money are doomed to failure.

9 The case of Shell is telling. In early 2004, the company had to reduce its published, highly overvalued reserve figures by 3.9 billion barrels – that is, by more than 20 per cent – to fulfil stock market supervision requirements (*Financial Times*, 25 August 2004). A major reason for such an 'error' and its correction is 'creative book-keeping'.

10 The Cheney Report lists eight countries of particular weight for US oil diplomacy: Mexico, Colombia, Russia, Azerbaijan, Kazakhstan, Nigeria, Angola and Venezuela. These countries are labelled by Michael Klare as the 'Alternative Eight' (Klare 2004: 115 *passim*).

Part II

Asia: social conflict, power and the American Empire

6   Neoliberal globalization, conflict and security

New life for authoritarianism in Asia?

Garry Rodan and Kevin Hewison

Introduction

In the postwar period, important watersheds have shaped conflicts that have arisen with regard to the establishment, consolidation and replacement of various economic and political regimes within Southeast Asia. In each case, these watersheds have entailed significant shifts in US foreign policy and economic leadership, thus shaping the complexion and outcomes of these conflicts. These watersheds include the emergence of the Cold War, the end of the Cold War and the 1997–8 Asian financial crisis. With each watershed, there has been a change in the USA's tolerance of and support for regimes that depart from economic and political liberalism. In particular, both the end of the Cold War and the Asian crisis led to new pressures for liberal economic and/or political reform. Presently, however, it is the War on Terror that represents a new potential watershed. Will it lead to an accentuation, reversal or uneven prosecution of these pressures?

The end of the Cold War left the USA as the world's sole superpower, and freed up resources and energy on the part of the US administration and business to lead and support an accelerated push for neoliberalism. Economic regimes in Asia that stood in the way of the neoliberal ideal came under increased scrutiny, and it became more difficult to rationalize Western support for authoritarian political regimes (Nye 2004a). The Asian crisis instantly generated confident neoliberal attacks on 'Asian capitalism', the developmental state and authoritarian regimes. These assaults came from both within and beyond the region, and involved a conjuncture of forces for economic and political liberalism whose agenda sometimes intersected.

Significantly, economic liberals did not target all forms of authoritarianism, while their criticism of the politics of Asian capitalism was not limited to authoritarian regimes. The principal targets for these critics were 'crony capitalist' regimes, or regimes in which there was endemic rent-seeking. An important point is that at this time, the neoliberal economic reform agenda was unrestrained by global security concerns. Consequently, US-dominated multilateral institutions promoted economic governance systems that were both functional for neoliberalism and fused with schemes to promote economic recovery in the region. The elevation of security concerns within US foreign policy in the War on Terror, however, heralds new challenges for the development of neoliberal globalization; this may see a return to the centre stage of the kinds of political concerns that motivated Cold War thinking. Whereas the post-Cold-War period witnessed an unprecedented privileging of the neoliberal economic reform agenda, is this now balanced by considerations of how to contain terrorism? Is the war on terrorism part of the global struggle to embed neoliberalism, as Harvey (2003a) and Lafer (2004) argue? More particularly, for the purposes of this chapter, what are the specific implications for political regime directions in Southeast Asia as a result of the US-led War on Terror? How will the concerted push for neoliberalism affect unresolved conflicts about the directions of authoritarian and post-authoritarian regimes?

In the discussion to follow, we examine this question by way of an analysis of Singapore and Thailand; these countries involve an authoritarian and a post-authoritarian regime, respectively. We argue that the US-led War on Terror has created new opportunities for the consolidation, refinement and restoration of authoritarian practices in both countries. These opportunities do relate not only to a strengthening of repressive powers that the state can use for political rather than security purposes, but also to an environment that is conducive to official ideologies that justify these and other measures that are hostile to political pluralism. Moreover, the USA's linking of trade access to co-operation in security is serving to enhance the status and credibility of those political leaders who are responsible for putting curbs on free political expression. Trade Representative Robert Zoellick's announcement that the USA was ready to extend free trade initiatives to 'can-do' Asian countries (*Far Eastern Economic Review*, 30 October 2003) bears a strong resonance to the historical pattern of US aid, trade and investment during the Cold War, which helped to prop up a range of authoritarian leaders in Southeast Asia. Rather than a straightforward replication of the Cold War period, however, there is also a subtle but important shift in rhetorical and ideological content in the latest geopolitical realignment. US neoconservatives seem to appreciate not just the role of certain authoritarian leaders in fighting a common enemy, as they did in the Cold War, but also their promotion of core values of social conservatism.

Singapore

The common feature in all authoritarian regimes is the systematic obstruction of political competition and an independent civil society, although the means by which this is achieved vary. In the Singapore case, crude forms of repression have, over time, given way to a greater emphasis on administrative and legalistic obstacles, on the one hand, and extensive structures of political co-option, on the other. The official ideological rationales for the virtual one-party state in Singapore have also been dynamic, with culturalist notions having been drawn on since the late 1980s in an attempt to justify authoritarian rule (Rodan 1996a; 1996b). The War on Terror is proving to be important to the regime in a number of respects. First, the Singapore government has been rewarded for its support of US foreign policy with a trade deal that enhances the economic strategies of the ruling party, and its international and domestic standing and legitimacy. Second, the 'war' is facilitating a consolidation and extension of more traditional forms of repressive legislation. Third, it has created a climate that is conducive to synthesizing and updating core ideological themes that rationalize existing social and political controls.

Strengthening the trade–security nexus

The Singapore case clearly bears out the point about a more acute nexus emerging between trade and security in the context of the War on Terror. The city-state had not been entirely shielded from heightened neoliberal pressures on developmental state economies following the advent of the Asian crisis. The Singapore government also became a strong supporter of FTAs in this period, with the view that ASEAN and APEC had failed and that there was a need to push ahead – even if only bilaterally – towards further trade liberalization. Indeed, since 1998, there has been unprecedented critical attention on Singapore's government-linked companies (GLCs) – which dominate the commanding heights of the domestic economy – by assorted interests in the financial sector, other elements of international capital and ideological champions of free markets, including within international financial institutions and the international media. Calls for various forms of privatization and liberalization to reduce the power of GLCs and usher in a more level playing field for private, and especially international, capital gathered momentum from 2001, when Singapore experienced its worst economic recession since Independence. The ensuing FTA negotiations between Singapore and the USA embodied some of this contention over GLCs.

The USA viewed Singapore as an economic hub for many of its interests in the region. It also saw the value in using an FTA with Singapore to set down some principles of domestic economic governance for subsequent agreements with other countries. Consequently, negotiations towards the United States Singapore Free Trade Agreement (USSFTA), first projected in late 2000, dragged on for two years and were only concluded in late 2002 and formally approved early the next year. The delay occurred largely because FTA negotiations brought a significant degree of scrutiny to bear on the GLCs and the institutional mechanisms through which their interests have been protected and advanced. The Singapore government's steadfast refusal to give ground on its right to impose capital controls in the event of an economic crisis was also a stumbling block. The issues at stake were not simply economic; the vast economic and social reach of the GLCs – and an equally important array of statutory bodies – is integral to the political economy of the authoritarian regime in Singapore. Ultimately, the capacities for political reward and punishment are affected by the control over resources that is embodied in these institutions.

Although there were matters in which Singapore was forced to shift ground in the course of the USSFTA, it was clear that the dynamics of the deliberations altered after 11 September 2001. From that point on, Washington's willingness to conclude deals intensified, and it took just a few more months for the treaty to be concluded. It was the first such accord between the USA and an Asian country.

Singapore has been a strong defence and security ally of the USA throughout the Cold War and beyond, including at times when others in the region were becoming wary about forging too close an alliance. When US forces were withdrawn from the Clark Air Base and the Subic Naval Base in the Philippines in the early 1990s, for example, the Singapore government offered them access to military facilities. More recently, Singapore developed the largest dock in the region, designed specifically to accommodate and support US aircraft carriers. In the wake of 11 September, the USA has been impressed by the Singapore authorities' unqualified preparedness to root out suspected terrorists from within and support the USA in international fora on security issues – in a region described by US Secretary of State, Colin Powell, as the 'second front' in the War on Terror (CNN.com 2004).

Between the time of the 11 September 2001 attacks in the USA and 2004, the authorities in Singapore had detained or placed restriction orders on fifty people (Boey 2004). This included the arrest of fifteen suspected terrorists in December 2001,[1] thus averting an alleged plot to bomb embassies and commercial interests of the USA and other Western countries. Such action was taken at a time when the USA faced difficulty in getting other governments in the region to co-operate fully in combating terrorism. Subsequently, the Singapore government took measures to curb money laundering activities and financial transactions that facilitated terrorism. It also arrested another twenty-one suspected terrorists in August 2002.[2] In October 2003, a Framework Agreement for the Promotion of Strategic Cooperation Partnership in Defense and Security was jointly announced by President Bush and then Prime Minister Goh Chok Tong. This agreement expanded bilateral co-operation in counter terrorism, counter proliferation of weapons of mass destruction, joint military exercises and training, policy dialogues and defence technology (Acharya 2004: 4). A Strategic Framework Agreement was formally signed in Washington DC by President Bush and Prime Minister Lee in July 2005.

Singapore's close co-operation with the USA in the fight against terror was further reflected in the opening of a legal attaché office of the FBI in the city-state. Moreover, the Singapore government lent strong support for the passage of United Nations Resolution 1441 and, eventually, the invasion of Iraq.[3] As a member of the 'coalition of the willing', Singapore made available transport and equipment support in Iraq as well as police and health care workers to assist with reconstruction. It also allowed US aircraft to fly in Singapore air space and use Singapore's military bases during the war. Thus, leading up to and beyond the signing of the USSFTA in early 2003, the alignment between the two governments on security matters went from strength to strength.

Crucially, the US Treasury had consistently taken a hard line on the need for provisions to 'ensure that US investors have the right to transfer funds into and out of the host country using a market rate of exchange' (quoted in US Chamber of Commerce 2003).[4] After 11 September, the USA settled for an agreement that guaranteed investors free transfer into and out of both countries, but which also gave Singapore the right to restrict capital flow via the Monetary Authority of Singapore.[5] Although the agreement also contained a number of provisions that were meant to introduce a more level playing field for competing with GLCs, they were modest and not all tied down to clearly defined or tightly scheduled reforms. As a result, the agreement is unlikely to reduce fundamentally the power of GLCs within the domestic market (see Rodan 2004).

An emphasis on the security dimension of USA–Singapore relations was a feature of lobbying in the USA by business interests associated with investment and trade between the two countries, as well as by assorted political groups that also sought to expedite the conclusion of the USSFTA after 11 September. The latter included the right-wing Heritage Foundation, which had long been effusive in its praise of the Singapore government despite the developmental state (Lee Siew Hua 2002). More significantly, Singapore is host to over 1,300 US companies, which account for more than half the city-state's exports to the USA. The USSFTA Business Coalition was specifically formed in March 2002 to muster the requisite political support for the deal. It was chaired by executives representing Boeing, ExxonMobil and United Parcel Services (UPS), and enjoyed institutional endorsement and support from the US–ASEAN Business Council and the US Chamber of Commerce.[6]

Another lobby group, the Singapore Congressional Caucus, emerged in October 2002 and came to work closely with the Business Coalition. It was a joint initiative of the US House of Representatives Republican, Curt Weldon, and a US Congress Democrat, Solomon Ortiz. Both were senior members of the House Armed Services Committee. The Caucus, boasting over fifty members, advocated stronger ties with Singapore for security and economic reasons (Hadar 2002).

The link between the USSFTA's speedy conclusion after 11 September and its rapid and uncontroversial passage through Congress was not a matter of dispute. Singapore's Foreign Affairs Minister, Lee Yock Suan, told the Asia Society in Texas that 'the real significance of the USSFTA goes beyond economic benefits' (Lee Yock Suan 2002). He contended that in view of the strategic trends concerning terrorism in Southeast Asia, 'concluding the USSFTA sends an important signal that the US intends to remain a dominant player in East Asia' (Lee Yock Suan 2002).[7] When asked if the expeditious conclusion amounted to a reward for Singapore's support for the US war in Iraq, Congress Republican Representative Pete Sessions responded: 'Singapore supported us not only on the day of the terrorist attacks, but has since been very involved in our war on terror.' He added: 'Countries which are our friends are those who will continue to reap the rewards of a closer relationship' (quoted in Leinin 2003). President Bush's visit to Singapore in October 2003 was only the second (after his father's in 1992) to the city-state by a US President (Fernandez 2003).

It is important to note that the security-conscious mood in the USA during the USSFTA negotiations meant that attempts by the Singapore government's human rights critics to influence debate were ineffectual. In particular, Singapore Democratic Party (SDP) Secretary-General Chee Soon Juan's efforts to raise such issues aroused little interest among US politicians (Chee 2003a). The considerable resources and networks of the Business Coalition and other supporters of a rapid conclusion to the agreement also helped ensure that such efforts were marginalized.

Shoring up repressive legislation

The capacity of existing authoritarian regimes to exploit the new geopolitical context for their consolidation is evident in Singapore. Among other things, the War on Terror has helped legitimize the controversial Internal Security Act (ISA), which allows for indefinite detention without trial and has, in the past, been used to silence the government's political adversaries; in recent years, this technique has given way to the use of defamation and libel suits through the courts (Seow 2004). Some opposition groups in Singapore had, prior to 11 September, sought to make the repeal of the ISA a major public issue. The Singapore government, however, came to demonstrate how swiftly it could tackle terrorism so as to deflect calls for a reform or repeal of the ISA.

Security concerns were also used to justify amendments to the Computer Misuse Act November 2003, allowing authorities to take pre-emptive action against 'cyberterrorism'.[8] The amendment, which carries sentences of up to three years in jail and a maximum fine of S$10,000, gives authorities extensive powers to scan the Internet and make arrests in anticipation of possible security threats. The law's similarity to the ISA prompted criticism from opposition groups, with SDP's Chee describing it as 'another disguised attempt by the ruling party to control the use of the Internet by Singaporeans and to curtail the spread of discussion and dissent in Singapore's cyberspace' (Chee 2003b).[9]

The immediate background to this accusation by Chee included a directive by the Singapore Broadcasting Authority in January 2002 to a group calling itself Voice of the Singapore Muslim Community to register as a political organization in order to continue publishing its seven-month-old web site, Fateha.com. The site contained a press release by Zulfikar Muhamad Shariff that criticized the Singapore government's alignment with the USA, and its having 'trivialised the concerns of the Muslim community for too long' (Zulfikar 2002). He also called for detainees under the ISA to be brought to trial (Associated Press 2002). Zulfikar subsequently found himself under police investigation for posting topics on the web site relating to the appointment of Ho Ching to Temasek, the banning of Muslim head-scarves in schools and the performance of the minister-in-charge of Muslim affairs (Tan 2003: 244–6). Under the spectre of charges for criminal defama-tion, which carried the prospect of up to two years in jail, Zulfikar fled Singapore to reside in Australia with the claim that he had no confidence in the independence of Singapore's courts (Rodan 2004: 104).

The Singapore government's readiness to use the new security context as a rationale for limiting dissent at times even embarrassed US officials. The US Ambassador to Singapore, Franklin Lavin, explained, for example, that the removal of peaceful protesters demonstrating against US policy in Iraq from outside the US Embassy in early 2003 was unnecessary:

> I don't see why a group of people who want to stand in front of my Embassy and tell me they don't agree with a policy of my country should not be able to do so. The right of peaceful expression of opinion is an important element of a successful society.
>
> (Lavin 2003)

Such sentiments, however, were overshadowed by the US government's strong endorsement of the regime's effectiveness in co-operating in the War on Terror.

As a result of the War on Terror, the extensive powers of state surveillance and intimidation may be enhanced through an even more centralized and co-ordinated set of structures. New agencies such as the Homefront Security Office and the Joint Counter Terrorism Centre are but part of a strategy of 'tighter networking and inter-agency co-ordination', according to the govern-ment's official document, *The Fight Against Terror: Singapore's National Security Strategy* (National Security Coordination Centre 2004: 15).

Security, ethnicity and authoritarian rule

Zulfikar's experiences and the confrontation with Fateha.com highlight the problematic and structural nature of the People's Action Party's (PAP's) brand of multiculturalism. As Rahim (1998) persuasively argues and docu-ments, despite absolute economic gains, ethnic Malays continue to be politically, economically and educationally marginalized compared to the dominant ethnic Chinese community. This is why Malays have historically constituted a disproportionate percentage of the non-PAP vote. The govern-ment's attempts to limit conflict in the relationship between ethnicity and socio-economic distribution have included ethnic quotas for Housing Development Board flats, diluting the electoral impact of organized Malay opponents, and state-sponsored ethnic community self-help groups such as Mendaki (Brown 1994; 2000). These measures have not been a complete success, as has been suggested by the formation of the independent Association of Muslim Professionals (AMP) in 1990 out of dissatisfaction with Mendaki, and its periodic friction with the government thereafter (Ahmad Osman 2000). The accelerated pace of economic restructuring associated with Singapore's wider embrace of globalization – and the increasing structural unemployment and social inequality that accompanies it – poses additional challenges for ethnic conflict management.

Moreover, of the fifteen initial arrests in December 2001, which the Singapore government claims foiled planned bombings in the city-state by three JI cells, thirteen of the detainees were Singaporean Malays. The government has argued that since the group included small business owners, and skilled and semi-skilled people, its motivation was religious and ideological extremism and not socio-economic factors (Lim 2002). Upwardly mobile Malays, however, are also more likely to encounter any subtle ethnic glass ceilings that exist, which could render them more vulnerable to ideological overtures from extremists. After all, the group was not exactly characterized by corporate high-flyers.[10]

To be sure, support for the USA-led War on Terror is not without its problems for the Singapore government. The importance of its relations with domestic Muslim constituencies and with its Muslim-dominated neighbours necessitates care in how it expresses support for US foreign policy. Singapore Defence Minister Teo Chee Hean's apparent endorsement in April 2004 of a proposal for US Marines to patrol the Malacca Straits to safeguard against maritime terrorism aroused a stern critical reaction from the Malaysian and Indonesian governments.[11] Singapore's neighbours not only resented the inference that they were not capable of protecting the shared waterway but were also adamant that a stronger US presence in the region would exacerbate terrorist threats (Sudha 2004). As a result, a new maritime security initiative, the Trilateral Co-ordinated Patrols Malacca Straits or MALSINDO, was launched by the Indonesian, Malaysian and Singaporean armed forces on 20 July 2004.

Then Prime Minister, Goh Chok Tong also took the opportunity during US Defense Secretary Donald Rumsfeld's visit to Singapore in June 2004 to make the point that, in relation to global terrorism: 'The US is essential to the solution but is also part of the problem' (quoted in DAWN.com 2004). Goh argued that 'the discomfort mainstream Muslims feel around the world with America's Middle East policies limits their ability to fight the ideological battles' (quoted in channelnewsasia.com 2004). Yet, Rumsfeld's appeal to Asian countries to 'work together' in the War on Terror also presents an opportunity for governments in the region to demonstrate their utility and commitment to US foreign policy.

Revitalizing PAP ideology

The concept of the War on Terror resonates powerfully with the PAP's long-fostered notion of Singapore's exceptional vulnerability to sudden and unexpected adverse forces. This spectre has been alluded to over recent decades to rationalize the need for highly elitist power structures. Its first manifestation was the ideology of 'survivalism', expounded by Lee Kuan Yew and his colleagues in the immediate aftermath of separation from the Federation of Malaysia in the mid-1960s (Chan 1971). Subsequently, the need to be constantly alert in pre-empting and/or addressing unforeseen threats has become a pervasive and more generalized aspect of official ideology (Leifer 2000). As the impact of this ideology waned in the context of social and political stability and rising economic prosperity, it was supplemented by concepts of how Asians were culturally predisposed towards elitist political orders (Rodan 1996b).

The advent of the War on Terror has presented the PAP with new opportunities to give expression to the ideology of imminent threat, or a politics of fear, and the related necessity of a powerful political elite. In *The Fight Against Terror*, for instance, the War on Terror is incorporated into a broader narrative of state mythology. It reads, 'Our Singapore story is the account of how a small island-nation overcame its vulnerabilities and prospered, despite overwhelming odds', and continues with, 'Like our forebears, all of us who call this island-nation home must work together to build a lasting legacy and write another shining chapter in the Singapore story' (National Security Coordination Centre 2004: 66). Historically, though, state rhetoric about 'working together' and 'political consensus' has been accompanied by the blunting of political pluralism. The government has also drawn on the War on Terror to claim legitimacy for contentious policies. According to Defence Minister Teo Chee Hean, for example, Singapore enjoys social cohesion rather than ethnic and religious conflict from these factors: the ethnic quota for Housing Development Board flats that accommodate over 80 per cent of the population, minority representation in Parliament through group representation constituencies (GRCs), and state-sponsored ethnic community self-help groups (*The Straits Times* 2004). Some scholars, however, have interpreted these same measures as involving forms of electoral engineering and state political co-option (Tremewan 1994; Chua 1995).

Thailand

Thailand presents an interesting contrast to Singapore, at least in terms of political starting points. Since 1992, Thailand's politics has been moving away from the authoritarianism that marked its past. The 1997 Constitution was seen by many as an attempt to entrench a more liberal political system, characterized by attention to rights, the recognition of civil society and competitive politics. The major recession brought on by the 1997–8 economic crisis and the 2001 election of the Thai Rak Thai (TRT) Party, led by businessman Thaksin Shinawatra, however, have tested the resilience of this new liberal politics. Since 2001, the War on Terror has proven important for the Thaksin regime in two respects. First, the government, dominated by business interests, has supported the USA in the hope of being rewarded through an FTA that will enhance the TRT's international and domestic legitimacy. Second, the War on Terror has buttressed authoritarian tendencies within the TRT government.

The economic crisis has had a major impact on Thailand's economy and capitalist class (Hewison 2004). Economic restructuring, based on a neoliberal model, meant reforms that required major changes to the way that domestic business was conducted. This saw considerable political fallout as opposition was mounted against the government's reform efforts, which were seen to be damaging Thailand's economic and social fabric (Hewison 2005).

The political outcome of this opposition was the emergence of the TRT Party. More so than any other party, the TRT represented the interests of big domestic business. Previously, big business had remained aloof from grubby electoral politics; it had not needed to be directly involved, for the government had long supported domestic business (Baker 2004). It was the threat to business interests and power posed by neoliberal policy reform that caused the remaining tycoons to conclude that domestic capital needed supportive government policies, which could only be achieved by taking control of the state. Many business rivalries were put aside as domestic business coalesced around Thaksin and the TRT. The TRT, thus, became the vehicle on which to *oppose* the neoliberal agenda, slow liberalization in some areas, and return a competitive 'edge' to domestic business. This was symbolized in the TRT's runaway 2001 election victory.

The TRT built an electoral platform that addressed the aspirations of many voters. Its slogan emphasized the theme that something new was required in politics: 'new thinking, new ways, for all Thais'. This inclusive slogan, and a party platform tinged with nationalism and populism, promised help for those suffering from the slump, and was especially appealing to poor and rural voters. The TRT also targeted small business, promising to make credit available for them. Most significantly, as noted above, the TRT's policies were designed to permit domestic capital to gain control of the state. The TRT's policies demonstrated that it was to follow a different path from that promoted by the previous government and the IMF. This different approach was dubbed 'Thaksinomics'; its success was demonstrated by the revival of the economy, which was buoyed by considerable pump priming by the government. It was symbolized in Thaksin's dramatic declaration in 2003 that Thailand was 'free' of the IMF's shackles after having repaid its credits early.

While the TRT continued to emphasize domestic consumption, it was clear that much of the good economic news was driven by recovery in manufactured exports. The reasons for the evolution of the TRT's economic policy reflected both the changing international economic environment – in particular, the emergence of China – and the rapidly changing geopolitical environment. The remainder of this section will focus on these geopolitical aspects.

Following the economic crisis, relations between the USA and Thailand had not been particularly warm. Thailand had long been a close US ally, and had permitted the USA to use a number of Thai bases for its operations against Vietnam, Cambodia and Laos. The USA's response to the economic crisis, however, left many Thais bewildered as it made clear, by way of Larry Summers and Robert Rubin, that Thailand would not be 'rescued'. In fact, Treasury Secretary Rubin (1998) emphasized the need for reforms in Thailand, explaining that these would actually 'benefit the American people'. Responding to criticism of the IMF, Rubin asserted that the 'United States needs an IMF that is financially equipped to help protect U.S. interests . . . If we close the door on the IMF, we hurt ourselves.' Speaking to the chairman of the Thai Federation of Industries, Rubin reportedly made it clear that US investors would not be back in Thailand until foreign ownership and investment restrictions were fixed (*Bangkok Post*, 1 July 1998). In other words, US support was contingent on policies that would benefit US investors. Thai policy-makers were taken aback by such comments as well as by US efforts to thwart Asian-led responses to the crisis, such as the Asian Monetary Fund.

Indeed, so strong was this sentiment that while the 11 September event garnered considerable sympathy from Thailand for the USA, Prime Minister Thaksin's initial response to the War on Terror was lukewarm. Thaksin emphasized the role of the UN, stating that Thailand would be 'strictly neutral' (*Bangkok Post*, 12 October 2001). Thaksin expressed 'support' for the USA but declined to comment on whether or not this would involve military commitments (*Bangkok Post*, 17 and 28 September 2001). The government did not immediately make a public offer for the use of Thai air bases for the US war in Afghanistan, and stated that it would consult with ASEAN if the USA made such a request (*Bangkok Post*, 12 October 2001). It was only in mid-December 2001 while visiting the USA that Thaksin said Thai troops would go to Afghanistan, while still arguing that a UN mandate was necessary (*Bangkok Post*, 15 December 2001).

This commitment followed somewhat tepid comments by Bush, who expressed US appreciation for Thailand's support for the War on Terror, which included efforts to track terrorists' funds and the passage of some new anti-terrorism measures. The two leaders did, however, state their 'determination' to expand co-operation on counter terrorism. At the time, there were conflicting reports from Thai government sources regarding the use of Thai bases during the initial period of the war against Afghanistan (*Bangkok Post*, 12 October 2001). It seems clear now that this was because there was more going on. The *New York Times* (Bonner 2003) has reported that

'American officials' stated that Thailand had been providing assistance secretly 'in several significant ways'. *The Wall Street Journal* (Lopez and Crispin 2003) reported that the Counter Terrorism Intelligence Center (CTIC), established in early 2001, works directly with the CIA and that facilities, information and equipment are shared 'on a daily basis'. The report also stated, 'Nowhere else in Southeast Asia are U.S. intelligence officials working as closely on the ground with a host government on matters of counterterrorism and intelligence.'

In hindsight, it appears that Thailand's proclaimed neutrality had two sources. *The Wall Street Journal* report quotes some operatives explaining that the stated neutrality was a way of presenting Thailand as being relatively safe for terrorists in the region, so that they could be tracked and observed in Thailand. At the same time, it has been suggested that the early statements of neutrality and that Thailand was safe from terrorism suited the government, for the economy relied heavily on tourism (Thitinan 2003a). Bush was apparently unhappy that Thailand was an unannounced supporter (Bonner 2003), but during Thaksin's visit to the USA, he welcomed the PUBLIC commitment to sign up to counter-terrorism conventions and Thaksin's offer to participate in the reconstruction of Afghanistan (Bush and Thaksin 2001).[12]

The events that finally revealed Thailand's role in the War on Terror were both political and economic. While the government regularly and publicly stated that Thailand was neither a base nor a transit country for Southeast Asian terrorists associated with JI or with al-Qaeda, damaging reports were apparently leaked from the FBI in 2002. These leaks accused 'rogue' Thai military elements and local gangsters of training JI members at a base in Thailand's Muslim-dominated south (Perrin 2002). This caused a falling out between Thai agencies and the FBI (Crispin 2003a), but captured the government's attention and forced it to address poor interagency co-ordination. It was the arrest of JI leader, Hambali, in August 2003 that revealed the façade. Captured in Ayutthaya in an operation that had US agents whisking him off to an unnamed destination, he was accused of plotting an attack on the October 2003 APEC meetings in Bangkok (see *Bangkok Post*, 16–19 August and 30 August 2003). In fact, it was around this time that it became clear that Thaksin had allowed the USA to use its air bases for the wars with Afghanistan and Iraq, and had permitted the CIA to bring suspected al-Qaeda members to Thailand for interrogation (Bonner 2003). The support for the War on Terror became overt as, according to Thitinan (2003a), the government sought to 'maximise . . . strategic assets and reap concessions'.

The Hambali arrest coincided with the hurried issuance of repressive decrees (which circumvented Parliament) that were allegedly enacted to deal with terrorism. These decrees also preceded the APEC meeting that Thaksin had used to promote his own image regionally. While the USA effectively hijacked the meeting for security issues, the economic gains that Thailand wanted soon became clear. As noted earlier, the USA had stated that it would support its friends. Thaksin's support for Washington's war against terrorism resulted in a decision to designate Thailand a 'major non-NATO ally' and a quick decision to move ahead with negotiations for a bilateral trade agreement (Crispin 2003b). The US administration made it clear that the agreement to proceed with the FTA had been contingent on Thailand's participation in the War on Terror, and with Thaksin's concurrence that security and economic prosperity were linked (*Bangkok Post*, 20 October 2003; *The Nation*, 23 October 2003). Despite domestic opposition, Thailand agreed to send a token military force of 447 to Iraq (Roberts 2003).

The opposition to Thailand's participation in the War on Terror included Thai Muslims. Even before the Thaksin government committed troops, there had been significant Muslim opposition to the USA-led war in Iraq, especially from Thailand's Muslim-dominated southern provinces (see Global News Wire, *Thai Press Reports*, 30 March 2003). According to *The Nation* (28 March 2003), Muslim organizations had urged the Thai government to take a clear position against the war on Iraq, while locally elected provincial bodies, village heads and religious scholars encouraged Muslims to fight the USA in Iraq. When the Thai government announced its commitment of troops, Muslim organizations and local leaders expressed considerable dismay over its support for the USA (*The Nation*, 24 August 2003).

Thailand's southernmost provinces are dominated by Muslims of Malay ethnicity, making this a region distinct from the largely Buddhist and Thai populated country (Che Man 1990; Virtual Information Center 2002). Yala, Pattani and Narathiwat, in particular, have long been the focus of separatist and nationalist movements, so it was no surprise that tensions in the region rose as the Thaksin government tied itself to US policy (Global Security 2004). In mid-2003, the Pattani United Liberation Organisation (PULO), one of several separatist groups, announced increased operations against the government, although much of this amounted to limited acts of banditry. In early January 2004, however, a Thai army camp was raided, with four soldiers killed and a cache of weapons stolen. At the same time, a spate of school burnings began. While the government shrugged off these events as a continuance of local banditry, subsequent events indicated that, in fact, the separatist organizations had moved to a higher level of activity. From an emphasis on nationalism and separatism, Islam appeared to gain a more significant role in the separatist movements. Since then there have been several deadly developments that have caused the situation in the south to worsen (see Chaiwat, this volume, for details).

The political and global significance of these events, together with the War on Terror, was indicated when the *Asian Wall Street Journal* editorial (29 April 2004) echoed a broadly neo-conservative view on political liberalism:

> The U.S., while appreciative of Thailand's contribution to the global war on terror, has been squeamish about endorsing its campaign against

southern insurgents. The U.S. State Department has been put off by tales of kidnappings and disappearances and accusations of torture by security forces. Of course, it is a favorite tactic of guerrilla armies to issue human rights complaints – even while they themselves are slaughtering innocents – to try to turn public opinion against the authorities. The State Department is particularly susceptible to such claims. It has accused Thailand of a 'worsening' human-rights record. Prime Minister Thaksin Shinawatra responded by calling the U.S. a 'useless friend' but his government has promised to investigate . . . If these attacks are any indication of what's to come, Thailand is in for a fight with radical Islam. What Bangkok deserves now is more support and fewer sermons from the State Department.

Apart from the fact that the language here is remarkably similar to that used during the Cold War when dealing with political opponents, it is clear that strong, pro-USA regimes are preferable to those that support democratic politics, human rights and liberal political values. Such advice is also supportive of the increasing authoritarianism evident in the Thaksin government.

The human rights record mentioned in the *Asian Wall Street Journal* has to do with not only the repressive anti-terrorism decrees and the deaths in the south, but also the Thaksin government's desire to expand the state's capacity to repress domestic dissent through a strengthening of security agencies, including the police and military (see Thitinan 2003a).[13] Thaksin has, since his 2001 election, sought to strengthen his government. Together with TRT members, he has threatened the independent agencies created under the 1997 Constitution, and attacked intellectuals, NGOs, international agencies and a range of other critics. The TRT and related groups also established considerable control over the media and managed their coverage, both domestic and international, to limit criticism of Thaksin, his government and the TRT. Thaksin has made the TRT a larger party by managing mergers with a number of smaller parties, such that the TRT came to control almost two-thirds of seats in the Lower House. This limited scrutiny of the government meant that there was little to worry about in managing Parliament. Indeed, Thaksin argued that Parliamentary opposition and government should be united in working for the 'best interests of the people', and he argues that adversarial politics may be a betrayal of the people (Thaksin 2002: 4).

In fact, by minimizing and managing opposition, the TRT has been making the government of business 'safe'. For Thaksin, the hope was that his government would stay in power for two or more four-year terms. This was a one-sided view, however, for whenever Thaksin or the TRT was criticized, the government vigorously attacked the critics. Its targets included the foreign press, the UN, independent local media, NGOs, organizations conducting opinion surveys, academics, and independent agencies created by the Constitution. The government has also attempted to limit funding to organizations that criticize it. For example, in 2003, the government attempted to force the Ministry of Foreign Affairs to pressure foreign donors to stop funding Thai NGOs (*Bangkok Post*, 10 May 2003). The military quietly reinstituted its surveillance of political movements (*Bangkok Post*, 20 and 21 May 2003), and the government moved to limit demonstrations (*The Nation*, 23 April 2002). In its brutal and bloody campaign against drugs, the government implemented policies that caused thousands of deaths – evidence that the days of excessive use of state violence had not passed. As noted, the capture of Hambali saw some repressive measures reinforced, and during the APEC meeting, Thaksin employed harsh measures to deny entry to NGO activists and to control demonstrations in Bangkok (*The Nation*, 9 October 2003). APEC security precautions also saw the discriminatory treatment of Muslims, including some government officials, and this caused considerable resentment (*Bangkok Post*, 14 October 2003).

Of course, such authoritarian policies, while opposed by many civil society groups, are attractive to those Regnier (2001: 22) identifies as the petty bourgeoisie. These emerge in SMEs and services, are politically right wing and attracted by populist and nationalist shibboleths.

Thaksin has also been able to consolidate control of the military and police by promoting his relatives and close associates to top positions in these organizations (*Bangkok Post*, 20 March 2003). It was critical to the recovery and development of domestic capital for Thaksin to stay in power and continue controlling the state. In early 2005, TRT was re-elected with an increased majority.[14]

The problem that now faces Thaksin's government is that its domestic policies of repression and its support for the USA may have let separatism off the leash in the south. Unsurprisingly, the measures taken by the government to stem resistance in the south have been heavy-handed and repressive, potentially threatening civil liberties and many of the democratic gains that have been made since 1992. In the view of one commentator:

> the behavior of the Thai forces cannot be written off as a matter for Thais alone. The unhappiness of Thailand's three southern, predominantly Muslim, Malay-speaking provinces has international implications – for the West in its self-proclaimed 'war on terror'; for ASEAN, in which Muslims are the largest religious group; and for Malays in Malaysia, who inevitably sympathize with their brethren across the border. The West has enlisted Thailand in its War on Terror, and Thaksin has been praised for his support, which has earned him the offer of a free trade agreement with the USA. Yet, his government's actions in the South have created just the kind of discontent on which Muslim fundamentalism thrives, and its resorting to strong-arm methods have engendered terrorism and violent reactions.
>
> (Bowring 2004)

Thaksin and TRT's re-election in early 2005 was by a landslide, everywhere *except* in the south. Hundreds of people have died in the three southern-most provinces, and violence and bombings continue. With the Thailand–US FTA still under negotiation, Thaksin has little to show for his support for Bush and the War on Terror other than this intensifying violence and a mounting death toll. While not yet an internationalized conflict, the southern violence may be primed for such an escalation and for militant Islam to gain broader support in an area where religion has traditionally been moderate.

Conclusion

The conclusion we have drawn is that this new phase of neoliberal globaliza- tion offers the prospect of a return to Cold War politics, in which there was a high level of tolerance and support for authoritarian political regimes in the interests of security. This means that, apart from those on the wrong side of the terrorism divide, authoritarianism will not be a measure that the USA will use in determining who its 'friends' are. In other words, 'freedom', that is being a strong US ally in the War on Terror, has been elevated above concerns for democracy and human rights. 'Freedom' also has an economic element, so the USA's potential allies need to show commitment to capitalism. Like it was during the Cold War, this may permit some variations in economic organiza- tion in the region, but without a necessary abandonment of the broad neoliberal agenda. Certainly, for the time being, the zenith of the neoliberal economic reform rhetoric of the Asian crisis period appears to have passed. In any case, US security concerns are likely to continue to compound existing conflicts and generate additional ones in East and Southeast Asia, and these may have unforeseen political and economic outcomes.

Compared to the Cold War period, there is a significant difference in the way that support for, or tolerance of, authoritarian regimes in Southeast Asia in the War on Terror is being presented by the USA and other liberal democratic and authoritarian governments. During the Cold War, authori- tarian governments were in an alliance *against* communism, whereas, in the War on Terror, there is a more positive notion of an alliance in *favour of* shared values that are being threatened by Islamic fundamentalism. These values, however, have not been clearly articulated. Given the composition of the coalition of the willing, the parties involved do not appear to be defined by an unwavering commitment to the principles of democracy, human rights and social justice. Modernizing authoritarian elites who embrace a mixture of market values and social conservatism can find various points of ideolog- ical intersection with President George W. Bush and his neoconservative allies. Indeed, the new emphasis in the USA on 'cultural politics', and the moral absolutist tone to it, may lay the basis for a more coherent ideological alignment with authoritarian elites than was possible during the Cold War.

Notes

1 The Singapore government alleges that thirteen of these people were members of Jemaah Islamiyah. See Chua (2002).
2 The Singapore government alleges that nineteen of these were members of Jemaah Islamiyah. For more general discussions of the extent and nature of terrorist activities in Singapore and Southeast Asia, see Kumar and See (2004), Wright-Neville (2004) and Desker (2003).
3 Foreign Affairs Minister S. Jayakumar explained: 'We must take a strong stand posed by weapons of mass destruction particularly after 9/11 because the danger of weapons of mass destruction falling into the hands of terrorists, terrorist organizations or extremist groups is not a hypothetical risk' (quoted in Lee 2003). He added that while no one likes war, the facts clearly showed 'that it is Iraq, not the US and not the UN, not the international community, which is in the dock' (quoted in Lee 2003).
4 The USA had previously not allowed any exceptions to the free flow of capital in its investment chapters of FTAs or in Bilateral Investment Treaties.
5 The agreement does not prevent a country from imposing controls, but it does require compensation for US investors when restrictions that 'substantially impede transfers' incur damages. This provision is based on the framework used in the USA–Chile FTA.
6 ExxonMobil, which built one of Asia's largest refineries in Singapore, is among the largest investors in the country. Apart from Singapore Airlines being a significant customer of Boeing commercial aircraft, the Singapore Air Force also buys fighter jets from Boeing's defence arm. The UPS interest in the USSFTA was slightly different – it sought to contain the ability of the Singapore postal service to cross-subsidize competing express mail services. The steering committee of the Business Coalition also included representatives from other powerful corporations such as General Electric, Federal Express, APL and Lockheed-Martin.
7 Just the month before, Singapore became the first port in Asia to participate in the Container Security Initiative, which allowed US inspectors to check USA-bound cargo for possible explosives (Acharya 2004: 3).
8 Senior Minister of State for Law and Home Affairs, Ho Peng Kee, explained that: 'Instead of a backpack of explosives, a terrorist can create just as much devastation by sending a carefully engineered packet of data into computer systems which control the network of essential services, for example power stations' (quoted in Reuters 2003).
9 Chee Soon Juan (2003a) Interview, Singapore, 11 July.
10 The occupations of detainees included condominium manager, dispatch driver, service engineer, printer, manager, technician and business person. Of the first twenty-one detainees, one person had a monthly income exceeding S$5,000 per month and two earned more than S$3,000 per month, but thriteen had incomes below S$2,000 per month. See Lim (2002).
11 The proposal was made by Admiral Thomas Fargo, head of the US Pacific Command, in March 2004. Some 200 ships pass daily and as many as 800 oil tankers pass per year through the Malacca Straits.
12 One US source notes that the deployment of army engineers to Afghanistan in March 2003 was the first coalition deployment of Thai troops with the USA since the Vietnam War (Harney 2004: 26).
13 It is important to recognize that the Thaksin administration has released the military and police from the constraints they had faced since their participation in the bloody events of May 1992, during which civilians were shot down in Bangkok's streets. Thaksin's government has allowed these forces to return to their normal repressive behaviour when confronted with demonstrators and

opposition. For a discussion of some of these tactics, see the report on the use of torture against suspected militants in the south (Crispin 2004).

14 In early 2006, Thaksin came under significant political pressure to resign over the sale of his family's business interests to Singapore's Temasek Holdings. The deal, worth about $1.8 billion, was conducted in murky corporate waters, including offshore tax havens and the limiting of tax liabilities in Thailand. This sale of Shin Corp was apparently interpreted by some elements within domestic business as a signal that Thaksin was more interested in promoting his family's interests over those of Thai domestic capital in general.

7 Indonesia

Order and terror in a time of empire

Vedi R. Hadiz

The post-Soeharto 'dis-order'

In relation to present-day, post-authoritarian Indonesia, two major issues have been a source of disquiet in so far as the imperatives of American Empire in Asia are concerned. First is the 'discovery' of the Jemaah Islamiyah (JI) in Indonesia and other parts of Southeast Asia (see International Crisis Group 2002; Barton 2004) soon after the World Trade Center attacks. JI and other assorted groupings of 'Islamic radicals', which are most certainly quite diverse in terms of origins and orientations, soon came to be almost uniformly seen as linked to Osama Bin Laden's Al Qaeda (Williams 2003; Abuza 2003). In the Indonesian case, prominent analysts have pointed out the likelihood that JI individuals have direct or indirect affiliations with 'legitimate' Islamic organizations such as mass organizations or foundations, and even political parties (Jones 2004: 25).

In the West, post-Soeharto Indonesia has been regarded as a site of economic and political instability in the region, and is considered fertile ground for the further spread of radical Islamic groups prone to acts of terror, especially in the absence of an effective central state authority. Several incidents have underlined Indonesia's status as a hotbed of terrorism: the Bali bombings of October 2002 that killed 200 people, a large number of whom were Australian tourists; the bombing of the Marriott Hotel in Jakarta in August 2003; and the bombing outside of the Australian embassy in September 2004.

The second source of worry concerns the viability of the Indonesian nation-state itself. After decades of centralized, iron-fisted rule under Soeharto's New Order, there are doubts whether Indonesia – in many ways the random product of an earlier age of European Empire – will stand the test of time (Aspinall and Berger 2001). In a nutshell, the question is: will there be a balkanization of Indonesia, a country of 220 million people spread unevenly over an archipelago of 17, 000 islands, in the foreseeable future?

East Timor, a former Portuguese colony invaded by Indonesia with US approval in 1975 (Milbank 2001), successfully attained independence following a referendum in 1999. Nevertheless, East Timor's status of being a part of Indonesia was never accepted internationally, so real fears have been worsened by bloody communal strife in Maluku, parts of Kalimantan and Sulawesi and, especially, by the resurgence of separatism in the resource-rich regions of Papua and Aceh. Aceh was placed under martial law until May 2004 and was until recently a site of concerted military operations to quash a long-simmering separatist rebellion even though the region has been devastated by the earthquake and tsunami of December 2004. All of these developments seem to strengthen the widely held perception that Indonesia is, today, an alarmingly fragile entity.

Not surprisingly, fears of Indonesian balkanization have been voiced not only domestically but internationally as well. This is partly due to the considerable ramifications of Indonesia as a genuinely 'failed state' to regional stability, not least in terms of aiding in the proliferation of terrorist networks. As Robert Gelbard, a former US Ambassador to Jakarta, once observed: 'Strategically, the security of most of Southeast Asia rests on a stable Indonesia and would be seriously threatened if a number of ministates emerged from a political collapse here' (Gelbard 2001).

It is significant that since the fall of Soeharto in 1998, Indonesia has frequently experienced volatility in its process of democratization. I argue here that Indonesia's path to democratization is deeply entangled in a variety of processes that are external to domestic constellations of power in Indonesia; it is intractably embedded in the processes of globalization, the mechanics of a USA-centred world order, and the unfolding of US security, political and economic interests in the region. As Johnson (2000) cogently argues, the present world order is characterized not only by unrivalled US economic, political and military hegemony but also by the increasingly free use of force by the USA in shaping the processes of economic globalization to meet its interests. Other authors specifically cite the primary interest of guaranteeing the ascendancy of US capital within world capitalism (Anderson 2002), through a combination of force and the manufacturing of worldwide consent for the USA's benevolent leading role in preventing a global descent into anarchy and chaos. Wood (2003), in particular, emphasizes the coercive aspects of the US-dominated 'empire of capital', which requires nation-states to maintain order – with the USA acting as the great imperial enforcer.

It may be useful at this point to recall that the entrenchment of a highly centralized, ruthless and predatory regime in Indonesia under Soeharto was a process that was deeply entangled in the international geopolitics of an era that has since come to pass. Established in 1966 while the USA was busy fighting an increasingly bloody war in nearby Vietnam, Soeharto's New Order was in many ways as much a direct product of the Cold War as it was an outcome of a prolonged, bitter conflict between domestic social and political forces in Indonesia.

In the current context, from the perspective of US interests, the issue at stake is making Indonesia's new democracy functional to broad requirements in the region. In very simple terms, the question concerns the possibility of crafting, in post-Soeharto Indonesia, an institutional framework of governance that would guarantee the following:

(a) The prevention of the break-up of the Indonesian nation-state.
(b) The containment of radical Islamic forces deemed hostile to Western interests.
(c) The security and predictability necessary for the operations of international, especially US, capital in Indonesia and the region.

It is noteworthy that since the fall of Soeharto, international development organizations such as the World Bank and USAID have been actively promoting programmes in the country under the headings of institution building, good governance, civil society promotion and the like. Although these programmes have origins that pre-date Soeharto's fall, the growing emphasis has been on the dissemination of democratic and 'civil' political practices and values for the construction of supportive social and institutional frameworks. It is, however, not just any kind of 'democracy' and 'civility' that is being pursued.

Organizations such as the World Bank, in particular, virtually revert back to 1960s modernization theory in highlighting the importance of a core of rational, market-friendly development actors and planners. In those documents that express its position on the virtues of administrative decentralization as a global development agendum, the World Bank emphasizes the advance of an institutional framework premised on market rationality (World Bank n.d.). While public accountability and transparency are widely discussed as well, such a framework is addressed in terms of directing public participation and citizenship in ways that are functional to the requirements of the market (Fine 2002: 220). The entrenchment of technocratic, market-friendly governance would also involve something akin to the 'low-intensity' type of democracy referred to by authors such as Gills (2000), in which distributional and other non-market-friendly coalitions are kept at bay. Thus, the sort of democracy being promoted in this vision of post-Cold-War globalization has much in common with the modernization theory of late 1960s' Huntingtonian revisionism, in that the latter privileged political order and stability as a marker of modernity and development (Huntington 1968).

The belief in benign and rational technocratic rule is ultimately related to the hope that, in the specific case of Indonesia, it can serve as a bastion against populist or predatory coalitions that may adopt nationalist and/or Islamic expressions. The Achilles' heel here, however, is that all systems of rule – even those directed by supposedly wise technocrats 'freed' from the pressure of particularist interest groups – require a social base. As Robison and Hadiz (2004) point out, such a social base does not really exist internally in Indonesia, partly because of the legacy of centralized, authoritarian rule that has deeply disorganized civil society, and produced a bourgeoisie and middle class that did not develop an abiding interest in free markets or liberal democracy. Traditionally, neoliberal market reform has been pushed for by international development organizations and a relatively small number of economic technocrats in the government, as well as by a handful of vocal middle-class public commentators. In the absence of a stronger social base, the additional factors of power and coercion become increasingly important. It is in this context that political illiberalism appears increasingly compatible with, and even functional to, the enforcement of a neoliberal market rationality. Thus, the cultivation or maintenance of some illiberal (even anti-liberal) types of political regimes appears to agree as much with the requirements of empire as with Iraqi-style 'regime change', despite all the hyperbole about the latter.

It is in this context as well that the most likely ally of US interests in relation to Indonesia is its long-time Cold-War-era partner, the Indonesian military. Following several years of a rather strained public relationship during the Clinton administration, the military is increasingly viewed as the glue that can hold Indonesia together and, simultaneously, as a bastion against the rise of Islamic radical groups. Some of the USA's closest allies in the region, including Australia and Singapore, have top officials who now seem to share a rather benevolent view of the Indonesian military, despite the latter's poor human rights record.[1] Australia, for example, resumed contact in June 2004 with Kopassus, the much feared Indonesian elite army unit with a record for human rights abuse (*Melbourne Age*, 18 June 2004). At a high-level regional security conference, Singapore's then Senior Minister Lee Kuan Yew urged the USA to support the Indonesian military as it is the only institution that can save the country from 'Islamic extremism' (*Tempo Interaktif*, 2 June 2002). There remains, however, some strong domestic opposition in the USA to overtly resuming ties with the Indonesian military. A large part of this hesitation stemmed from the belief that the military was responsible for the murder of American schoolteachers in Papua in 2002 (Goodenough 2004). Still, the Bush government appears intent on forging stronger links with the Indonesian military in the context of the War on Terror.

The Indonesian military itself is, of course, eager to demonstrate its indispensability to Indonesian national unity. Army Chief General Ryamizard Ryacudu, for example, drove the point home in a public speech in which he asserted that there are those 'who are constantly trying to bring about the collapse of the Unitary State of the Republic of Indonesia (NKRI) either from within or from outside of the country' (Detik.com, 12 May 2004). Obviously, the more fragile Indonesia appears to be, the greater the legitimacy of the military's claim for a broad role in post-New-Order politics.

Thus, a strange feeling of déjà vu may easily descend upon any long-time observer of Indonesia. If the threat during the Cold War was the spread of global communism, the threat today has been identified by the USA as an increasingly globalized type of violent, anti-Western Islam. The remedy for the current global disease is remarkably similar to the old 'cure' as well – the emergence of free markets under a benevolent pro-Western and modern technocracy that is backed up, if necessary, by a powerful military. Thus, the Indonesian military is turning out to be a major beneficiary of both Cold War and post-Cold-War US geopolitical strategies; however, serious complications and contradictions may yet emerge.

Indonesian authoritarianism, US power and the Cold War

It is necessary to recall the Cold War origins of New Order authoritarianism to make sense of the turbulent process of democratization in the post-Cold-War context. General Soeharto attained power through a bloody campaign of eradicating communism that was supported by the Western powers (Cribb 1990). The exact death toll of this nationwide campaign is unknown, although the consensus is that it is in the vicinity of 800,000 lives. In addition, several hundred thousand suspected communists and sympathizers were detained without trial for many years. The impact on Indonesia's subsequent trajectory is hard to overstate. The New Order's successful eradication of communism facilitated policies for disorganizing civil society in general; this resulted in a centralization of state power that was never to be attained by the authoritarian rulers of neighbouring countries such as the Philippines and Thailand, despite their own strident efforts.

Soeharto's rise to power – and the demise of his predecessor, the nationalist hero and firebrand, Soekarno – was facilitated by a coalition of interests led by the military, which included elements of the propertied, rural elites and the urban middle class. These were social forces that were all either threatened by the radical, left-wing populism of the PKI (Indonesian Communist Party) or harmed directly by Soekarno's hyper-inflationary, autarchic economic policies. Once in power, Soeharto embraced economic policies that were pro-Western. These policies established the basis for a long period of economic growth and political order that would, ultimately, end with the Asian economic crisis of 1997–8.

The military was a particularly important component of the New Order during its early years, and its rise was a long and gradual process that was facilitated by Indonesia's entanglement in global Cold War politics. As numerous analysts have noted (for example, Mortimer 1974), Soekarno grew closer to the PKI in his final years in power, although this was done partly to check the growing power of the Indonesian military. The latter had, for example, taken control of many foreign firms that were nationalized in the late 1950s. The military was also increasingly dominant in the operations of local governance, due to the promulgation of martial law in response to regional rebellions in West Sumatra and North Sulawesi (see Kahin and Kahin 1995).

The Indonesian Communist Party was the only viable competitor to the Indonesian military at the onset of the 1960s. In the increasingly intense contest between the PKI and the military, particularly the army, the USA was clearly on the side of the generals. A close relationship with the military's top brass was partly forged through assistance programmes, including the training of officers in the USA as well as the supply of military hardware. Such a policy was particularly pursued after the US government recognized the failure of the previous policy of undermining Soekarno through the covert support of separatist rebels (Kahin and Kahin 1995: 193).

It should be recalled that Western analysts and some of Soeharto's domestic supporters expected him to establish a democratic and market-friendly regime.[2] The New Order, of course, turned out to be ruthlessly authoritarian. Indeed, Soeharto's legacy was effectively to kill the possibility of real party politics as he institutionalized an authoritarian corporatist system that pre-empted independent, autonomous organizations. Workers, for example, were forced to join a single state-dominated labour organization (Hadiz 1997; Kammen 1997; Ford 2003), as were the peasantry, youth, women and so on. Moreover, even though Soeharto remained firmly committed to the US camp as far as Cold War politics was concerned, he directed Indonesia towards a remarkably predatory form of capitalism. In this, he was aided by international development assistance and by windfall oil revenues in the 1970s. In the process, Western-trained economic technocrats in Indonesia were often marginalized (Robison 1987; Winters 1996), though they continued to present the world with a façade of economic rationality in the country.

These economic technocrats were a product of US policy from the 1950s, which was partly based on nurturing a select group of pro-USA actors in a range of important institutions. It is well documented that a host of Indonesian Cold-War-era intellectuals, bureaucrats and policy-makers were educated and trained in the USA by way of a number of assistance programmes. The Ford Foundation, for example, helped to develop the infrastructure for 'modernizing' Indonesian intellectuals at leading universities such as Cornell, where Indonesian (and Southeast Asian) studies particularly flourished.

The Ford Foundation was most famously instrumental in developing the Faculty of Economics at the University of Indonesia, an institution that provided the Soeharto bureaucracy and Cabinet with a steady stream of individuals with technocratic expertise and skills.[3] Some of the earliest beneficiaries of this programme came to hold various economic and development portfolios for decades, and were dubbed the 'Berkeley Mafia' in reference to their Alma Mater (Ransom 1970).

Of course, the developments in Indonesia were not unique. It is generally accepted that the activities of several US private foundations in Latin America and Asia in the 1950s and 1960s were frequently linked to US geopolitical strategies and interests; not surprisingly, there have been credible allegations of links to the CIA.[4] It was no less than Dean Rusk, a former top State Department official and head of the Rockefeller Foundation, who suggested at the height of the Vietnam War that 'communist aggression' in

Asia needed to be confronted not only by the training of US combatants, but also by the opening up of US 'training facilities' for 'increasing numbers' of the USA's Asian allies (Ransom 1970: 40). Thus, a modern pro-Western technocracy, together with the military, came to be regarded essentially as the twin pillars of anti-communism in Indonesia. It was no doubt useful that some of the clear beneficiaries of the New Order policy were, ultimately, giant US-based corporations like the oil company Caltex, which operates in Riau, and the mining giant Freeport, which operates in Papua.

It was only in the wake of the Asian economic crisis that Soeharto's New Order finally unravelled. In the evolution of the New Order, a ruling coalition of interests – cemented by Soeharto himself based upon political–business families and large corporate conglomerates that emerged from the apparatus of the state – had earlier taken possession of the state to an astonishingly instrumental degree. This capitalist oligarchy not only was able to wield control over state institutions but also hijacked and shaped the process of economic liberalization (Robison and Hadiz 2004). As Indonesia's economy became even more integrated in the 1980s, particularly into new global financial markets, an internally decrepit and unconstrained economic system thus became entrenched; it would eventually become fatally over-borrowed before collapsing altogether.

Tensions between US interests and those of Soeharto's increasingly predatory and rapacious oligarchy became evident at the height of the Asian economic crisis, less than a decade after the end of the Cold War. The unambiguous statement by then Secretary of State, Madeleine Albright, that Soeharto should step down in the face of growing popular opposition in May 1998 was, perhaps, symbolic of the latter's dispensability.[5]

It was the effective withdrawal of support from the International Monetary Fund (IMF) that delivered the real external body blow to the Soeharto regime. A dispute between the IMF and Soeharto had been simmering for a while; its source was Soeharto's refusal to comply with IMF economic reform policies that would have jeopardized the economic position of leading conglomerates, including those controlled by his own family. The situation that developed conformed broadly to Desai's general description of the relationship between US interests and those of 'crony' capitalism in Asia, as expressed by the advocates of post-Cold-War neoliberal globalization. For Desai (2004: 174), the 'ideological attack' on crony capitalism in Asia after 1997 was an indication that 'what was once fostered and tolerated for Cold War purposes' had become 'not only dispensable but constituted an obstacle to the interests and intentions of metropolitan capital'.

It was the IMF chief, Michel Camdessus (1997), who declared that the Asian crisis had revealed the faults of the previously heralded model of Asian state-led developmentalism, and that wide-ranging reforms were required in places like Indonesia, although these have yet to transpire. In fact, just as Soeharto's cronies hijacked markets in the 1980s (Robison and

Hadiz 2004), elements of the old New Order regime have now reconstituted and appropriated the institutions of governance by reinventing themselves in parties and parliaments. Thus, the Indonesian post-Soeharto experience shows that predatory relations of power can survive the unravelling of an authoritarian regime. Moreover, the demise of such relations of power does not appear to be automatically connected to the outright subjection of Indonesia to forces that might exert pressure for greater transparency and accountability in governance. For example, those foreign businesses that might have had a vested interest in neoliberal market reforms attempted to defend the privileges they gained by way of corrupt deals with the New Order regime; therefore, they demonstrated (yet again) the compatibility of investor interests and predatory politics under certain circumstances. This was perhaps best illustrated , the Indonesian state-owned electricity company. Soon after the fall of Soeharto, US business interests, personally supported by the US ambassador to Jakarta, threatened PLN when its director sought to cancel Soeharto-era contracts (*Far Eastern Economic Review*, 21 October 1999: 63–4). These contracts were widely believed to have been the product of high-level corruption – the kind that Indonesia was supposed to abandon. The case underscores that the primary concern of international investors is not necessarily transparency or 'good governance', but certainty and predictability, which can be offered by various kinds of regimes. As Max Weber once observed, there is a key difference between predictable and unpredictable forms of corruption (Weber 1978: 240; 1095).

The main problem with Indonesia's democracy, from the point of view of these investors, is that the demise of the highly corrupt but also highly centralized New Order – and the decentralization of power both from the executive body of government to parliaments, and from Jakarta to the regions and localities – has given rise to highly decentralized and unpredictable corruption (Hadiz 2004b). It is mainly in response to such unpredictability that a Singapore-based business daily highlighted the possibility of an exodus of fairly long-established international business operations from Indonesia (*Business Times*, 20 May 2004).

It is in this context of 'dis-order', juxtaposed to the 'orderliness' of the Soeharto era, that Cold-War-era ideas about rational, modernizing elites are invoked. This is often achieved by recourse to the fashionable literature on 'rational choice' or 'social capital', which embodies many of the assumptions of modernization theory (see Leys 1996: 80–103; Fine 2001). Presently, the emergence of rational, modernizing elites – typically through good governance assistance programmes – is not envisaged as an antidote to communism, but to the dreaded 'failed state'. As mentioned earlier, however, such a technocracy cannot simply be wished into being. Moreover, given the context of the US-led War on Terror, it is the Indonesian military rather than any 'rational' technocracy that can offer the assurance of thwarting a descent into the 'failed state'.

The military and Indonesia's disorderly democracy

As power is reorganized in Indonesia, concrete struggles over the control of state institutions and resources underlie the process of democratization. The main actors in these contests have been, predominantly, interests who have been nurtured by the old regime and have been able to reconstitute themselves through new vehicles and alliances (Robison and Hadiz 2004). Though relatively marginalized since 1998, the military remains a powerful force; in fact, it has been displaying signs of a comeback of sorts in more recent years after being pressed into retreat in the early post-Soeharto period.

The apparent political 'rehabilitation' of the military was epitomized by the rise of General Wiranto, who was nominated for the presidency in 2004 by Golkar, the New-Order-era state party. Regarded as a loyal protector of the Soeharto family interests, Wiranto remains embroiled in numerous cases of supposed human rights abuse. He was no less Soeharto's personal adjutant, and then Minister of Defence as well as Commander of the Armed Forces. The eventual winner of the presidential race, however, was General Susilo Bambang Yudhoyono, the former Chief of Political Affairs of the armed forces. Yudhoyono had somehow managed to graduate from the New Order without a human rights record that was nearly as blemished as those of his peers. Nevertheless, he was a top general in Jakarta when the military stormed an opposition party headquarters – that evolved into Megawati Soekarnoputri's PDI-P – in July 1996, during which event an unknown number of political activists disappeared or were killed (*Jakarta Post*, 8 June 2004). Yet, the PDI-P, the victor in the first post-Soeharto democratic elections in 1999, is itself not a clearly reformist vehicle. Akin to virtually all the major political parties of the post-Soeharto era, it is a vehicle for motley interests, including those incubated in the old New Order as business cronies, generals, political operators and enforcers (Hadiz 2004c).

It would be an exaggeration, however, to suggest that these results suggest popular support for a highly centralized authoritarian regime (Sugianto Tandra 2004). There is, no doubt, a longing for a time of greater certainty, especially among sections of the urban propertied and middle class (Gazali 2003; Kurniawan 2003). It is also significant that the terms of the public debate in Indonesia have shifted considerably from '*reformasi* versus the status quo' in the early post-Soeharto period, to 'disorder versus order and stability', with the Soeharto regime representing a time of orderliness, stability and relative prosperity in the imaginations of many.

The juxtaposition of order to chaos in much of the domestic discourse bears an uncanny resemblance to Washington's rhetoric about world politics, especially after the events of 11 September 2001. The latter emphasizes the duty of the USA to safeguard economic and political security in the world, particularly in the face of destabilizing forces such as global terror networks of radical Islamism. Indeed, the stated aims of US power – as expressed in speeches by the likes of George W. Bush and in the writings of others (see Dobriansky 2003) – is to make the world safe for democracy and to ensure the stability required for global economic prosperity based on an international system of global markets. The increasingly perceived wisdom in Washington, however, is that such a system would need to be at least partially sustained by force and coercion, and may require direct strikes against presumed sources of threat (Schmitt 2003).[6] The overall outcome is an apparent reversion to the Cold War practice of supporting the most horrendous of dictatorships and authoritarians, as long as they support US interests (Rodan and Hewison 2004).

There is little doubt that the post-9/11 international context has contributed to the Indonesian military's regain of some of the confidence it had lost, though this must also be attributed to the ineptitude of Indonesia's civilian political leadership. The governments of Abdurrahman Wahid and Megawati Soekarnoputri, two former leaders of the *reformasi* movement of 1998, each failed to meet the high expectations of their early days in power. Notably, however, the predominantly 'nationalist' Megawati government also displayed some hesitance in supporting the US-led War on Terror. Aware of the former President's vulnerability in relation to organized political Islam in Indonesia, Islamic parties had thwarted her first attempt at the Presidency in 1999; thus, she was cognizant of the dangers of further alienating Muslim political groups.

According to the journalist Tatik Hafidz (2003), the Megawati government had an internal debate on whether or not Indonesia should take the so-called 'Musharraf Road'. This is, of course, a reference to the Pakistani military dictator's ability to garner US support through his government's unambiguous support for the US-led War on Terror. In the case of Musharraf, this entailed turning against many of the radical Islamic political groups that his government had helped to cultivate in previous rounds of domestic political struggle. Hafidz suggests that military intelligence czar General Hendropriyono was the main advocate of the Musharraf Road, although some of his colleagues remained more wary.

It is, perhaps, useful to recall that sections of the Indonesian military leadership had sometimes cultivated relationships with these same groups for domestic political purposes. General Prabowo Subianto, Soeharto's son-in-law and a notoriously ruthless commander, was known to have provided patronage to militants; this was partly a corollary of the late New Order strategy of courting various Islamic groups (Hefner 1993). In this connection, groups of thugs, such as the Front Pembela Islam (Islamic Defence Front), donned Islamic regalia and symbols and allegedly enjoyed the protection of New Order generals like Djaja Suparman, a former chief of the elite Kostrad unit, as well as Wiranto himself.[7] Indeed, even the Lasykar Jihad, the group that sent armed fighters to Maluku, apparently maintained close links to the military. Indonesian observers like George Aditjondro (n.d.) have strongly suggested that sections of the military were responsible for initially fanning the flames of violence in Maluku. More recently, it has been suggested by the respected weekly *Tempo* that the reigniting of communal strife in Ambon in early 2004 was the work of Kopassus troops (*Tempo*, 13 January 2003: 46).

The irony is that the military is supposed to be the force that holds Indonesia together, yet it reputedly also has an interest in the perpetuation of violence in Indonesian regions such as Aceh (Kingsbury and McCulloch 2004). Indeed, analysts have long speculated that periodic anti-Chinese rioting and church burnings in the 1980s and 1990s were instigated by at least some sections of the military leadership in a bid to demonstrate their indispensability to political stability. This is a 'tradition' that goes back quite a long way – General Ali Moertopo, Soeharto's most valuable aide in the early New Order period, was known to have cultivated Islamic radicals, including individuals linked to cleric Abubakar Ba'asyir, the alleged spiritual leader of the Jemaah Islamiyah. Such 'alliances' were always considered 'tactical' and tenuous; the New Order turned against militants when it became convenient for it to do so (International Crisis Group 2002).

It does not follow, however, that the resurgence of the Indonesian military indicates the demise of Indonesia's new democracy. While recent global and domestic developments may have been favourable for its resurgence, few would expect the military to be able to dominate Indonesian politics and society as it did, particularly in the early years of the New Order – even with a military man in the presidency since 2004, just six years after the fall of Soeharto.

The major interest of the military as an institution is, arguably, to maintain enough influence and power to safeguard access and control over certain economic resources. Rather than overturn the post-Soeharto reorganization of power, it needs to find a niche within it. The military, for example, has long been in control of a range of companies and foundations that provide extra-budgetary revenue, and extra income for officers (Mohammad and Pamuntjak 2004; International Crisis Group 2001: 13). Not surprisingly, military companies and foundations have been the sites of some of the worst and most long-standing cases of corruption in the country. The military is also believed to be involved in organized crime, with interests in gun running, drug dealing, prostitution, illegal gambling and extortion rackets (e.g. Kingsbury and McCulloch 2004). It is, perhaps, useful to recall that the national budget reportedly covers only a quarter of the financial needs of the military.[8]

In practice, safeguarding the institutional interests of the military also involves perpetuating the so-called 'territorial structure' within which local military commanders serve as counterparts to civilian administrations at each level of government (Mietzner 2003). This territorial structure allows local military commanders the opportunity to enter into local political and business alliances. In the current context of decentralization of fiscal and administrative governance, it is conceivable that some local military commanders are finding such alliances more lucrative than ever (Mietzner 2003). Significantly, the Indonesian military chief, General Endriartono Sutarto, maintained in a controversial statement that military officers would be allowed to contest local elections in 2005 (*Tempo Interaktif*, 27 April 2005), a development that was regarded as a clear setback by democracy activists.

The international rehabilitation of the Indonesian military has not proceeded without hitches. The shadow of the 1999 post-referendum military-sponsored murderous frenzy in East Timor still looms large in the background, and although the USA lent financial assistance to Indonesian security forces for the purpose of combating terrorism (Carothers 2003), military aid remains severely restricted. This situation could change fairly soon, however, as Indonesia has been readmitted to the so-called IMET (International Military Education and Training) programme. It is no less than the US Secretary of State, Condoleezza Rice, who has been at the forefront of efforts to 'rehabilitate' the Indonesian military's standing in the USA (http://www.theaustralian.news.com.au/common/story_page/0,5744,12392715%5E2703,00.html).

Indonesian democracy activists are rightly concerned – the military was instrumental in the establishment of martial law in Aceh after exploiting recent domestic and global developments. Most disturbing is that the military tried, although unsuccessfully, to put forward a law that would have effectively placed it in a commanding position in times of national emergency (Jones 2004). Activists also fear that new anti-terror laws will be abused. Alarm bells rang because of the ambiguity with which 'terrorism' was defined, which allowed for the deployment of the legislation against separatist movements in Aceh or Papua (Sebastian 2003: 364–5; Jones 2004: 26). Prior to this, there were already fears of a return to a security state when some student activists in Java and pro-independence Acehnese activists were arrested on the basis of the Indonesian Criminal Code (Jones 2004: 25). Moreover, after the Marriott bombing, it was increasingly opined that Indonesia *should* have an even more draconian Internal Security Act in the style of Singapore and Malaysia. The idea was first floated by Matori Abdul Djalil, the Defence Minister in the Megawati government, and was supported by, among others, current President Susilo Bambang Yudhoyono, who was then Coordinating Minister for Politics and Security (Balowski 2003).

In sum, global and domestic developments since 2001 have produced new opportunities for the military to regain some lost political ground. The military, in particular,

> used the post-Bali climate to push for a strengthening of its own intelligence capacity down to the village level, in a way that would serve only to reinforce the existing territorial command structure – the gradual dismantling of which had generally been seen as an essential step towards moving the army out of daily political life.
>
> (Jones 2004: 26–7)

More importantly, a new law that was passed on the military in 2004 left the territorial structure untouched.

The illiberal consequences of empire

Anti-US sentiments are very much alive and well within post-Soeharto Indonesia. Even at the levels of provinces, *kabupaten* and towns, political leaders express disbelief that those convicted of the Bali bombings, for example, are the real culprits. Frequently, the idea of a global, USA-led conspiracy against Islam is invoked. For example, the East Java boss of the PPP (United Development Party), the 'Islamic' party produced by the New Order, believes that the Bali bombers were merely the hired hands of bigger players – 'educated people' trained overseas and lacking in nationalism.[9] A Surabaya local parliamentarian, A. Wachid, expresses disbelief that those accused of carrying out the Bali bombings had the technical capacity to do so, thus speculating on the role of US and Israeli agents. The aim, he suggests, is to define Indonesia as a terrorist state, thereby placing the country in a vulnerable position.[10] A Golkar Member of Parliament in Gresik, East Java, argues that too much attention to human rights will disable the Indonesian military from carrying out its duty to defend national integrity.[11]

These views are particularly ironic given the increasingly order- and security-oriented agenda of the USA in the region. It is, however, in the interests of political conservatives in Indonesia – whether 'secular–nationalist' or 'Islamic' – to exploit anti-US sentiment, which in turn increases US anxiety about terror groups in the country. Thus, a mutually sustaining process of creating fear and anxiety is evidently at work.

In reality, nothing appeals less to US interests in Southeast Asia than having to deal with a chaotic process of Indonesian balkanization. Thus, in spite of the stated aims of US hegemony, of defending 'freedom and democracy, little attention has been directed by Washington to the role of US companies such as Exxon and Freeport in bankrolling the pervasive brutality of the Indonesian military in conflict-ridden places like Aceh and Papua. The indifference was apparent in the lack of response to the assassination of an important Papuan political leader even though the murder was publicly praised as an act of patriotism by one of Indonesia's most powerful generals.[12] This apathy also manifests itself in the USA's restrained reaction to military violence in Aceh.

The overwhelming concern with order and security has been expressed vigorously by a number of commentators in the USA. One of the most notable examples may well be Sebastian Mallaby, a columnist for the traditionally 'liberal' *Washington Post*. In the journal *Foreign Affairs*, Mallaby (2002: 2–7) quite remarkably argues that the USA must assume the position of an imperial power or risk a descent into global chaos, and the proliferation of 'failed states' that are potentially threatening to the USA. For

Mallaby, modern institutions are never going to take off in these 'failed states', all of which are potential sources of world instability and fertile ground for the emergence of hostile terror networks. The implication is that international assistance programmes are only of limited use, and that it is now the duty and burden of the USA to sort things out by *enforcing* conditions that could lead to the emergence of market rationality and good governance in the most inhospitable of contexts.

Not surprisingly, the ideal of human rights and a more genuinely empowering democracy have been the major casualties of the securitization of US policy in Indonesia. Thus, the Indonesian military intelligence service has gotten away with applying the sort of pressure on critical NGOs that has not been seen since the late Soeharto period, when political activists were regularly harassed and brutalized on the claim that the latter's activities are a threat to national security and interests (Tjhin 2004).[13]

The effects of American Empire have also been unsupportive of democratic struggles in Indonesia in various ways. First, as we have seen, the post-Cold-War/post-9/11 US agenda seems to be throwing a lifeline to some of the most conservative elements of the Indonesian body politic. As NGO activists in Indonesia have remarked, the war on Iraq benefited presidential hopeful General Wiranto's chances by stripping human rights arguments of their moral force.[14] Second, recent developments have shown that governments such as those in Indonesia or China have enjoyed great latitude in defining domestic opponents as security threats in the context of the War on Terror. China, for example, branded a pro-independence movement in the largely Muslim province of Xinjiang as 'terrorist' (Roberts 2002), in the same way that the Indonesian government tried to in relation to Acehnese separatists (*Jakarta Post*, 21 November 2003). Third, the rhetoric of the Bush administration about making the world safe for democracy, freedom and human rights has tainted the activities of democracy and human rights activists in Indonesia, thereby further weakening the reformist impulse in Indonesian society. This has especially been the case since the revelation of abuse of suspected terrorists in Guantanamo Bay and, more so, after the very graphic disclosure of the systematic torture of prisoners by US military personnel at Abu Ghraib.

Events such as these may have more than just passing relevance in so far as the struggle to shape Indonesia's new democracy continues. The USA would seem to have lost what little moral authority it had in Indonesia to preach the language of justice and human rights, even while keeping in mind an awareness of several decades of Cold War-era support for military juntas worldwide. In other words, it has lost much of the basis of what Nye (2004a) has called its 'soft power' – the appeal of the values that it is supposed to represent. Indeed, one Muslim political activist in Indonesia points out that the images of US soldiers humiliating Iraqi prisoners would ensure that no one would take seriously US claims of championing human rights (Alhadar 2004). Even the Kopassus appears to be relishing the situation – its spokesman pointed out that the US military has not adhered to the human rights principles that Indonesia's military was supposed to have learned according to past US rhetoric (*Jakarta Post*, 19 May 2004). On the other hand, Indonesian foreign ministry officials perceive that the USA is pursuing double standards, and they express their bewilderment that past criticism has now given way to an encouragement of authoritarian controls.[15]

In effect, the US agenda, especially after the events of September 2001, has reinforced the already strong basis for resistance to political liberalism in Indonesian state and society. This is not merely an unintended consequence of policy in the sense of Johnson's 'blowback' (Johnson 2000). Instead, political illiberalism, and even anti-liberalism, have been understood to be necessary in enforcing the kind of world order envisioned by the advocates of US Imperium, as this chapter has shown. In the Indonesian case, the main beneficiaries so far have been the most anti-democratic forces in the country, while the main casualty has been the struggle to uphold the ideals of human rights and the establishment of a more genuinely empowering democracy.

Notes

1 See the transcript of a joint press conference by Australian Minister of Defence, Senator Robert Hill, and US Deputy Secretary of Defense, Paul Wolfowitz, at the Shangri-la Hotel, Singapore, on 1 June 2002 at http://www.minister.defence. gov.au/Hilltpl.cfm?CurrentId = 1558. Also see the transcript of a speech by Senior Minister Lee Kuan Yew on the occasion of the 1st International Institute for Strategic Studies Asia Security Conference, Singapore, 31 May 2002, Singapore Government Press Release, Media Division, Ministry of Information, Communications and the Arts, at http://sg.news.yahoo.com/020530/57/2qiur.html.
2 For views on modernizing liberal pluralists in Indonesia at the time, see Bourchier and Hadiz (2003: especially Ch. 2).
3 For a detailed early look at this programme, see Dye (1965). Also see Ford Foundation (2003).
4 This theme is revisited, for example, in Petras (2001).
5 As noted in the chronicle of events directly leading to and following Soeharto's fall provided by Sinansari Ecip (1998: 129).
6 This article, originally published in the *Los Angeles Times*, is found on the web site of the Project for the New American Century, of which the author is Executive Director. US Deputy Defense Secretary, Paul Wolfowitz, is a leading participant.
7 See the report in http://www.laksamana.net/vnews.cfm?ncat = 2&news_id = 4545 (8 January 2003) about a meeting in 2000 that involved these generals and top Muslim militant groups.
8 For example, according to Ikrar Nusa Bhakti, a researcher at the Indonesian Institute of Sciences. Read the interview in 'Government Must Act on Military Businesses', *Jakarta Post*, 20 May 2000.
9 Interview with Moeslimin in Surabaya, 15 December 2002.
10 Interview with A. Wachid, 16 December 2002.
11 Interview with Koesmulyanto, 18 December 2002.
12 See his comments as reported in 'Jenderal Ryamizard: Pembunuh Theys Hiyo Eluay Adalah Pahlawan', *Tempo Interaktif*, 23 April 2003.

13 Not all NGO activists, however, have taken the threat seriously. Bonnie Setiawan, head of the Institute of Global Justice, an anti-globalization group, claims that no such list really exists and that military intelligence chief Hendropriyono was just making empty threats (personal communication, 11 June 2004).
14 Interview with staff members of Indonesia Corruption Watch, 14 June 2004.
15 Interview with Iwan Wiranataatmadja, Director for Special Political Affairs, Indonesian Foreign Ministry, and Hassan Kleib, Director for International Security and Disarmament Affairs, Indonesian Foreign Ministry, 11 June 2004.

8 Islamic opposition in Malaysia

Political idiom, moral economy and religious governance*

Khoo Boo Teik

September 11 has been the major excuse for perpetrating unspeakable brutality on the world of Islam; the USA-led War on Terror has become a crusade of imperial terror against recalcitrant Muslim states, radical Muslims and, virtually, Islam itself. For Malaysia, which is neither recalcitrant nor radical but a state that constitutionally maintains Islam as its official religion, the impact of September 11 has been ironic rather than destructive.

September 11 was an opportune moment for Prime Minister Dr Mohamad Mahathir and his ruling party, the United Malays National Organization (UMNO). Since September 1998, neoliberal forces had castigated Mahathir for imposing capital controls and opposing the pro-market reforms that the International Monetary Fund (IMF) had prescribed for solving the East Asian financial crisis. Since April 2001, there had been protests against the Mahathir regime's resumed use of the Internal Security Act (ISA) to carry out pre-emptive arrests and detention without trial.[1] With September 11, however, neoconservative geopolitics overshadowed neoliberal economics; Mahathir's 'economic fault' was overlooked while his 'security sin' seemed to be vindicated. Thus, September 11 provided Mahathir with an opening to make amends with the interests driving American Empire.

On 29 September 2001, Mahathir declared that Malaysia was an 'Islamic state'. This was a contradictory stance because over two decades, Mahathir's policies, including Islamization, had never been anything but 'secularist'. On the other hand, the notion of an 'Islamic state', which bears a vision of theocracy, was the proclaimed goal of the opposition Parti Islam SeMalaysia (PAS or Islamic Party). Mahathir's '929'[2] stance, however, boldly signalled his way out from disrepute and UMNO's way out of threatened 'irrelevance' (after its rejection by a majority of its Malay constituency in the 1999 general election).

Implicit in that stance was a dichotomy between a moderate, progressive and 'secular' Islam that would serve domestic transformation and engage with global changes (that is, the Islam of Mahathir and UMNO) – and therefore favoured by the USA – and an extremist, fundamentalist and theocratic Islam caught in a recoil against modernity (that is, the Islam of PAS). While such a dichotomy may be good for domestic and international politicking, it is too formulaic for appreciating the contested meanings of 'Islam and politics'. Instead, in this essay, I explore Islam as it is embedded in the historical specificities of national and local politics, the practicalities of moral economy compelled by financial constriction, and an infusion of governance with piety. This essay does not dwell on the regime whose officially sanctioned Islam is well publicized, or the regime's alleged shadowy enemies, of whom hardly anything is reliably known to researchers. Rather, in this essay, I focus on PAS, an Islamic party that is experienced in managing 'opposition governments' in Kelantan and, to a lesser degree, in Trengganu. I will pay particular attention to Islam as a political idiom, economic management under severe constraints, and the meanings of Islamic governance.

An idiom from two movements

In Malaysia's first post-independence general election in 1959, PAS leapt from obscurity to rule the states of Kelantan and Trengganu, thus staking a big claim on the allegiance of the Malay–Muslim electorate. PAS's startling success prompted many prejudiced academic responses that were coloured by variants of modernization theory and an empathy with the ruling Alliance coalition. PAS was regarded as an extremist party, not so much in an Islamic ideal as a 'Malay chauvinist' mould. PAS's leaders, many of whom were (non-English-educated) religious teachers, were cast as traditionalists, fanatics and even charlatans who appealed demagogically to the poorly educated, communalist and parochial masses that populated Malaya's economically and socially backward regions. Kershaw (1969), Kessler (1978) and Funston (1980) offer notable exceptions to prejudiced academic representations of PAS. Kessler, who approached PAS as 'the product of enduring tensions within Kelantan's predominantly Malay society', argued that for PAS and its supporters, 'Islam [was] a politically persuasive idiom for the apprehension of mundane social experience' (Kessler 1978: 35). Kessler concluded that PAS represented 'like many populist movements . . . a *conservative movement of radical discontent*'[3] whose typical supporter belonged to a 'threatened smallholder peasantry' who in 'seeking the restoration of an idealized past . . . is gradually radicalized by his forlorn attempt to remain traditional' (Kessler 1978: 167).

Neither the social restoration nor political radicalization noted by Kessler came to pass. This was partly because PAS ceased to be an opposition party for several years after it joined the BN, the enlarged ruling coalition that replaced the Alliance after the ethnic violence of 13 May 1969. It was also partly because the implementation of the New Economic Policy (NEP) contained rural discontent in at least three different ways. First, the settlement of landless peasants in the land schemes managed by the Federal Land

Development Authority (Felda) assuaged, to some extent, the rural popu-
lace's poverty and 'hunger for land' (Husin Ali 1978). Second, the NEP
inducted large sections of rural youth into the new export-processing zones,
in which multinational corporations commenced a programme of export-
oriented industrialization. Third, the state sent tens of thousands of Malay
students into educational institutions at home and abroad, and created
employment and business opportunities for other Malays. Broadly, this was
not a milieu to favour the vitality of Islam as a 'politically persuasive idiom'.

Indeed, the revitalization of Islam as political discourse in Malaysia did
not come directly from PAS but via a global 'Islamic resurgence' centred in
the Middle East. This resurgence was politically churned by war, imperialist
interventions in the affairs of the *ummah*, and revolution (Esposito 1998:
158–65). Inasmuch as it bespoke 'a development crisis', namely 'the failure
to overcome problems associated with uneven and skewed development', the
resurgence attracted 'groups [that] have their own reasons to bear a grudge
against the state for its failure to deliver economic dividends in the wake of
urbanisation and education'; that is, 'the young', the 'new middle class' of
professionals, technocrats and students of non-religious subjects, and the
'urban dispossessed' (Ahmad Fauzi 2001: 23). As much as the resurgence
manifested a 'Muslim reaction against a universal crisis of modernity'
(Ahmad Fauzi 2001: 23), Islamists opposed most 'social ills such as break-
up of family life, individualistic and materialistic attitudes to life,
widespread divorce, sexual freedom, crime and immorality in general'
(Ahmad Fauzi 2001: 24). Hence, and to invert Kessler's formulation, the
Islamic resurgence may be seen as a *radical movement of conservative discontent* that was radically opposed to the state but which conservatively
espoused 'religion as a doctrinaire remoulder of society' (Thubron 1995: 42).

In Malaysia, the Islamic resurgence was influential among Muslim
students in universities and colleges, and was visible through *dakwah*
activism organized by such groups as the Angkatan Belia Islam Malaysia
(ABIM; Malaysian Islamic Youth Movement) and the Jamaah Islah (Islam)
Malaysia. In some universities in the UK and the USA, Muslim activists
among the large number of government-sponsored Malaysian students
founded organizations such as the Islamic Representative Council,
Malaysian Islamic Study Group and Suara Islam. In time, the domestic and
'foreign' organizations developed links with Islamists in both the 'core' and
the 'periphery' of the world of Islam, from Egypt to Pakistan, for example.
Other expressions of the Islamic resurgence in Malaysia included the Darul
Arqam. This began in the 1970s and became an almost self-contained and
self-reliant Islamic community, complete with its own economic, educational
and social institutions. The state Islamized itself to some extent, with its
most notable slate of policies being Mahathir's broad programme of
'Islamization'.

For the Malaysian Islamists, the period of the NEP was not a time of
personal privation; on the contrary the NEP[4] brought them a 'crisis of

development' – not one of underdevelopment, but the multi-dimensional outcome of rapid and far-reaching development. They bore witness to the socially and culturally dislocating changes that accompanied the capitalist transformation of Malay society, led partly by the state and partly advanced by multinational corporations. The Islamists were also not subjected to political ravage even though they regularly came under state scrutiny and suffered bouts of police repression; however, they were conscious of the global *ummah*'s terrible conditions. Like Islamists elsewhere, they spurned the idea that the solutions to domestic and global problems could be supplied by capitalism or communism, each of which had intervened in the Middle East with disastrous consequences. They would also not turn to nationalism, which had frequently failed, or to the 'secularism' that was often imposed by force. Hence, although 'it would be extremely offensive to attribute their "discovery" of the Islamic message to other causes which suggest "escapist" explanations and misuse of Islam as a political tool' (Ahmad Fauzi 2001: 29), the Malaysian Islamists discovered in Islam an undivided fountain of religious identity, personal piety, social consciousness and political engagement. As Nik Abdul Aziz Nik Mat, Kelantan's Mentri Besar (Chief Minister) since 1990, often says, 'Politics for us didn't begin when the West invented socialism, capitalism or pragmatism. For us, politics began with Islam. Therefore, when we have problems, we don't turn to socialism, capitalism or pragmatism. We return to Islam for our solutions.'[5]

Significantly, in Malaysia, the call among Islamists of different orientations for a 'return to Islam' – not to observing it as mere 'official religion' but to its practice as *ad-Din* (a way of life) – came amid the turmoil that beset PAS from 1977 to 1982. In 1977, a split in Kelantan's PAS-led government, abetted by UMNO intervention, led to PAS's withdrawal from the BN, the declaration of a state of emergency in Kelantan, and PAS's heavy defeat in the 1978 general election. Bereft of its regional power base and discredited by its sojourn in the BN, the PAS leadership (then under Mohamad Asri) was toppled by a group of *ulama*. This latter group was made up of young and old, many of who had furthered their religious education in the Middle East (but also elsewhere at times). PAS's new *ulama* leadership, including Yusof Rawa, Fadzil Mohd Noor, Nik Abdul Aziz Nik Mat and Abdul Hadi Awang, represented a conjunction of the old, local 'conservative movement of radical discontent' and the new, global 'radical movement of conservative discontent'.[6]

Thus was Islam revitalized 'for the apprehension of mundane social experience' but under conditions that required doctrinal reinvention by Islamists in general and, for PAS, an ideological turn towards what Muhammad Ikmal (1996: 61) called 'conservative (that is, puritanical) radicalism'. Social life had been much altered by the state's pursuit of a nationalist–capitalist project, beginning with the NEP and continuing with Mahathir's 'Malaysia Incorporated'. Two decades of high economic growth had produced enormous wealth but there were glaring inequalities within rural society –

between rural and urban communities, and between new politico-corporate elites and the rest of society. For instance, Kelantan, the poorest state, was not only economically lagging behind Klang Valley, the richest region. The capitalist, corporate and consumerist world of metropolitan Kuala Lumpur was remote from the communitarian environments of rural and small-town Kelantan.[7] For that matter, appeals to ethnic commonality, expressed in 'Malay nationalism' vis-à-vis the non-Malays, could scarcely bridge the gulf between the spectacularly rich 'Melayu Baru' (New Malays) of the major cities and the rural poor of the so-called 'Malay heartland'. For those who held on to Islam as *ad-Din*, the rich were also corrupt and not coincidentally un-Islamic.

At least until the early 1990s, Malaysian politics was subject to the intensification of inter-ethnic disputes over the implementation of the NEP, opportunities for small businesses, culture, language and education. Given the residential and cultural patterns of Malaysian society, the 'relationship' between the Islamists and PAS leaders, and non-Muslims (especially the Chinese), was characterized by distance, mutual incomprehension and unease. Yet, those who were part of the global Islamic resurgence found little purchase on 'Malayness'. UMNO had monopolized that marker of identity as a rallying point. Besides, the 'Malay nationalism' of the Asri leadership was discarded by PAS's new *ulama* leaders, who lived and thrived in social environments that were distant from the majority of the non-Muslim communities.[8] Pledging a purer universalistic Islam, various Islamists sought to dissociate themselves from ethnic chauvinism and, even, 'to reject ethnic discrimination and privileges, including the NEP and Bumiputraism, as inimical to the spirit of Islam' (Jomo and Cheek 1992: 98).

The above summary can only hint at the totality of social division, changing conditions and waves of discontent of the mid-1980s, from which PAS renewed its challenge to UMNO. By then, 'social life in rural areas with clear and strong opposition to the government, such as in Kelantan, Kedah and Perlis, [had been] split along party lines'. 'Dissenting voices from marginalized groups' sought refuge in PAS, whose programme offered 'more than vulgar material concerns' (Halim 1999: 191). Old rural discontentment found new expression. In Felda schemes, for example, inconclusive conflicts between the settlers' aspirations of land ownership and Felda management practices that seemed to proletarianize the settlers could be 'Islamized':

> For instance, [PAS supporters] argue that they are forced into the forbidden system of usury (*riba*) as shown by payment of interest on their loan repayment by virtue of being in land schemes. Likewise, they argue that the block system provides them with a forbidden (*haram*) income because Islam forbids a follower to deprive others of their labour which is possible under the block system.
>
> (Halim 1992: 116)

Table 8.1: Governments of Kelantan, 1957–2004

Period	Party (coalition) in power	Comment
1957– 9	UMNO (Alliance)	Based on 1955 Legislative Council election
1959– 74	PAS	Victory from first post –Merdeka election
1974– 7	PAS (Barisan Nasional)	Ended after a PAS split abetted by UMNO
1977– 8	State of Emergency	Rule by National Operations Council
1978– 90	UMNO (Barisan Nasional)	With Berjasa, party of PAS breakaway
1990– 6	PAS- S46	Angkatan Perpaduan Ummah coalition
1996– 9	PAS	S46 was dissolved in 1996
1999– 2004	PAS	With Keadilan in Barisan Alternatif
Since April 2004	PAS	Nominally in coalition with Keadilan

Table 8.2: Governments of Trengganu, 1957–2004

Period	Party (coalition) in power	Comment
1957– 9	UMNO (Alliance)	Based on 1955 Legislative Council election
1959– 61	PAS	Victory in first post –Merdeka election
1962– 4	UMNO (Alliance)	Defections caused fall of PAS government
1964– 99	UMNO (Alliance/BN)	Long UMNO rule
1999– 2004	PAS (Barisan Alternatif)	PAS return on *Reformasi* wave
Since April 2004	UMNO (BN)	Dramatic reversal of 1999 election result

Thus, during its revivalist phase in the early 1980s, PAS:

> aligned itself with contemporary trends in Islamic resurgence by repudiating nationalism of all sorts ... Bent upon discarding its nationalist and traditional image, PAS revived demands for an Islamic state, remodelled its arguments with Islamic political vocabulary, resorted to universal principles of justice and equality to woo non-Muslims, and presented itself as the voice of the oppressed masses. PAS' fierce assaults against government policies criticised injustices of the New Economic Policy and oppressive legislation, [cast] doubts on 'cosmetic Islamisation' and raised concern at the lack of initiatives to tackle rising problems of corruption and moral decadence.
>
> (Ahmad Fauzi 2003a: 81–82)

Persistent divisions, rejuvenated ideology and determined challenges, however, were no guarantee of political recovery. The non-Muslim vote was still closed to PAS as the typical non-Muslim voter supported either the BN's non-Malay parties or the opposition Democratic Action Party (DAP). With inter-ethnic disputes unabated but NEP-driven growth benefiting a large section of the Malay population, UMNO's 'Malay nationalist' appeal, vast financial resources and powers of state held the Malay electorate against PAS incursions. Despite the fervour its leaders generated before the 1986 general election, PAS had a dismal election result: merely one seat in Parliament out of eighty-seven contests against UMNO.

As it turned out, political developments not directly connected to religion returned PAS to power in Kelantan and then in Trengganu. In 1990, after being out of the government for thirteen years, PAS won Kelantan in coalition with Parti Melayu Semangat 46 (S46 or The Spirit of 46 Malay Party). The latter was a party of UMNO dissidents forced out of UMNO following the party's bitter election of 1987. In 1999, another UMNO crisis (over the dismissal and persecution of Anwar Ibrahim) helped PAS to retain control of Kelantan and, after thirty-seven years, regain power in Trengganu. This time, PAS was the leading member of an opposition coalition, Barisan Alternatif (BA or Alternative Front). Yet, any degree of jubilation or trepidation over an ever-rising PAS was corrected by the March 2004 general election, during which PAS gained the slimmest of victories in Kelantan but was toppled by a resurgent UMNO in Trengganu. It is to this recent PAS rule in Kelantan and Trengganu that I turn for insights into the compatibility of Islam with democracy and the meanings of Islam in administration.

Democracy and the electoral process

As Tables 8.1 and 8.2 show, Kelantan – and to a lesser extent, Trengganu – exists as close to a 'two-party system' as has been seen in Malaysian politics.[9]

One might even call this a 'two-Malay-party system' since an important reason for this atypical situation lay in the absence of inter-ethnic disputes in overwhelmingly Malay-populated Kelantan and Trengganu. The electorate could choose between UMNO and PAS without worrying about non-Malay intrusions. Thus, politics in Kelantan and Trengganu turned on an even UMNO–PAS divide, so that a small but definite vote swing could decisively affect electoral outcomes. At more than one election, internal strife in one party provided that swing by prompting its members and supporters to defect to the rival side (Halim 2000: 3).[10]

A second important reason was PAS's perseverance in electoral contestation despite having to endure very unequal terms of contest as well as periodic repression. Proclamations by PAS leaders of the party's commitment to democracy and the electoral process are often met with scepticism. Yet, PAS's record is not without substance; the views of PAS leaders such as the present PAS President, Abdul Hadi Awang, deserve serious consideration:

PAS definitely participates in elections and the system of democracy practised in this country . . . Previously PAS won in Kelantan and Trengganu, fully accepted the fall of its governments in these two states, and continued to struggle via elections until PAS regained victory. The people can reject us if we fail.

(Abdul Awadi Awang 2002: 24)[11]

On the topic of which party was a threat to democracy, Hadi was neither disingenuous nor provocative when he reminded voters not to be 'fooled and tyrannized by the media and the abuse of laws':

PAS patiently endured the fall of its governments in Trengganu in 1961, in Kelantan in 1978, the results of UMNO's extremist actions. In Trengganu, the fall occurred via money politics and administrative and media pressures; in Kelantan via an emergency arranged with play-acting demonstrations. PAS firmly supports democracy by participating in elections but UMNO displays its extremist attitude and is prepared to destroy democracy if it loses because it will not patiently suffer even a reduction in votes and seats.

(Abdul Awadi Awang 2002: 49)

There may be more to PAS's position than its leaders' sincerity. PAS has not been a militant party advocating violent struggles[12] nor has it had to be so when 'policies towards Islamists have stressed accommodation and co-optation rather than overt coercion [so that] we see Islamic resurgence blossoming in a non-militant form' (Ahmad Fauzi 2001: 29). Further, PAS has held power in two states, has had opportunities of governing (and for extended periods in Kelantan) and had previously been a member of three nationwide coalitions, namely BN, APU and BA. Consequently, unlike those Islamic parties in other countries that consistently suffered violent repression, PAS's hopes of electoral success were not illusory – even if its hopes had exceeded its experience.

Despite setbacks in the 2004 election – which PAS denounced as 'unfair' because of UMNO's 'money politics', intimidation by the regime, media distortion, and the Election Commission's gerrymandering and manipulations – PAS 'accepted the fact of the outcome'.[13] In fact, PAS politicians, at least in private interviews, do not deny the party's errors. The latter include renominating 'non-performing' incumbents or fielding unsuitable candidates[14] neglecting young voters,[15] underestimating the negative impact of limited PAS-led economic development, and being complacent about retaining power in Kelantan and Trengganu. It was a realistic PAS Vice-President Mustafa Ali who rejected any suggestion that the party should boycott elections: 'if PAS boycotts the elections and the people do not, then there is no effect at all. It doesn't serve any purpose' (Pereira and Zubaidah 2004).

In its defeat, PAS leaders derived solace from religious fortitude: 'The Islam of our struggles is true; defeats occur due to the errors and weaknesses of those who advance the struggle, not because of weaknesses and errors in Islam' (Abdul Hadi Awang 2002: 24). Yet others should not so readily dismiss PAS leaders' appreciation of the possibilities – not merely instrumental or strictly doctrinal – that democracy and Islam may hold for each other:

> although democracy is a creation of the West, not of Islam, and is full of pronounced weaknesses and deviations, Islam accepts the liberties and rights conferred by democracy and profits from them in order to express the teachings of Islam, conduct *dakwah*, enjoin righteousness and prohibit sin.
>
> (Abdul Hadi Awang 2002: 23)

Moral economy and Islamic governance

Away from the electoral process, one critical matter for PAS was that of managing a government. There were at least three different kinds of difficulties. First, the Kelantanese state civil service (but less so than in Trengganu) was constitutionally placed under the authority of the Sultan and not within the office of the Mentri Besar. Senior officers of the state civil service were not, ultimately, accountable to the PAS administration.[16] Second, payments of various kinds – notably, mandatory federal government contributions to state revenues and development funds – were delayed, withheld or 'rechanneled' via federal agencies. Third, from 1990 to 1995, for example, although UMNO did not hold a single state seat in Kelantan:

> the Federal Government has sent its army known as the JPP. We create *penghulu* and they create *penghulu*. We appoint *penggawa*, they appoint *penggawa*. We make DO's, they make DO's. We appoint the MB, they appoint an MB, too.[17] Formerly they charged that we had two *imam*,[18] now they have two of everything . . . In no other democratic country in the world do people work this way
>
> (Abdul Aziz 1995: 149–50)

The federal government's hostile tactics, not peculiar to the PAS-led Kelantan experience, were effective. This was because Malaysian 'federalism' creates such a great discrepancy in scope and degree of power, and types and levels of resources between the federal government and any other state government, that the former holds the latter at its mercy. Similar tactics, practised over a decade, helped to remove the Parti Bersatu Sabah government in 1994. Avoiding the risk of having to face them was one reason why the Parti Gerakan Rakyat Malaysia rump had joined the BN two decades earlier.

What, then, can Islam mean to an administration that is so hemmed in? At one level, Nik Aziz strove to infuse his government with austerity, thrift, care and transparency. He set a personal example by living modestly in his own house that was close and accessible to his community. He reduced his salary and official allowances, and limited use of his official car. Other members of the State Executive Council took a 10 per cent salary reduction and contributed to various funds. In turn, Nik Aziz exhorted civil servants to adopt 'the spirit of contract, not a spirit of salaried work' (Abdul Aziz 1995: 13) and only to expect remuneration that was proportionate to their effort. Since Kelantan could hardly implement amply financed large-scale socio-economic projects under severe funding constraints, Nik Aziz tried to maintain a popular government that remained close to the people by 'stressing values of social collectivism, civil justice and redistribution through Islamic practices' (Hilley 2001: 194).

It was hoped that both the government and the people might, thereby, *membangun bersama Islam* (develop with Islam). A sociocultural route to this goal was expected to recover the richness of Kelantan's communitarian traditions:

> Faced with our state's poor condition, a condition caused by [the federal government's] neglecting us as if we're [its] stepchild, Praise be to God, we can develop by *muafakat jimat-cermat* [thrift by consensus] and *gotong-royong* [mutual aid] . . . That's why I've always maintained that Kelantan's being short of money doesn't really matter as long as the people support [the government]. The people's support is like money, of an extremely high value.
>
> (Abdul Aziz 1995: 38)

Another path was offered by a kind of 'moral economy' that envisaged an acceptance of 'a lower standard of material existence . . . not incompatible with the existing capacity of the people' (Halim 2000: 3). While the 'existing capacity of the people' was bolstered by the easy availability of relatively cheap produce and consumer goods from Thailand,[19] the thrust of PAS's 'moral economy' was to lighten the economic burdens of everyday and community life by offering small remedies – whether popular, practicable or administrative. For example, since federal funding for large-scale infrastructure projects unjustly lay beyond PAS's control,[20] Nik Aziz was proud that the people:

> were prepared to carry out *gotong-royong*; [to] establish *wakaf* [bodies for public benefaction] . . . build small roads . . . build small mosques . . . build small prayer rooms. The *gotong-royong* practised by the people of Kelantan is clear proof that they love the present government.
>
> (Abdul Aziz 1995: 48)

The government transferred its monetary deposits from interest-bearing accounts to 'interest-free Islamic banking' accounts in accordance with the Quranic injunction against *riba* (interest). By the same injunction, the state established pawnshops that did not levy interest charges, and private pawn-shops were encouraged to follow suit.[21] The Kelantan government also removed the 'service charge' that was previously levied on loans to civil servants (Abdul Aziz 1995: 127). Similarly, the government called for the termination of (federal-government-imposed) fees for television licences, renewal fees for driving licences and road tax (Abdul Aziz 1995: 4–6).[22] Land, the one state-controlled resource, and agriculture were important for PAS – in Kelantan (and later in Trengganu), PAS attempted to improve land administration so as to process more efficiently applications for land.[23] Hadi Awang's government granted ninety-nine-year leases for residential land because 'housing is a pillar of life', but only three-year temporary occupation licences for agricultural land – until the 'tiller' proved himself worthy of continued land occupation and ownership.[24] Nik Aziz characteristically preferred 'industries based on agriculture and animal husbandry' because these 'truly benefit [poor] target groups we consider important and deserving of priority', whereas 'other industries, such as manufacturing, don't just benefit outsiders economically (because the factories are owned by foreign investors), they have an adverse impact on our social system, especially on our youth' (Dinsman 2000: 137). Finally, PAS was not opposed to tourism, although in terms of hotel development, PAS preferred hotels that were true to their original homely purpose of providing safe lodging to travellers and tourists, not hotels that were turned into sites of vice or embodiments of 'Western cultural domination' (Ismail 1999: 29).

When PAS regained control of Trengganu, it seemed imminent that a well-endowed PAS government would at last demonstrate if it could 'progress' beyond a limited moral economy to show what 'Islamic development' might mean. The federal government, however, immediately dashed that possibility. For twenty-three years while UMNO/BN ruled Trengganu, Petronas – the national petroleum company – paid the state government an annual royalty for oil taken off Trengganu waters. Petronas, at the bidding of the federal government, unilaterally terminated payment to Hadi Awang's government. Instead, the money, approximately RM850 million a year, was reclassified as *wang ehsan* (goodwill money) that was rechannelled to Trengganu via federal development agencies and projects. Thus, more than just PAS politicians would find contemptible UMNO's ceaseless sneer of 'no development under PAS' or, as Nik Aziz once remarked, 'The federal [government] should not show it is the champion in an economic race and we are a tortoise because we cannot race under conditions that restrict us.' These were conditions imposed by '"desperadoes" who want to see Kelantan tortured and who wait to say the state government has failed to advance' (Ismail 1999: 5).

Apart from economic issues, governance meant demonstrating the quality of Islamic leadership, which did not separate religion from politics. Many of PAS's elected representatives, notably the *ulama*, regularly led prayers at their mosques and organized other religious–communitarian activities. Again, Nik Aziz led the way: on most Friday mornings, Nik Aziz delivered his *kuliyyah* (lecture) in the heart of Kota Bharu. He led the faithful men and women, seated in the streets and on pavements, in reading the Quran before giving his *tafsir* (interpretation) of selected verses. These Friday sessions were marked by piety and sobriety while enjoying an air of 'market festivity'. People, including out-of-state visitors who came specially to listen to 'Tok Guru' and tourists, milled in the main areas that were closed to traffic but open to makeshift stalls. Nik Aziz's *kuliyyah* would be transcribed and repro-duced in books, cassette tapes and video compact discs to be sold around the country. These Friday *kuliyyah*, at once religious and political, may be likened to a hybrid of a *pondok* (religious school) class and a party *ceramah* (political talk) that effectively 'localized Islamist discourse' (Farish 2003). These lectures made no distinction between Kelantan as Serambi Mekah (The Verandah of Mecca) – an old sobriquet of Kelantan – and as Universiti Politik Terbuka (Open University of Politics) – a title bestowed on it by Nik Aziz.[25]

Once, in an inventive sequential conflation of the several identities of a people that had chosen to Develop With Islam in the face of adversity, Nik Aziz greeted them thus: 'We Muslims, particularly we Malays, more particu-larly we Kelantanese, and even more so we who live in a state whose government is based upon Islam as a way of life' (Abdul Aziz 1995: 10). Surely such a people were 'select' enough to face material blandishments without being corrupted. Hence:

> if someone wants to give [you] money, take it; give sugar, stir it; give cloth, wear it; give a cow, lead it away; then vote Angkatan. Try repeating this! Give money, take it; give sugar, stir it; give cloth, wear it; give a cow, lead it away; then vote Angkatan. If those Kelantanese who like *dikir barat* want to make a song of this, they can, too.
>
> (Abdul Aziz 1995: 159)

A state such as Nik Aziz's Kelantan demanded that PAS's elected representa-tives should be accountable to the electorate. Not all would all live up to the ideal,[26] and some did not:

> nearing this election, I've to say there are among the elected representa-tives we chose those whom we must change. We must change a bit, have new screws and new nuts. Hopefully that will give us satisfaction although it's definitely not possible to satisfy everyone.
>
> (Abdul Aziz 1995: 48)

Nik Aziz claims he replaced thirteen PAS incumbents for the 1995 general election because of complaints he received about them.

Of course, such an Islamic administration could earnestly *require* of its people that *they* lead a pious and moral 'way of life', and the PAS govern-ment attempted this aim in three different ways: facilitation, enforcement and deterrence. Facilitation came in the form of government-sponsored programmes for *pembersihan jiwa* (soul cleansing), mostly to expand and deepen religious education, understanding and observance. Some measures could readily be taken to foster an Islamic vision of development as 'a balance of spiritual and material development'. For example, time had to be set aside for personal reflection and family life. Kelantan (and later Trengganu) shortened the work-week for civil servants to five days, while the federal government maintained a five-and-a-half day work-week, and declared one of the non-working days as 'Family Day'. The state civil service in Kelantan (and later in Trengganu) extended fully paid maternity leave from forty-two to sixty days for female personnel. There were other programmes that needed funding; the 1999 Kelantan state budget, for instance, ranked expenditure for the 'religious sector' second only to 'administration' (Ismail 1999: 502–3). Alternatively, individuals, organizations and businesses were encouraged to contribute to the Tabung Serambi Mekah, a fund to help the poor in Kelantan (Ismail 1999: 163–5).

The enforcement of moral conduct was carried out through regulation, restriction and prohibition. There was a ban on all forms of gambling, which Islam forbade and which, according to PAS, the representatives of other religions only acceded to.[27] Outlets that sold or served alcohol (but only to non-Muslims) were not banned since the consumption of alcohol was not prohibited by other religions, although they were reduced in number. The Kota Bharu Municipal Council closed video game and *karaoke* centres, and other types of entertainment and service establishments suspected of being sites of *maksiat* (vice). *Menutup aurat*, minimally to cover one's head, was expected of Muslim women and required of their civil service counterparts while Muslim men were encouraged to adopt articles of dress that were emblematic of Muslim identity (Dinsman 2000: 110–11). The 'free mixing of the sexes' in public places was discouraged, to the extent that supermarkets and departmental stores had to maintain separate check-out lanes for the different sexes. Malay or Kelantanese artistic and cultural expression, deemed 'pre-Islamic' or anti-Islamic, were prohibited or ceased to be performed, following either a *fatwa*[28] issued by the Majlis Agama Islam Kelantan (Kelantan Islamic Council) or the revocation of licences by the Kota Bharu Municipal Council (Dinsman 2000: 114–17).[29]

Third, and probably most controversial of all, was deterrence – itself an indispensable element of the Islamic penal code usually referred to as *hudud*. PAS maintained that *hudud* was fundamental to an administration that was based on the Quran and Sunnah. Muslims, including ruling party politicians, were generally reluctant to oppose *hudud* openly, for fear of being judged 'un-Islamic'. Non-Muslims were promised the right to choose between *hudud* and existing civil and criminal laws. Yet, any attempt to introduce *hudud* was widely feared and opposed principally because of its harsh penalties for certain criminal offences. In 1993, the Kelantan government sought to pass the Syariah Criminal Code Enactment, while in July

2002, the Trengganu government passed the Syariah Criminal Offences (*Hudud* and *Qisas*) Bill. Neither state enactment could have become law then because each was *ultra vires* the federal Constitution.

Thus, the totality of PAS's administration, barely gleaned here, was crucially formed from a mix of Islamic concepts, doctrinal appeals, communitarian concerns and pragmatic policies. The ideal was to demonstrate the superiority of Islamic government, which infuses governance with morality, and balances material development with spirituality. The important reality of it was to survive the hostility of the federal government long enough to be able to prove anything at all.

Conclusion

Under PAS rule, neither Kelantan nor Trengganu was an 'Islamic state' – if the term connoted a theocratic system. Rather, their politics was embedded in linkages amid the revitalization of Islam as a political idiom, PAS's uneven recovery of power under 'fortuitous' conditions, and an *ulama* leadership's strained effort to govern 'peripheral' states in defiance of a powerful centre. Each of these developments added to a rich texture of socio-political life that was not reducible to formulaic interpretations of an undifferentiated 'Islamic fundamentalism'.

PAS's core experience of 'governing in opposition' has been intensely local, and largely confined to popular measures and a moral economy far removed from globalization. Unlike UMNO, which superintends a state-led nationalist–capitalist project, PAS has not had to confront neoliberal pressures for market liberalization, deregulation and the adoption of new frameworks for investment and governance. This is not to say that globalization can have no impact on a state like Kelantan, but in so far as PAS has no prospect of securing power at a national level, it is likely to approach 'global' matters – or at any rate, non-religious ones – with local lenses. For example, when the federal government announced a token Cabinet salary cut during the East Asian financial crisis, Nik Aziz replied that Kelantan and its leadership had been on salary cuts and a 'thrift drive' since 1990 (Ismail 1999: 382).

Finally, Nik Aziz was once asked, 'Was UMNO correct in saying PAS used religion to oppose progress?' (Abdul Aziz 1995: 102). It was an Australian journalist who asked this question, but he or she could have been any 'secularist' who intuitively separated politics from religion, and left religion out of progress. Nik Aziz replied:

> I say, if I don't want progress what's the point of my being head of government . . . it'll be better if I'm just a leader of prayers teaching the Quran to children, teaching *fardu ain*.[30] When I'm tired, I sleep, and whatever happens outside the prayer room, let it be.
>
> But I'm head of government, I search for funds, I prepare the budget. My officers work, my friends in government think of ways to carry out

progress. The only difference between us [PAS] and them [UMNO] is, the progress we bring is progress that saves the people from this world to the next world. I won't have anything to do with progress that can only be brought about by money if with the money comes God's wrath.

(Abdul Aziz 1995: 102–3)

Nothing in Nik Aziz's reply precludes the leap in imagination from local to global that PAS needs to negotiate globalization, but nothing in it presupposes that a PAS global–local interface must be made in the neoliberal image.

Notes

*   For their kind assistance, when I was in Kota Bharu and Kuala Trengganu in May 2004, I am indebted to Haji Ubaidah Yaakub, Abdul Shukor Taib, Tuan Khairul Anuar Tuan Yusuf, Mohamed Zainal Abidin Hussin and Zaihan Daud. I wish to thank Husam Musa, Rohani Ibrahim, Norazaman Abdul Ghani and Romelah Harun in Kota Bharu, and Dato' Haji Hadi Awang and Dato' Mustafa Ali in Kuala Trengganu, for making time to meet and speak to me. I also interviewed several senior civil servants, but as some of them requested anonymity, I have decided not to name others either. This in no way diminishes my gratitude to them. I am much obliged to Halim Salleh and Siti Hawa Ali for their hospitality and instruction in many matters of Kelantan politics and social life. I also wish to thank Ahmad Fauzi Abdul Hamid, Roger Kershaw, Francis Loh and Kevin Hewison for various forms of assistance.

1   His regime had imprisoned without trial two groups of dissidents. One group was well known – the leaders of the *Reformasi* movement that arose after Mahathir's dismissal and maltreatment of his deputy, Anwar Ibrahim, in September 1998. Of the other group of detainees – alleged 'Islamic militants' of a supposed underground movement – little was known.

2   For a summary and critique of such views, see Kessler (1978: 32–3).

3   Emphasis added.

4   'But for these Malays – like many middle classes elsewhere who no longer have to scramble for subsistence but who prioritize rights and social justice instead – Islam is the metaphor for their aspirations for a more ethical society and for their ensuing disgruntlement' (Martinez 2004: 38).

5   As he said when he spoke at the Seminar Politik Kelantan, Kota Bharu, 23 May 2004. This excerpt was noted and translated by the author who was present at the seminar.

6   Harper (1999: 339) noted that a confluence of Islamic dissent and radical Malay nationalism, bringing the 'diaspora of Malay radicals' into PAS, strengthened the party under Burhanuddin al-Helmy.

7   For instance, the changing social relations in Kota Bharu under an incipient capitalism in the mid-1970s (Halim 1981) were far removed from, not to say 'far behind', the economic and cultural conditions of the major towns

8   'The years since the ascendancy of the new PAS leadership in 1982 have seen a curious mix to greater ideological consistency combined with strategic incoherence. Acutely aware of the Malay nationalist underpinnings of the party's espousal of Islam under Asri, the new leaders have tried to articulate a more pristine version of Islam, inadvertently surrendering Asri's turf to Mahathir, Sanusi and Anwar's "born-again" Muslim UMNO' (Jomo and Cheek 1992: 97).

 9 Changes of state government had taken place in Penang (1969) and Sabah (various times) before. But after Parti Gerakan Rakyat Malaysia joined the BN in 1974, no opposition party has ever ruled Penang. The situation in Sabah was more complex: different parties had assumed power, supported by or eventually joining the ruling coalition.

10 In 1990, 'PAS gains were mainly a consequence of UMNO internal divisions and weaknesses. Not only was this reflected in the formation of Semangat 46, state UMNO organizations throughout the northern rural states had become deeply factionalized and alienated from the electorate' (Funston 2004: 170).

11 PAS 'in contrast with most other Islamic parties in the Muslim world, has since its inception participated in the Malaysian electoral process competing in a semi-democratic political system that heavily favours the UMNO-led coalition government' (Ahmad Hussein 2002: 101).

12 'The unexpected and unprecedented (as far as PAS was concerned) harshness of the repression of 1985, expecially the Memali incident, shocked PAS militants into recognizing the repressive character and potential of the state. Indications since then would suggest that most PAS members, including the national leadership, have chosen to back off. Despite much PAS rhetoric about the martyrdom (a fate exalted in Islam) of the victims of Lubok Merbau and Memali, the PAS leadership probably recognized that PAS was hardly prepared mentally, let alone physically and organizationally, for violent struggle. Cynical observers have commented that UMNO called PAS's bluff and won' (Jomo and Cheek 1992: 99). In 2001, Nik Aziz's son was detained under the ISA. This was as close to a repressive blow against Nik Aziz himself as could be imagined. Yet neither Nik Aziz nor PAS have been anything but 'constitutional' in their protests.

13 Interview with Abdul Hadi Awang, Marang, Trengganu, 25 May 2004.

14 Husam Musa, a member of the Kelantan State Executive Council, thought that PAS lost seven seats in 2004 because of unsuitable nominations. Interview with Husam Musa, Kota Bharu, 21 May 2004.

15 Interview with Norazman Abdul Ghani, Kota Bharu, 20 May 2004.

16 A colleague has suggested that this was a considerable difficulty for the Nik Aziz adminstration. The author was unable to obtain detailed information on this matter. But the Mentri Besar's control over the state civil service was probably less problematic when PAS ruled with S46 since the latter supplied intimate links to the royal house.

17 JPP stands for Jabatan Pembangunan Persekutuan, or Federal Development Department. Kelantan is administratively divided into *jajahan* or districts, for each of which there is a District Officer (DO). Each *jajahan* is divided into several *daerah* (nominally sub-district), with each *daerah* being headed by a Penggawa. Each *daerah* is further divided into several *mukim* (sometimes translated as 'parish'); each *mukim* is headed by a Penghulu who oversees several *kampung* (villages). The MB, *Mentri Besar*, of a state is its Chief Minister.

18 The issue of two *imam* (leader of prayers), seen as dividing the *ummah*, was blamed on PAS in the 1980s. But as Kershaw (1969: 52) observed, the divisiveness was much older: 'whereas before 1959 incipient modernity and tradition could co-exist within such received institutions as the family, reciprocal hospitality connected with private and public ceremonies, and Islam, politics has brought a bitter polarization even within families and between men who were accustomed to worship as brothers at the same mosque. Mosques and suraus have become identified with one or other of the two parties and attract the corresponding part of the village population. Shops draw their clientele from one political faction in the same way. The cementing function of hospitality has declined . . . and today invitations are generally restricted to supporters of one's own party. A big feast of reconciliation is held to mark a man's change of allegiance. There is much

genuine despair on both sides at this evil which has overtaken Malay society.' See, too, Kessler (1978: 130–60) for local details of 'an unremitting intensity of party conflict in Jelawat', not attributable to PMIP instransigence alone, that affected everyday life, sports, prayers and control of local councils. Even then there was a two *surau* (mosque) problem.

19 More than one resident or observer of Kelantan had remarked so to me thus. Thailand and Kelantan engage in considerable trade at three gazetted border-crossing points.

20 Examples of how the federal government squeezed Kelantan via restrictions on funding for several infrastructural projects are found in Abdul Aziz (1995: 206–7).

21 State-owned pawnshops were operating by this basic principle in Trengganu under UMNO/BN rule.

22 Note that this section referring to the different licences and fees comes from an excerpt of a speech made by Tengku Razaleigh Hamzah in 1995 while he was S46 President and S46 was still PAS's ally.

23 Between 2002 and 2003, the Department of Land and Mines in Trengganu processed over 50,000 applications for land, compared to an average of 1,000 applications per year before 1999. A former civil servant, who spoke to the author, remarked that PAS was earnest about resolving the land application delays and problems inherited from the UMNO/BN administration. Confirmation on this point was provided during the interview with Abdul Hadi Awang, Marang, Trengganu, 25 May 2004.

24 The use of the word 'tiller' is the author's, but 'land to the tiller' would be a usage in the spirit of Hadi's distinction between different 'rights' to different categories of land. Interview with Abdul Hadi Awang.

25 'Because of *pondok-pondok* [religious schools] such as this and other *pondok-pondok* before them, Kelantan has been known as Serambi Mekah. We don't actually know who gave this name of Serambi Mekah to Kelantan' (Abdul Aziz 1995: 42). Nik Aziz said of this 'open university of politics' that it 'is not covetous of certificates, is not covetous of any kind of qualification' but 'only desirous of consciousness, desirous of understanding that is so deep as to reach the next world' (Abdul Aziz 1995: 42). After the 2004 election, when it was still unclear if PAS had won, Nik Aziz gathered the elected PAS representatives in the Hotel Ansar, Kota Bharu, for three days, presumably to prevent any defection to UMNO.

26 The federal government followed by adopting a five-day week for civil servants two weeks in a month!

27 See Husam (2003) for an extended criticism of gambling and the federal government's 'complicity' in it.

28 Legal ruling by Muslim jurists.

29 Two types of 'dance dramas', *makyong* and *menora*, were prohibited by *fatwa*, while *wayang kulit* and *main puteri* performances ceased.

30 Individual duties required of each Muslim, including daily prayers and fasting during Ramadan.

9   The American Empire and the southern Philippine periphery

An aberrant case?*

Patricio N. Abinales

In January 2002, 660 US troops joined the Armed Forces of the Philippines (AFP) in joint exercises in southeastern Mindanao Island, where a Muslim separatist rebellion and a gang of Islamic kidnappers had bedevilled the Philippine government (*Newsbreak Magazine*, 13 February 2002; *Philippine Daily Inquirer*, 26 January, 1 March 2002; henceforth *PDI*). Filipino nationalists criticized 'Balikatan 02–1' as yet more proof of 'US imperialism' (*Unmasking the U.S. War on Terror*, 2002). The public, however, thought otherwise. Polls showed that a large percentage (84 per cent) of respondents favoured the US deployment (Social Weather Station, Special Media Release, 30 January 2002). Among Filipino-Muslims, 60 per cent supported Balikatan 02–1, while 26 per cent disapproved of it (Social Weather Station, Special Institutional Sponsor Release, 6 August 2002).

How can we account for this discordance? Scholars point to a deeply embedded 'colonial mentality' that prevents Filipinos from seeing the reality of US global power. This false consciousness supposedly has an unusual vivacity that is fed by the state's ideological apparatuses (such as education and the media) that promote pro-USA views and impose US consumerist values on Filipinos. The argument scores political points but has little explanatory value in present times. It understates, among other things, the capacity of Filipinos to defy US ideological power, and ignores the manifold ways in which various 'weapons of the weak' have also been used to defang an ostensibly powerful US culture through expropriation and indigenization. Moreover, it does not account for changes in national culture in the late twentieth century, during which Filipinos became exposed to other external cultural agencies – from Japanese *anime* to Mexican soap operas and Taiwanese pop stars.

I would suggest that US popularity in Muslim Mindanao can be better explained by looking at the intersection between US geopolitical interests, national politics and local power in the Muslim areas throughout history. The triangulation of three nodes of power reveals an unexpected portrait; instead of an all-powerful US actor demanding compliance from Filipinos and Muslims, power is actually located more on the local side, with Muslim elites and communities manipulating US power as a means of protecting their local power from an intrusive national state. They also mean to entrench their standing further in the community and, finally, to contain possible threats from groups beyond their control. In short, Muslim responses to US presence in southern Philippines suggest a perspective that regards the 'the power of the local' as being an equally, if not more, important factor in evaluating the extent to which the politico-military agenda of US neoliberalism has succeeded in those countries that the USA has targeted as battlefields in its War on Terror.

This bottom-up perspective likewise enhances our understanding by placing the relationship among US imperialism, the Philippine nation-state and the southern Philippine periphery in historical perspective. This is not the first time that the US military has been in Mindanao: a century ago, a US expeditionary force set up camp in the Muslim areas to pacify the 'uncivilized peoples' of the area and install the colonial state. The USA's formation of a colonial state set up the institutional frame that defined the relationship among imperial, national (colonial) and peripheral actors. This triangular relationship persisted into the post-colonial period, reinforced by the decentralized nature of post-war Philippine politics. The attempt by President Ferdinand Marcos to centralize the nation-state through authoritarian rule did not eliminate this triangulation; instead, it gave it a durability that accounts for its resurfacing in today's debates.

Colonial origins of separatism and accommodation

In another paper, I argue that two distinct processes of colonial state formation occurred in the first decade of US rule. For the lowland Catholic-dominated areas, a civilian regime, anchored on a close collaboration between a nascent Filipino elite and US officials, was established. In the 'non-Christian' highlands of northern Luzon and among the Muslims of southern Mindanao – areas that the preceding Spanish colonial regime had been unable to control effectively – the US Congress gave the US Expeditionary Army sole power in determining the best way to govern the 'wild tribes' of the regions (Abinales 2003: 148–81). The 'Moro Province', an autonomous regional structure covering almost two-thirds of the island and deemed 'ungovernable' territory in Spanish accounts, was governed entirely by the army. US fidelity to the principle of separation of church and state, however, compelled top administrators to seek alternative ways to administer their 'wards'. They observed neighbouring Dutch Java and British Malaya for possible lessons to be learnt in handling religious matters (Thompson 1975).

What struck US officers immediately about the British and Dutch 'models' was the importance given to local Muslim leaders in sharing the burdens of governing (Amoroso 2003: 118–47). This was readily copied and, by 1906, the Americans had appointed Muslim *datu*s (traditional local leaders) and sultans as 'tribal ward' leaders who were responsible for tax collection and keeping lines open between local communities and the military authorities. These administrative measures were positively received by many *datu*s, and their support was further cemented when many were conferred additional official titles and made to join the basic administrative units – the district councils. By the end of the first decade of US rule, Muslim Mindanao was declared stable and peaceful.

This success also created a dynamic with long-term consequences for southern Mindanao's relations with the rest of the Philippines. Throughout most of colonial history under Spain, Muslim communities never saw themselves as part of Las Islas Filipinas, and their views of Filipinos and, initially, of Americans were coloured by their participation in a much broader Southeast Asian world. Muslim elites regarded the inhabitants of central and northern Philippines mainly as sources of human booty to be traded for other commodities in the profitable Southeast Asian maritime trade. The tide turned in the latter's favour only after the Spanish acquired coal-powered gunboats in the mid-nineteenth century and ended the decades of 'Moro slave raids' that had haunted many lowland communities in central and northern Philippines This shift in favour of the Spanish, however, came too late. Spain was already on the way out; in fact, a few years after the first gunboats destroyed Muslim *cottas* (forts), colonial rule began to unravel when a nationalist rebellion started to spread throughout the rest of the colony (Gowing 1977: 26–42). A few years later, the Americans declared war on Spain.

Weakened but not thoroughly powerless, *datu*s and sultans saw the nationalist revolution and the coming of the Americans as a chance to preserve or recover some of their former power. With the breakdown of Spanish rule, Muslim leaders such as the brilliant Datu Piang of Cotabato reached out to the US Army, which he viewed as a potential protector of control of the local trade. Others, like the Sultan of Sulu, welcomed the coming of *Los Americanos* as an opportunity to re-establish themselves as players in the Southeast Asian maritime trade (Abinales 2000a: 193–228). The only problem was that the Americans were committed to ending the slave trade and cutting off Muslim links to maritime Southeast Asia. Some *datu*s rebelled but many others, with their independent local power practically dissipated, began to explore other options. They were increasingly alarmed by the efforts made by Filipino leaders to win US recognition of southern Mindanao as an organic part of the Philippines. To protect their gains from Filipino encroachment, *datu*s agitated for the separation of Moro Province from the rest of the colony and found an unexpected sympathizer in the US Army (Glang 1969: 16–17).

The army's mandate allowed it to govern the Moro Province differently from other Philippine provinces. It was understood that the programme's success depended on the army being unhampered in its pursuit of civilizing the Moros (Bliss 1909: 4; Wood 1904: 21). Army officers took pride in their work, especially when they saw how unevenly the civilian pacified areas were being governed; the more they learned about 'Moro history', the more they realized how brittle ties were between southern Mindanao and the Philippines. This attitude merged with their contempt for the spread of patronage politics in Manila and their suspicions that the Filipino rhetoric calling for the full integration of Mindanao was prompted by a desire to get hold of the island's rich natural resources at the expense of the Muslims and 'non-Christian tribes' (*Mindanao Herald*, 5 December 1906). These misgivings were soon validated by the attempts made by Filipino politicians to control the Moro Province's budget and question military rule in southern Mindanao.

In the resolve to keep Mindanao autonomous and shielded from Manila and the Filipinos, this unusual *de facto* alliance of disempowered Muslim *datu*s and army bureaucrats deployed various political and bureaucratic weapons. The army issued glowing reports of success but diluted these with warnings that 'Moro Mindanao' remained unstable and prone to explode in rebellion (Government Printing Office 1907: 342–3, 355–6). The most audacious act of the army was to propose separating Mindanao from the Philippines and creating 'the Mindanao Plantations', which were to be populated by US settlers and administered by the Army (Hoyt 1909: 3–4). There is little written evidence of Muslims' opinion at this time, but their constant appeals to US authorities for separate rule for Mindanao suggests their support for the army's position.

In the end, no separatist movement came to fruition as Washington removed the army from its 'nation-building' responsibilities and Congress ordered it home after the organization of a local constabulary force was completed. Since US imperial policy was grounded in the eventual transfer of power to Filipinos, separatist agitations eventually fizzled out. The failure of early US settlements in turning Mindanao into the next American West further undermined the cause (Hartley 1983: 75; Hayase 1984: 76–9). By the time Woodrow Wilson won the presidency in 1912 and the Democratic Party made good its promise to speed up 'Filipinization', the separatist dream was no more.

In 1914, the Filipino-controlled Philippine Assembly, together with Governor-General Francis Burton Harrison, created the Department of Mindanao and Sulu, which enabled Filipinos to extend their power and influence in the special provinces (Abinales 2000a: 30–40). Muslim leaders began to accept the new political reality of Filipino dominance and Mindanao integration, and sought to find a niche for themselves in the new order (Kalaw 1931: 74). Still, separatist sentiments were not completely extinguished and Muslim elites retained a certain loyalty to the USA, especially to the army overlords. Filipino leaders were aware of this; yet, while they insisted on their right to govern the Muslim areas, they also entered into some form of mutual accommodation with Muslim leaders in which, in exchange for the latter's allegiance, politicians such as Manuel Quezon promised not to interfere in Muslim religious affairs. They also vowed to bring the *datu*s or their progenies into the orbit of Filipino patronage (Malcolm 1936: 45; Kasilag 1938: 12–23).

Since they were latecomers to the colonial game – isolated for a decade by the US Army – Muslim leaders had to catch up, acquiring basic knowledge from the public school system along with skills vital to a political career. The few who made it to college were also the most qualified to ascend the social and political ladder (Beckett 1975: 60–1). The Second World War temporarily derailed this educational and political journey, but war also gave them the opportunity to cement ties with Filipino leaders by joining the anti-Japanese resistance – by forming an army or subordinating armed followers to the authority of a guerrilla unit that was officially recognized by the allied forces (Baclagon 1988). Other Muslim leaders collaborated with the Japanese for reasons ranging from opportunism to the astute recognition that it would be crucial to have control of the administrative apparatus when the Americans returned (Quirino 1984: 29–41, 43–4, 51–62). In either case, by the time of the Second World War, few Muslim leaders held any separatist sentiments; for all intents and purposes, they had become Filipinos.

The politics of accommodation

After the war, the USA granted the Philippines independence and a repub-lican state that combined patronage, the rule of a few wealthy provincial families and local strongmen with democratic rituals such as elections and the 'four basic freedoms'. The practice of 'Cacique democracy' tacitly condoned the presence and occasional interference of the USA in Philippine affairs; this element lasted through the first three decades of the post-war period (McCoy 1993: 10–19; Anderson 1998: 206–9). Within this decentralized order, Muslim leaders – already at ease with the new order – simply firmed up their authority over their local 'bailiwicks'. They were also aware, however, that they were operating from a position of relative disadvantage. Most of Muslim Mindanao remained underdeveloped and backward, and the residents were not as rich as their Christian counter-parts. Moreover, although the Muslims may have had their guerrilla armies intact, their overall resources paled in comparison to the political clans of central and northern Philippines. The Muslim leaders would overcome this deficiency by making 'ethnicity' and 'religion' valuable political assets. The more successful among them became adept in mixing these 'primordial ties' with the trappings of modern-day politics. A Muslim academic observed in 1962:

> The Alontos of Lanao, the Pendatuns, Sinsuats and Ampatuans of Cotabato and the Abu Bakrs of Sulu are all of royal blood; although occasionally in distantly collateral lines. Their gradually waning tradi-tional influence is now rather significantly buttressed, if slightly in nature, by the considerable resources of the constitutional system (such

as patronage, public works funds, police systems, etc.). The *datu* class now controls sizable blocs of votes, which are often the basis of constantly shifting political alliances. It appears to be a fact that the most effective leaders are those who combine both traditional and constitutional authority.

(Saber 1962: 14)

This blending became especially crucial during elections, during which Muslim politicians could promise to deliver 'the Moro vote' to their patrons or allies in the national centre in exchange for the latter's support.

Given the history of internecine warfare between Muslim and Christian Philippines, however, social tensions between the communities were never fully resolved in the post-war period. Filipinos remained suspicious of Muslims for religious reasons and past battles against 'Moro slave raids'. The image of Mindanao as a volatile frontier reinforced this Filipino view, even as a massive influx of settlers from the Visayas and Luzon made the Muslims fear that they would soon lose their lands and livelihoods to the children of former slaves (George 1980: 114–15). These anxieties fed a common Muslim view that the national government was insensitive to Muslims' interests and aspirations, and hostile towards their attempts to be heard. They also provided opportunities for Muslim politicians to impress upon national leaders their political value.

Muslim leaders thus managed to anchor their political ambitions by being able to mediate between the suspicious, increasingly aggrieved Muslim minority and the determined national state that was associated with the Christians. In reaching a mutual level of accommodation between the Muslims and the settlers, Muslim leaders increased their power at the local level and brought prestige and influence to the national capital (Bentley 1985: 70). These political exchanges were most prominent during national and provincial elections, during which Muslim politicians mobilized voters to ensure victory for their non-Muslim allies and national patrons. These politicians were crucial in moderating the unresolved tensions of the US colonial period; they were also responsible for an unprecedented twenty years of stability in the country's largest frontier (Bentley 1993: 248–50; Abinales 2000b: 135–6).

The success of this 'Janus-faced gentry' (Shue 1988: 89) also explains the persistence of pro-Americanism in southern Mindanao. After independence, several remained loyal to the USA, including the heirs of families and individuals that governed Muslim districts under the Americans and fought side by side with them during the Second World War, and politicians such as Ali Dimaporo of Lanao Province and Salipada Pendatun of Cotabato. Pendatun was proud of his wartime collaboration with the US anti-Japanese guerrilla movement in Mindanao; after the war, he fashioned himself the Magindanao Douglas MacArthur and demanded that everyone call him 'General' when he was in Congress. A staunch anti-communist and one of the country's top warlords, he became one of the most avowedly pro-USA politicians and was a favourite of the US embassy (Cowen 1950). When President Ferdinand Marcos faced Congressional opposition to his plan to assist the USA in Southeast Asia, Dimaporo – who was also a wartime guerrilla – 'helped shepherd through Congress [the] controversial bill sending Philippine troops to Vietnam' (Bentley 1993: 251).

There were no nationalist challenges to this sentiment and no debates over 'neo-colonial relations' on the frontier, unlike in the capital where students and nationalist senators were already questioning US interference and intervention in Philippine affairs. In addition, the limited presence of US institutions and agencies in Mindanao dulled the effectiveness of nationalist rhetoric. There was no concrete 'imperialist' target on the island that propaganda could be directed towards, and the minuscule representation of US presence, namely, Peace Corps volunteers and a roving movie-and-book programme run by the US cultural mission in Davao City, were received positively by communities. The latter were starving for information and education, which the Philippine government and its pitiable educational system could not provide.

Marcos's vigorous push for the inclusion of Mindanao in national development plans was a turning point (Salas 1961). With Mindanao's resources and growing electorate – over 1 million people settled in Mindanao from central and northern Philippines from 1946 to the mid-1960s – Marcos also saw it as a means of breaking the hold of the 'traditional elites' and old oligarchs on national political power. First, however, he needed to undermine the power of local Mindanao strongmen who were allied to his enemies, and those with independent power to obstruct his plans. In doing so, Marcos tipped the delicate balance between state and strongmen by creating his own network of local allies, who were less autonomous and more beholden to him, which he then unleashed on his enemies. Marcos sent the military to break up the 'private armies' of his Muslim enemies, and split Muslim ranks by encouraging his allies to establish rival Muslim associations and challenge those under the control of local opponents. By doing so, he created the conditions for the typical weapons of competition, patronage and elections, to be displaced by the more coercive methods of political combat (Abinales 2000b: 163–71). Conflict then spread to the communities and involved Muslims and Christian settlers, with the latter receiving support from the military (George 1980: 129–77).

The breakdown of stability and the decline of Muslim politicians' power brought new actors to the frontier – young Muslim students who saw the need to organize 'the Moro masses' for an inevitable confrontation with the state and its local strongmen allies. These students initially joined forces with anti-Marcos warlords and propped them up by reconstituting their political machines into organizations with armed capacities, and by establishing some form of a united front called the Mindanao Independence Movement (MIM). For the first time since the early days of US colonial rule, an anti-

USA sentiment took shape in the Muslim provinces (George 1980: 200–1). When Marcos declared martial law, the stage was set for Muslim Mindanao to engage in war.

Rebellion and breakdown

The MIM had a short life span; soon after Marcos declared martial law, the students, under the leadership of university professor Nur Misuari, established the Moro National Liberation Front (MNLF) and launched a separatist war against the AFP (Madale 1984: 180–1; Abat 1993). The rebellion lasted for only three years, with the MNLF saddled with military inexperience, in-fighting among its leaders, and division within the various Muslim groups. The two most serious breaches, however, were the ones involving ethnic disunities and class differences. The first involved the two most dominant 'ethnic' groups in the Muslim community: the Taosugs, to which Nur Misuari belonged; and the Magindanaos, which formed the biggest group inside the MNLF. What began as ideological differences soon turned into disagreements over war strategy and equal representation within the organization as well as in the Organization of Islamic Conference (OIC). The OIC turned down appeals from Hashim Salamat, the leader of the Magindanao bloc and representative of the group of religious scholars trained in the Middle East, to abandon the 'leftist' Misuari, trained at the University of the Philippines. Instead, the former broke away, formed the Moro Islamic Liberation Front (MILF) and began to rebuild an armed capacity in the provinces of Cotabato in southwestern Mindanao (Vitug and Gloria 2000: 106–135).

The second split was between the conservative and traditional *datu* 'politicos' and the radical non-traditional activists. The former joined Misuari and his comrades in the rebellion after the dictatorship began to confiscate their weapons and dismantle their private armies. The alliance, however, did not last long once Marcos opened the door to compromise and once the politicians realized that the rebellion could not be sustained. They made peace with Marcos and, together, proceeded further to undermine the MNLF's cause by organizing a 'moderate alternative'. Cotabato's Pendatun formed the Bangsa Moro Liberation Organization, a purported third force that was committed to the pro-Muslim and anti-communist struggle (Che Man 1990: 128–9; Gonzales 2000: 116–18).

Reassertion of local politics

The second split reopened the space for traditional politics to reassert itself in the Muslim arena (Gutierrez 2000: 55–61). There were new faces that joined the likes of Pendatun and Rashid Lucman of Lanao, MNLF commanders who surrendered to Marcos in return for access to state patronage and AFP officers who entered into politics after military service (Abinales 1998: 122).

These new actors shared with their elders a penchant for keeping politics local and for limiting their dealings with external forces (whether the state or MNLF) to those who helped consolidate local power. They also preferred a continuing impasse on the battlefield to an all-out war that could have devastating consequences for their own hold on power, especially since the presence of the national army could often complicate the conduct of politics in their localities. The case of Amelil Malaguiok, Chairman of the MNLF's Kutawato Regional Committee, was one classic example. 'Kumander Ronnie' surrendered to the government after being offered the governor's seat in a newly created 'regional autonomous government of Region 12', which encompassed central Mindanao, and awarded a logging rights concession to a vast forested area in the same area (Vitug and Gloria 2000: 125).

This fragmentation and shift back to localist politics insulated southern Mindanao from the intensifying polarization of national politics in the 1980s. The massive protest demonstrations that followed the assassination of leading Marcos opponent, former senator Benigno Aquino Jr, in 1983 were replicated in Cotabato City, Marawi City, Jolo, and Zamboanga City in the Muslim provinces. One notable feature in the mobilizations in the national capital was, however, absent in their local echoes – the absence of 'anti-imperialist' themes. Radical messages were muted or non-existent in many of these Mindanao rallies; instead, the protests were calls for the restoration of 'democracy' and, predictably, included returning the anti-Marcos Muslim politicians to their perches.

Thus, after the fall of Marcos in 1986 and the restoration of Philippine constitutional politics, the only remarkable source of conflict between Muslim Mindanao and President Corazon Aquino was the extent to which her government 'intervened' to replace pro-Marcos mayors and provincial governors with her own allies. This conflict did not prove lasting, as pro-Marcos politicians simply switched sides and declared fealty to Aquino or struck deals with the new government (Bentley 1993: 267–8). There was no rhetoric or politicking with regard to US support for the new regime then or in 1991, when the Philippine Senate began debates on a renewal of the US–Philippine military bases agreement. None of the fiery exchanges between nationalists and pro-Americans in Manila made an impact on Muslim Mindanao.

The decline of US interest in the Philippines after the shift of strategic worries to China and withdrawal of military bases reinforced the inward-looking nature of southern Mindanao politics. The Aquino government's general weakness prevented it from pursuing peace talks with the MNLF with any degree of consistency. It was left to Aquino's successor, Fidel V. Ramos, to complete the process (Joaquin 2003: 124–32). Again, negotiations with Misuari's dwindling force did not include a discussion of the 'American factor', even as the Filipino leftists raised the alarm that Ramos' economic liberalization programme would allow the USA to reassert its imperial interests in Mindanao (*Kilusan* 2002). The appearance of the MILF and the Abu Sayyaf in the 1990s, however, would change all this.

'Radical Islam' and the US War on Terror in Mindanao

While its rhetoric was Islamicist, the one thing notable about the MILF was that, oddly, it was a moderate force. The army it built (15,000 strong by the late 1990s) and the communities it established, complete with their own *sharia* courts, prisons and educational systems, did not hide the fact that its leaders regarded Islam as a moral question and that they had 'not yet fully thought [the] idea of what constitutes an Islamic state' (Vitug and Gloria 2000: 111). Hashim Salamat doubted the applicability of existing 'models' of Islamic governance (for example, Pakistan and Saudi Arabia) to 'our different culture' (Vitug and Gloria 2000: 114), and had conflicting notions of *jihad*. Some argued that it meant declaring war on the Philippine government for being an occupying force, while others saw *jihad* as something dictated by circumstance. It was right to invoke *jihad* against the Marcos dictatorship but the principle was not applicable in the post-Marcos era, since a more democratic regime was open to negotiation (Vitug and Gloria 2000: 115–16). Finally, an 'ideological gap between the leaders and the rank and file [was] wide and palpable' (Vitug and Gloria 2000: 116); while its leaders were devout students of Islam, ordinary Magindanaos exercised a form of folk Islam that combined animistic beliefs with invocations from the Koran. They joined the MILF for reasons that had nothing to do with religion – they wanted to avenge the deaths of family and friends at the hands of the military or because the MILF represented one of the few opportunities in one of the poorest regions in the country (McKenna 1998: 183–4, 191–6).

Until Ramos's successor, President Joseph Estrada, ordered a full-blown assault on the MILF camp, there was no clear-cut antagonism between the state and the MILF. President Arroyo reversed Estrada's all-out-war policy, and went back to the bargaining table even as armed skirmishes between the two forces carried on. The MILF agreed to negotiate and, in a move that surprised everyone, sought the help of the USA in co-ordinating with Malaysia in the role of mediator (*Newsbreak*, 19 May 2004: 29–30; Santos 2003). This response likewise enabled the MILF to tap the services and support of a select group of traditional politicians who became *de facto* spokespersons for the rebel group outside Mindanao (McKenna 1998: 213–19). This shrewd balancing act has excluded the MILF from the USA's list of 'terrorist organizations', despite reports that it once received support from Osama bin Laden and had sent fighters to Afghanistan. The move has also enabled the MILF to develop a wide range of support, from Islamic countries to European aid agencies that are now taking the lead in rehabilitation programmes in Muslim Mindanao (Vitug and Gloria 2000: 110 and 118; Fuentes 1998: 25–33).

Given that the Abu Sayyaf's (ASG) history has been extensively covered elsewhere, I would like to focus on one angle that is relevant to this chapter: that of location. The ASG operates mainly on Basilan Island in the Sulu archipelago and in the Sabah–Borneo area; the farthest it has operated is in Zamboanga City north of Basilan. While it is reported to have links with Al Qaeda and other Islamic terrorist groups, the ASG's main largesse comes from its kidnapping activities and the protection racket it runs in partnership with local politicians and military commanders (Gutierrez 2000: 64–77). This live-and-let-live relationship with the two other forces in Basilan led to the classification of the ASG as local insurgents who were 'containable' (Vitug and Gloria 2000: 218–19).

The protective mantle of localism unravelled, however, once the group began raiding communities outside Basilan, expanding its kidnapping targets to include non-Filipinos and establishing ties with suspected Al Qaeda leaders in Mindanao. The ASG attack on the town of Ipil in Zamboanga del Sur broke an accord with the military and gave the AFP command an excuse to order active pursuit. The kidnapping of European tourists on the Sabah resort island of Sipadan and a group of vacationers in Palawan Island, including an American missionary couple, not only infuriated the Philippine government but also drew the ire of the US government. Even before 9/11, the USA had been increasingly concerned with 'world terrorism, including what was happening in the Philippines Mindanao backdoor' (*Newsbreak*, 13 February 2002: 7–8). The kidnapping of Garcia and Martin Burham gave the USA the justification to approach the Philippine government and offer assistance in its war against the ASG.

Thereafter, mutual accommodation between local politicians and the ASG began to unravel as the politicians increasingly came to view the group as a liability. For the local politicians, the USA's pursuit of the ASG was opportune. The inflow of kidnapping 'revenues' to friends and kin of ASG members in Basilan and Jolo had disrupted these politicians' networks of patronage, since the ASG had become an alternative source of patronage. The arrival of the Americans not only gave the politicians a chance to eliminate this rival but also alerted them to a new source of largesse. US development aid, promised along with military training, could replace the ASG's kidnap funds, which were expected to dry up soon. When the Balikatan exercises began, the Manila media reported that people in Sulu had mixed feelings towards the US presence (*Newsbreak*, 31 March 2003: 8–10), although there were no second thoughts among the various congressmen, governors and mayors of the area (*Philippine Daily Inquirer*, 7 February 2002). They lent firm support to the two Balikatan 02–1 exercises. In this new stage in the political play in Muslim Mindanao, the Manila government was relegated to a supporting role.

Conclusion

There is no question that the USA's neoliberal economic agenda is enjoying global dominance today (Rodan and Hewison 2004: 394–8), yet we can also see that its impact is unevenly felt around the world. We cannot conclude that because 'neoconservatives' are ascendant in the government of the USA, and have been able to combine neoliberal economic agendas with neoconservative political goals, that US aspirations, as a consequence, can be realized without effort and strain. As the protests in Davos and Porto Alegre indicate, there is strong resistance in many parts of the world. More significant, however, are the many actions of those who have been subjected by neoliberalism to deflect, undermine and compromise on the proponents of this agenda. In this chapter, I have attempted to show how the latter process can come about, once we leave the metropolitan capital and venture into the 'peripheries' of the nation-state. Here, intricate arrays of social and political forces create obstacles and limit the acts of the national state and imperial actors, forcing the latter at times to negotiate and compromise (Migdal 1988, 31–2; Shue 1988; Kohli 1990: 385). Refocusing our analytical lens so as to privilege the peripheries also enables us to tweak out historical nuances, which are often concealed by an inordinate concern with politics at the top.

The recent US military adventure in the southern Philippines has been a puzzle to many Filipino scholars because the very communities suspected of hosting and protecting 'Islamic terrorists' have received it positively. By giving a broad historical overview of the development of the triangular relationship involving US overlords, Filipino leaders and various Muslim political forces in the last century, this chapter has provided a possible alternative explanation to this puzzle. The decisions of Muslim politicians and rebels in favour of or against the US presence were driven by calculations that view the Americans as a deterrent to intrusions made by the national state. Imperial power had also become an alternative resource that Muslim politicians or rebel leaders could tap into, since these could not be provided by the national state. Basilan Governor Wahab Akbar's profuse declaration when US forces brought in road-building equipment to his province aptly sums up this perception: 'My happiness is indescribable, my dream is now starting to materialize . . . I know I can die 10 times and not be able to purchase this equipment for my people' (*Philippine Daily Inquirer*, 7 February 2002).

The long-term consequences of the US military presence in the southern Philippines thus hinges as much on how it would affect local power as it does on the interplay between international relations and national politics. This circumstance is a reality that is unique not only to the Philippines, for the USA presently confronts similar situations in Iraq and Afghanistan.

Notes
* This essay is based on a working paper presented at the workshop 'In Whose Interest? The Future of the US Military in Asia', held at the East–West Center, Hawaii, on 20–22 February 2003. An earlier version was published under the title 'The Good Imperialists? American Military Presence in the Southern Philippines

in Historical Perspective', in *Philippine Studies*, 52, 2 (2004). I wish to thank Donna J. Amoroso, Sheila Smith, Katharine Moon, Naoki Kimamura, Paul Hutchcroft and Vedi Hadiz for their criticisms and comments. All shortcomings are mine.

10 Fostering 'authoritarian democracy'

The effect of violent solutions in Southern Thailand

Chaiwat Satha-Anand

On 16 July 2004, there was a closed-door roundtable on 'A Proposal from the Civil Society Sector on Southern Violence', organized by the Peace Information Center and *Fa Diew Kan* magazine, at the Faculty of Political Science of Thammasat University, Bangkok. Some thirty participants, including academics, members of the media, religious leaders, NGO activists from Southern Thailand and others from Bangkok, attended the seminar. A professor from a state university in Pattani said that after the killing of Buddhist monks, which began on 22 January 2004, her daughter returned from school and complained that her friends refused to speak to her. When pressed for the reason behind their attitude, some said that their mothers had forbidden them from speaking or playing with the young Muslim girl because 'the Muslims killed the monks'. The professor then said that on 28 April, at the height of the violence, she and her children travelled from Pattani to nearby Narathiwat. Her daughter cried all the way as she was afraid of falling victim to militant violence. Similarly, her daughter cried every night whenever the professor's husband, a noted public intellectual in the south and presently an opposition Member of Parliament, went out on his frequent speaking engagements because she was afraid that he might not return home. Presumably, he could have been taken away by state authorities, as has been the fate of more than a hundred people in the area. In desperate bewilderment, the professor asked a religious leader from the south who was sitting next to her, 'How could democracy turn out to be so barbaric?' (*Fa Diew Kan* 2004: 159).

It is important to come to terms with the strange phenomenon when 'democracy' takes an authoritarian turn, as is presently the case in Thailand and other places in the world. Given the situation in Southern Thailand, in the context of the 'war against terrorism' championed by the American Empire, I am interested in understanding what violence does to democracy. If it is possible for democracy to have a 'personality', could that personality sometimes turn out to be authoritarian, especially when touched by 'excessive' and sustained violence employed by the state itself?

This chapter is an attempt to address this quandary through an examination of the effects of the violent solutions carried out by the Thai government in Southern Thailand. The combined effects of four major incidents in Southern Thailand on 4 January, 22 January, 28 April and 25 October 2004 intensified a new cycle of violence when the drastic actions of Thai state officials were met with violent responses from their shadowy opponents in the south. This violence and counter-violence, in turn, is transforming Thai society into an 'authoritarian democracy'. The argument in this essay will be formulated in the form of a series of related questions: How has the emergence of recent violence in Southern Thailand been different from the violence of the past half-century? What has been the Thai government's response? What does violence do to society? Can similar effects of violence on democracy be seen elsewhere in the world? I conclude this chapter with a discussion of the notion of 'authoritarian democracy' as an attempt to address a query raised by the political philosopher Alexis de Tocqueville at the end of his *Democracy in America* (1835): 'What sort of Despotism Democratic Nations have to fear' (Tocqueville 1956: 301).

Muslims and Thai society

Muslims constitute the largest minority group in Thai society, comprising about 5 per cent of Thailand's 60 million people, according to official figures. It is important, however, to understand that Muslims in Thailand are not homogeneous. While there are Chinese Muslims in the north, Cambodian and South Asian Muslims in Central Thailand as well as Arab and Indian Muslims elsewhere, most are Malay Muslims. The latter reside in the five southern border provinces, where they constitute a numerical majority of 64.75 per cent (Chaiwat 2004b).

The violent episode of 28 April 2004 between government forces and Muslim men, mostly armed with knives and machetes, took the lives of 111 people, including five policemen. The event marked a significant shift in the more than half-century of violence in Southern Thailand. There are several ways to understand violence in the south. Many choose to link the recent violent incidents, especially those that have taken place in the past two years, with separatist movements, regional or global terrorist organizations, local criminal elements, or local and national animosity between two major political parties – the present prime minister's Thai Rak Thai Party and the main opposition Democrat Party (Kavi 2004).

I find it useful to view the phenomenon from two dimensions, vertical and horizontal. The vertical dimension points to relationships between the state, broadly defined, and the southern population in general. Given the history of Pattani, violence between government officials and locals in the south should come as no surprise (Scupin 1998). Pattani was involuntarily annexed to Siam in 1909 and this changed the centralizing tendency of the modern nation-state, which had begun in 1902 amid the colonial shadow of the British in the west and the south, and the French in the east. Pattani's border has also been hazy given its geographical proximity to Malaysia. The River

Golok that separates Kota Bharu from Narathiwat is often considered by locals to be nothing more than an inconvenient monsoon drain, with relatives, associates and interests existing on either side of it (Nadzru B. Azhari 2004). The area has suffered injustices perpetuated by some government officials while a larger percentage of people in Narathiwat (34.07 per cent) live below the poverty line compared to the national average of 10.43 per cent (in 2002, according to the NESDB (National Economic and Social Development Board)). The area has also suffered from a prevalence of illegal businesses, including smuggling, drug trafficking, casinos and brothels, together with religious–cultural differences and a demographic concentration of Malay Muslims in the area. What has been unusual, however, is the horizontal relationship among locals, Muslims and non-Muslims, which has been marked by a high degree of cultural sensitivity to differences. For example, a recent study found that non-Muslim shop owners in the town of Yala prefer to employ Muslim women who wear the *hijab* (Muslim women's headscarf) and speak Malay. The employees would be expected to do many things, including cash registration duty, but would not be asked to work in the owners' kitchens or buy them non-Muslim food (Prair 2003). Such a state of affairs is possible because Muslims and non-Muslims alike in the south possess a sufficiently high degree of cultural sensitivity – necessary for living together in such a context. If peace and security are understood from a cultural politics perspective, then they cannot be protected by mere military might. Instead, the ties that bind people with differences, despite some prejudices, into a political community are the tools that sustain peace and security.

The new violence

On 4 January 2004, the Fourth Development Battalion in Narathiwat was robbed of 413 weapons, namely 380 M16s, two M60 machine guns, seven rocket-propelled grenade launchers and twenty-four 11 mm pistols (*Bangkok Post*, 19 July 2004.) One source reported that the 380 stolen M16s were probably split into three lots and distributed among militants to stir up violence in Thailand, and among Kampulan Mujahideen Malaysia (KMM) and Acehnese rebels who took part in the raid (*Bangkok Post*, 16 July 2004). In this highly organized and efficient operation, during which communications lines were cut and obstacles were quite comprehensively placed on several roads to block possible pursuit, four non-Muslim soldiers were killed. Though violence against government officials was not a new occurrence, this particular incident was significant because the target was a military camp, although not that of a fighting unit. Unlike most past incidents, in which the victims of violence on the side of the government were policemen or civilian officials, the victims this time around were soldiers. Non-Muslim soldiers were separated from others and brutally killed. As a matter of fact, this attack was undertaken by more than a hundred people, yet the government has learnt precious little about it. Even at this time of writing, eleven months after the incident, Thai officials still have been unable to locate the missing weapons. In this sense, the incident of 4 January may be seen as a demonstration of new heights in vertical violence, characterized by the highly organized way in which it was carried out, the military target of the operation, and the degree to which state power was directly challenged.

On 22 January in Narathiwat, two men on a motorcycle used a long knife to slit the throat of a 64-year-old Buddhist monk who was returning from an early morning round of asking for alms. Two days later, three other monks were attacked in both Yala and Pattani. Two of them were left dead, the younger of them a 13-year-old novice. Deputy Prime Minister Chavalit Yongchaiyudh remarked that cold-blooded attacks on Buddhist monks were 'too unusual to be the work of locally trained rebels'. In fact, it was unheard of in Southern Thailand for monks to be killed. I have argued that the killing of Buddhist monks in provinces that have a Muslim majority is a very dangerous development in the continuing phenomenon of violence. Recently, Buddhist monks from temples in Kelantan – and there are nearly 100 temples built by the Thai Malaysian communities in border towns and in Kota Bahru – decided to shelve plans to visit the southern provinces. Phra Suk Sathawarom (50) of Wat Bang Nai in the town of Tumpat said he had given up his annual visit for the year because he 'feared for his life' since 'I've heard about the violence, the explosions and killings. I heard a monk in Yala was killed while collecting alms and soldiers have had to step up security at temples'. Phra Chamras (30) of Wat Pothiviharn said that all planned visits have been cancelled because of the volatile situation (*Bangkok Post*, 23 July 2004). I would argue that the cultural connotation of using knives to kill Buddhist monks in a provincial context in which Muslims constitute a majority, yet in a national context where they constitute a minority, is explosive since the knives did more than rob the Buddhist monks of their lives. They cut deep into the cultural ties that bind a community in which different people have to live together. Thus, they have caused great damage to the horizontal relationship, historically marked by some degree of acceptance and tolerance (Chaiwat 2004a).

On 28 April 2004, some 300 militants attacked twelve police and military posts in the three southern provinces of Yala, Pattani and Songkhla. The clashes began at about 5.30 a.m. and ended in the early afternoon when the military attacked the ancient Kru-ze Mosque in Pattani, killing all thirty-two militants inside the mosque. There were 111 deaths in all, including those of three soldiers and two policemen. Most of the 106 dead militants were between 20 and 30 years of age. A few were under the age of 18 and the oldest casualty was 62 years old (Bhumiputra 2004). The authorities found twenty-six guns among the militants, including ten M16s and three HK33s, while knives and machetes made up the rest of their weapons. Copies of the Qur'an as well as prayer mats were found on the bodies of some of the militants. Those who had heard the shouts of the militants as they launched their attack on the authorities had no doubt that they were going into battle prepared for death. Some of the militants had told their relatives prior to 28 April that they would die for God, and that neither should their bodies be washed nor prayers offered; instead, they should be buried in accordance with the traditions of *shahid* (those who die at the hands of non-Muslims in the battle to defend Islam). It turned out that with or without prior instructions from the deceased, most of the militants' relatives did not wash the bodies or offer prayers, which meant that they did treat the militants as *shahid* (Janjira 2004). The then Army Commander-in-Chief, General Chaisit Shinnawat, remarked that the militants were a 'bunch of ignorant kids', 'drug addicts' and 'crazy', which was why they were 'inhumanly courageous'. 'They were bloody crazy which means they must be high on drugs. [I] have never seen [normal] people who are as courageous and crazy' (*Matichon*, 29 April 2004). Most officials believed that the Thai state had won an important battle against the Muslim militants because in terms of sheer numbers, more than a hundred of 'them' were killed while only five of 'us' died.

It should be noted that between 1992 and 2001, there were 441 violent incidents in the southern border area, including Songkhla. These resulted in 42 deaths and 144 wounded (A Special Committee on Bombing and Other Violent Incidents in the southern Border Provinces, House of Representatives 2004: 47–50). According to the Thai Army, from 4 January to the first two weeks of November 2004, excluding the incidents of 28 April and 25 October, 257 people were killed (142 common people in the south and the rest government officials, including soldiers and police) and 433 injured. The most violent month was November, which saw ninety-eight incidents in just the first two weeks (*Bangkok Post*, 21 November 2004). In the first six months of 2004 in Pattani alone, Governor Sanoe Chantra reported that there had been 615 violent incidents in the province since 4 January; this had resulted in thirty-nine deaths and about 5.8 million baht in damage (*Bangkok Post*, 16 July 2004). I would argue that the 28 April incident has changed the landscape of violence in Southern Thailand for three related reasons. First, militants attacked government posts armed mostly with knives and machetes. In one important case, they could have escaped after acquiring some weapons from the police post they robbed, but they chose not to flee. Instead, they moved into the Kru-ze Mosque, waiting to be attacked and eventually killed by government forces. This indicates that their understanding of victory might not have been defined by the number of people they killed, but from the way in which they died.

Second, the political significance of the 28 April incident could be assessed by the way in which the militants' deaths will be remembered. Most were buried unwashed and without prayers, thus their deaths were considered *shahid*. Even in those cases where the bodies were washed and prayers were offered before the burial, some journalists who returned to the graves about two months after the incident found that the signs on the tombs had the names of the deceased ending with the term *shahid*. Third, in choosing 28 April as the date of the attack, the incident could be linked to the most violent uprising in the history of Pattani – the Duson Nyor uprising. According to some Malay historians, this uprising took place on 28 April 1948, when some 400 Malays along with thirty policemen were killed in battle (Ibrahim 1985: 74). I would argue that by symbolically linking the present attack to a past uprising, the militants successfully entered into the collective memory of the south as a new breed of martyrs. In this sense, it created an atmosphere in which both the vertical and horizontal relationships were adversely affected and could generate much more damage to peace and security in the future.

Responses of the state

After the incident of 4 January, continuing daily violence in the south produced both Muslim and non-Muslim victims. A respected army general told me in early 2004 that the military's task was not merely to find lost guns but also to re-establish state power in the fear-dominated region. Yet, it seems that in times of crises, the Thai state goes back to the most fundamental and, perhaps, most common of qualities that characterizes the 'nature' of the state itself: the extraction or use of money and violence (Passerin d'Entreves 1967: 2). The government, in defining the region as 'poor' and 'underdeveloped', has thought up many remedies, including developing a *halal* (food religiously permissible for Muslims) food industry and tourism, creating a new Islamic university, reforming *pondok* (traditional religious) schools, and extensive public relations campaigns, among other measures. The aim is to turn the insecurity in the south into an industry characterized by plentiful resources, monetary and otherwise. On the other hand, the Thai state has moved back and forth between adopting hawkish measures and dovish tactics, since many in the security community also know that this is a war to win over the hearts and minds of the people. On 26 July, the government decided to reinstate General Thammarak Isarangkura na Ayudhaya as head of military operations in the south. The general maintained that the government would have to change its tactics from an emphasis on political education and development to greater use of military means. He said: 'Concentrating on political work has resulted in the people remaining in the grip of fear. We need to rebuild the people's confidence' (*Bangkok Post*, 28 July 2004).

Fear is infecting even the forces that have been brought in to rid the region of it. At present, there are some 12,000 security forces in the south, and nearly all the troops are from other areas of the country; in fact, most of the infantrymen are from the northeast. It was reported that many carry thirty or more amulets for good luck, to ward off misfortune and guard against harm. They feel that the amulets give extra protection and keep their spirits high in the face of danger. Sgt Somkid Roopkom (45) from the 6th Infantry

Division's 1st Battalion, based in the northeast, left home wearing nine amulets, with another thirty in his satchel. He said that he worshipped every amulet he was carrying as they kept him out of harm's way, and that he needed these objects of reverence as sources of spiritual support because, 'It's a battlefield out there', and the soldiers could be ambushed at any time (*Bangkok Post*, 21 July 2004).

In late July 2004, however, the Prime Minister dismissed General Thammarak. It could be argued that the southern violence has been responsible for many changes in government personnel at the top levels of the Ministries of Defence and the Interior, the army as well as the police. The government later appointed a deputy commander at the Army Supreme Command to take responsibility for the overall operation of the southern border area, while the fourth regional army commander responsible for the 25 October incident was removed (*Matichon*, 6 October 2004). In an unprecedented development, the Queen herself granted an audience to 930 invited guests, to heed her call for unity and order by inviting people to find ways to end the violence, and to continue the military presence in the area. She also warned human rights advocates that those killed daily were also innocent victims. She called on the government and the Thai people to help 300,000 'Thais' (meaning members of the minority Buddhist communities) in the three provinces by freeing them from the threat of violence. She talked about the impossibility of relocating these 300,000 people, while stressing their right to life and livelihood. She ended her speech with a promise that at the age of 72 years, she would train herself to shoot a gun without the use of spectacles (*Daily News*, 17 November 2004). After listening to her speech, the Prime Minister called for an end to violence. He also insisted that those who refused to stop resorting to violence 'will not be considered "Thais" worth keeping'. Yet, he also proposed that everyone in the country fold millions of origami cranes or 'peace birds', as a way of expressing their love for the people of the south on the event of His Majesty the King's birthday on 5 December (*Bangkok Post*, 17 November 2004).

With such mixed messages and confusion among the government agencies responsible for dealing with violence in the south, it is perhaps more useful to analyse two particular responses by the Thai state in order to understand the changes that have transpired within the state itself. These are the failure of the initiative proposed by Chaturon Chaisaeng before the violence of 28 April and the brutal suppression of the Tak Bai demonstration on 25 October 2004.

In early April 2004, Prime Minister Thaksin Shinawatra asked Chaturon Chaisaeng, a former student leader and one of his current deputy prime ministers, to look into ways to solve the crisis in the south. After meeting with more than a thousand people in the south, both government officials and ordinary citizens, Chaturon proposed a seven-point peace proposal. Before submitting the proposal for Cabinet approval, he recommended three documents to the Prime Minister. These were a King Rama VI Report on the southern region, which recognized cultural differences of the people in the area as a given reality (A Special Committee on Bombing and Other Violent Incidents in the southern Border Provinces, House of Representatives 2004: 90–100); and my study, which was originally published by the National Security Council as *Prime Ministerial Order 66/43: The State, Problems of State Culture and Conflict 'Management' in the New Century*. My work suggests that given the new realities that produce new and complex types of conflict, Thai society needs to rethink its methods of coming to terms with them (Chaiwat 2003: 130–153). The third document was *Security Policy for the south 1999–2003*, formulated by the National Security Council and already approved by the Cabinet; the document maintains that cultural diversity is the strength of Thai society and that security in the south depends on the capacity of Thai society to allow Muslims to live as Muslims in Thailand (*Matichon*, 5 April 2004). The 'Chaturon Chaisaeng initiative' has four important features. First, killings and abductions by the state apparatus must stop, and police forces from Bangkok should be returned to the capital city. Second, amnesty will be provided to all those related to southern violence, provided that the persons have not committed any criminal offences. Third, the *pondok* as a cultural institution should be left alone. Fourth, the dual citizenship that is currently enjoyed by more than 100,000 people in the south should not be considered a security threat but a national asset, as these citizens can communicate in more than one language, work in more than one country and, as such, bring more wealth into the country.

When the media asked me about the Chaturon initiative, my reply was that it does have potential for success but would, instead, be rejected (*Matichon*, 9 April 2004). It goes without saying that the fostering of a sense of insecurity benefits a large number of parties involved on different sides of the conflict. There are at least three reasons why I thought the initiative would have been rejected and, indeed, it was thrown out of the Cabinet three times. First, the initiative was primarily proposed from a bottom-up or local-to-centre perspective, which is quite unusual for a peace/security-oriented proposal recommended by a deputy prime minister. Second, the initiative is radical in its recommendations – to stop the killings and the abductions, the forces from the centre, who were thought to be primarily responsible for these atrocities, had to be removed. To leave the *pondok* alone, cultural control in the form of ordering the registration of all *pondok*, which would then produce legal and illegal *pondok*s, had to be abandoned. This would mean a departure from the state's well-established understanding of *pondok*s as obstacles to the construction of the national identity that it considers desirable. The provision of amnesty to all requires a complex arrangement of legal provisions that would then separate those who violated the law politically from those who did so criminally. Third, it required a rethinking of some of the widely accepted notions related to national security, such as the concept of dual citizenship. It is important to understand that the initiative itself was not designed to solve all problems in the south; however, from a prophylactic perspective, it was a modest effort to mitigate existing violence and prevent the situation from delving deeper into the whirlpool of violence.

On 25 October 2004, thousands of Muslim demonstrators gathered in front of the Tak Bai Police Station in Narathiwat to protest against the earlier arrest of six village security guards who were charged with giving false testimonies and stealing official weapons. The protesters demanded their release and after a stand-off that lasted several hours, the military commander of the Fourth Regional Army on location decided to use force to disperse the protesters. Six protesters were shot dead, eleven were injured and more than 1,300 were arrested. While transporting the detainees from Narathiwat to military camps in Pattani some 150 kilometres away, the usual two-hour drive took more than six hours, and seventy-eight people in all were found dead on several trucks. The cause of the deaths was said to be asphyxiation, resulting from the way in which the detainees were loaded onto the trucks: face down, hands tied behind their backs, stacked in layers three to four deep with no room to move, their bodies crushed and muscle cells destroyed. In some cases, the last resulted in kidney failure that required dialysis treatment at Songkhla Hospital (Chirmsak 2004; Senate Foreign Committee 2004).

I would argue that the violent incident of 25 October is important because it is quite different from other incidents described earlier. First, unlike the violence that took place on 28 April, the people who gathered at the Tak Bai Police Station were, by and large, peaceful demonstrators who were met with brutal state violence. Some of those arrested died in custody even before they were charged; the responsibility clearly lies with government officials, who employed excessive violence. It was reported by a senator that when those lying in the trucks cried out for help, the soldiers in charge stomped on them, hit them with their rifle butts and said, 'So you would know that hell exists!' (Chirmsak 2004: 4). When a government forensics expert from the Justice Ministry explained to the public that these seventy-eight people died of asphyxiation and had no trace of torture on their bodies, the statement was generally accepted (*Bangkok Post*, 19 November 2004). Yet, at a recent meeting organized by the National Commission on Human Rights, a Muslim lawyer who investigated the incident showed pictures of those killed, with their faces bruised and swollen. The faces were so disfigured that some of the relatives of those killed refused to claim the bodies because they could not recognize them. The lawyer also said that his investigations showed that 80 per cent of those who were killed were physically abused.

Second, I believe that some Muslims had differing feelings towards the incidents of 28 April and 25 October. In the former case, where militant Muslims initiated the attack, many Muslims in Bangkok were somewhat indifferent. In the second case, however, they clearly expressed their frustration and anger at the way the government had treated the Muslims. Right after the incident, I attended a Friday prayer session at a local mosque in Bangkok that is frequented by international visitors and local office workers in the area. The *imam* (prayer leader) delivered his *qutbah* (Friday sermon) in tears. Without directly speaking about the Tak Bai incident, he told those in the congregation to brave God's test with patience because, in the very end, victory will come to those who follow in God's path. He then gave the example of David, who fought the fearsome Goliath and defeated the well-armed Philistine with nothing more than his slingshot and faith in the Almighty. It seems that in the eyes of some Bangkok Muslims, the violent response unleashed by the government on the armed militants could be accepted with some legitimacy on the grounds that they were responding to the attacks. The Tak Bai incident, however, was received with disbelief and anger.

Third, despite the brutality of excessive state violence, general public approval for the way in which the government dealt with the issue was evident from remarks made on or sent to talk shows on public television, radio programmes and in cyberspace. This trend of approving the government's use of violence in the context of the increasing distance between Muslims and non-Muslims in the area is, perhaps, the most disturbing change in present-day Thai society.

It is important to note that approval for solving problems through violent methods in Thai society did not begin with the Tak Bai or the incident of 28 April. According to a recent survey of 4,817 people in twenty-five provinces between 2 and 17 July 2004, other developments that eroded public faith in the Thaksin government included rising fuel prices (63 per cent), rising price of goods (55 per cent) and unrest in the deep south (53 per cent). This does not, however, signify a lack of approval for the use of violence by the government because 94 per cent said that they were most satisfied with the government's drug war initiative (*Bangkok Post*, 19 July 2004). In the sixty-page report, *Not Enough Graves: Thailand's War on Drugs, HIV/AIDS, and Violation of Human Rights*, Human Rights Watch states: 'The Thai government crackdown began in February 2003. Within 3 months, an estimated 2,275 drug suspects were shot dead. There were altogether almost 3,000 unexplained deaths, and thousands had been forced to have drug treatment in military boot camps' (http//hrw.org/english/docs/ 2004/ 07/08/ thaila9012).

In addition, since Thaksin came to power in February 2001, sixteen environmentalists have been murdered, and almost all of these murders remain unsolved. For example, Charoen Wataksorn, a leading opponent of the Bo Nok coal-fired power plant in Prachuap Khiri Khan, was fatally shot on 21 June 2004 in his home province after he and a local leader testified before a senate panel that was investigating public land-grab allegations (Euayporn 2004: 14–17, 45). A Bangkok senator, Sophon Suphapong, said the Prime Minister's obvious dislike of opponents to state projects and his 'pro-violence tendency', as evidenced in the way he has handled the southern unrest and the war on drugs, has sent influential figures the signal that violence is an acceptable way to resolve conflicts and deal with opponents.

Under Thaksin, economic growth in Thailand has jumped about two years ahead of expectations, but social justice, public safety and peace have been set back twenty to thirty years. In his thirty years of working on environmental protection, Sophon has never seen a government like the Thaksin administration, which bears great hatred towards community leaders and social activists. Sunee Chaiyaros, a human rights commissioner, accused the government of failing to deal with the conflicts when they emerged between villagers and state agencies or private investors. Instead, the government instructed developers to clear local opposition to their projects. Allowing members of the private sector to deal with project opponents is akin to asking for trouble as these powerful people will often use illegal means, including death threats and even murder, to silence villagers. Other critics, however, say that the Thaksin administration does not bear all the blame. There are other problems, including the weakness of independent agencies such as the Constitutional Court and the Election Commission, the lack of public support for environmental and human rights movements, the media's inadequate concern over the issue, and the inertia of non-governmental organizations (*Bangkok*, 19 July 2004).

Some scholars argue that in the past two decades, the far south has found a way to live in an uneasy balance with the Thai state, but Thaksin's policies and outside pressures 'had disturbed this balance in a tragic way' (Pasuk and Baker 2004: 239). This has happened in the context of a unique Thaksin style of managing Thai society, where organized dissent has been stifled, the media controlled and public intellectuals silenced. In order to promote prosperity – defined primarily as economic growth – and under pressure from globalization, the government has sacrificed rights and freedoms. Through a mix of social contract theory and modernist Buddhism, the Prime Minister as a 'good', disinterested leader could justify himself and his government, while publicly relegating democracy to a tool (Pasuk and Baker 2004: 134–71). In fact, in a speech delivered in December 2003, the Prime Minister categorically stated that: 'Democracy is a good and beautiful thing, but it's not the ultimate goal as far as administering the country is concerned. Democracy is just a tool, not our goal' (quoted in Pasuk and Baker 2004: 171). Another commentator maintains that Thaksin has changed the face of Thai politics by carefully cultivating an unprecedented degree of political stability under democratic rule that is, among other things, 'impressive even by the standards of bygone military-authoritarianism' (Thitinan 2003b: 287). He also notes that the way in which the Prime Minister wields power, both centralized and personalized, under his almost complete domination of the political environment has become increasingly authoritarian (Thitinan 2003b: 278).

The Thai state's violent responses to troubles in the south, as seen from the rejection of the Chaturon initiative and the suppression of the Tak Bai demonstration, are yet another indication of the rise of a more authoritarian tendency that accepts violence as a dominant strategy in solving conflicts –

and this with a high degree of popular approval. To understand this tendency, it is important to ask: what does the use of violence do to democracy in Thai society? I would argue that violence as used by the state, in this case, has been responsible for introducing a dangerous side of democracy.

The effects of violence on democracy

The Thai political scientist Thitinan Pongsudhirak coined the term 'demo-cratic authoritarianism' to describe the irony of the 'more democracy than ever' 1997 Constitution and the reality of the increasingly authoritarian 'Thaksin rule'. He believes that Thai society is undergoing 'authoritarian rule under democratic disguises' (Thitinan 2003b: 278). On the other hand, Kasian Tejapira, a noted public intellectual, argues that Thaksin is building a regime of 'elected capitalist absolutism' (Kasian 2004: 133) characterized by:

1) Absolute political power – using state power to solve problems with a strong inclination to violate the rights of its citizens, overstep constitutional boundaries, monopolize politics, and patronize rural people.
2) The capitalist political CEO, who uses business-style centralizing strategies.
3) Grassroots Keynesianism – using domestic economic forces and the state sector to successfully move the Thai economy forward at a time when the US, Japanese and European Union economies are suffering from recession, a cash flow trap and low growth rates, respectively.
4) Capitalist populism, which emphasizes cross-class coalition politics for economic redistribution in the full service of capitalism.

(Kasian 2004: 131–64)

Kasian concludes that this 'elected capitalist absolutism' is important because it has engaged in an ambitious project of changing Thai society by oppressing the small-scale peasant class and weakening Thai civil society (Kasian 2004: 237–8).

Thitinan's formulation emphasizes the discrepancy between what is 'on paper' and the actual practice. He is, therefore, less hesitant to call the phenomenon 'authoritarianism', with the term 'democratic' serving as a light qualifier. Kasian, on the other hand, underscores the interplay of the different ways that power has been used by the regime, especially in the areas of rights and economics.

Other democracies in the world are also displaying authoritarian charac-teristics. It is as if the world itself is undergoing a transformation that is revealing an unusual and even paradoxical face of democracy. At the end of the last century, some theorists, following Francis Fukuyama, maintained that human history has come to an end with the idea of democracy emerging triumphantly over other competing ideas (Fukuyama 1989). While the notion that 'the end of history' has arrived was always highly debatable, there has indeed been a phenomenon in the international community whereby a body of standards, joint statements or declarations of policy or intention, and resolutions have been adopted at different global forums. International commitment takes the form of 'soft laws', agreed guidelines that could be constitutive of building blocks that may eventually become customary rules and laws (Cassese 2001). In a world transformed by the spectre of violence fuelled by the threats from and war against terrorism, however, even these 'soft laws' have been seriously undermined.

For example, in July 2002, the first permanent and independent judicial body that could prosecute crimes of international concern, including genocide, war crimes, other crimes against humanity and the yet to be defined 'crimes of aggression', the International Criminal Court (ICC) was born under the Rome Treaty. Presently signed by 139 states and ratified by nearly a hundred, yet different from the International Court of Justice, which deals with states, the ICC deals with individual criminals and organizations wherever they are. In August 2002, however, the US Congress passed the American Soldiers Protection Act, which allows the US government to invade the court and seize US soldiers if and when they are surrendered to the ICC by state parties. In July 2004, the US House of Representatives attached an anti-ICC 'Nethercutt Amendment' to the Foreign Operations Bill. This allows the US President to cut off economic support to all countries belonging to the ICC but which have not signed the Bilateral Immunity Agreement with the USA (Balais-Serrano 2004). After US voters put George W. Bush back in the White House in 2004 together with stronger Republican representation in the Senate, it is very likely that the US Senate will approve this bill. In fact, the US Congress passed an anti-terrorist act on 8 November 2004 that would reduce the number of migrants, especially from Latin America and South Africa, to the USA as a way of curtailing the threat of terrorism. A more controversial outcome is that it makes it possible for the USA to indict children or family members of convicts in terrorism cases (*A Day Weekly*, 12–18 November 2004: 41). Elsewhere in Europe, the Hungarian Minister of Defence recently informed the media that the government has adopted a secret resolution that permits the shooting down of any civilian aircraft suspected of being used to carry out terrorist attacks. What is more worrying is his claim that every NATO member must have a similar resolution (*The Budapest Times*, 28 June–4 July 2004). In England, after two deadly Irish Republican Army bombings in London at the beginning of the last decade, closed-circuit television (CCTV) has been so widely used that, presently, an average Briton is scrutinized by some 300 cameras a day. While human rights advocates decry Britain for having turned into 'the surveillance capital possibly of the world, certainly of Europe', others hail these cameras as 'a kindly and watchful uncle or aunt' (Wardell 2004).

From a human rights perspective, dangerous trends have been emerging in the world since the September 11 incident. First, multilateral and diplomatic approaches to solving international problems may surrender the ground to unilateral and more forceful approaches. Second, approaches to solving international problems based on the rule of law will give way to approaches that are security driven. Third, the legal definition of 'terrorism' would be rendered unproblematic, with critical debate about it suppressed by the official definitions and policies. Fourth, the spread of polarized political language and imprecise rhetoric have created an environment in which certain groups of people – especially religious and ethnic minorities, and migrants and dissidents – whose rights can be easily threatened will become increasingly more vulnerable to repression. Fifth, recourse to military solutions as the first rather than the last resort to problems of deadly conflict could create new risks in many parts of the world. Sixth, the problem of economic injustice is being relegated to marginal importance (International Council on Human Rights Policy 2002). Faced with chronic inequality and increasingly brutal repression, some victims might then view the use of violence as a justified means for allowing their voices to be heard and for altering unjust power relations. This would, in turn, fit well with the dominant security discourse, which both produces and justifies the state's use of violence and the curtailment of citizens' rights. In this way, the cycle of violence is politically produced and sustained.

More important, from the perspective of the effects of violence on democracy, the random examples cited above reflect some common features. First, they take place in countries that are largely governed by democratically elected governments. Second, these countries perceive themselves to be under the threat of violence, usually from 'global terrorists' or from civil war. Third, their responses to these security threats have been dominated by the use of violence against groups that oppose the government, while the rights of their own citizens as well as others who enter their sovereign territories have been significantly curtailed. Fourth, there has been considerable public approval for these states' use of violence and their curbing of civil rights.

Israel offers a most fascinating case study. Within the context of increasing violence resulting from the War on Terror, and the realities of the Israeli occupation of Palestinian land, what has emerged in the country is a 'political–military partnership' that has the professional officer class increasingly involved in policy making due to the collapse of the distinction between military and civil decision making (Peri 2002: 13). It goes without saying that the democratic quality of the state is compromised when security policies are formulated by state agencies without popular accountability because of the 'increasing interpenetrability of the military and civilian spheres, both structurally and culturally' (Peri 2002: 13).

During the Second World War, Harold Lasswell advanced his 'garrison state thesis', which maintains that a state that is constantly at war cannot remain a democracy and that its society will cease to be an open society. The needs of national security will severely restrict civil liberties, and the military will become the dominant institution of government (Lasswell 1941). The types of war and violence that democratic societies face at the beginning of the twenty-first century, however, are quite different. The context of global violence – characterized by global terrorism, which in itself is a response to conditions of glaring injustice – and the state's violent responses have produced some unusual realities. Since terrorism can affect anyone at any time or place, it successfully robs a society of that precious sense of certainty that allows members to continue leading their lives in normalcy. In this sense, the present terror and the continuing war against it together undermine the basic foundation of any political society: that is, a sense of certainty guaranteed by the normal functioning of the state, the least of which is the protection of citizens' lives. With the absence of normalcy, the society that mourns the tragic fate of its victims is transformed into a society of victimizers (Chaiwat 2002: 158). It is as if present violent conditions have sunk the world into a state of 'pure war'.

'Pure war' exists in the sense that the whole of society is mobilized militarily at all times in the name of fear (Virilio and Lotringer 1983), so much so that in the USA, there is daily notification on television of terrorist threats, in different colour categories of seriousness, not unlike weather forecasts. Yet, the continuing violence, such as the daily battles in Iraq and Afghanistan or events in Southern Thailand as well as the cultural violence that appears in the form of profiling groups of people as potential terrorists (as evident in the media), is not hidden. Instead, every armed hostility and, in fact, conflicts between governments and those who oppose them can be conveniently seen as figments of the imagined war against terror. Depoliticization in this new 'pure war', therefore, takes place not because violent confrontations have been eclipsed by any grand catastrophe, but because they have been militarized and their discourse heavily securitized. In such circumstances, political solutions are absent, ordinary citizens' rights are sacrificed, and civil society groups that oppose the state are punished or silenced, at times summarily. The moment a political society has to live under the shadow of such 'pure war' is the instant when democracy turns authoritarian under the curse of violence.

It goes without saying that the notion of 'authoritarian democracy' is problematic. One of the most obvious reasons is that democracy itself is a highly contested concept. According to Norbert Bobbio, a meaningful discussion of democracy must be based on an understanding that it is made up of a set of rules grounded in four basic ideals: tolerance as a corrective ideal against the fanatic monopoly of 'truth' and the use of force to impose it on others; non-violence as an alternative ideal for resolving political conflict without bloodshed and to regard the adversary not as an enemy but an opponent whose existence, and not destruction, will make the political process meaningful; the gradual renewal of society as an energizing ideal through free debates by which citizens' ways of life could be suggested and modified; and the ideal of brotherhood/sisterhood, through which a kinship that unites all human beings in a common destiny can be recognized (Bobbio 1987: 23–42). There are also three minimum conditions that need to be met. First, rules must be established with regard to which group will be authorized to make collective decisions, and the power to choose rests on a large number of members from that group. Second, decision-making procedures are arrived at based on the rule of the majority. In order for decisions to be binding for the whole group, at least the majority needs to approve them. Third, those who are called upon to make these decisions must be offered 'real alternatives' and be in a position to choose among these alternatives.

Bobbio's 'rules of the game' are important in the context of the questions raised here. I would argue that a society that uses violence continuously in a situation of 'pure war' risks compromising the minimum conditions through which it could remain a democracy. There are five reasons why these conditions would be compromised by violence. First, in a situation where rights are suspended and alternatives curbed by the security discourse in the name of possible threats to security, it is less likely that the majority can make meaningful political choices. Second, in a context of 'pure war', 'truth' is generally monopolized and the official version is imposed on society. Third, in war – whether ideological or ethno-religious – a demonization of the other is as important as a monopoly of 'truth'. Fourth, violence tends to push a society away from the possibility of gradual renewal due to the fact that, in war, free debate becomes a luxury. Fifth, creating a clearly defined enemy, doing away with free debate and alternatives as well as curtailing citizens' rights will, in time, shatter the idea of the common destiny of all human beings through the sense of impending violence. Although some other rules may continue to be observed, it is questionable if society will continue to be democratic when political alternatives are not possible.

For how long must violence continue before it has such an effect on society? Some have argued that in crises such as civil wars, liberal and constitutional governments might not be able to rule effectively, and states with vast security apparatuses will suspend constitutional rights. It could, therefore, be concluded: 'the greatest threats to human liberty and happiness in this century have been caused not by disorder but by brutally strong, centralized states' (Zakaria 1997: 32). This phenomenon is not something unprecedented; in the nineteenth century, Alexis de Tocqueville observed that 'Democratic governments may become violent, and even cruel, at certain periods of extreme effervescence or of great danger; but these crises will be rare and brief' (Tocqueville 1956: 302). Both theorists, from different centuries, share the belief that crises in democracies are exceptional and brief, but today times of crises cease to be the exception and are the norm. Faced with the dangerous normality of 'pure war', it is a kind of 'authoritarian democracy' that now surfaces.

Conclusion: an authoritarian democracy?

At the end of his *Democracy in America*, Tocqueville points out that there was a possibility that despotism might have been established among the democratic nations of his day, though it would have assumed a different character, more extensive and mild at the same time and degrading people without tormenting them. He also wrote that:

> the species of oppression by which democratic nations are menaced is unlike anything which ever before existed in the world: our contemporaries will find no prototype of it in their memories. I seek in vain for an expression which will accurately convey the whole of the idea I have formed of it.
>
> (Tocqueville 1956: 302)

After describing the people in that political society as a multitude of equals, all alike but atomized because 'he exists but in himself and for himself alone', Tocqueville proceeds to describe this new kind of oppression as follows:

> That power is absolute, minute, regular, provident and mild. It would be like the authority of a parent, if like that authority, its object was to prepare men for manhood; but it seeks, on the contrary, to keep them in perpetual childhood: it is well content that the people should rejoice, provided they think of nothing but rejoicing. For their happiness such a government willingly labors, but it chooses to be the sole agent and the only arbiter of that happiness; it provides for their security, foresees and supplies their necessities, facilitates their pleasures, manages their principal concerns, directs their industry, regulates the descent of property, and subdivides their inheritances; what remains, but to spare them all the care of thinking and all the trouble of living?
>
> (Tocqueville 1956: 303)

Tocqueville's new despotic democracy is a society without citizens, in the sense of people who actively participate in politics. In an atomized world, the purpose of living as part of a larger political community is lost. At the same time, a person's daily existence is provided for by the state to the extent that there is no need to think; as such, there is no meaning left in living itself. Though Tocqueville's portrait of despotic democracy is sharply recognizable at the turn of the twenty-first century, it does not capture the transformation of a democracy more or less shaped by the effects of violence, precisely because he thought that the violent phase would be 'rare and brief'. Today, normalized violence has produced what I would call an authoritarian democracy.

The notion of 'authoritarian democracy' used here is inspired by the concept of 'authoritarian personality', advanced half a century ago by T. W. Adorno and others. In his preface to *The Authoritarian Personality*, Max Horkheimer discusses the rise of 'the authoritarian type of man', who combines ideas and skills typical of a highly industrialized society with irrational beliefs, enlightened and superstitious, proud to be an individualist and inclined to submit blindly to power and authority (Adorno *et al.* 1969: ix). Moreover, the role of violence is crucial for the authoritarian personality. Adorno argues that violence is essential for fascism's basic psychodynamic principles because fascist propaganda incites sadistic violence against 'the enemy', while a masochistic aggression is directed against the self in the form of self-destruction, and ritual violence is used to bind the members together (Crook 1994: 12–13). It is violence that helps sustain hatred of the enemy, an inclination to hurt oneself and a longing to be a part of a community. *The Authoritarian Personality* is important precisely because it is a study neither of fascists in Italy nor Nazis in Germany; instead, it looks at the potential of Americans to be influenced by fascist propaganda. It is important to note that a democratic society *is* the context for the existence of the authoritarian personality. When a democratic society goes through a period of heightened conflict, it is easier to imagine it turning in an authoritarian direction.

If democracy could be thought of in terms of personality, and not merely as a model of governance, then there could be authoritarian and non-authoritarian democracies. An authoritarian democracy, like an authoritarian personality, would be characterized by hostility to others, espe-cially minority groups; ambivalent relations to authority marked by obedience to superiors and cruelty to those below; a lack of meaningful rela-tionships with others; and an instrumental appreciation of violence. It is also possible that, like an authoritarian personality, an authoritarian democracy would emerge as a result of certain circumstances – notably violence and war – that manifest themselves as hostility to enemies, insecurity within one's self, meaningless relationships with others, and the readiness to rely on mili-tary means and violence as tools of the state.

The term 'authoritarian democracy' is introduced here because, like Tocqueville, I am searching for a way to explain the new phenomenon when democracy turns out to be barbaric right before our very eyes. The term is useful because it takes into account that a democratic government can, in reality, be barbaric. To distinguish between democracy and constitutional liberalism – maintaining that constitutional liberalism, defined as respect for civil liberties marked by the rule of law, a separation of power and the protection of basic liberties, is the precondition that would prevent violence and ethnic conflicts in a divided society (Zakaria 1997: 35) – is to overlook what has transpired in countries with evident 'constitutional liberalism' yet plagued by incessant conflict and violence (the cases of Northern Ireland and Sri Lanka) or brutal engagements in war (the US invasions of Afghanistan and Iraq).

On the other hand, to acknowledge the use of illiberal means in a democ-racy but relegate them to a time of exception, in case of emergencies (Zakaria 1997: 33), is to misapprehend the sign of the times when violence and hostility against 'the enemies' become the norm. More importantly, the concept of authoritarian democracy considers seriously the legitimacy of the democratic government that turns barbaric. In the past, military dictatorships that unleashed their force on unarmed demonstrators easily lost their legitimacy, yet it is much more complicated when that violence against citizens is unleashed by a properly elected government with a popular mandate to continue fighting drug wars, global terrorism or separatist movements. In this sense, the concept of authoritarian democracy is an attempt to express the present condition of democracy in all its complexities when it is touched by the curse of violence.

11 China's response to US neoconservatism

Zhiyuan Cui

The rise of China: from the 'Washington Consensus' to the 'Beijing Consensus'

It is commonplace today to view China as the emerging economic giant that will eventually challenge, and perhaps even surpass, the economic might of the world's only recognized superpower at present – the USA. China is therefore regarded as a serious potential challenger to the current supremacy of American Empire. China has in fact undergone rapid economic growth and incredible social transformation in the last two decades, with an average annual GDP growth rate of 9 per cent (see Figure 11.1). This is especially remarkable in light of the economic decline of the

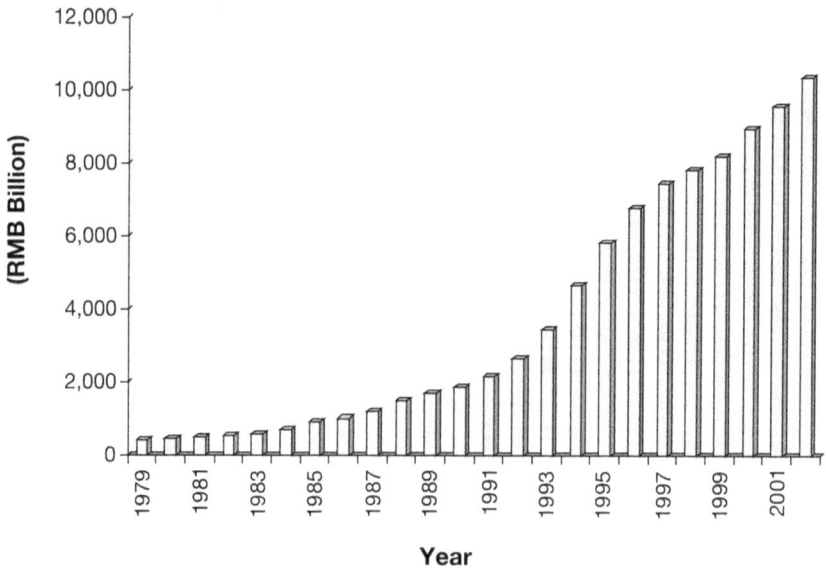

Figure 11.1: China's GDP, 1978–2002

former Soviet Union and the slowdown of the world economy after the Asian financial crisis of 1997–8.

How is China's phenomenal economic growth to be explained? There are some competing explanations.

The conventional explanations for China's economic rise tend to downplay the significance of the specific institutional underpinnings of China's economic growth. One school of conventional thought argues that there is nothing significant or unusual about China's economic growth given its large rural population. In the words of two leading development economists:

> China faced the classic problem of normal economic development, the transfer of workers from low-productivity agriculture to higher-productivity industry . . . The large labor allocation effect in China reflects the existence of a large amount of labor employed in low-productivity agriculture and the success of the post-1978 Chinese reforms in creating higher-productivity jobs in the industry and service sectors.
>
> (Sachs and Wing 1994: 102–45; Sachs and Wing 1997)

I would like to emphasize the importance of the special institutional arrangements that have characterized China during this period of incredibly rapid growth. Together, these constitute nothing less than what might be called 'institutional heresies'. They are heresies because they do not conform neatly to the dictates of the Washington Consensus that urges liberalization, fiscal discipline, privatization and macroeconomic stability[1] (Williamson 2000: 251–64; Williamson 2002) – all of which have become the cornerstones of the neoliberal economic orthodoxy. These institutional heresies – comprising such practices as the collective ownership of rural land, an extensive share-holding co-operative system in rural industry, and a three-tier shareholding system in the incorporated urban industrial sector – played a crucial role in generating economic growth in China (see Cui 2005). These practices have been all but ignored in most readings of China's remarkable economic success story.

Another school of development thinking argues that China's economic growth is mainly driven by foreign investment and export. As Table 11.1

Table 11.1: The share of exports by foreign invested enterprises in China

Year	Share of exports by FIEs (%)	Year	Share of exports by FIEs (%)
1986	1.9	1993	27.5
1987	3.1	1994	28.1
1988	5.2	1995	31.3
1989	9.4	1996	40.7
1990	12.6	1997	41.0
1991	16.7	1998	44.1
1992	20.4		

Source: Korea Security Exchange, Annual Report (2004).

shows, however, it was only after 1992 that foreign investments began to play an important role in China's exports; thus, China's growth in the 1980s was largely domestically driven. Such recognition constitutes nothing less than another form of heresy to the purveyors of the Washington Consensus and its perceived economic 'wisdoms'.

Nevertheless, it has clearly not been smooth sailing all the time. China is now faced with a number of problems which, taken together, pose fundamental questions: Can the institutional heresies that were crucial to its success be maintained? Are they merely ephemeral adaptations of the 'conventional' path of economic development that will, ultimately, be swept away by the supposedly all-powerful, inexorable force of neoliberal economic globalization? Are they instead, and more tantalizingly, the starting point for an alternative path, an alternative model to the one inspired by the Washington Consensus and that has become the orthodox route among most communities of international development planners? The answers to these questions are crucial not only in relation to the future of economic development in China but also in terms of posing alternatives to the most dogmatic forms of economic neoliberalism, which are often expressed in policies imposed by the West on developing countries, as was shown during the Asian economic crisis of the previous decade.

It is significant that the economic achievements of China over the past two decades have been threatened in recent years. In the public sector, there has been an increasing number of bankruptcies among state-owned enterprises (SOEs). The related problem of widespread unemployment, both urban and rural, is no less serious. Already, news of peasant and labour protests, previously almost unheard of in China, has sometimes made its way to the foreign press. The special favours that the export sector has been receiving from the central government (such as in the form of export tax rebates) have become increasingly unsustainable, given the fiscal drain on the central government's coffers. Social, regional and sectoral income inequalities have also been increasing. This is reflected in China's Gini ratio, which stood at 0.341 in 1988 but has been steadily increasing to stand now at 0.457. Corruption – the conversion of public office to private advantage, especially with lower level government officials – is a serious threat to the legitimacy of the Communist Party, which has been successful thus far in presiding over China's economic transformation. China's increasing degree of global economic integration, for example through membership in the WTO, will accentuate all these dynamics of challenge and threat.

It is fair to say that if not for September 11, Chinese policy-makers and intellectuals may not have realized the significance of the Chinese development experience as a possibly more enduring adaptation and alternative to the conventional path prescribed by the Washington Consensus. The post-9/11 policies of the USA, which have included placing political pressure on China to appreciate its currency, forced Chinese policy-makers to give serious thought to the lessons of the country's own concrete development experience as well as possible alternatives.

Thus, a Beijing Consensus appears to be emerging, with main elements such as the prominence of institutional innovations and flexibility (of the kinds mentioned above), and more emphasis on equitable development – the latter perhaps a reaction to social tensions due to existing economic inequalities:[2]

> The Washington Consensus was a hallmark of end of history arrogance; it left a trail of destroyed economies and bad feelings around the globe. China's new development approach is driven by a desire to have equitable, peaceful high-quality growth, critically speaking, it turns traditional ideas like privatisation and free trade on their heads.
>
> (Ramo 2004: 4)

The importance of the emergence of such a Beijing Consensus should not be underestimated, given that the whole world is searching for a substitute to the dominant paradigms of economic and social development as espoused by international development institutions. Both Marxism and social democracy had lost much of their political and intellectual momentum by the end of the Cold War, and this was underscored by the ascendance of economic neoliberalism as once codified in the Washington Consensus. The disillusionment with neoliberalism, however, is also growing, as evidenced by the recent events in Seattle, Mumbai and elsewhere. China, first among the continental peripheral countries and economically dynamic but politically resistant to reform, occupies a position of utmost importance for this worldwide search. Its official ideology is characterized by the confused co-existence of a shrunken form of Marxism with a fossilized type of neoliberalism. Thus far, its intelligentsia have been unable to make sense of the country's achievements or comprehend the nature of the dangers that can yet derail them; September 11 served as their wake-up call.

It is significant that three tendencies in contemporary politics and political thinking reinforce one another in China. Domestically, there are 'cautious neoliberals' who reject the pressures exerted by big global financial interests and insist on strengthening China's social safety nets. There are chastened social democrats who, in the name of recombining US-style economic flexibility with European-style social protection, end up with the same two concerns: of limiting dependence on international financial interests and insisting on more commitment to social welfare. Also, there are ex-leftists who have lost faith in statism and want institutional alternatives, but without knowing what these are, they have arrived by default at the same position as the former two. It is ironic that these three groups want to be enemies, yet do not know how to.

It has become increasingly clear that to continue its advance in a progressive direction, China must go beyond these three positions. Caught between residual statism and crude neoliberalism, there is a common desire in China neither to surrender to neoliberal globalization completely nor to insist on a simplistic nationalist rejection of global markets. The unintended consequences of September 11 and the Bush Doctrine (discussed below) for China may be that they have made Chinese policy-makers and intellectuals more conscious of an emerging Beijing Consensus.

If China continues to rise – whatever the merits of a new economic model and in spite of the problems and uncertainties mentioned above – there will clearly be important consequences for power in the region and, indeed, in the world. While the West has welcomed the opening up of the Chinese economy over the last decades and has embraced the opportunities presented in terms of investment and huge new markets, there remain very strong reservations about the broader political ramifications of China's continuing rise. It is well known, for example, that the so-called 'neoconservative' group that has been so influential in charting the political agenda of the George W. Bush administration has especially viewed China's growing might with considerable trepidation. One of the stated aims of the famous security and foreign policy paper of the early 1990s penned by Paul Wolfowitz (see Introduction, this volume; Beeson, this volume) was to ensure that no power, including China, could emerge to challenge the political, economic and military dominance of the USA globally.

It should come as no surprise that Chinese policy-makers and intellectuals have been fully aware of the concerns, particularly ascendant among sections of the US political elite, about the real and potential challenge posed by China. The rest of this chapter is an attempt to elaborate on some responses within China to the US post-Cold-War political agenda, especially as it relates to China and the East Asian region. Specifically, I discuss China's response to rising US neoconservatism, which has produced the Bush Doctrine, one of the hallmarks of what is often referred to in contemporary literature as 'American Empire'. One of the arguments I make is that the sharp break that many view as having taken place in the US agenda following the rise of the Bush administration is not perceived in exactly the same way in China. Instead, the view from China is that there has been remarkable consistency in the US post-Cold-War agenda, in spite of the shift in rhetoric and policy emphases from the Clinton to the Bush Jr administrations. For Chinese elites, this cannot be separated from abiding US geopolitical interests in the East Asian region and on the broader world stage.

The Bush Doctrine: a US post-Cold-War grand strategy

It is widely believed in North America and Europe that that the so-called Bush Doctrine is strongly rooted in the neoconservative thinking and movement that have become increasingly ascendant politically in the USA. The elements of the Bush doctrine were elaborated on 1 June 2002 in an address by President Bush at the famed American military academy, West Point. It was here that President Bush announced the three basic elements of the Bush

Doctrine. First, the USA would no longer rely solely on 'Cold War doctrines of containment and deterrence'. Instead, it would actively pursue the strategy of 'pre-emptive strikes' and 'take the battle to the enemy, disrupt his plans and confront the worst threats before they emerge'. Second, the USA would endeavour to export democracy globally, since 'the requirements of freedom apply fully to Africa and Latin America and the entire Islamic world'. Indeed, on a different occasion, Bush declared that 'The liberty we prize is not America's gift to the world, it is God's gift to humanity' (Merry 2003: 12–15, 94–9). Finally, the USA would ensure that its military supremacy would be beyond any challenge arising from anywhere in the world, 'thereby making the destabilizing arms races of other eras pointless, and limiting rivalries to trade and other pursuits of peace' (Kaplan and Kristol 2003: 74). The idea is that the USA should become so powerful militarily that any other country would find it futile to compete with it. Thus, the three elements of the Bush Doctrine were declared as: pre-emptive strikes, democracy promotion and military supremacy. Soon after, in September 2002, President Bush signed a document entitled the 'National Security Strategy of the United States', which essentially formalized the three elements of the doctrine he had earlier expounded.

As discussed elsewhere in this volume, the US agenda under Bush has had a longer history than would appear at first glance. Indeed, its evolution and shape owe much to the contribution of a number of policy-makers and thinkers over the last decade or decade and a half. Most significantly, Paul Wolfowitz's aborted 1992 Defense Planning Guidance had already contained the three elements of the Bush Doctrine and presented them in very stark terms; interestingly, however, it was largely devoid in its original version of the 'idiom of freedom, peace and liberty' (Merry 2003: 96). This idiom was only to acquire greater emphasis as the Wolfowitz vision was incorporated into the policy and rhetoric of the Bush Doctrine. In 1997, the Project for the New American Century was founded by such prominent figures as Dick Cheney, Donald Rumsfeld, Paul Wolfowitz, William Kristol and Robert Kagan (see www.newamericancentury.org), among others; it has since become a beacon of US neoconservative as well as more traditionally conservative thought. Clearly, the Bush Doctrine owes much to the views of this group of policy-makers and thinkers. In 1997, Irving Kristol – already the recognized leading spirit of the US neoconservative movement as well as the father of the influential political commentator, William Kristol – predicted that 'One of these days, the American people are going to awaken to the fact that we have become an imperial nation, even though public opinion and all of our political traditions are hostile to the idea.' For Kristol, this 'fact' did not result from any 'overweening ambition' on the part of Americans to define their destiny in this way, nor was it the consequence of 'any kind of conspiracy by a foreign policy elite'. US imperialism 'happened because the world wanted it to happen, needed it to happen, and signaled this need by a long series of relatively minor crises that could not be resolved except by some American involvement' (*The Wall Street Journal*, 16 August 1997). In this connection, it is noteworthy that Bush awarded the Presidential Medal of Freedom to Irving Kristol on 9 July 2002, effectively recognizing his influence and contribution to shaping the post-Cold-War US grand strategy.

Many analysts have drawn analogies between the policies and views of contemporary neoconservative figures in the USA and some aspects of the political thought of the long bygone era of Imperial Rome (Merry 2003: 96; Johnson 2005). Certainly, there is no lack of classical scholars among the leading neoconservative thinkers in the USA.[3] If the USA is the new Rome in the minds of some of the neoconservatives, it is then not surprising to discover that the strategy of 'pre-emptive strikes' was similarly a key element in Roman Imperial strategy. This was expressed by no less than Cicero, the great Roman political philosopher:

> how can you believe that the man who has lived so licentiously up to the present time will not proceed to every extreme of insolence, if he shall also secure the authority given by arms? Do not, then, wait until you have suffered some such treatment and then rue it, but be on your guard before you suffer; for it is rash to allow dangers to come upon you and then to repent of it, when you might have anticipated them.
>
> (Tuck 1999: 21)

How do Chinese intellectuals and policy-makers now perceive and respond to the Bush Doctrine given the economic rise of China, the new economic problems described earlier, and the recognition that the USA harbours an interest in restraining or at least controlling the process of China's emergence as a regional and world power? Of course, as should be expected, there are various viewpoints on this matter. It is clear, however, that the main view adhered to by Chinese policy-makers and intellectuals is one that identifies remarkable continuity in post-Cold-War US thinking and strategy. This view emphasizes the similarities of the Bush Doctrine with Clinton's foreign policy, and recognizes that it was during the supposedly less aggressive Clinton period that US military force began to be used more freely and frequently around the world. The standpoint is one that understands the emergence of the Bush Doctrine as the culmination and maturation of the US post-Cold-War grand strategy.

We can appreciate the Chinese perspective described above by contrasting it with the views of some of Europe's leading intellectuals. For example, Jurgen Habermas, the well-known German public intellectual and philosopher, has emphasized the newness of the Bush Doctrine. Habermas, like many other leading European intellectuals and commentators, perceived the Bush Doctrine as signalling a significant break with, rather than the more or less logical culmination of, the foreign policy agenda initiated during the Clinton administration. The result has been the loss of the USA's moral authority to talk about democracy and human rights to the rest of the world. According to Habermas, 'The United States has, with the Iraq war . . . given up the role of a guarantor of power in international law; with its violation thereof she sets future superpowers a disastrous example.' He further laments: 'Let's not kid ourselves: America's normative authority lies shattered' (Habermas 2003: 33). For the Chinese, however, the 'normative authority' that Habermas mourns has been lost with the actions of Bush Jr was not there in the first place. In the rest of this chapter, I will outline some of the basic geopolitical and philosophical reasons for the Chinese understanding of the Bush Doctrine as the culmination of the US post-Cold-War grand strategy.

The geopolitical bases of the Chinese response

While the Cold War ended in Europe by 1990, it never fully ended in East Asia. Few in the West would appreciate the importance of this fact. Few Europeans or North Americans are aware that the war on the Korean Peninsula has never actually ended – no peace treaty was ever signed to conclude the war, and only a ceasefire agreement officially stands in the way of open warfare. This is just one example of how the Cold War remains a lived reality in East Asia. As a major legacy of the Cold War era, there is also deep distrust among all the major powers in the region, with regard to one another's motives and intentions. It is not only the USA and the West that cast a worried glance over the rising economic and political power of China; some countries in East Asia are also fearful of the repercussions of an overwhelming Chinese economic dominance in the region. For its part, China is continually concerned that Taiwan will seek independence with the backing of the USA and Japan, especially given the developments there marked by the demise of the Kuomintang's political hegemony and the recent rise of political forces that quite openly and frequently espouse the aim of independence (see Lee and Yang, this volume). As is well known, the idea of Taiwanese independence stirs up great nationalist feelings within China. Given these circumstances, it is perhaps not too surprising that Chinese elites tend to be more sensitive and vigilant than their European counterparts with regard to the consequences of the USA's seemingly increasing aggressive unilateralism. They are apprehensive about the possible repercussions for the issue of Taiwanese independence.

The Chinese view about the continuity between the Bush agenda and Clinton-era foreign policy is basically grounded in philosophical reasons – the Chinese see very little disjuncture between the stated aims and objectives of Clinton's 'liberalism' and Bush's 'neoconservatism', insofar as the dissemination of proclaimed universal values is concerned. The dissemination of these values as elements of 'democracy export' is regarded as part of the requirements for maintaining global US economic and political hegemony. This perception of continuity seems to be confirmed by some prominent spokesmen of the neoconservative cause itself among the US intelligentsia. For example, Kaplan and Kristol claim that 'Bush would hardly be acting without precedent if he acted unilaterally against Saddam. After all, President Clinton resorted to force without U.N. approval on several occasions', and each time received the support of his fellow Democrats. US 'exceptionalism', however, is not merely expressed by just neoconservatives. For example, top US diplomat Richard Holbrooke, formerly the USA's representative to the United Nations, is quoted by Kaplan and Kristol as saying: 'Act without the Security Council, or don't act at all' (Kaplan and Kristol 2003: 90).

Furthermore, Chinese elites have noted Madeleine Albright's rather arrogant boast that the USA is an 'indispensable nation' that 'stands tall' and sees 'further into the future' (http://www.saidwhat.co.uk/quote4229.html.). Albright, of course, was Clinton's Secretary of State. In addition, Zbigniew Brzezinski, a former national security advisor during the Democratic presidency of Jimmy Carter, has explained the US post-Cold-War grand strategy in particularly crude terms. According to this still influential figure within US foreign policy-making circles, the aim of the USA is ultimately 'to prevent collusion and maintain security dependence among the vassals (Europe) . . . to keep barbarians from coming together' (McCormack 2003).

Given such statements, it should not be surprising that from the point of view of those in China, aggressive US unilateralism, as expressed in what is now known as the neoconservative-inspired Bush Doctrine, is only one step further along in the direction of US post-Cold-War grand strategic thinking. What has been the Chinese response so far?

There have been several concrete Chinese responses to the US grand strategy. These include such policies as (a) using China's vote in the United Nations Security Council; (b) supporting the role of the euro as a competitor to the US dollar by diversifying China's foreign currency holdings; (c) attempting to develop more trade and monetary co-operation with other Asian countries; and (d) developing trade and security co-operation with Russia and neighbouring states in Central Asia (in what is known as the Shanghai Co-operation Organization or Shanghai Six). The last possibly poses the most immediate worry to the USA, given the possible ramifications of the global scramble for the rich oil and gas reserves believed to be situated in Central Asia (see Altvater, this volume). An economically growing and energy-hungry China is likely to become an increasingly active participant in such a scramble. Thus, China and Kazakhstan recently agreed to explore the possibility of building a gas pipeline from Kazakhstan to China. China also secured a commitment from Kazakhstan to help it counter Islamic separatists in Xinjiang Province on the border with Kazakhstan. In return, China promised to support Kazakhstan's bid to join the World Trade Organization (WTO) (*Straits Times*, 5 July 2005).

In general, Chinese efforts at 'counterbalancing' US power have to date remained very limited. For a long time, Chinese leaders have been keen for China to keep a fairly low profile in international affairs for the purpose of not being perceived as a direct 'threat' to US interests, in particular. China's low profile is partly indicated in the UN Security Council's records on vetoes on its resolutions. As indicated from these records, China has used its veto power only five times since becoming a member of the UN Security Council, as compared to the Soviet Union/Russia (120 times) and the USA (76 times). Even more revealing is that almost all of China's veto power has been used on issues relating to Taiwan (Cui 2004).

China's long-standing 'low-profile' policy does not, however, mean that China's responses to the Bush Doctrine, in particular, and to the post-Cold-War US grand strategy has had no real policy effects. In the longer term, the increasingly close co-operation between China and the European Union may be the most important of China's responses to the Bush Doctrine and the more openly aggressive policy of unilateralism that it embodies. The EU itself has clearly welcomed this development, which is not surprising given the tensions and contradictions within Europe itself with regard to being led by the USA in a world now marked with the distinct absence of the kind of global communist threat that had once ensured that major capitalist powers would acquiesce to US leadership. Thus, the policy paper adopted by the EU Commission on 10 September 2003 sets out a framework that is intended to guide EU policy and action towards China over the next two to three years. The paper identifies six priorities for relations in the coming years, including sharing responsibilities in promoting global governance, supporting China's transition to an open society based upon the rule of law and respect for human rights, and promoting China's economic opening domestically and externally. The paper also contains a number of concrete proposals with a view to enhancing EU–China relations in key areas, including economic and trade relations and China's internal reform process (see http://europa.eu.int/rapid/start/cgi/guesten.ksh?p_action.gettxt= gt&doc = IP/03/1231|0|AGED&lg = EN&display =).

The philosophical bases: Chinese perceptions of US neoconservatism and liberalism

It has been stated that a key idea of this essay is that, from the point of view of Chinese elites, there is more continuity than disjuncture between the agendas of the Bush Jr and Clinton administrations. This perception is ultimately based on the observation that US neoconservatism shares with its liberal counterpart the vision of the USA as a 'redeemer' endowed with 'special providence' or a 'special mission'. The perception of the USA that predominates among China's elites is, thus, essentially a reaction to the notion of US exceptionalism, in the way that it is espoused by a range of US political figures and thinkers, as mentioned earlier. For the Chinese, it is no coincidence that both Clinton and Bush Jr have made the claim of basing their foreign policy objectives on such notions as 'democratic peace' and the extolling of human rights above national sovereignty, at least in relation to countries outside of the USA itself. Thus, in the most basic ideological sense, they are similar – whatever their differences otherwise in terms of means and emphases. The most evident difference is merely that these stated objectives are pursued in a way that is more overt, aggressive and forceful under the Bush Doctrine than under Clinton, as I will explain further.

The perception of continuity between such seemingly disparate streams of thought may seem strange to many Americans, but to appreciate this sense of continuity, one needs to recognize the forward-looking character of US neoconservatism, which contrasts very starkly with, for example, the traditionalism of British conservatism. The latter's world-view has been succinctly summarized in the words of a leading thinker of British conservatism, Michael Oakeshott. He suggests that 'What is esteemed [in conservatism] is the present; and it is esteemed not on account of its connections with a remote antiquity, nor because it is recognized to be more admirable than any possible alternative, but on account of its familiarity.' He goes on to argue that to be:

> conservative, then, is to prefer the familiar to the unknown, to prefer the tried to the untried, fact to mystery, the actual to the possible, the limited to the unbounded, the near to the distant . . . the convenient to the prefect, present laughter to utopian bliss.
>
> (Oakeshott 1962)

Nothing could be more different from the world-view espoused by American intellectuals such as Irving Kristol, regarded by many as the father of the US neoconservative movement. Kristol explicitly rejects the idea that conservatives should be respectful of and value what exists in the present, and is derisive of the 'secularism' of British conservatism. Kristol declared Oakeshott to be 'irredeemably secular' compared to his characterization of himself as a 'Jewish conservative'. For Kristol, 'It is impossible for any religious person to have the kinds of attitudes toward the past and the future that Oakeshott's conservative disposition celebrates.' He notes that the Jewish scriptures and daily prayer book provide a link 'to the past and to the future with an intensity lacking in Oakeshott's vision' (Kristol 1995: 373) Therefore, US neoconservatism, imbued with a particular kind of religious inspiration – at least at its point of origin – is in fact forward looking and even revolutionary in nature. It is no surprise that it shares with the US liberals the so-called 'democratic peace' theory, as famously proposed by Princeton political scientist Michael Doyle in the 1980s, insofar as democracy is installed as the main pivot of a benign vision of a future world order.

As is well known, Doyle's 'democratic peace' theory came to gain a great degree of prominence among US policy-makers of different political orientations. By the early 1990s, Doyle's ideas formed part of the validation for growing US arguments about the virtues of exporting or promoting democracy worldwide. In the context of the seemingly growing number of states deemed 'failed' or 'rogue', the democratic theory proposal had a lot of appeal for Washington policy-makers, who were dealing with what at times seemed like a much more chaotic world than that which existed during the Cold War. Fundamentally, Doyle's theory holds that democratic, liberal states have a greater inclination to maintain peace among themselves while 'these republics would engage in wars with nonrepublics'. The reason democracies do not go to war with one another, according to Doyle, is that 'Institutional features lead to caution'. Specifically, he points out that the consent of the citizenry to a war is a requirement under a democratic system (Doyle 1986: 1151–69).

Though Doyle claimed that his 'democratic peace theory' is rooted in Immanuel Kant's famous 1795 essay 'Perpetual Peace', it is useful to point out that he has quite fundamentally misinterpreted the Kantian thesis. For Kant, 'the consent of the citizens is required to decide whether or not war is to be declared', but 'it is very natural that they will have great hesitation in embarking on so dangerous an enterprise'. Kant recognized that:

> this would mean calling down on themselves all the miseries of war, such as doing the fighting themselves . . . having to take upon themselves a burden of debt which will embitter peace itself and which can never be paid off on account of the constant threat of new wars.
>
> (Kant 1991: 100)

Kant provided a two-fold reason for explaining why republics are reluctant to go to war: citizens have to be engaged in any war as combatants directly and then they would have to bear the burden of ensuing public debt. This line of reasoning, however, is outdated and not particularly relevant to the conditions of modern democracies that have large professional armies, and to states that have the capacity to issue debt to foreigners. Kant's thesis is particularly inappropriate in explaining the foreign policy of the USA, given its huge professional military force and its status as the world's largest debtor. Thus, the 'democratic peace' theory is premised on very flawed assumptions.

Historical facts also cast doubt on the premises of the democratic peace theory. Kenneth Waltz points out, for example, the fact that the USA has often overthrown democratically elected leaders of governments, such as Salvador Allende in Chile and Juan Bosch in the Dominican Republic, when this has served its interests (Waltz 2002: 34). More importantly, Doyle's claim that 'liberal states do maintain peace among themselves' while at the same time 'these republics would engage in wars with nonrepublics' (Doyle 1986: 1159) totally misrepresents the Kantian thesis. Kant's dual reason for the reluctance of republics to go to war claims nothing at all about the nature of the enemy that is being faced (Cavallar 2001: 233).

Given such blatant misrepresentation, it is hard to see why Doyle's reading and adoption of the Kantian perpetual peace thesis has gained such wide acceptance among academics and in influential policy-making circles.

The answer to this puzzle can only be found if Doyle's 'democratic peace theory' is linked to a justification of an imperial project. Doyle, in fact, stated that 'the protection of cosmopolitan Liberal rights thus bred a demand for imperial rule that violated the liberty of Native Americans, Africans and Asians' (Doyle 1997: 273). This goes against Georg Cavallar's reading of Kant, which highlights that Kant himself argued against the European imperial project. According to Kant:

> The natives can turn strangers away on condition that this does not cause their death. The (European) strangers in turn are obliged to behave 'in a peaceable manner', and if they don't, the natives act 'wisely' if they place restrictions on them.
>
> (Cavallar 2001: 241)

Doyle also conveniently ignores Kant's fifth thesis in 'perpetual peace', which holds that 'No State shall forcibly interfere in the constitution and government of another state' (Kant 1991: 96). This forgotten thesis clearly bears much relevance to the frequently heated exchanges between Chinese and Western governments over the years about the condition of human rights and the lack of democracy in China. The problem becomes increasingly thorny from the point of view of Chinese policy-makers when political conditionalities are linked to trade and economic issues. This is especially so given the widely accepted understanding that one objective of the broad US geopolitical strategy is to contain the potential Chinese challenge to US global economic and political dominance.

Conclusion

It is significant that the Bush Doctrine places 'democracy export' together with the other main principles of executing pre-emptive strikes on perceived threats and maintaining US military supremacy. To Chinese policy-makers and intellectuals, this is a clear signal that US pronouncements on democratization and human rights – and the pressure it has frequently exerted on China in these areas – cannot be disentangled from the broader US geopolitical strategy and interests in the region and elsewhere.

It should be understood, however, that this is not an argument to justify any Chinese resistance to democratization. Rather, China must face the challenge of democratic innovations in both the economic and political spheres. The best response to the Bush Doctrine is for the new generation of Chinese intellectuals, policy-makers and common people to develop new institutions of democracy and market economy, to contribute to the progress of human civilization beyond the narrow horizon set by Bush and his peers. Interestingly, we can already observe that since September 11, China is moving beyond the so-called Washington Consensus and is developing something called the Beijing Consensus. Of course there are many hurdles, and one huge task is resolving the many social problems stemming from rising inequalities. If successful, China's efforts represent the offer of a competing model of economic development to the one outlined within the strict precepts of the Washington Consensus. The latter still has the status of dogma among development practitioners in Western governments and international development institutions.

Blindly adhering to the confines of these precepts is not the answer to the problems that can threaten the sustainability of the Chinese economic miracle. In the words of the famed Third World revolutionary, Franz Fanon, 'If we wish to turn Africa into a new Europe, then let us leave the destiny of our countries to Europeans. They will know how to do it better than the most gifted among us' (Fanon 1965: 312). The emerging Beijing Consensus represents an attempt by the Chinese to take hold of their destiny and chart their own path – in the context of a world order characterized by American Empire and the ascendance of neoconservative ideology in the USA.

Notes

1 The term 'Washington Consensus' was coined by John Williamson in 1989 to refer to policies that he thought everyone in Washington would agree were needed in Latin America. He coined the phrase 'to refer to the lowest common denominator of policy advice being addressed by the Washington-based institutions to Latin American countries as of 1989'.

2 The term 'Beijing Consensus' was coined by Joshua Cooper Ramo to describe the Chinese alternative to the 'Washington Consensus'. Ramo interviewed 100 Chinese policy-makers and intellectuals over a year and summed up the overall picture, which emerged as the 'Beijing Consensus'. Another element of the Beijing Consensus that was identified is a non-symmetrical national defence strategy aimed at limiting US power and actions in the immediate region. See Ramo (2004).

3 See Saul Bellow's (2000) novel *Ravelstein* for a story about Paul Wolfowitz's relationship with Allan Bloom, a prominent scholar of the classics at Cornell in the 1960s. Wolfowitz was influenced by Bloom as an undergraduate. Also, Donald Kagan, the father of another leading neoconservative, Robert Kagan, is a leading scholar of the Roman Empire at Yale University. His brother, Frederick, is also regarded as a leading neoconservative historian.

12 The post-Cold-War world order and domestic conflict in South Korea
Neoliberal and armed globalization

Sonn Hochul

Introduction

The 'spectre of globalization' is haunting the world and it manifests today in two forms: first, in 'neoliberal economic globalization'; and second, in 'armed globalization', which is today well represented in so-called 'preventive wars' as is the case in Afghanistan and Iraq.

With the end of the Cold War, some scholars envisioned that the post-Cold-War world order would be characterized by peace and, ultimately, prosperity for all. Fukuyama (1992), for instance, argued for the end of history, that is the final triumph of liberalism globally. Instead, neoliberal and armed globalization, which characterize the post-Cold-War world order, have now intensified conflict internationally and domestically in many countries. On this basis, this chapter will analyse how neoliberal globalization and armed globalization have each shaped and influenced the nature of domestic conflict in South Korea.

'Armed globalization', coined by Claude Serfati (2002), is a term designating '"the recent militarization of the planet" and the unlimited war associated with the globalization of capital'. The key assertion is that contrary to neoliberal discourse, globalization does not represent the highest stage of peace. On the contrary, the globalization of capital and the militarization of the planet are closely linked. The former leads the world to the 'criminalization of social resistance' to neoliberal globalization, and the belief that those who do resist deserve punishment in military fashion. According to Serfati, who cites US Congressional research documents, the number of armed US military interventions around the world in the 1990s exceeded those for the entire period of 1945 to 1990.

Serfati also points to a report produced in June 2000 by a Commission on American National Interests, which included members of Congress. The report identified the defence of globalization as a vital US interest that should be ensured, with military force if necessary. Thus, for Serfati:

> McDonalds cannot prosper without McDonnell Douglas, the enterprise which designed the F-15 fighter for the Air Force, because the market

only functions and prospers on condition that the rights of property are guaranteed and protected, which demands a political framework itself backed up by military force.

(Serfati n.d.)

Historical legacies: the Cold War and Korea[1]

Korea had been a Japanese colony for thirty-six years. With the end of the Second World War, Korea was divided into two antagonistic nations by the two superpowers, the USA and the Soviet Union. This division and the subsequent outbreak of the Korean War in 1950 made South Korea a front-line state of the Cold War; therefore, it was one of the most anti-communist and militarized nations in the world. It was only in the 1980s that South Korea experienced a renaissance in radicalism, as a response to the massacre of innocent citizens by the military in May 1980. Throughout the Cold War, the labour movement was severely repressed due to accusations that it was communist in nature. The Korean War also transformed South Korea (from now on, Korea, unless noted otherwise) into one of the most USA-dependent countries politically, economically and, particularly, militarily. Korea has allowed the USA not only to deploy its army in the country but to also exercise command over the Korean military.

In the 1970s, however, Korea succeeded in transforming itself into one of the economic success stories of the Third World. It owed this to a combination of factors, including the destruction of the landlord class through successful land reform that was instituted to compete with North Korea; the weak labour and people's movements, which enabled gross exploitation by Korean industrialists; a state-initiated outward industrialization policy that was pushed by the military, which took power through a 1961 coup; and the favourable policies of the USA towards Korean industrialization due to the Cold War.[2] In the 1970s, the image of Korea changed from that of an 'aid-junkie' to a country that was economically successful, in spite of political failure as symbolized by the military dictatorship. In contrast, North Korea, which had once belonged to the elite group among socialist countries and had been expected to surpass South Korea in terms of economic performance, started to fall well behind.

The Cold War system in Korea began to be challenged in the 1980s with the rapid growth of the people's (*minjung*) movement (see Koo 1993), which succeeded in ending the military dictatorship in 1987. Korean democratization led to the blooming of various progressive movements, albeit short-lived ones. The collapse of the existing socialist countries in the late 1980s brought to Korea a resurgence of conservatism and anti-communism. Therefore, in spite of the end of the Cold War globally, the Korean peninsula has remained a final stronghold of the Cold War.

It is true that the Clinton government pursued post-Cold-War-oriented policies with regard to North Korea; besides, Kim Dae Jung, the long-time

Table 12.1: Share of foreign capital in Korean stock market

June 1997	Dec. 1998	Dec. 1999	Dec. 2001	Dec. 2003	May 2004
3.2%	10.9%	21.8%	36.9%	40.1%	43.7%

Source: Korea Security Exchange, Annual Report (2004).

liberal opposition leader, succeeded in taking over power thanks to the economic crisis of 1997, which occurred just before the presidential election, and pursued the so-called Sunshine policy towards the North (Moon and Steinberg 1999). The Bush Junior administration, however, has since succeeded in turning back the clock in the Korean peninsula.[3]

The post-Cold-War period and the Korean case

There are two issues that require some preliminary discussion at this stage. First, the nature of the post-Cold-War international order itself; and second, the way that it broadly affects social and political developments in the Korean case. One book worth mentioning and related to the first issue is the well-known and contentious *Empire* by Hardt and Negri (2000). Arguing that the key characteristic of post-Cold-War global order is the emergence of 'Empire', the book presents us with four basic assumptions regarding the post-Cold-War international order (see Sonn 2004):

1   That 'Empire' is inevitable.
2   That it is desirable.
3   That the old 'leftist' strategy of anti-globalization is 'damaging' and 'reactionary'.
4   That the alternative is, rather, to accelerate globalization in order to make possible the emergence of counter-Empire as soon as possible.

In conclusion, the book advises that 'rather than resist capital's globalization, we have to accelerate the process' (Hardt and Negri 2000: 206).

Despite having many merits, Hardt and Negri's work is tainted with both Eurocentrism and ultra-leftist idealism.[4] The authors' position is contradictory to mine: borrowing from Callinicos (2003: 21), I argue that neoliberal globalization constitutes nothing less than a savage capitalist war against the planet (Marcos 2002: 270) and the interests of humanity. Neoliberal globalization exacerbates the destructive ecological tendencies of capitalism, causes extreme social polarization, places everyone in a race towards the bottom, and leads us to the militarization of the planet.

Furthermore, I contend here that *Empire* fails to pay attention to one very important aspect of the post-Cold-War world order, that of armed globalization. Armed globalization, as represented by the invasions of Afghanistan and Iraq by the USA, shows that the world is far from the one imagined by Hardt and Negri.

The Korean case has special relevance to the question of the impact of neoliberal and armed globalization on social and political development and conflict in Asia. Even though virtually no country today is free from the pressures of globalization, the case of Korea is illuminating in many respects. First of all, prior to the Asian economic crisis of 1997–8, Korea had been one of the most 'protected' markets in the capitalist world. It was particularly closed in terms of capital markets and foreign direct investment. Rather than foreign direct investment, foreign loans had been the dominant form of financing from abroad;[5] thus, the share of foreign capital in the Korean stock market just prior to the economic crisis stood at a mere 3 per cent (see Table 12.1).

The Asian economic crisis, however, changed everything. Before analysing the consequences of the crisis, we need to examine its causes. The mainstream neoliberal school as represented by the IMF, which had previously regarded Korean success as a result of effective state intervention, suddenly changed its position and argued that the cause of the crisis was the 'crony capitalism' in the developmental state, and that the right prescription for the economic ailment was the market.[6] Others, however, attribute the crisis to the tendency for over-accumulation in capitalism itself, which produced an unprecedented amount of speculative capital at the global level. Still others argue that the rapid economic liberalization process initiated by the Kim Young Sam government just before the crisis was the main cause; in short, they blame neoliberalism for the crisis. It is true that at the deepest level, the over-accumulation tendency was an important cause of the Korean crisis. It does not, however, explain why it was Korea and not any other country that suffered the crisis at that particular time. In order to answer the question, we need more concrete analysis, for example by taking account of the tangible effects of the end of the Cold War (Cumings 1998). During the Cold War, the USA tolerated the East Asian economic model because it needed an economically strong East Asia to act as a bastion against communism. With the end of the Cold War in 1997, however, the USA had developed an interest in opening up markets globally for transnational capital. Ultimately, it was the worst combination of the old model during the Park Chung Hee era and neoliberal economic policy that constituted the main cause of the crisis:[7]

> Whatever the cause of the crisis, Korea was to experience drastic upheavals as a result of the pressures of neo-liberal economic globalization in the wake of the Asian economic crisis. It was forced to accept the harsh IMF 'bail out' package to avert economic collapse. The package stipulated a strict austerity policy, liberalization of trade and capital markets, the privatization of public companies, increase in labour flexibility, abolition of restrictions on foreign ownership, lowering of

*chaebol*s' (family-owned Korean conglomerate) debt ratio to the global standard, and so forth.[8] The harsh policies that the IMF dictated to Korea disregarded the differences between Korea and Latin America, and led the IMF to admit later that it had made mistakes.

(Stiglitz 1998; 2003)

The scope of this change can be discerned from the share of foreign capital in the Korean stock market, which skyrocketed to 43 per cent in 2004 – a by-product of the neoliberal reforms designed by the IMF and implemented by the Kim Dae Jung government (see Table 12.1). Besides, a number of major Korean companies that had previously been symbols of Korean success were sold at cheap prices. For instance, Daewoo Motors and Samsung Motors were taken over by GM and Renault, respectively. The major national banks were taken over by foreign finance capital; the First Bank of Korea, into which the Korean government had injected 1,700 billion won (US$1,500 million) after the economic crisis, was sold to New Bridge Capital, an American speculative capital group, for a mere 500 billion won (US$420 million). As a result, the share of foreign ownership in the banking industry rose to 63 per cent in 2004.

Neoliberal globalization, thus, has resulted in internal fractures within the Korean ruling bloc. In contrast to their full support for a neoliberal labour policy intended to enhance labour flexibility, *chaebol*s have vigorously opposed reform measures that have been targeted at them, including regulations on investment and management restructuring. They have claimed that these measures are part of a conspiracy by foreign capital to take over the Korean economy. In particular, Kim Woo Jung, the owner of the Daewoo Group and the President of FKI (the Federation of Korean Industries) – the most powerful business association – resisted vigorously. *Chaebol*s failed to mobilize public opinion, however, because of anti-*chaebol* sentiments among the Korean people; in fact, most Koreans blame the *chaebol*s for the economic crisis. Besides, the Korean government held strategic power over the *chaebol*s. As the virtual owner of the major national banks, the government controlled the financial sources that the *chaebol*s desperately needed to overcome the financial crisis. Therefore, the clash between the global neoliberalism-oriented Kim Dae-Jung government and the Wall Street–Treasury–IMF complex, on the one hand, and Park Chung Hee's national capitalism-model-oriented *chaebol*s on the other, ended in victory for the former. Kim Woo Jung, the spokesman for the latter, had to flee the country to avoid prosecution as the Daewoo Group sank into bankruptcy.

It could be argued, then, that the Korean state is now acting more and more like 'the executive committee', presiding over the interests of foreign finance capital rather than those of domestic capital. In other words, the Korean state has increasingly become a 'denationalized foreign capital-luring state' rather than a classical 'national competition state' (*der nationale Wettbewerbstaat*) or a 'Schumpeterian competition state'.[9]

Finally, the Korean case has special meaning as well, given a particular paradox that it has long embodied. In spite of a deeply entrenched and strong sense of 'economic nationalism',[10] Korea has been one of the countries most dependent on the USA in the area of military defence. The USA has not only maintained a permanent military base in Korea but also wielded command of the military operations of the Korean Army. Significantly, the US military presence has sometimes aroused popular anger at the perceived trampling of Korean national sovereignty, as exemplified by the year-long candlelight protests against the death of two high school girls run down by a US tank in 1997 (as discussed further below). Popular anger led the Bush administration to plan for, in the near future, moving US troops from Seoul to a rural area that would attract less attention from the Korean people (*The Korea Times*, 6 March 2003).

Impact of neoliberal economic globalization on Korean society

In spite of the economic nationalist and protectionist tendencies of a succession of Korean governments,[11] Korea has actually long been unable to completely escape the pressures of neoliberal economic globalization. The first set of neoliberal economic policies was forced on the Korean government by the IMF as early as 1979, and included measures such as a fiscal austerity policy and a reduction in food subsidies. These measures were geared to overcome an economic crisis caused by the Park Chung Hee government's over-investment in heavy industry, and the second global oil shock of the 1970s. Even if the Park Chung Hee government was indirectly toppled by popular uprisings targeted against economic hardship caused by the neoliberal austerity policies, these policies continued to be pursued by successive military governments (see Sonn 1987: 309–28). In addition, in the mid-1990s, the Kim Young Sam government implemented neoliberal economic policies as well, in order to address the requirements of the Uruguay Round. In particular, the government liberalized the financial market in 1994 in order to join the OECD, which resulted in a drastic increase in foreign borrowing that contributed to the economic crisis of 1997.[12] Neoliberal economic policies, however, was launched in Korea in full

Table 12.2: Major poverty indicators

	Gini index	*Absolute poverty index**
1996	0.298	5.91%
2002	0.358	11.46%

*Absolute poverty index = households below the absolute poverty line/total households.
Source: Statistics Office of Korea, Social Indicators of Korea 2003.

force only after the Asian economic crisis, and in the subsequent Kim Dae Jung government.

Neoliberal economic policies implemented in South Korea since the Asian crisis have resulted in dramatic social polarization and have exacerbated social conflict between the rich and the poor, for example in the form of labour disputes, which will be discussed below. Table 12.2 tells part of the story quite succinctly.

In this connection, it is useful to pay particular attention to the changes in Korea's Gini index. The Gini index reached its highest point in Korean history (since the government started to measure it in the late 1970s) following the implementation of Kim Dae Jung's neoliberal economic reforms. The irony is that Kim, previously a long-time opposition leader and democracy activist, was widely regarded as the most 'progressive' and egalitarian of the politicians. Kim's reputation led successive military governments to accuse him of being pro-communist. It is well known that he suffered under the military government of Korea for his political activism, for which he eventually came to be awarded the Nobel Peace Prize in 2000. Furthermore, even when he did pursue neoliberal policies as President, he named his own party the Common People's (*Somin*) Party. Ironically, Kim contributed to the polarization of Korean society in more ways than any other previous president, including the harshest of the military dictators.[13]

Comparative data may be useful in shedding some light on recent changes in Korean society, especially as far as social inequality is concerned. Before the full thrust of neoliberal economic globalization, Korea, in terms of social inequality, was located somewhere between conservative and liberal regimes.[14] In other words, Korea was more egalitarian than the USA and the UK, but less so than some continental European countries.

After the IMF-induced reforms in the wake of the Asian crisis, however, social inequality in Korea became worse than what exists in established (neo)liberal societies (see Table 12.3). Even more shocking is the pace of social polarization in Korea – the Gini index has risen by 0.060 in four years after the implementation of neoliberal economic policies, whereas the index

Table 12.3: International comparison of Gini index

	1987(a)	1996(b)	2000(c)	(b– a) or (c– b)
Social Democratic	0.235	0.239	–	+0.004
Conservative	0.263	0.267	–	+0.004
Liberal	0.307	0.339	–	+0.031
Korea	–	0.298	0.358	+0.060

Source: Sonn (2005).
Note: The classification of Social Democratic (for example, Sweden), Conservative (for example, continental Europe) and Liberal (for example, the UK and USA) statuses is based on Esping-Anderson's (1980) well-known work.

has risen only by 0.031 in ten years in those societies in the West that have experienced the fastest degree of polarization.

One outgrowth of increasing social inequality has been the intensification of labour disputes in Korea. There has been a kind of 'Korean exceptionalism' in relation to progressive movements, in general, and labour movements, in particular, when Korea is compared to Europe or Latin America (Sonn 1997; Koo 2001). The Korean experience is meaningful in a dual sense: the 'earlier absence' of such movements due to strong anti-communism that resulted from the Cold War division of the Korean peninsula into two antagonistic states; and their 'late blooming', particularly after the Kwangju massacre (for details, see Katsiaficas 2003) by the military in 1980. In particular, since democratization in 1987, the Korean working class have succeeded in establishing the long-awaited national federation of independent and militant trade unions, that is the Korean Confederation of Trade Unions (KCTU or *Minju-nochong*). The labour movement successfully launched the first general strike in Korean history against the Kim Young Sam government when the latter planned to legalize layoffs in such a way as to enable Korean capitalists to introduce neoliberal flexible production strategies.[15]

With the economic crisis of 1997, however, the IMF-prescribed neoliberal policies changed everything. Utilizing the crisis as a good opportunity to crack down on the militant Korean labour movement, both state and capital executed a series of unprecedented attacks against labour in the form of massive layoffs, legalization of unilateral dismissal by employers, and the privatization of major public corporations such as Korea Heavy Industries,

Table 12.4: Annual working days lost due to labour disputes (per 1,000 workers; unit = days)

	Korea	Japan	Germany	UK	USA
1995	30.7	1.4	7.7	18.9	52.4
1996	68.4	0.8	3.1	58.3	43.7
1997	33.6	2.0	1.6	10.1	36.7
1998	119.1	1.9	0.5	11.9	46.6
1999	109.1	1.6	2.4	10	11.9
2000	144.1	0.7	0.3	20.3	155

Source: Korean Labour Institute, World Labor Statistics (2002).

Table 12.5: Number of workers prosecuted after labour disputes

1996	1997	1998	1999	2000	2001	2002
149	43	219	129	97	241	200

Source: KCTU, White Papers on Labour Oppression (2003).

Korea Electric Power Corporation, Korea Telecom and Pohang Iron & Steel Co., which resulted in a large number of public sector workers being laid off. For instance, in the three-year period from 1998 to 2000, the public sector saw 131,100 workers, or 18.3 per cent of all public workers, laid off (The Ministry of Planning and Budget 2002). In response, Korean workers have had to carry out some painful defensive struggles against state policies. For instance, at the initial stage of the crisis, the KCTU presented work-sharing as the alternative to massive layoffs and fought for it, yet the government simply ignored the proposal and, instead, legalized massive layoffs (Korean Tripartite Commission, http://www.Img.go.kr).

There is a host of statistical data that demonstrate the intensification of labour disputes arising from the implementation of neoliberal economic reforms. The average number of annual working days lost due to labour disputes per 1,000 workers in the last three years just prior to the economic crisis (1998–2000) was 44.2 days. This figure rose to 124.1 days after the crisis (see Table 12.4) and other sets of data show the same troubling pattern. The number of workers annually prosecuted for labour disputes, for instance, has almost doubled from 96 persons to 177 persons (see Table 12.5). Furthermore, in September 2003, six labour leaders committed suicide in protest against neoliberal globalization policies.

Another major consequence of neoliberal globalization is the deepening of internal differentiation within the Korean working class, particularly as reflected in the dramatic increase in the number of casual workers (Koo 2002). These workers, who had comprised about 46 per cent of the Korean workforce in 1997, surpassed the number of regular workers in 1999. By 2000, casual workers constituted 52.1 per cent of the Korean workforce; however, a new study shows that if we apply OECD standards of classification to Korea, casual workers comprise an astounding 58.4 per cent of the workforce in 2000 (see Table 12.6).

This dramatic increase in casual workers has introduced two new phenomena into the Korean labour movement. It has, first of all, intensified internal disputes within the working class, particularly between regular and casual workers, and between male and female workers (a high proportion of casual workers are female); thus, it has been increasingly difficult for cohesive action among the working class. Casualization of the workforce has also encouraged new efforts to organize casual workers and build new forms of solidarity. In fact, even though efforts have been far from satisfactory from the point of view of social solidarity, there have been instances of regular

Table 12.6: Proportion of casual workers to the total number of workers

1996	1997	1998	1999	2000
43.2%	45.7%	46.9%	50.6%	52.1% (58.4%)

Source: Sonn (2004).

workers going on strike to fight for the rights of their colleagues who are employed on a casual basis. For instance, the trade union of Kumho Tire, a world-famous tyre company, succeeded in 2003 in making the company promise to apply the same wage structures to casual workers. The KCTU also threatened to launch a general strike against the government's plan to give capital greater freedom in employing more casual workers in October 2004, which prompted the government to postpone deliberations on the law to the next session of the National Assembly.

The peasantry are another group that has suffered from neoliberal globalization. Like many other East Asian countries, Korea is highly populated in terms of a human/land ratio; as a result, Korean agriculture has a very low level of international competitiveness because of the lack of economies of scale. Since neoliberal globalization has meant a virtual death sentence for Korean agriculture, Korean peasants have vigorously fought against it. For instance, to protest the government's policy to open agricultural markets, including the rice market – the staple of the Korean diet – and to stop the government's purchase of rice from farmers, a Korean peasant protested by committing suicide in public in September 2003 at Cancun, Mexico. This episode succeeded in preventing an important WTO meeting, which would have seen a discussion of the liberalization of the world's agricultural sector (*The Korea Times*, 15 September 2003).

The most severe domestic conflict linked to agricultural issues was caused by neoliberal globalization policies related to an FTA (Free Trade Agreement) signed between Korea and Chile in 2004, to promote the export of Korean manufactured goods to Chile. The Korean peasantry, the most obvious losers of the treaty, would have lost the domestic fruit market to Chilean farmers and tried, unsuccessfully, to carry out firm protests against it. The issue became very emotional, and even the National Assembly was divided – not along the usual party lines, but along pro-rural and pro-urban lines.[16]

One major development against neoliberal globalization has been the founding of a new organization in 2000, the National People's Solidarity (*Minjung-yondae*). This umbrella organization comprises different sections of Korean society, which, until recently, seldom worked with one another. It has become increasingly evident to anti-globalization activists that workers, the peasantry, the urban poor and various organizations representing disaffected sections of society need to set up a united front to carry out their struggles more effectively. As a result, in March 2000, thirty-five progressive organizations including the KCTU, the National Coalition of Peasants (*Chunnong*), the National Confederation of the Poor (*Chunbinyon*), the Korean Democratic Labour Party (*Minju-nodongdang*) and the National Association of Professors for Democratic Society (*Mingyohyup*) formed the National People's Solidarity. In addition, due largely to the economic hardship suffered by many people as a result of neoliberal economic reforms, the Korean Democratic Labour Party (KDLP) succeeded in winning 13 per cent of total votes and ten seats in the 2004 Parliamentary elections. It became the third largest political party in the National Assembly, and it was virtually the first time in Korean history that an ideologically progressive political party had succeeded in winning seats in the National Assembly. In contrast to the conservative parties, the KDLP opposes neoliberalism and fights for various progressive programmes such as free education, free health care and 'taxing the rich'. It is true that anti-communism still works as an obstacle against the KDLP, while regionalism, which had been the dominant cleavage in Korean politics since democratization in 1987 (for details, see Sonn 2003b), hinders the further development of the KDLP. Neoliberalism, however, is helping the KDLP gain support from the economic losers.

The struggle among some sections of society to resist neoliberal globalization policies has produced internal splits within social movements as well, and these are especially centred on which strategies to adopt. After democratization in 1987, the democratic camp in Korea has been divided into two broad movements.[17] One is the more traditional *minjung* (people's) movement that is basically class based, particularly low-class based, and has more or less radical tendencies. The other is a newer movement, a citizens' movement that can be regarded as a Korean version of the so-called cross-class new social movements that have emerged in the West in the last couple of decades. The new citizens' movement is primarily represented by the moderately reformist and liberal-oriented sections of the middle class that tended to distance themselves from the radical *minjung* movement, particularly in its early stages.

Once the citizens' movement succeeded in establishing itself in Korean politics and gaining social legitimacy in the early 1990s with the help of the conservative mainstream mass media, it maintained an ambivalent relationship of co-operation and conflict with it. The full-fledged arrival of a neoliberal globalization policy under the Kim Dae Jung government in the late 1990s, however, introduced a new source of conflict and ideological struggle between the two groups. Considering the old Park Chung Hee model of an authoritarian, state-controlled economy as the 'principal enemy' of Korean society, the citizens' movement largely endorsed the policies of Kim Dae Jung and of his successor, Roh Mu Hyun. The logic that it held on to was that neoliberal reforms would dismantle the old, statist Park Chung Hee model. In contrast, the *minjung* movement has targeted the growing, seemingly inexorable force of global neoliberalism and not the already dying

Park Chung Hee model as the principal enemy of Korean society. These two different positions are related to the above-mentioned different diagnoses of the causes of the Korean economic crisis in 1997.

One example of friction between the people's and citizens' movements concerns a disagreement over how to reduce the powers of the *chaebol*s. An organization called People's Solidarity for Participatory Democracy (*Chamyo-yondae*), the most powerful and radically inclined among the citizens' organizations, sought to achieve the goal by merely enhancing the power of small stock holders. In fact, it had gone so far as to sue *chaebol*s such as Samsung on behalf of foreign small stock holders, that is speculative finance capital, with the argument that in the age of globalization, the nationality of the stock holder does not matter.[18] In contrast, the *minjung* movement has argued that the real alternative is to promote workers' control of *chaebol*s (see People's Solidarity for Social Progress 2000).

Another example of conflict concerns the electoral process. The citizens' group campaigned against corruption and devoted itself to urging people not to vote for corrupt politicians in the 2000 and 2004 Congressional elections. The *minjung* group, on the other hand, criticized the anti-corruption campaign for distracting people from punishing the government at the polls for its neoliberal policies (see Kim Song-koo 2000).

The unprecedented impeachment of President Roh by a National Assembly, which was under the control of the Cold-War-oriented and conservative Grand National Party, also triggered a series of fierce debates between the two camps. Believing the impeachment to be a 'Parliamentary *coup d'état*', the citizens' groups launched a full-fledged rescue mission for Roh. On the other hand, the hard-liners of the *minjung* movement criticized the rescue effort, and argued that the real danger was not the reactionary counterattack represented by the Grand National Party – the giant conservative opposition party – but the 'neoliberal reform fascism' of President Roh (see http://www.another0415.net for these radical arguments).

Finally, neoliberal globalization has intensified conflicts within the ruling bloc. As discussed above, whereas the Kim Dae Jung and Roh Mu-hyun governments have implemented neoliberal *chaebol* reform policies, the *chaebol*s have resisted them. There has been growing conflict between the government and the Grand National Party, which has been far more sympathetic towards the *chaebol*s' complaints on the issue.

Impact of armed globalization on South Korea

The impact of armed globalization on domestic conflicts in Korea is epitomized in the remarkable rise of anti-Americanism in Korea, as well as in internal disputes related to that issue. Historically, owing to strong anti-communism sentiments, Korea had been relatively free from anti-Americanism; however, the Kwangju massacre by the military in 1980, approved by the US military in Korea,[19] triggered a strong wave of anti-

Americanism among students and social activists. That first wave was limited to the narrow circle of radical students and *minjung* movements, and weakened after the breakdown of actually existing state socialist countries from the late 1980s. Neoliberal economic policies in the late 1990s triggered a second, broader wave of anti-Americanism, which involved 'common people', including the relatively privileged middle class. These policies were seen to be dictated by the Wall Street–Treasury–IMF complex.

The development of armed globalization made matters worse. Throwing away Clinton's *détente* policy towards North Korea and demonizing North Korea as well as Iraq as part of an 'Axis of Evil', George W. Bush not only pursued a policy of isolating North Korea, but also forced South Korea to slow down its so-called Sunshine policy of appeasement. Besides, the USA was believed to have forced the Korean government to send its troops to the unjust and unpopular war in Iraq, even though the majority of the Korean population was against the war.[20]

The situation was exacerbated by the already-mentioned terrible incident in which two high school girls were killed by a US Army tank on 13 July 2002; the US military court, however, found the soldiers responsible not guilty on 22 November 2002 (*The Korea Times*). The incident triggered daily candlelight ceremonies nationwide that hundreds of thousands of ordinary people participated in voluntarily. This helped Roh Mu-hyun, who promised

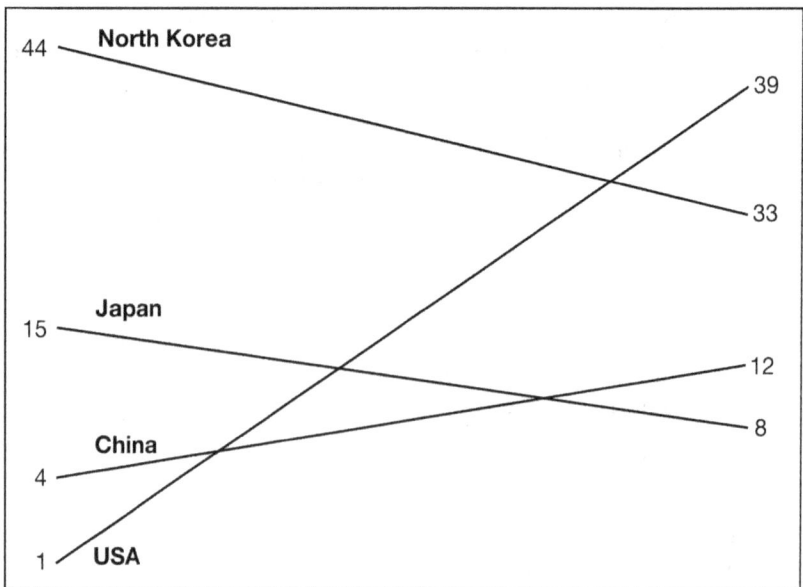

Figure 12.1: Rise of Anti-Americanism in Korea

Source: Dong A Ilbo, 15 June 2004, on the basis of Korean Gallup, R & R surveys.

a more independent foreign policy from the USA, win the presidential election of December 2002.

The spectacular rise of anti-Americanism worldwide after the invasion of Iraq prompted a US research centre to conduct a survey on anti-Americanism in fifteen countries. According to the survey results announced in May 2004, 50 per cent of Koreans answered that they had negative feelings towards the USA, whereas 46 per cent said that they had positive feelings. According to a different survey conducted by a Korean newspaper, 80 per cent of Koreans said that the country should not follow in the USA's footsteps as the Korean and US governments held different opinions on security issues related to the Korean peninsula; 20 per cent of Koreans held the opposite view (*Hankyoreh*, 12 May 2004).

The rise of anti-Americanism is best demonstrated in the change in the Korean people's perception of security threats. About ten years ago, in 1993, 44 per cent named North Korea and only 1 per cent named the USA when asked which country posed the most dangerous threat to Korea's national security. According to a recent survey conducted in January 2004, however, the USA ranked first with 39 per cent of respondents identifying it as the greatest source of threat to Korea's national security. In other words, the USA surpassed North Korea by six percentage points as the country that most Koreans felt posed the greatest threat (Figure 12.1) (*Donga Ilbo*, 15 June 2004).

Significantly, armed globalization has intensified not only anti-Americanism in Korea but also internal disputes in Korea concerning several key issues, such as policy towards North Korea, policy towards the Iraq War, Korea–US relations and other matters. For instance, George W. Bush's hard-line policy towards North Korea encouraged Cold-War-minded ultra-right-wing groups in Korea to start criticizing the *détente*-oriented Sunshine policy of the Kim Dae Jung government. This was followed by fierce South–South conflict (between the supporters and opponents of the sunshine policy) on the issue of South–North (Korean) relations (Sonn 2003a). A related and noteworthy issue is the recent activation of ultra-rightist movements. Until recent years, right-wing forces in Korea had not felt any need to organize themselves as social movements, since Korean politics had guaranteed a virtually monopolistic hegemony of their anti-communist position. The sunshine policy and growing anti-Americanism in Korea, however, have made them feel the need to organize. For instance, in December 2000, old anti-communist organizations and fundamentalist Christians organized a national alliance called Liberty Citizens Solidarity (*Jayusimin-yondae*) to fight liberal and progressive forces in Korean society. Korean civil society, therefore, has become a battlefield of three social forces: progressive (*Minjung-yondae*), liberal (*Sinminsahoi-yondaehaei*) and ultra-right (*Jayusimin-yondae*). Fortunately, up till now at least, the battles between these social forces have been manifested only in the form of cyberdebates, demonstrations and counter-demonstrations rather than physical violence. Yet, no one can guarantee that they will not accelerate towards physical violence.

Conclusion

This chapter has analysed how the post-Cold-War international order characterized by neoliberal globalization and armed globalization has shaped and influenced domestic conflicts in Korea. As mentioned earlier, neoliberal and armed globalization constitute nothing less than 'a planetary war' against humanity, that is a 'Fourth World War' (to borrow the words of Subcommandante Marcos 2002: 270) that has already begun. To win this war, we need to counter neoliberal globalization with the globalization of people's movements, and armed globalization with the globalization of the peace movement. In particular, if we fail to counter armed globalization with a globalization of the peace movement, then with the re-election of President Bush, the worst scenario in the Korean peninsula – an outbreak of another war in the peninsula –could materialize in relation to the North Korean nuclear issue.

Notes

1 For the best textbook on the Korean modern history, see Cumings (1997).
2 There is a voluminous literature from different schools of thought on the topic. To name a few works, see Hamilton (1986), Deyo (1987),White (1988) and Evans (1995).
3 This does not mean that the recent US–North Korean conflict is completely the Cold War conflict. On the contrary, the conflict is deeply related with the post-Cold-War order as well. To put it more precisely, the US–North Korean conflict is related to the armed globalization mentioned earlier. The fact that President Bush included in the 'Axis of Evil' not only North Korea but also Iraq, which bears no relation to the Cold War supports this thesis. In conclusion, the recent US–North Korean conflict has the characteristics of a combination of the Cold War and the post- Cold-War order (especially armed globalization).
4 For the debate on the book, see Balakrishnan (2003).
5 Eurocentrism is a tendency to perceive and analyse the social world from the perspective of the Western advanced countries (see Said 1978). For instance, even Marx argued in his early period that however brutal it might have been, colonialism was an inevitable historical process for historical development (Marx 1972). We also can define ultra-leftist idealism as a tendency to present an extreme political position on the basis of a one-sided analysis which ignores complex social dynamics and the long process of historical development. For example, one could call ultra-leftist idealism the argument that the progressive forces of the Third World must support the advancement of colonialism since it will shorten the coming of socialism.
6 Curiously, in his earlier book that was published during his exile in the USA in the mid-1980s, Kim Dae-Jung criticized the Korea economy for being 'over-closed'. According to him, in 1981, the total accumulated amount of foreign direct investment comprised only 5.7 per cent of the total accumulated foreign capital in Korea, whereas it was 85.1 per cent and 64.2 per cent, respectively, in Singapore and Taiwan (Kim 1985: 32).

7 See, for instance, Kang (2002). For a different view, see Wade (1988).

8 Contrary to the analysis of the IMF, the radical liberalization of financial markets in 1994 by the Kim Young Sam government, undertaken in a bid to join the OECD, was one of the main causes of the Korean crisis. The overemphasis on neoliberalism, however, makes us ignore many problems produced by the old Park Chung Hee model.

9 For instance, it demanded that the average debt ratio of 70 *chaebol* groups be reduced from 400 per cent to 200 per cent within two years.

10 For the concepts of 'national competition state' and 'Schumpeterian competition state', see Hirsch (1995) and Jessop (2002: 95–139), respectively. According to them, the state in the West has recently transformed from the Keynesian welfare state to a Schumpeterian competition state whose main goal is to enhance international competitiveness in the global market. In the case of Korea, however, with the introduction of neoliberal policies, the main goal of the state was changed to lure foreign capital rather than enhance the international competitiveness of domestic capital against foreign capital. Therefore, the state has been more concerned in satisfying foreign capital rather than domestic capital. I name this kind of state a 'denationalized foreign capital-luring state', distinct from the Keynesian or Schumpeterian competition state that Hirsch and Jessop observed in Western advanced countries.

11 This does not deny that Korean capitalism is dependent capitalism.

12 It does not mean that Korea had pursued autarky-oriented policies. On the contrary, as is well known, Korea had integrated into the world capitalist system actively by pursuing export-oriented industrialization. In other words, Korea had pursued its own version of 'globalization', but not neoliberal globalization.

13 The total accumulated foreign borrowing more than tripled during the period 1994–7.

14 For the classification of different regimes of modern capitalism, see Esping-Anderson (1980). In this path-breaking book, he classified the Western countries into three categories. The first group is made up of social-democratic regimes such as Sweden, which emphasize the principle of universalism and responsibility of the state. The second group consists corporate–conservative regimes such as those in continental Europe (Germany, France, etc.), characterized by the preservation of status differentials and traditional families. The final group is made up of liberal regimes such as the USA and the UK, which depend on the market.

15 Some radical scholars attribute the cause of the economic crisis in 1997 to this general strike (Chang 2001). They argue that the general strike defeated the government's plan to implement major economic restructuring by increasing labour flexibility, and also made the government a lame duck, which in turn contributed to the acceleration of the economic crisis.

16 *The Jung-Ang Daily*, 16 February 2004.

17 See Sonn (1995), also Koo (2002: 118–20) and Kim Sunhyuk (2000).

18 This recalls what Petras (2001) has labelled 'NGOs in the service of imperialism';

19 For the controversy surrounding the role of the US Army in the massacre, see Clark (1988).

20 According to a national survey, 57.5 per cent of Koreans were against sending Korean troops to Iraq, whereas 38.2 per cent were for it (*Hankyoreh*, 22 September 2003).

13 The USA, China and identity politics in Taiwan

Lee Wen-Chih and Yang Der-Ruey

Introduction

Taiwan as a society comprises many waves of migrants who have arrived from the Chinese mainland at different times. They have formed diverse ethnic groups and, historically, have often aligned with polities outside Taiwan to boost their domestic political position. Consequently, interventions by foreign polities have always played a pivotal role in Taiwan's historical development.

Politics in contemporary Taiwan is primarily characterized by the ethnic-based political struggles between the *waisheng ren* (外省人 or 'mainlanders') who moved to Taiwan after the Second World War, and the *holo lang* (or 福佬人 'Hokkien') who migrated to Taiwan before 1945 and used to be the island's dominant ethnic group. In addition, there exist other minor migrant groups, the most notable of these being the Hakka (客家人), now the third largest ethnic community on the island. In this chapter, we contend that the changing relationship between the USA and China during the Cold War and post-Cold-War periods has exacerbated ethnic-based political tensions in Taiwan. We will also show that as ethnic-based conflict becomes increasingly significant in shaping domestic politics in Taiwan, it has also come to have a direct bearing on broader regional stability issues in so far as the geopolitical interests of China and the USA are concerned.

Despite the fact that one's political orientation is not determined by one's ethnicity, the contest between the two contrasting positions on the future status of Taiwan – 'reunification' (with China) and 'independence' (for Taiwan) – has, nevertheless, been gradually ethnicized as a struggle between the two largest migrant populations. Brought about by the dramatic changes of the post-Cold-War era, this conflict has become increasingly prominent in Taiwan's domestic politics. By projecting a tough pro-'indigenization' and pro-independence image, the Democratic Progress Party (DPP) has successfully assumed the role of political representative of Taiwan's ethnic majority, the *holo lang* (Hokkien-speaking population). As such, in the presidential election of 2000, the DPP defeated the long-standing Kuomintang (Chinese Nationalist Party) to become the ruling party in Taiwan. The political agenda of the DPP sharply contradicts China's stated intention of protecting its 'territorial integrity' but won a considerable measure of support from the USA. Disregarding furious protest from Beijing, the George W. Bush administration not only allowed Taiwanese President Chen Shui-Bian to transit and stop over in New York in 2001 and 2003,[1] but also approved the largest arms sale to Taiwan in recent decades.[2] These developments triggered a serious sense of crisis on the part of *waisheng ren* (mainlanders), who embrace a pan-Chinese identity and endorse reunification with China. Meanwhile, in fear of the possibility that Taiwan may eventually obtain independent status and become an instrument of US interests in the region, the People's Republic of China has sought allies within Taiwan.

The shifting nature of the relationship between Beijing and Washington complicates Taiwan's domestic politics. In the context of the Cold War (as well as the Vietnam War), the USA and China had forged an alliance against the Soviet Union (*Lian Zhong Zhi Su* or 聯中制蘇 , Sutter 1991), which helped produce US commitment to a One-China policy. This development – which came to pass after years of conflict between the two countries, including a history of military confrontation during the Korean War – severely damaged the standing of the then ruling anti-communist Kuomintang Party in Taiwan. This, in turn, encouraged the growth of a democracy movement in Taiwan that came to be increasingly identified with separatist political and cultural inclinations.

It is important for Taiwan that even in the present context – characterized by the ascendance of what many have dubbed an American Empire – the USA and China are increasingly locked in a relationship of mutual dependency. US power has pressured China to liberalize its economy and open up its markets to provide US capital with new and vast business opportunities. China's co-operation is also regarded with importance for the US war against terrorism. The USA, however, does not want to see an economically robust China emerge as a superpower that could challenge its global supremacy (Brzezinski 1997: 151–93); thus, US policy towards China requires nuance and balance. The baseline is that although co-operation is pursued, the USA could still confront Beijing in the event of a major collision of interests (Rice 2000: 55–7). On the other hand, despite all its suspicion and hostility towards the USA, China needs a healthy USA with a vibrant economy, since the latter's consumer market is literally the engine for China's much admired export growth. As such, Taiwan – as a political entity that is, in many ways, a direct product of the Cold War – cannot help but find itself being given the role of a US tool for containing China's regional (and global) ambitions in the US-dominated, post-Cold-War international order. Taiwan, however, is not quite ready to act out the role assigned to it by American Empire. Since the early 1990s, ethnic-based political struggle on the island has continuously intensified; thus, the impetus for Taiwan to declare outright independence is steadily escalating. Consequently, domestic politics in Taiwan holds the fuse that might trigger a cross-Straits war that could potentially draw the USA, the world's only superpower, and China, potentially a challenger, into a head-on collision.

The international context

Since the later half of the nineteenth century, access to and control over the Pacific Ocean has become a vital part of US geopolitical strategy (Solan 1988: 87–111). After its forays into Asia in the nineteenth century, most notably in the Philippines, the USA had an excellent opportunity after the Second World War to gain control over much of the Pacific. China was crucial to this plan as the USA hoped to utilize China in containing the rising ambitions of the Soviet Union, and to hold a commanding position in its potentially huge post-war market (FRUS 1947I: 775; FRUS 1948I; Hathaway 1984: 302). Yet, this plan was foiled by the Chinese Communist Party's victory in 1949. As a result, the USA applied the Truman Doctrine in East Asia and established the 'insular strategy'. This connected the countries on the first island chain of the Pacific – including Japan, South Korea, Taiwan and the Philippines, among other Southeast Asian countries – to form a naval line to contain the influence of communism that was emanating from the Asian continent, primarily from China.

The main theme of the USA's Asia–Pacific policy in the 1950s and 1960s was to synchronize the interests of the USA and its Asia–Pacific allies by means of bilateral security pacts and economic aid, in order to form a regional strategic system led by the USA. The situation, however, changed dramatically with the Vietnam War. In the late 1960s and early 1970s, the Nixon administration decided to carry out the 'align with China [in order] to restrain USSR (Lian Zhong Zhi Su)' policy (Sutter 1991). Consequently, the strategic importance of the naval line established along the first island chain, including the weight of Taiwan in it, was largely reduced, while China's strategic importance increased dramatically (Spanier 1985: 174–90; Sutter 1991: 5–7). This historic shift, which culminated in the severing of official US–Taiwanese diplomatic relations in 1979, virtually set the entire context for much of the ensuing difficulties and upheavals that Taiwan has since had to undergo.

Although China has replaced the USSR as the primary challenge to US hegemony in the Asia–Pacific since 1989, its economic reforms and open-door policy have made US policy-makers maintain good diplomatic relations with China, in terms of achieving regional stability and developing global markets (Brzezinski 1997: 158–73); this in spite of the continuing rule of the Chinese Communist Party in Beijing. The Bush Senior government clearly pointed out that US policy towards China was one of 'constructive engagement' in order to induce 'positive change' or 'peaceful evolution' for a democratic market economy (Baker 1991; Bush 1991). Almost at the same time, however, Bush approved the sale of long-awaited F-16 fighter jets to improve Taiwan's capability to defend itself against China, which demonstrated US concern for containing China's superpower ambitions (see Cui, this volume).

On the other hand, in more recent times, China has set out to redefine its economic and geopolitical relationship with the newly industrialized economies of ASEAN by means of 'good neighbour diplomacy' and by strengthening regional economic ties in an attempt to distinguish the interests of East Asia from those of the USA and Japan (Lee 1996: 130–1). Significantly, China has also improved relations with post-Soviet Russia.[3] In a joint declaration signed in Beijing in December 1992, China and Russia assured each other that neither would participate in any military or political alliance against the other. In September 1994, they went on further to declare a 'constructive partnership'. Later, the two countries together with the former Soviet republics of Kazakhstan, Kyrgyzstan and Tadjikistan commenced the Shanghai Five summit. This summit resulted in several agreements on boundaries, the reduction of military forces in border areas and measures to promote mutual trust in military affairs. It is significant that through these agreements, the former Soviet republics effectively reduced potential support for the separatist inclinations of some Islamic ethnic minorities, particularly in China's Xinjiang Province (Misra 2001).

During the Clinton administration (1992–2000), however, it became more apparent that the USA was actually pursuing a policy of simultaneous engagement with and containment of China (Lieberthal 1994: 36; Shambaugh 1995: 243–4) or so-called 'congagement'. Again, the aim was to open up China economically while, at the same time, preventing possible challenges to US supremacy (Carlucci *et al.* 2000: 65–6). On the one hand, this congagement strategy is illustrated by the use of WTO membership to encourage China to accelerate the opening up of its economy. On the other hand, there was the advent of the Theatre Missile Defences (TMD) project, involving Japan, Taiwan and South Korea, which aimed to deter the threat of China's powerful missile system to countries in the region (Allen *et al.* 2000).

At the beginning of the twenty-first century, we thus see that China has become the first potential source of challenge to US hegemony in the Asia–Pacific, and even globally. Following the main theme of the Nye Report of 1995 (Nye 1995; DoD 1995), the two important reports published by the US Department of Defense (DoD) in 2000 – the Joint Vision 2020 and Asia 2025 – clearly reflect this development. They both suggest that the USA should respond to the rise of China by preparing to deal seriously with it as an emerging military superpower. Condoleezza Rice, US Foreign Secretary under George W. Bush, once also suggested a redefinition of the USA–China relationship from one of 'strategic partner' to one of 'strategic competitor' (Rice 2000: 56). Even though 9/11 encouraged the USA to seek China's co-operation in the War on Terror, little has really changed. Not surprisingly, the Annual Report on the Military Power of the People's Republic of China, published by the US DoD in May 2004, acknowledges that China has already posited the USA as its top potential adversary, thus the USA should prioritize the containment of China as its most important strategy in the Asia–Pacific.

It is within this regional and global political context that recent political leaders in Taiwan have been tempted to invent the term *xin Taiwan ren* (新臺灣人 or new Taiwanese). As we shall see, the changing nature of USA–Chinese relations and US policy and geopolitical strategy in the region has promoted separatist sentiments in Taiwan, whether directly or indirectly. The exacerbation of domestic conflict between pro-independence and pro-reunification forces, which are often ethnically defined, is intricately connected to these regional and international developments.

Taiwan's identity politics: from 'China irredentism' to 'indigenization' (Ben Tu Hua, 本土化)

During the Cold War era, the ideological appeal of the Kuomintang regime was built on three canons: anti-communism, pro-Americanism and irredentism. Its policies of anti-communism and pro-Americanism won US support against the People's Republic of China, while the Kuomintang employed irredentism to call for the support of overseas Chinese and to legitimize its authoritarian rule in Taiwan. After the 1960s, this irredentism and authoritarian rule incurred animosity, especially from the Hokkien and Hakka ethnic groups. Kuomintang rule not only oppressed human rights and circumscribed political participation for all citizens of Taiwan (regardless of ethnicity), but also 'punished' the non-mainlanders for their 'blemished Chineseness' (or 'pseudo-Japaneseness') by regulating access to all sorts of public (political, cultural and educational) resources on the basis of Mandarin education. In the economic sphere, Kuomintang rule was characterized by coercive measures that involved land reform, food confiscation, property forfeiture and the like; these were geared to provide for the numerous immigrants who arrived in Taiwan with the Kuomintang in the 1940s. Although these measures benefited tenant farmers as well as some landlords-turned-new industrial/commercial capitalists, inevitably they alienated many middle-class and comparatively well-off non-mainlanders.

As US–Chinese relations entered a new phase in the 1970s and the USA began to reduce its all-out support for the Kuomintang regime, Kuomintang rule began to experience serious trouble not just domestically but also in terms of its international standing (Lee 1988: 23–4; Chu and Lin 1998). The direct result of the USA's new policy of appeasing China was Taiwan's expulsion from the United Nations in 1971 and the severance of Japan–Taiwan diplomatic relations in 1972. In addition, the oil shocks of the 1970s also seriously damaged Taiwan's economy and provided ammunition for various dissident groups that called for democracy and human rights, and/or the resolution of Taiwan's ambiguous international status once and for all (Chu 1992: 18–32).

The Kuomintang regime's response was to widen the opportunity for political participation by non-mainlanders. Hence, elections for so-called 'supplementary' Parliamentary seats, local councils and some local administrative headships were instituted. Although this helped the Kuomintang in the short run, the unintended consequence was the rise of localism and indigenism, which was potentially fatal to a regime that was dominated by mainlanders (Lee 1988: 21–3; Chu 1992: 48–98). The Kuomintang also launched a Keynesian-style Top Ten Construction project to win the allegiance of the broader citizenry by providing better economic welfare for all. This measure, however, exacerbated the long-standing north–south and urban–rural imbalance by clustering highly polluting industries such as petrochemicals and steel manufacturing in southern Taiwan while pooling most of the investment for transportation infrastructure in northern Taiwan. Consequently, the residents of southern Taiwan (mostly Hokkiens) suffered most of the negative effects (decades of heavy pollution) while receiving less of the benefits (higher income and better living standards) from Taiwan's economic development. Hence, they are inclined to view Taipei (臺北 which literally means 'north of Taiwan'), the seat of the central government and where the majority of large firms have their headquarters, as the site from which mainlanders exploit 'native Taiwanese' – a reference to the Hokkien-speaking population. Ironically, the Top Ten Construction project, which was aimed at strengthening the legitimacy of the Kuomintang regime, laid the social, economic and psychological foundations for broader dissent. Eventually, southern/rural Taiwan became the stronghold of anti-Kuomintang, anti-mainlander, pro-independence and Hokkien-centred political forces.

The legitimacy of the Kuomintang was further damaged when the Carter administration ceased official diplomatic relations with Taiwan in January 1979. The precarious position of the Kuomintang contributed to the outbreak of the largest political riots since its retreat to Taiwan – the Formosa Event of December 1979 in Kaoshiong, the largest city in southern Taiwan.[4] Since then, the emerging 'democracy movement' has tended to be identified with ethnic political movements in Taiwan, as they have both been involved in the Hokkien struggle against the authoritarian regime that was constructed by mainlanders and has since been monopolized by them (Wu 2002: 76–7). Even worse for the Kuomintang was the conservative and fervently anti-communist Reagan administration. Instead of receiving more favourable treatment as might have been expected, the Kuomintang government in 1982 was presented with the 817 Communiqué, in which the USA promised China that it will gradually reduce the quality and quantity of arms sales to Taiwan. This was surely one of the greatest diplomatic setbacks for the Kuomintang, and it certainly further damaged the legitimacy of its rule in Taiwan.

Moreover, the USA further pushed its allies to 'internationalize' and 'liberalize' their economies while waving the flag of free trade. With the demand from the USA, the Kuomintang government was obliged further to relax its stringent regulations on foreign exchange and tariffs, to privatize state-owned industries, and to allow multiple interest groups (in fact, the underlings of US companies in Taiwan) to access Taiwan's decision-making process so as to further open up Taiwan's markets to foreign capital (Chu 1992: 137–42). These had profound ramifications for local society and politics. In terms of politics, the most important implication was the waning of the authoritarian regime that has been laboriously entrenched by the Kuomintang since 1949. Privatization broke the linkage between the Kuomintang regime and the interests of a sizeable part of the population, while the opening up of the decision-making process increased the opportunity for diverse, conflicting social interests to intrude into the party–government system and thus gradually break up the cohesion of the party and officialdom. As a result, members of society gradually shunned away the control of the once overwhelming state and began to reassert their autonomy in the form of widespread civil disobedience (Chang 1989).

In sharp contrast, China's initiatives in relation to Taiwan during the same period were largely ignored. In fact, ever since the USA unilaterally terminated its official relationship with Taiwan, China began to launch a series of 'peace offensives' towards Taiwan. These included 'Nine Principles for the Peaceful Reunification with Taiwan' proposed by Yie Jianying in 1981,[5] the 'One Country, Two Systems' initiative in 1982,[6] which was applied to Hong Kong in later days, and 'Six Conceptions for Peaceful Reunification'[7] by Deng Xiaoping in 1983. The hope, obviously, was that these initiatives would find a base of domestic support within Taiwan and discourage the rise of separatism. It would not be unfair, however, to say that these 'peace offensives' produced little that was tangible.

In view of how the Kuomintang regime was besieged by a series of failures on the diplomatic front and incessant cases of civil disobediences on the domestic front, various dissident forces in Taiwan decided to seize the opportunity to make a groundbreaking move: the creation of an opposition party. Thus, the Democratic Progress Party (DPP) was founded in 1986. To the surprise of many, instead of suppressing the new party by force, the waning Kuomintang in 1987 repealed martial law that had stood in Taiwan for four decades, shortly after the founding of the DPP.

Despite the Kuomintang's attempts to appease its critics by giving concessions and extending democratization *ad locum*, the unrealistic nature of one of its ideological canons – Chinese irredentism – was subjected to suspicion and ridicule. Thus, the DPP, especially its militant separatist elements, was persuaded to distance the party's stance further from the Kuomintang's by making even stronger appeals to 'localization' or 'indigenization'. As a result, the DPP issued 'Resolution on Taiwan's Future' in 1988, which insisted that 'Taiwan's future should be decided by Taiwanese themselves'.[8] Apart from appealing to the 'localization' or 'indigenization' agenda, the DPP at that time was very quick to form a common front with all sorts of anti-establishment forces, including left-leaning activists friendly to communist China. Hence, the DPP managed to rise hand in hand with the burgeoning labour, farmer environmentalist and student movements in the late 1980s (Chu 1992: 99–124).

Faced with the vibrant united front of the DPP and various social movements, the waning Kuomintang government, then headed by the dying President Jiang Jingguo,[9] became increasingly sluggish. Soon after President Jiang Jingguo's death in 1988, however, Lee Deng-Hui, the first native Taiwanese to become the Chairman of the Kuomintang and President of the Republic of China (Taiwan), began his twelve-year rule that ushered in a new era of fresh uncertainties for Taiwan. Craftily sidelining the mainstream mainlander cliques within the party – many of whom later came to form the pro-reunification New Party – Lee gradually consolidated his grip on the Kuomintang, replacing its former Chinese irredentism with a vision of a Taiwanese society that was much more distinctly separate from mainland China in its treatment of national identity.

The politics of indigenization: the experience of Lee and Chen

'The Lee Deng-Hui "line"'

The economic liberalization of China encouraged the growth of Taiwanese investments in the mainland, which were attracted there by cheap labour costs and geographical proximity to and the size of the Chinese market.[10] Yet, the People's Republic of China, which regards Taiwan as a renegade province, did not look too kindly on recent political developments on the island. Although Taiwan–China economic links were becoming stronger, political tensions continued to escalate. The boiling point was almost reached in 1996 when China threatened Taiwan with missile launchings and ominous military drills – this was probably the closest to an outbreak of open warfare that China and Taiwan (and the USA) had ever approached since the 1950s.[11] Faced with a seemingly out-of-control emergency, the USA sent two aircraft carrier battle groups, the *Independence* battle group from Okinawa and the *Nimitz* battle group from the Arabian Gulf, close to the Taiwan Straits to prevent a fast approaching war (Global Security 2003). Being thus implicated in the ongoing political tension, economic links between Taiwan and China inevitably became problematic. Hence, in 1994, Lee launched the 'Go South' policy, which was aimed at encouraging Taiwanese investors to seek opportunities in Southeast Asia rather than in China (Lee 2003: 23–6).

Ironically, Lee was able to capitalize on the 'China threat' to consolidate his popularity further and marginalize the remaining mainlander politicians. In 1995, he put up the slogan 'New Taiwanese', which in its rhetoric meant encouraging 'mainlander Taiwanese' to switch their national identity from Chinese to Taiwanese. Nevertheless his 'mainlander' adversaries came to be tainted with accusations of disloyalty to Taiwan and complicity with Chinese designs on the island. The employment of such a domestic political strategy helped Lee to victory in Taiwan's first direct presidential elections in 1996. Largely by emphasizing the 'China threat', Lee won the election with more than 50 per cent of the votes, thus making him the single biggest asset of the growing Taiwan independence movement; China's threats had backfired by benefiting Lee.

Apart from utilizing the 'China threat' to present Taiwan as an innocent victim of devious internal and external forces, Lee actively sought to portray Taiwan as a champion of US values. Responding to the USA's 'congagement' policy towards China, Lee Deng-Hui attempted to link Taiwan's 'democratic consolidation' with the US vision of the globalization of democracy. Of course, the indirect and unflattering comparison was to the People's Republic of China, which was ruled by a totalitarian Communist Party. By this time, the Lee Deng-Hui 'line' had been developed in its full-fledged form, which was to link any competition or mutual suspicion between China and the USA with the requirements of the separatist versus reunification conflict in Taiwan. Thus, Lee equated Taiwan's democratization with 'peaceful evolution', and local pro-reunification forces with the 'China threat'.[12]

While inevitably promoting xenophobia, and an 'us versus them' mentality within the Taiwanese body politic, the strategy was successful. The proof of this was the demolition of the pro-reunification New Party in the 2001 legislative body election. The New Party won 12.95 per cent of the votes in the 1995 elections but only 2.86 per cent of the votes in the 2001 poll (NCCU 2004). Thus, the old ideological orthodoxy in Taiwan – characterized by anti-communism, pro-Americanism and irredentism – was replaced by a new ideology that was pronouncedly anti-China, pro-USA and pro-Taiwanese self-determination/independence. Those who subscribe to at least some part of the old orthodoxy, usually 'mainlanders', were indiscriminately characterized by this newly ascendant ideology as being anti-democratic and pro-authoritarian reactionaries. At the same time, the pro-Lee forces insisted that the USA would definitely protect Taiwan from military threat or invasion from China, just as it had done in the Taiwan Straits missile crises 1995–6 (Lin 2002). Hoping to lay the ground for a quasi-military alliance with Japan and the USA, Lee first expressed his willingness to join the US-initiated Theatre Missile Defence (TMD) system in 1996. Tang Fei's, Taiwan's Minister of Defence, comment about this initiative delivered in February 1999 testified to the main purpose of this attempt: 'the introduction of a TMD system would bear a political significance bigger than its military significance' (Allen *et al.* 2000: vii).

In July 1999, Lee went a step further by publicly characterizing the Taiwan–China relationship as 'a special state-to-state relationship' that clearly challenged the 'one-China policy' that had been jointly agreed to by the USA and China since the 1970s. This statement was only met by cautious US and Chinese responses (Lee 2000: 43–53). Interestingly, Lee's actions directly contradicted US President Bill Clinton's so-called 'three No's' policy towards Taiwan that was expressed in a 1998 visit. This consisted of 'No support for Taiwan independence', 'No recognition of a separate Taiwanese government' and 'No backing for Taiwanese member-ship of international organizations' (*Taipei Times* Sunday, 19 December 1999: 1).

The Lee Deng-Hui 'line' proved triumphant again in the 2000 presidential election, which pitted two candidates from the Kuomintang: Song Chuyu (James Song), a mainlander who was forced to leave the party in November 1999; and Lian Zhan, the official candidate of the Kuomintang with an ambiguous Hokkien background.[13] Their loss was partly due to the internal split that took place within the Kuomintang, precipitated by the actions of Lee himself. The winner was Chen Shui-Bian, the candidate of the DPP and a representative of the 'pure' Hokkien population of Taiwan. Political power in Taiwan had been finally transferred to an indigenous Hokkien-dominated party, thus symbolizing the achievement of victory of the Lee agenda that had been cultivated over the previous twelve years.

Changes and continuities: the Chen Shui-Bian 'line'

Essentially, Chen Shui-Bian has continued along the political lines set by his predecessor, Lee. There were, however, many problems in doing so, one of the most important being the 9/11 attacks on the Twin Towers in New York City. The attack compelled the US government to approach China to secure its support in the War on Terror. As a matter of fact, China's co-operation has been essential for the USA in building up a comprehensive global anti-terrorist network because China has always played an important role in various areas, including the non-proliferation of WMD, the collection and exchange of intelligence concerning Islamic 'extremism' (western China and Chinese borders in Central Asia are the sites of government conflict with Islamic separatist forces) and the North Korean nuclear programme.

The possibility of improved relations between the USA and China, which had been damaged by such events as the mistaken bombing of the Chinese Embassy in Belgrade in May 1999 and the collision of US EP3 and Chinese F-8 aircraft over the South China Sea in April 2001, was regarded as a threat to the DPP agenda in Taiwan. Chen Shui-Bian's response was to propose yet another new characterization of the cross-Straits relationship, 'one state on each side [of the Taiwan Strait]'; this was arguably even more agitating to China than Lee's earlier formulation. On the domestic front, the Chen government officially 'endorsed' the initiative of the United Front of

Taiwan that was raised by Lee Deng-Hui[14] to promote two cutting-edge movements: 'Correcting Taiwan's Name' and 'Referendum on Taiwan's Independence'. Chen also proclaimed at the DPP's birthday celebration on 28 September 2003 that he would hold a referendum in 2004, establish a New Constitution of Taiwan by 2006, and ratify the new Constitution via another referendum in 2008.

The new international development, however, meant that reactions from China and the USA were muted enough not to exacerbate domestic tensions between 'Pan-Blue' pro-Kuomintang forces and 'Pan-Green' pro-DPP and United Front of Taiwan forces; thus, like Lee, Chen was unable to capitalize from the 'China threat' factor. It was arguably only the incident of the assassination attempt on Chen – that was thought to have, in the public imagination at least, been hatched by pro-China forces – that secured his victory at the March 2004 presidential election, an election he had earlier been widely tipped to lose.

It was only in April 2004, after the DPP victory was assured, that China put forward the National Unification Law as a response to the DPP's increasingly bold statements about a possible timetable for an independence referendum (*China Times*, 22 May 2004: A13). With the prospect of a change in the status quo and of being drawn into an unwanted military confrontation with China that runs against its interests, the USA has also responded by issuing official warnings to the Taiwanese government not to provoke China by making provocative gestures towards independence. Interestingly, there is widespread belief in Taiwan that Chen Shui-Bian's inauguration speech was reviewed beforehand by the US government (*United Daily News*, 5 May 2004: A4).

In order to soothe the USA's disaffection at Chen's behaviour during the presidential election and to counter China's threats, the re-elected Chen Shui-Bian announced on 2 June 2004 a massive arms purchase from the USA amounting to US$18.4 billion. This announcement came despite the fact that Taiwanese voters had already refused to endorse more expenditure on new weapons through the first national referendum that had been held concurrently with the presidential election on 20 March 2004.[15]

Conclusion

We have illustrated how Taiwanese society has been conditioned by domestic ethnic politics and the changing international context of the Cold War and post-Cold-War era. In particular, the evolution of USA–China relations has fed the sources of ethnic-based conflict within Taiwan's domestic politics. The manifestation of the influence of USA–China relations, however, has been different during distinct phases of the Cold War and post-Cold-War periods. Moreover, since the demise of the bipolar system of global power in the late 1980s and its replacement by a more distinctly unipolar system centred on the USA, Taiwan has at times enjoyed comparatively greater autonomous space in the way that it negotiates in the international arena. We have shown that the way in which this process of negotiation has taken place – largely driven by the forces of pro-independence and indigenization – has once again ignited the impulse of long-suppressed ethnic politics, which has translated into political party and electoral competition. Most significantly, it has spilled over considerably into fundamental questions about Taiwan's national identity and political status, all of which in turn shape the relationship between China and the USA. Thanks to the mobilization of ethnic/cultural biases by political elites representing 'mainlanders' and Hokkiens, the 'unity' of Taiwan – achieved only as a result of the exigencies of the Cold War – is now being eroded. Taiwanese society is becoming increasingly polarized along ethnic lines and orientations towards reunification or independence.

Although there still exist cultural commonalities – such as national symbols centring on the Republic of China; the national language, which is a more or less Hokkien-accented version of Mandarin; and the official narratives of national history – throughout Taiwanese society today, these have been downplayed in the course of domestic power struggles in recent years. At the time of writing, the possibility of a Chinese invasion of Taiwan timed to take place before the 2008 Summer Olympic Games in Beijing is being widely debated. There is also speculation on how the USA, the great hegemonic power in the Asia–Pacific and the world, would react to such an invasion should it ever take place. Ironically, therefore, while the Cold War has been long over, a state of heightened tension reminiscent of the Cold War era still lingers in this part of the world.

Notes

1 Taiwan's political leaders have never enjoyed this level of hospitality from the USA since the official diplomatic relationship between USA and the Republic of China (Taiwan) was terminated in the 1970s. President Lee Deng-Hui, who had also tried to transit US airports a few years earlier, was required to use only the airports in the West Coast region and was not allowed to enter the USA.

2 The money value of this arms sale, which included advanced weaponry, amounted to US$20 billion.

3 Since the demise of the USSR, China has become the top buyer of Russian advanced weaponry, from jet fighters (SU-27/UBK and SU-30MK), submarines (Type 877/636, Kilo class), destroyers (Sovremenny Class), air-to-air missiles (AA9/AA10), surface-to-air missile (S300/S400), helicopters (Mi 17), to tanks (T80/T90) and so on (*China Times*, 14 July 2000: 14).

4 The Formosa Event refers to violent clashes between police forces and protesters, led by the editorial board of the biweekly political journal *Formosa*, who ignored government prohibition and boldly marched on the street. Although no one was killed, hundreds of protesters as well as policemen were injured; and more than 100 people, including almost all the elite dissidents in Taiwan, were arrested. The incumbent Vice-President of Taiwan, Lu Hsiu-Lian, and some ex-Chairmen of the Democratic Progress Party were among the detainees. Current President Chen Shui-Bian started to build up his political career by serving as one of the

lawyers of those detained. US politicians actively intervened in the aftermath. In 1980, the last US ambassador to the Republic of China (Taiwan) paid a special visit to Taiwan in order to express the concerns of the US government. The day after the visit, the Chairman of the American Institute in Taiwan met the families of those who were detained and accepted their petition. Later, the Democratic presidential candidate, Edward Kennedy, appealed to the US government to stop the Kuomintang regime from continuing its oppression of the democratic movement in Taiwan.

5 For the full text, refer to http://www.chinataiwan.org/web/webportal/W5027158/A5111749.html.

6 For the full text, refer to http://www.chinataiwan.org/web/webportal/W5098650/A5526296.html.

7 For the full text, refer to http://www.chinataiwan.org/web/webportal/W5098650/A5183425.html.

8 The DPP publicized the '417 Resolution on the Independence of [Taiwan's] Sovereignty' on 23 April 1988. This insists on the sovereignty of Taiwan in the international community and declares that the sovereignty of Taiwan belongs to the people of Taiwan according to the principle of 'people's sovereignty'. In 1991, the DPP went a step forward to advance the idea of 'building up the Republic of Taiwan' in its party programme. The clause read as follows: 'In view of the actual situation of Taiwan's sovereignty, [our party] seeks to build up Taiwan as an independent state, to institute a new Constitution for it so as to make its legal/political system fitting the reality of Taiwan's society, and to strive for Taiwan's rejoining of the international community according to the principles of international law.'

9 He was the son of Generalissimo Chiang Kai-Shek, a founder of the Kuomintang, who led the central government of the Republic of China and the Kuomintang retreat to Taiwan in 1949 when the Chinese Communist Party under Mao conquered the whole of mainland China.

10 Taiwanese investments to China began to skyrocket after the second southward tour of Chairman Deng Xiaoping in 1992, and quickly exceeded Taiwan's investment in Southeast Asia from 1993; this trend has never been altered since. Similarly, trade between Taiwan and China is also rising at an increasing speed. For example, the rate of mutual dependence in trade between the two sides of the Straits speedily increased from 5.36 per cent in 1993 to 9.3 per cent in 1994 and to over 12 per cent in 1999. This clearly proves that the mutually dependent relationship between Taiwan and China in the economic/trading sphere is actually strengthening despite the attempt of the 'Go South' policy to weaken it. Meanwhile, the trade surplus that Taiwan earned from China also grew – from just over US$10 billion in 1993 to US$16.7 billion in 1999, and then to around US$25 billion in 2002. In contrast, trade between Taiwan and Southeast Asia showed no signs of escalation except during the two years immediately after the institution of the 'Go South' policy in 1994. In 1995, exports to six Southeast Asian countries constituted 13.5 per cent of the total export of Taiwan, which is an unprecedented high point. Since 1996, the rate fell back slightly to around 13 per cent and has remained there for years, except in the two years immediately after the Asian financial crisis in 1997. In 1998 and 1999, the rate dropped back to its usual level before the institution of the 'Go South' policy, which was around 10 per cent. Generally speaking, however, trade between Taiwan and Southeast Asia is still growing, albeit at a much slower speed (Lee 2003: 24–5).

11 The 'Taiwan Strait missile crisis 1995–6' refers to a series of missile tests conducted by China after President Lee Deng-Hui visited the USA in June 1995. During the first stage of the missile test (in July and August 1995), China set the target zone on the sea surface 85 to 80 miles (136 to 128 km) north of Taiwan. Later, in March 1996, the distance between the target zone for the tested surface-

to-surface missiles and Taiwan was reduced to half of that in 1995, which was far too short for the safety of major airline and shipping routes. Of the three missiles launched, two landed 23 miles (37 km) north of Taiwan's northern coast, which is very close to the Keelung Port approximately 30 miles (48 km) northeast of Taipei. The third missile landed 35 miles (56 km) southwest of Taiwan's southern coast, very close to the Kaohsiong Port. These two port cities, Keelung and Kaohsiong, are the entryways for more than 70 per cent of commercial shipping to Taiwan. The proximity of these missile tests to the ports and major airways effectively caused serious disruption to Taiwan's international sea and air traffic, as all incoming and outgoing ships and aircraft were forced to avoid the test areas during the exercise. Besides, both the scope and nature of the March 1996 tests sharply heightened the risk of a real military conflict should there have been some miscalculation or accident (Global Security 2003).

12 The statements above are based on the extensive discussions we had with government officials and consultants in Taiwan. We hereby express our deepest gratitude for their contributions to this chapter.

13 Mr Lian was born in Xi'an City, China, in 1936 and was brought to Taiwan by his father, Lian Zhendong (a Taiwan-born gentleman), after Japanese colonial rule in Taiwan ended in 1945. Lian, therefore, was categorized as 'ban shan' (半山 'half-mainlander') instead of an authentic 'sweet potato' (the metaphor for native Hokkien-speaking Taiwanese). His unusual background was taken by fundamentalist Taiwan separatists as grounds for questioning his loyalty to Taiwan. They suspected that he might sell Taiwan's interests to China if he got the chance to handle the cross-Straits interaction, due to the 'sentimental attachment' he was supposed to have had with China.

14 By then, Lee had already been expelled from the Kuomintang on 21 September 2001 because he had established a new party on 24 July 2001. This was the Taiwan Solidarity Union, a rival to the Kuomintang in that year's Congressional election.

15 There were two questions asked in the referendum. The first question was: 'If China refuses to remove her missiles targeting on Taiwan and to openly insure that they would never use military force against us, would you agree that the government should try to acquire more advanced anti-missile weapons to strengthen Taiwan's self-defence?'. The other question was: 'Would you agree that our government should negotiate with China in order to establish a "peaceful and stable" framework for cross-Strait transactions so as to nurture a cross-Strait consensus and to promote the welfare of the peoples on both sides?' Both questions failed to pass the minimum requirement for an effective referendum as less than half of eligible voters cast their vote for either question.

14 US imperialism and Bengali nationalism*

Habibul Haque Khondker

Iraq's future won't be decided in No. 10, in the Oval Office or by the UN – it will be decided in the streets and communities of Iraq.
(Journalist Rageh Omaar in an interview with Dickson Hooper, BBC Bristol, 14 May 2004)

America is a curious mixture of what is considered hard-headed realism and a vague idealism and humanitarianism.
(Jawaharlal Nehru 1946: 539)

Introduction

One of the salient contributions of sociology has been an exploration of the world of the unintended consequences of various social phenomena. Regardless of whether the post-Cold-War international order will stabilize after the contemporary troubles of wars, violence and destruction on a massive scale, it is worthwhile to explore the various consequences – both intended and unintended – that imperialism and global power play bring to the trajectories of specific societies. It is with this objective in mind that this chapter seeks to explore the ramifications of the US political, economic and military roles in South Asia on the geopolitics of, and conflicts within, the region. One of the most important geopolitical developments in South Asia in the last quarter of the twentieth century was the emergence of Bangladesh out of the ashes of the old Pakistan. This chapter explores the role, albeit unintended, of the USA as an imperial power in the trajectories of Bengali nationalism in the context of the Cold War. The implications of the Cold War are still unravelling in various parts of the world, to the extent that it may be premature to state categorically that the Cold War has come to an end.

These issues are especially important in relation to the current War on Terror, in which countries such as Bangladesh and Pakistan are often considered the incubators of violent fundamentalist Islamic forces; but US policy, particularly during the Cold War, is at least partly responsible for the decline of secular politics in these countries.

At a roundtable meeting organized by the Bangladesh Workers' Party in Dhaka on 18 March 2005, one of the party's leaders, Fazle Hossian Badsha, noted the irony that the US government does not consider the Jamaat-i-Islami of Bangladesh – part of the coalition in power – a fundamentalist party. At the same time, he recollected that it was the USA that had essentially created the Taleban in Afghanistan (*The Daily Star*, 19 March 2005). It is remarkable that the role of the USA in creating and nurturing an Islamic Right in the South Asian context is now being publicly discussed in Bangladesh; yet, the unholy alliance between the forces of imperialism and the religious Right, under conditions of the Cold War, and their long-term implications have not been sufficiently examined. What I would like to explore in this chapter is the long-standing role of the USA in the politics of the Indian sub-continent – with special reference to Bangladesh and Pakistan – and its contemporary consequences. A careful understanding of nationalism in Bangladesh must include the context of the Cold War and the superpower rivalry within it that leaders of East Bengal, both communist and non-communist, played an important role in by taking a conscious position against US power in the region.

More recently, the emergence and consolidation of the unipolar world order following the end of the Cold War was unmistakably demonstrated by US military action against Iraq in the previous year, in defiance of the United Nations and some of its traditionally close allies. This post-Cold-War phase has been variously dubbed by theorists as that of a 'new imperialism' (Harvey 2003a; 2003b), a 'new militarism' (Mann 2003), a new age of 'empire' (Garrison 2004), or a US-led 'empire of capital' (Wood 2003). On one level, some argue that the increasingly aggressive role of the USA can be explained by its economic interests, or at least those of some economically dominant groups in America. Others, such as Mann (2003), contend that the imperialist ambition of global economic dominance is not best served by the militaristic postures of the current US government. For Mann, the requirements of militarism and capitalism are not always in harmony; therefore, he portrays the USA as an 'incoherent empire' (Mann 2003). Other writers, such as Gowan (2004a), observe continuity in the dominance of the US government by 'business interests' throughout the twentieth century, or suggest that the presence of the Soviet Union provided a major basis for the emergence of unilateral imperialist ambitions that were often at odds with the interests of other capitalist powers such as Germany and Japan. Following the demise of the Soviet Union, the USA retained its old unilateral posture that was formed under previous circumstances.

Despite the rhetoric and impression of 'newness', there is evidence of a certain degree of continuity. The slogans of democracy, human rights and freedom, and the self-assumed role of the USA in promoting global enlightenment, belie the existence of various important internal contradictions in policy, which have remained remarkably consistent since the Cold War. During the Cold War, the USA was the 'indefatigable champion' of freedom and democracy and it remains so in the so-called post-Cold-War world. What we know, however, is that the USA supported authoritarian regimes as long as they were friendly to its economic and geopolitical interests, and it was often an accessory to gross atrocities and human rights violations in Asia and elsewhere. In fact, the social theorist Derrida viewed the events of 11 September 2001 as 'a distant effect of the Cold War itself'. Derrida was referring to the fact that the USA provided training and weapons to the enemies of the Soviet Union in Afghanistan and elsewhere 'who have now become the enemies of the U.S.' (Derrida quoted in Borradori 2003: 92). Chalmers Johnson (2000) made a similar argument about the consequences of the clandestine operations carried out by the USA, which have now come back to haunt the superpower in the form of a 'blowback'.

In this chapter, I explore earlier episodes of superpower politics, in which similar contradictory policies were evident as ideological commitments were put on hold when *realpolitik* demanded it. While the sole superpower today continues to preach such ideals as world peace, human rights and democratic values, one may have reason to be a little sceptical in view of many episodes in recent history. I choose to revisit certain episodes from the political history of Bangladesh and Pakistan, events that stem from the war of liberation in Bangladesh and its immediate aftermath in the 1970s.

It is notable in this connection that during the war of national liberation in Bangladesh in 1971, the Marxist parties in Bangladesh and their leaders turned to the People's Republic of China for support and assistance, but only to be disillusioned. They found out that China, rather than supporting the cause of national liberation as would have been expected, staunchly supported Pakistan and was on the same side as the USA. The problem was that by then, the myth of ideological divide between capitalism and socialism was starting to give way to the new geopolitical realities of globalization that brought together the USA and China as new partners. The USA, however, was also a source of disappointment in Bangladesh's early days of independence. When the country was threatened by famine in 1974, the US government actually called off food shipments on the pretext that Bangladesh was a communist ally – this decision contributed to the creation of a terrible national tragedy.

The changing ideological alignments and realignments since the official end of the Cold War continue to disadvantage the poverty-stricken nations of the world, which are arguably even more vulnerable in today's unipolar world. From time to time, one sees some client states attempt to squeeze concessions from the global hegemon, as in the relationship between Pakistan and the USA after 9/11, but these are largely exceptional. With there being no counterweight to US power, as was the former Soviet Union, poor countries like Bangladesh are powerless when it comes to policies of economic assistance or preferential treatment in terms of access to the US market.

One underlying premise of this chapter can be stated in the following manner: the policies of superpowers such as the USA can have a deep and durable impact on the internal politics of weaker nations like Bangladesh, so much so that in the long run, some of these policies may backfire dramatically, very much in the sense of Johnson's 'blowback'. For example, the formation of Bangladesh can be explained – partly, if not completely – in terms of responses to US policies in South Asia since the Cold War. The US policy of containment of the Soviet Union and the spread of socialism led to its unqualified support of Pakistan in the 1970s; this was within the context of a regional arms race and competition for supremacy between Pakistan and India, the latter a Soviet ally. The political uncertainties and difficulties involved in consolidating democracy in Pakistan eventually gave way to the creation of Bangladesh, a third state in the Indian sub-continent. US policies have since actually led to the erosion of secular and democratic forms of politics in South Asia, as well as the rise of authoritarian regimes that frequently legitimize their position by calling on religion. Both the democratic process and secularist ideals were to be sacrificed in so far as the interest of US policy was the containment of socialism. Thus, the environment for the emergence of anti-US Islamism in the region, including in Bangladesh, was partly facilitated. The consequences of these past policies are all too glaring to overlook in today's world. A major contention of this chapter is that we need to look at the contemporary political situation in many parts of the world – including Bangladesh, where democratic secular politics has been under continuous and severe assault – in light of the historical legacies of superpower politics of a previous era.

Given this background, it is ironic that in the summer of 2004, Mr Harry Thomas, the US Ambassador to Bangladesh, expressed concern over the rise of Islamic radicalism in the country. Uncharacteristic for a diplomat, Thomas was very frank and candid in his remarks and noted that fundamentalism would destroy all, and he asked for the arrest of Bangla Bhai, a self-styled Islamic extremist (*The Daily Star*, 29 June 2004). He showed little awareness of the strong link between the USA's past policies in the region and the prominence of fundamentalist Islamism in the politics of contemporary Bangladesh, which resulted in the eclipse of secular social and political forces. This is because the military dictators of Bangladesh, like the military rulers of Pakistan, have been supportive of the USA and, in turn, have received patronage from their Big Brother. These military dictators not only derailed democratic processes but also proclaimed themselves champions of Islam in order to court the support of the God-fearing masses. They did so also as a means of exercising control over domestic sources of political opposition. President General Ziaul Haque in Pakistan, President General Ziaur Rahman and, later, President General Ershad all used Islam to bolster their legitimacy – with deleterious consequences for future stability.

In recent times, a number of incidents in Bangladesh have sent out chilling signals that religious extremism has spun out of control. Three secular-minded professors at Dhaka University, once a bastion of openness and intellectual freedom, have been threatened with death, unless they return to the path of Islam, by a group that calls itself 'Committee for the Resistance of Atheism' (*Mridu Bhashan*, 5 July 2004). On 21 August 2004 at an opposition rally of the secularist Awami League, grenades were hurled at the former Prime Minister, Sheikh Hasina. She escaped unhurt, although scores of politicians, including a senior leader, and party workers were killed. In mid-December 2004, a professor at Rajshahi University who was a former freedom fighter was murdered by a group that was apparently linked to the religious Right. On 26 January 2005, three days after a news story published in the *New York Times* hinted at the possibility of the rise of fundamentalism in Bangladesh, a grenade attack killed another senior leader of the Awami League and a former finance minister, together with a number of party members. Again, suspicion was cast on the fanatical groups linked to the religious Right.

It should also be noted that since the overthrow of the socialist-inclined government of Sheikh Mujibur Rahman in 1975, the military has been the dominant force in Bangladeshi politics and has been the lynchpin of various authoritarian governments. Interestingly, the authoritarian tilt in Bangladeshi politics coincided with the start of pro-market economic reforms. These reforms took off in the 1980s and 1990s as full-fledged, Western-supported, neoliberal economic policies that included curtailing government expenditure, currency devaluation, trade liberalization, withdrawal of state subsidies and privatization of economic activities. While the result of this was the achievement of a measure of macroeconomic stability in the 1990s, a stark process of wealth concentration was to take place as well, which saw further economic marginalization of Bangladeshi peasants and workers. According to Nuruzzaman, neoliberal economic policies – in large part sustained by authoritarian governments – have produced a small group of 40–50 families that effectively control all of Bangladesh's industrial and financial assets (see Nuruzzaman 2004: 33–54). This conceivably provides some of the context for the emergence of groups that were dissatisfied with the status quo and attracted to more radical, and sometimes violent, Islamic politics.

The USA and the Indian sub-continent

A detour to the political history of the Indian sub-continent is necessary for placing the arguments of this chapter in their proper historical context. It is a commonly held view that prior to the independence of Pakistan and India in 1947, the USA was either indifferent to or ignorant of political developments in the Indian sub-continent. Although the USA under the presidency of George Washington appointed a consul in Calcutta, the capital of British India, in 1792 (Kux 1993: 3), the relationship did not flourish. Thus, prior to the Second World War, US interest in British India was quite limited (Cohen 1999: 190) and was fuelled with missionary zeal more than commercial interests. Moreover, the Indian nationalist leadership of the early twentieth century was imbued with anti-imperialist values and was critical of the USA, especially of its role in Latin America. In 1928, a year after an international congress against colonial oppression and imperialism, Nehru wrote: 'It is the United States which offers us the best field for the study of economic imperialism' (Kux 1993: 5).

Nevertheless, relations between Indian nationalism and the USA markedly improved during Franklin Roosevelt's administration. President Roosevelt's social welfare policies under the New Deal of the 1930s and his anti-colonial stance, which eventually led to the decision to grant the Philippines independence in 1946, created a favourable opinion of US policies in India. But India, still under British rule, had yet to achieve any timetable for self-rule. The Roosevelt administration began to put it across to the British government that colonialism might not be in the latter's best interest; this suggestion was largely ignored and created some bitterness among the British leadership. The Truman administration also placed some indirect pressure on the British administration to change its policies towards India. Although Churchill declared that he 'did not become the first Minister of the Crown to preside over the disintegration of the British Empire', the empire did begin to unravel in the aftermath of the Second World War. After the Labour Party's Atlee replaced Churchill as Prime Minister, it was only a matter of time before India achieved independence and the British Empire disintegrated. As the British Empire came to an end, however, a new empire emerged on the horizon – one that would deeply affect the politics of the Indian sub-continent.

USA–Pakistan: a special relationship

In spite of the USA's role in supporting India's independence, the former was to develop a special relationship with Pakistan, which was carved out of India in 1947 to form a 'homeland' for Muslims in the sub-continent. The relationship has been such that many commentators in the USA have expressed unease about its nature and consequences. These sentiments are expressed in occasional outbursts, such as in a recent editorial in the *International Herald Tribune*, in which Pakistan's President, General Pervez Musharraf, was taken to task for destroying democracy, supporting the religious Right and even overlooking illegal transactions involving dangerous nuclear technology (*International Herald Tribune*, 13 July 2004). Some writers try to explain the special relationship in terms of Pakistan's support for the US campaign against Islamic radicalism, especially against the Taleban in Afghanistan and elsewhere in the region, although as far as the USA is concerned, Pakistan has long been a favoured state. It is important to situate this special relationship in a historical context. Although Pakistan emerged on the grounds that the Muslims of the Indian sub-continent needed a homeland of their own, the new country was not a theocratic state and its leader, Muhammad Ali Jinnah, was a liberal-minded, secular person.

The newly created Pakistan's struggle to establish a democratic polity coincided with a pro-Western tilt in so far as foreign policy was concerned. This policy was underscored by Pakistan's founding leader Ali Jinnah, who stated in September 1947 that: 'Pakistan is a democracy and communism does not flourish in the soil of Islam. It is clear therefore that our interests lie more with the two great democratic countries, namely, the U.K. and the U.S.A., rather than with Russia' (Kux 2001: 20). Pakistan's leadership continued to pursue a pro-Western foreign policy after the death of Jinnah on 11 September 1948, barely a year after the nation was created. Moreover, Pakistan sought to enlist the support of the Western powers, especially the USA, in establishing its claim over Kashmir, a territory held in dispute with India.

Jinnah's successor, Liaquat Ali, was even less ambiguous in his support of the USA in the context of the new Cold War when he refused to visit the Soviet Union and, instead, headed for the USA on 19 April 1950 on a personal invitation from President Truman. Here, too, the rivalry between India and Pakistan was an apparent factor in Liaquat Ali's rejection of the Soviet Union. During this trip, according to one author, 'the Prime Minister's only substantive meeting seems to have been at the Pentagon with Secretary of Defense Louis Johnson and Chairman of the Joint Chiefs of Staff General Omar Bradley' (Kux 2001: 35). The US response to Pakistan's request for arms was lukewarm; at that juncture, the USA had yet to support Pakistan fully in its growing rivalry against India.

On 17 April 1953, a former ambassador to the USA, Mr Mohammad Ali (Bogra), was installed as Pakistan's Prime Minister by Governor-General Ghulam Muhammad, in a move that was not unlike a *coup d'état*. John Foster Dulles, the staunchly anti-communist US Secretary of State at the time, then declared that Pakistan was 'a bulwark of freedom in Asia' (Ali 1983: 51). In January 1954, William F. Knowland, the Republican majority leader in the US Senate, called Pakistan 'one of the key, important countries in the entire world in relation to the defense against Communism' (Spain 1954: 742).

It is possible to understand the pro-US tilt in Pakistani politics in view of the latter's military and diplomatic confrontations with India. The relationship between these two neighbours soured from the very early stage of their separation, over the issue of Kashmir. The principle for a division of the Indian sub-continent was religion, and Kashmir was an overwhelmingly Muslim majority state, thus it was claimed by Pakistan. The Hindu rulers of Kashmir, however, were encouraged by the Indian government to incorporate the state into India. This led to an armed confrontation between Pakistan and India in 1949 that ceased only at the behest of the United Nations.

While Pakistan needed a superpower patron that could provide both military and development assistance, the USA itself needed a foothold of some strategic importance in the space between the Middle East and

Indochina, thus Pakistan came to play the role of a surrogate for the USA since the 1950s. Pakistan needed a patron, and the USA was anxious to complete the containment ring around China and the Soviet Union. An alliance with Pakistan seemed to be an ideal match, with 'each side meeting the immediate needs of the other' (Thornton 1999: 173). Pakistan joined pacts such as the Southeast Asia Treaty Organization (SEATO) and the Central Treaty Organization (CENTO) in the 1950s to build closer ties with the US-backed Western powers. SEATO, a pact signed in 1954 by eight nations – Pakistan, Australia, France, New Zealand, the Philippines, Thailand, the UK and the USA – in Manila, was a bulwark against the spread of communism in Southeast Asia (Government of Pakistan 1998: 85). Pakistan also joined the Baghdad Pact, which later became CENTO on 23 September 1955, with the participation of Iraq, Turkey and the UK (Government of Pakistan 1998: 100).

The already close relationship between Pakistan and the USA reached a new high point after the entrenchment of the military rule of General Ayub Khan. General Ayub showed such a strong pro-USA orientation that it was rumoured the CIA aided him in his rise to power. Ayub is said to have remarked at a Cabinet meeting soon after the military takeover in October 1958: 'There is only one embassy [in Pakistan] for us and that's the American Embassy' (Ali 1983: 219–20). With US support, Ayub ruled Pakistan until 1969, including several years on the basis of martial law.

The roots of the struggle for Bengali autonomy

The growth in demand for autonomy from the Bengali-speaking province of East Pakistan can be explained by a number of factors, including the exploitation of East Bengal (East Pakistan) by the dominant classes of (West) Pakistan; regional disparity; and an unequal power structure. One should not, however, overlook the differences in attitudes towards the USA's role in this region. According to Tariq Ali:

> the Western alliance gave Pakistan a certain geopolitical importance. The army and bureaucracy agreed to make the country an American base. In the autumn of 1953 General Ayub, then the Pakistani military chief, negotiated military aid for Pakistan. In April 1954, a Pakistan–Turkey alliance was signed in Karachi: its aim was to extend the American sphere of influence along the Soviet frontiers and to isolate India.
>
> (Ali 1983: 51–2)

The warming of relations between the USA and Pakistan was viewed favourably in West Pakistan (present-day Pakistan) and played a role in the creation of a rift between the central government and the provincial government of East Pakistan (present-day Bangladesh). US Vice-President Nixon's visit to Pakistan in December 1953 was hailed by the Karachi-based *Dawn*, which claimed 'the prospect of a military pact between Pakistan and the USA was "heart-uplifting news"', and commented that 'the people of Pakistan will be found overwhelmingly in favor of such an alliance'. Further, US military aid was heralded as well as 'a glorious chapter in our history' (Burke 1973: 242–3).

The central government of Pakistan may have been establishing an alliance with the Americans due to mutual interests, but this did not go down well with the politicians of East Pakistan. The military–bureaucratic elites of Pakistan were imbued with sectarian and regional interests, and their pre-eminence in internal politics was buttressed by their close relationship with the USA. The provincial leaders, however, did not benefit from the privileged relationship with the USA and continued to be subordinated by Karachi. This contributed to the rift between the two wings of the artificially created country. The most outspoken critic of Pakistan's pro-US posture was Maulana Abdul Hamid Khan Bhashani, a Left-leaning leader and a key founder of the Awami League, a party that subsequently played the vanguard role in the liberation and establishment of Bangladesh. Other East Pakistani leaders expressed unease with military assistance from the USA. The Nixon visit to Pakistan was even criticized by Mr Suhrawardy, a some-what pro-Western leader of the Awami League, who allegedly said that a military treaty with the USA would be a blow to Pakistan's independence and initiative (Burke 1973: 244).

A major electoral defeat on the part of the Muslim League, the founding party of Pakistan, in provincial elections in East Pakistan in 1954 delivered a message – that the people of the region were unhappy with a regime in which Bengalis were poorly represented, and in which military–bureaucratic elites appeared to be propped up by the West. It may not be farfetched to suggest that the Muslim League's defeat in East Pakistan was not totally unrelated to Nixon's visit, in particular, as well as the overall pro-USA posture of the central Pakistani government.

In these elections, an East Bengal United Front, composed of an alliance between the Awami League and other parties, won an absolute majority. Mr A. K. Fazlul Haque became the Chief Minister of East Bengal, but in May 1954 as well, barely two months after the formation of the provincial government in East Bengal, the central government dismissed the elected government and appointed Major-General Iskander Mirza the Governor of East Bengal. Earlier in the same month, Pakistan rejected the Soviet protest that was lodged in March against USA–Pakistan military co-operation. In May 1954, Pakistan and the USA signed a Mutual Defense Assistance Agreement in Karachi. The people of East Bengal felt betrayed as their elected government was summarily dismissed by the central government on no convincing grounds. In October 1954, the Prime Minister of Pakistan declared that Pakistan did not believe in neutralism because it was no longer possible to remain indifferent to the conflict between the two major blocs in the world (Government of Pakistan 1998: 86). Thus, Pakistan followed an unambiguously pro-US policy right after the death of Ali Jinnah and, by 1954, even the trappings of neutrality were completely removed.

As is well known, the Cold War that began in Europe gradually spread to other parts of the world, including South Asia. The Soviet Union and the USA, after having split Europe into their respective spheres of interests in the aftermath of the Second World War, were locked into a similar position in the Indian sub-continent. As Pakistan was drawn into the US orbit, India leaned heavily towards the socialist camps of the Soviet Union and China. The friendship between India and the Soviet Union intensified after the Sino-Soviet rupture and the subsequent military conflict between India and China in 1962 over territories in the Himalayas. These realignments had profound consequences for the geopolitical developments in the region, which culminated in Bangladesh's independence in 1971.

As noted earlier, the liberation war of Bangladesh was an outgrowth of years of resentment, mistrust and regional exploitation as the eastern province began to see itself as a colony of West Pakistan. The leaders of the Awami League, a predominantly provincial party, began to demand regional autonomy, social and economic parity, and equal rights. The movement had manifold objectives, including the exercise of free and fair elections.

This resentment first surfaced strongly when a movement against the rule of General Ayub began in the late 1960s, especially after the celebration of the ten-year anniversary of the *coup d'état* of 1958, in the face of growing opposition to his draconian rule. It did not help that the Pakistani military was perceived to have performed poorly in another armed confrontation with India in 1965. Ayub was forced to leave power in the hands of the army chief, General Yahya Khan, who promised elections based on an adult franchise. The Awami League was victorious in these historic elections of 1970, garnering 151 of the 313 National Assembly seats, including almost all of the seats allocated to East Pakistan. In view of the Awami League's victory, the government postponed the session of the new National Assembly, thereby spawning mass agitation in the east. Developments then took a violent turn and, ultimately, escalated into an open war of national liberation in East Pakistan.

Following a period of intense negotiations, Pakistani troops on 25 March unleashed a reign of terror by attacking Dhaka University and killing students, teachers and anyone else who sympathized openly with the cause for an independent Bangladesh. On 28 March 1971, the *New York Times* reported: 'The Pakistani Army is using artillery and heavy machine-guns against unarmed East Pakistani civilians to crush the movement for autonomy in this province of 75 million people' (Quadir 1997: 89). On 29 March, *Der Spiegel* reported: 'The West Pakistanis, although in a minority, oppressed the Bengalis and exploited them in the best traditions of the colonialists' (Quadir 1997: 90). This war, which Pakistan portrayed as an internal matter within a sovereign country, was supported by many Muslim-majority nations. Islamic countries outside the region also lent support to Pakistan. As late as 2 December, just weeks before the end of the war, Libyan leader Qaddafi reiterated his firm support for Pakistan's independence and sovereignty.

In contrast, on 4 April 1971, the Prime Minister of India, Indira Gandhi, called on Indians to give their full support to the people of East Pakistan; meanwhile, millions of refugees crossed over into India to avoid genocide. On 18 May, UN Secretary-General U. Thant issued a worldwide appeal for aid to Bengali refugees in India, whose numbers eventually grew to an estimated 9 million. As the possibility of a wider war loomed, Pakistani President Yahya Khan stated in an interview on CBS on 8 November that China would intervene if India were to attack Pakistan. On 28 November, US President Nixon sent messages to Yahya Khan, Indira Gandhi and Alexei Kosygin, asking that they do everything possible to prevent a full-scale war in the sub-continent.

On 3 December, Pakistan military planes attacked a number of Indian air bases, some of which were deep within Indian territory. India retaliated and a full-scale war broke out on both the eastern and western fronts. The Soviet Union, India's staunchest ally, exercised its veto power to stem any motion for a ceasefire in the United Nations Security Council. On 6 December, the US State Department announced that it was cutting off US$87.6 million in development loans to India. On 10 December, the USS *Enterprise*, a nuclear-powered aircraft carrier, and a flotilla of supporting ships left Saigon en route to the Bay of Bengal (Brown 1972: 226) in a clear show of support for Pakistan. The presence of the US Navy failed, however, to scare off either Indian troops or pro-independence Bengali fighters. Defeated and demoralized, the Pakistani military in East Pakistan (Bangladesh), under the command of Lt. Gen. Niazi, surrendered on 16 December 1971 to Lt. Gen. Aurora of the joint command of Indian forces and the liberation forces of Bangladesh.

The war of liberation for Bangladesh broke out because the Pakistani military refused to hand over political power to a democratically elected government. The USA was in a dilemma: on the one hand, it was ideologically supposed to support democracy in South Asia; on the other hand, it also wanted a stable Pakistan that would work closely with it in the fight against communism. Pakistan was also important to the USA for its strategic location, and its role in helping Kissinger carry out his secret mission to China in July 1971 was something that the USA wanted to reward. At this time, the Nixon administration was trying to reach a negotiated settlement of the Vietnam War with the support of the People's Republic of China.

Seymour Hersh commented on the genocide in East Pakistan, which had been ignored:

> The full extent of the administration's eagerness for the rapprochement became obvious only in the last half of 1971, as Yahya Khan's govern-

ment mounted a war of genocide inside East Pakistan in a futile effort to stop a rebellion and prevent the emergence of the independent nation of Bangladesh. Hundreds of thousands of Bengalis were massacred by Pakistani troops in the spring and summer, as the USA looked away out of fear that any intervention would distress China, Pakistan's ally, and mar the President's summit. Nixon and Kissinger, refusing to listen to the bureaucracy, which came close to open rebellion on the issue, chose to support Pakistan. They maintained that position in the famous 'tilt' of late 1971, even as the war escalated to a near showdown with the Soviets, who were supporting India, Pakistan's perennial enemy, in its objection to the terror tactics in Bangladesh. In his memoirs, Nixon quoted Kissinger's statement at a key point in the conflict, as the potential for a Soviet-American clash deepened: 'We don't really have any choice. We can't allow a friend of ours and China's to get screwed in a conflict with a friend of Russia's.'

(Hersh 1983: 368)

It should be mentioned that while the war of liberation was organized under the leadership of the Awami League, leftist leaders joined in the struggle for independence and played a major role. On 21 April 1971, Maulana Abdul Hamid Khan Bhasani, leader of the main socialist party, the National Awami Party (NAP), sent an appeal for support to world leaders. These included Chairman Mao Tse Tung, Prime Minister Chou En-lai, the USSR's Podgorny, Brezhnev and Kosygin, the USA's President Nixon, French President Pompidou, British Prime Minister Heath and Yugoslav President Tito, among others (Quadir 1997: 73). Leftist leaders in Bangladesh, however, were quickly disillusioned at the lack of response from their comrades in China, who were starting on the process of reconciliation with the USA.

On its part, the Nixon administration opposed the prospect of a divided Pakistan; thus, it promoted a peaceful settlement. Nevertheless, the US Consul-General in Dacca (Dhaka), Archer K. Blood, forwarded a cable in protest at official US silence towards human rights violations in East Pakistan (Kux 1993: 292). Blood sent a telegram dated 28 March 1971 with the subject heading 'Selective Genocide', barely three days after the Pakistani military's brutal crackdown on Bengali inhabitants. The note read:

Here in Dacca we are mute and horrified witnesses to a reign of terror by the Pak military. Evidence continues to mount that the MLA [Martial Law Authorities] authorities have a list of Awami League supporters whom they are systematically eliminating by seeking them out in their homes and shooting them down . . . Full horror of Pak Military atrocities will come to light sooner or later. I, therefore, question continued advisability of present USG [United States Government] posture of pretending to believe GOP [Government Of Pakistan] false assertions and denying, for understood reasons, that this office is communicating detailed account of events in East Pakistan.

(Blood 1971: memo no. 00959)

The 'Blood Telegram' denounced the USA's complicity in 'genocide' in former East Pakistan, and prompted Blood to be recalled from his post in Dhaka. The crackdown left at least 10,000 civilians dead in the first three days, with the eventual civilian death toll perhaps as high as 3 million. Some 10 million Bengalis, about 13 per cent of East Bengal's population, fled across the border into India.

In their cable, Blood and his fellow signatories charged:

Our government has failed to denounce the suppression of democracy. Our government has failed to take forceful measures to protect its citizens while at the same time bending over backwards to placate the West Pakistan-dominated government. Our government has evidenced what many will consider moral bankruptcy, ironically at a time when the U.S.S.R. sent President Yahya Khan a message defending democracy.

(Holley 2004)

Writer Christopher Hitchens, in his book *The Trial of Henry Kissinger* (2001), described the cable as 'the most public and the most strongly worded demarche, from State Department servants to the State Department that has ever been recorded' (Holley 2004).

Seymour Hersh, however, observed:

For Nixon and Kissinger, there was no issue. Yahya Khan held the key to Nixon's re-election; their conduit to the Chinese would not be challenged. The policy was easy to rationalize. Those who were against Yahya Khan were pro-India and pro-Soviet Union . . . There was no question where Nixon stood. He ordered Archer Blood transferred out of East Pakistan.

(Hersh 1983: 445)

Blood and his colleagues in the Dhaka office were unaware of the top-secret negotiations taking place between China and the USA, in which Pakistan played the role of middleman.

Furthermore, in the aftermath of independence, Bangladesh was faced with severe economic problems, but the USA was lukewarm in helping this impoverished nation and even suspended food aid during a crucial shortage. When Bangladesh was faced with a famine in 1974, the USA diverted ships carrying food to Bangladesh ports on the basis of a flimsy charge that Bangladesh did not qualify for US assistance because of its trade links with Cuba, a communist country. In reality, Bangladesh had a largely negligible trade relationship with Cuba, to which it merely exported jute bags (McHenry and Bird 1977; Sobhan 1979), but US law apparently forbade assistance to countries that had trade links with communist countries. This was bitter irony as the USA itself was establishing links with the world's most populous communist country – the People's Republic of China.

Significantly, the post-liberation economic crisis in Bangladesh contributed to the erosion of the legitimacy of the Awami League government. In August 1975, a small section of the army, in cahoots with some retired military officers, overthrew the government in a bloody coup that left dead the secular nationalist leader, Sheikh Mujibur Rahman, and members of his family. His two daughters survived as they were overseas. While taking on a pro-USA stance, the military also began a process of Islamization in this culturally pluralistic society. In contradiction to the idea of a necessary link between neoliberal economic reforms and liberal democratic politics, Bangladesh's military-dominated governments were largely to preside over an economic liberalization and structural adjustment process, especially from the 1980s, which resulted in increasingly gross inequalities in Bangladeshi society.

Conclusion

In this chapter, I have tried to sketch the nature of the Cold-War-era geopolitics that eventually produced the country of Bangladesh following its war of independence in 1971. Relations between the new country and the USA were strained in these early years given the USA's support for Pakistan. Since the death of Sheikh Mujibur Rahman, however, relations between Bangladesh and the USA have markedly improved, largely under conditions of military-dominated authoritarianism. Significantly, not only has Bangladesh been moving away from a democratic path, it has also been straying from its early secular commitments and in the direction of a more Islamic path. In fact, the leaders of both Bangladesh and Pakistan have become closer allies of the USA while turning a more Islamic shade. Islamization in South Asia – or, at least, the emergence of radicalized Islamic groups – was not viewed with great alarm by the USA within the context of the struggle to contain communism in the region. Today, however, it has returned to haunt the global hegemon as a major form of 'blowback'.

There are at least two lessons to be drawn from the above discussion. First, the Cold War is, in some senses, far from over; the fallout from the Cold War continues to influence the politics of the sub-continent. The nature of today's South Asian politics and the role of the world's sole superpower is a legacy of Cold-War-era conflicts. The second is that domestic politics in South Asia has been shaped by the dictates of the superpowers but has also simultaneously contributed to shaping the foreign policy agenda of the superpowers.

The Cold War may be officially over but the role of the USA remains central to the geopolitics and conflicts of South Asia. Many in Bangladesh today remain sceptical of US designs in the region – actual or perceived – given the experience of the Cold War. Bangladesh found the USA on the opposite side in its own struggle for national self-determination and democratic rights, so when Bangladeshis hear the US administration championing democracies worldwide, they have good reason to show some scepticism.

Moreover, the US government is now dominated by neoconservatives who have launched a global *jihad* against the so-called 'rogue states', at a time when the behaviour of the current US administration appears to be increasingly 'roguish'. Interestingly, the litany of complicities, assassination attempts and other unsavoury practices carried out by the USA for seventy years after the Bolshevik Revolution have prompted one writer to use the phrase 'rogue state' to describe the only superpower today, even prior to the unilateral invasion of Iraq and before 9/11 (Blum 2000).

In *America's Strategy in World Politics*, published in the early 1940s, N. J. Spykman states:

> The statesman who conducts foreign policy can concern himself with the values of justice, fairness, and tolerance only to the extent that they contribute to, or do not interfere with, the power objective. They can be used instrumentally as moral justification for the power quest, but they must be discarded the moment their application brings weakness. The search for power is not made for the achievement of moral values: moral values are used to facilitate the attainment of power.
>
> (Quoted in Nehru 1946: 538)

It seems that very little has changed in the last six decades.

* I wish to thank Ambassador Farooq Sobhan, Ishtiaq Hossain and Vedi Hadiz for their helpful comments.

15 Hindu fundamentalist politics in India

The alliance with the American Empire in South Asia

Anand Teltumbde

Introduction

Hindu fundamentalist politics has long been a thorn in the lives of India's religious minorities, Dalits[1] and Adivasis,[2] who together constitute about 40 per cent of the country's total population. Historically stemming from the interests of high-caste Hindus, Hindu fundamentalist politics also has a fascist genealogy that can be traced to the Hindu Mahasabha (Great Council of Hindus), an organization founded in 1915 that opposed the Muslim League and aspired to establish a Hindu Rashtra or Hindu state. The fascist heritage of Hindu fundamentalist politics has been examined by scholars such as Cassolari (2000: 218–8).

The amorphousness of Hinduism,[3] which hindered the building of a strong political movement, was first overcome by the ideological constructions of V. D. Savarkar. Savarkar provided it with the political creed of Hindutva, which literally means 'Hinduness' and which was purported to be the basis of Hindu nationalism. In addition, the Rashtriya Swayansewak Sangh (RSS or National Volunteers Corps), founded in 1925 in Nagpur, has always sought to create a paramilitary force of ideologically indoctrinated volunteers to realize the goals of Hindu Rashtra. Today, Hindu fundamentalism is represented by a plethora of organizations and outfits created for and catering to every segment of Indian society. While most of them have been floated by the RSS and, therefore, have been collectively called Sangh Parivar (family of the RSS outfits), there are a few like the Shiv Sena (Army of Shivaji) in Maharashtra, which, despite being independent of the RSS, is also zealously committed to Hindu fundamentalism.

Hindu fundamentalism derives its ideological orientation from a kind of Brahmanism that naturalizes a hierarchical structure of the world and, therefore, does not harbour serious ideological contradictions with many forms of political and cultural domination, which explains its various paradoxes. While committed to Hindu nationalism, it never came into serious conflict with British colonial rule and, rather, opposed anti-colonial struggle. While subscribing to the Gandhian vision of development, its adherents were responsible for Gandhi's death; while having lived under Muslim rulers for seven centuries, they bear an inveterate hatred of Muslims; while the movement is well disposed towards the Christian world, its members frequently terrorize Christians in India; while many Hindu fundamentalists admire Hitler,[4] they are at the same time friendly with Israel; while Hindu revivalist doctrine does not negate the serfdom of Dalits, it awkwardly tries to co-opt them along with its icon, Ambedkar; and while *swadeshi* or self-reliance is emphasized in rhetoric, the political organs of Hindu fundamentalism have embraced the neoliberal economic agenda as fervently as any neoliberal evangelist.

It is contended here that Hindu fundamentalism – the BJP (Bharatiya Janata Party) being its main representative – has been a well-matched partner of the USA in India, having been engaged in a prolonged relationship of mutual benefit with the global hegemon, politically as well as economically. While the post-Cold-War order means that the USA no longer faces any direct military threat from the likes of the erstwhile Soviet Union, it does face a world with numerous, diffuse and unpredictable sources of threats of diverse natures. The concerns of American Empire partly emanate from the need to manage this unwieldy international system, which requires the support of gendarmes in strategic regions of the world. While in power, Hindu fundamentalists, represented by the BJP, proved to be its reliable regional allies.

During the Cold War period, the USA always considered India a pro-Soviet country and therefore favoured Pakistan, but the collapse of the USSR changed many things. While Pakistan continues to be vital to the USA, India has come to assume more importance in the economic and political arenas. Neighbouring China is a strategic competitor of the USA. Nearby Central Asia is not only at the crossroads of Europe and Asia, but also a major source of oil and gas outside of the Middle East. Thus, from a geo-strategic point of view, it becomes imperative for the USA to bring India into its fold. India can serve as a counterweight against the threat of China, against Islamic fundamentalism and also against Pakistan's tendency to make increasingly extravagant demands in return for its services in the War on Terror.[5]

The political rise of Hindu fundamentalist forces over the last few decades has been the result of many factors. Not least among them was the discernible rise of communal tension in the 1980s, creating an environment within which Hindu fundamentalist forces could, within a decade, rearticulate their ideology more aggressively and transform themselves into serious contenders for power. Initially, it was the nationalist movements (for example, those of the Sikhs and Kashmiri) in many parts of the country in the 1980s that impelled Prime Minister Indira Gandhi and, later, Rajiv Gandhi – both from the BJP's main rival, the Congress Party – to use religious idioms to mobilize the support of the Hindu majority for their governments (Chandhoke 2000). Ironically, the growing communalization of Indian politics occurred at the same time that India was beginning to open up its economy to the forces of neoliberal globalization that, in some theoretical constructs, is supposed to lead to the rise of a secular civil society. The opening up of India's economy began modestly, coinciding roughly with the first disbursement in 1981 of an IMF loan of US$5 billion to India.

It was in this general context that the BJP launched a movement in 1989 for the 'liberation' of Ram Janmabhoomi (birthplace of Lord Ram), which meant building a Ram temple in place of a sixteenth-century Babri mosque[6] at Ayodhya. The episode is well documented – the resultant tensions set off a series of communal riots between Hindus and Muslims in many cities in the state of Uttar Pradesh. The communal frenzy was further fanned by a Rath Yatra (chariot journey) of BJP politician L. K. Advani in 1990; he traversed 10,000 kilometres from Somnath, a temple town on the west coast, to Ayodhya, and this sparked off another series of deadly riots. Significantly, in the 1991 general elections that followed, the BJP reaped a bumper crop, emerging as the second largest party in Parliament with 119 seats; it had expanded its share of the vote from 11.4 per cent in 1989 to 20.1 per cent. The year 1992 saw the eventual demolition of the Babri mosque, followed by nationwide Hindu–Muslim riots that resulted in thousands of casualties.

In this chapter, I seek to delineate the essential characteristics of Hindu fundamentalist politics, an important social force in a contemporary and increasingly economically globalized India, through its historical development and to its present operations. I also seek to identify the areas in which Hindu fundamentalist politics is complementary to the concerns of American Empire in the post-Cold-War period and the global agenda of economic neoliberalism.

Post-Cold-War concerns of the American Empire

As mentioned earlier, the USA considered India to be in an alliance with the Soviet Union during the Cold War and, therefore, sided with Pakistan, India's long-term nemesis in the region. Relations between Washington and New Delhi reached their lowest point in the 1970s and early 1980s after the USA took the side of Pakistan in the 1971 India–Pakistan War, which ended in the humiliating defeat of Pakistan and the liberation of Bangladesh. The USA further courted China when India had serious border disputes with the country. In the late 1980s and early 1990s, when the CIA-sponsored Mujahidin were fighting the Russians in Afghanistan, the USA allowed Pakistan much leeway, even in the latter's development of a nuclear weapons programme (Bothra 2002).

The end of the Cold War, however, also brought about a sea change that favoured better Indo-US relations.[7] China's emergence as a major challenge to US predominance in the Asia–Pacific; Russia's potential resurgence; the emerging strategic partnership between Russia and China; and Islamic fundamentalist challenges in the Gulf, Afghanistan, Pakistan and some of the Central Asian Republics (Kapila 2000: 22 April) were all reasons that impelled the USA to court India as a potential partner for maintaining stability in the region.

Besides geo-strategic and political considerations, the geo-economic interests of US multinational corporations (MNCs) operating in South Asia have also significantly influenced the USA's shift towards India. India's sheer size, its growing market and an expanding base of middle-class consumers and, more importantly, the synergy between its economy and that of the USA – particularly in knowledge-based industries like pharmaceuticals, information technology, biotechnology and entertainment – spell tremendous business opportunities. US trade with India has shown impressive growth since India embarked on substantial economic reforms in July 1991. Total US merchandise trade rose from US$5.7 billion in 1991 to US$15.9 billion in 2002, representing a growth of 279 per cent. Total Indo-US trade, including IT/software exports in 2002, amounts to US$24.7 billion, making the USA India's largest trading partner.[8] The economic and strategic potential of India's IT industry and its dovetailing with US businesses have also been an added boon (Kapila 2001).

The political roots of Hindu fundamentalism

Historically, the origins of Hindu fundamentalist politics can be traced to the ideas of the Hindu Sanghatan (Hindu consolidation), which germinated in nineteenth-century Bengal just after the Sepoy rebellion of 1857 that had shocked the colonial establishment by demonstrating the political potential of Hindu–Muslim unity. While the British succeeded in quelling the rebellion with brute force, they came increasingly to realize the need to build a base of support among kings and landlords, and the usefulness of communal division between Hindus and Muslims. It may not be surprising, therefore, that one of the earliest Hindu nationalist texts of the colonial era was the celebrated novel *Anandmath* (*Abbey of bliss*), written in Bengali by Bankim Chandra Chatterjee.[9] Chatterjee was the first Indian to have been directly appointed to the post of Deputy Magistrate in the year 1858. *Anandmath* has two distinct thrusts: hatred of Muslims and admiration for British rulers, which suggests that Hindu nationalism was conceptualized at its inception mainly in opposition to Muslims. The novel is replete with passages in praise of Santans (rebel hermits) plundering and killing Muslims:

> they came down to the Muslim villages and torched their houses. The Muslims were worried for safety of their lives and the Santans robbed them of everything.
>
> (Chatterjee 2000: 112)

At the same time, the novel exudes love for the British colonialists: 'There is no possibility of restoring the Santan-virtue without the Englishman becoming King' (Chatterjee 2000: 192). 'Therefore, we would make the Englishman our King . . . The subjects would be happy in the English kingdom – they would practice the virtue without any trouble' (Chatterjee 2000: 193).

Significantly, the British encouraged the formation of the United India Patriotic Association (UIPA) in the 1880s. This was an organization of the declining classes of landlords, kings and other nobility, both Hindus and Muslims (Puniyani 2003a). The UIPA resolved to cultivate Indian loyalty to the British crown, and later served the colonial policy of divide and rule by giving way to the Muslim League on one side and the Hindu Mahasabha–RSS on the other (Puniyani 2003b). The RSS was, in fact, formed as a right-wing response to the nationalist mass upsurge against the Rowlatt Act in 1919. It was also a response during the Non-Cooperation movement to the emergence of a working-class movement with the founding of the All India Trade Union Congress in 1920, the rise of several communist groups and workers' and peasants' parties and, most importantly, the rise of an anti-caste Dalit movement (Basu *et al.* 1993: 16–17; Ahmad 1998; Ahmad Fauzi 2001).

The direct influence of European fascism on Hindu fundamentalist politics goes back to at least the early 1930s. One of the prominent leaders of the Hindu Mahasabha, Dr B. S. Moonje, was a mentor to Dr K. B. Hedgewar, the founder of the RSS. Moonje took time out from the Round Table Conference in London in 1931[10] to visit Italy for the purpose of studying the ideology, structure and operations of Italian fascism. He even had a personal audience with Mussolini, and recorded in his diary that he was impressed with the fascist leader (Moonje 1932–36). After his return, he founded a military school and reorganized the Hindu society in Maharashtra along fascist lines.[11] The RSS that was already created under his mentorship came to be further developed on the basis of this blueprint. Moonje 1932–6 declared:

> I have thought out a scheme based on Hindu Dharm Shashtra which provides for standardisation of Hinduism throughout India . . . But the point is that this ideal cannot be brought to effect unless we have our own swaraj with a Hindu as a dictator like Shivaji[12] of old or Mussolini or Hitler of the present day in Italy or Germany.

In his preface to *The Scheme of the Central Hindu Military Society and its Military School*, Moonje 1932–6 wrote:

> This training is meant for qualifying and fitting our boys for the game of killing masses of men with the ambition of winning victory with the best possible causalities of dead and wounded while causing the utmost – possible to the adversary.[13]

The political practice of Hindu fundamentalism

The RSS concentrated on apolitical activities like *shakha* (unit) training and pedagogy-based discourses called *bouddhiks* (intellectual sessions) in the pre-Independence period, although the vision of a Hindu Rashtra that was espoused was itself a political statement. The ostensibly apolitical character of the RSS can be understood as a means of not antagonizing the colonial powers, given the anti-colonial stirrings that had become widespread. This apolitical mask, however, was soon to be discarded. After its takeover in 1940 by M. S. Golwalkar, the *sarsanghchalak* (supreme leader) following Hedgewar, the RSS articulated an even more discernible fascist form of politics.[14] As Puniyani (2003c) suggests:

> Golwalkar . . . crystallized the Hindutva politics in very strong and blunt ways. His hatred for minorities and communists comes out transparently. His appreciation for the eternal relevance of the laws of Manu[15] is a clear pointer to the status of Dalits and women in the RSS vision of India, which is that of a Hindu Rashtra. It was from the Golwalkar era that, rather than direct political activity, the RSS emphasized infiltration of its trained volunteers into the bureaucracy, army and media.

It is important to note that the RSS did not initially recognize the national flag, institutions such as the Constitution or the Parliament of independent India. When the Congress Party adopted *poorna swaraj* (full independence) at its session in Lahore in December 1929 and called upon the people to observe 26 January 1930 as Independence Day (by unfurling the tricolour flag), Hedgewar issued a circular to all RSS *shakhas* to worship the *bhagwa jhanda* (saffron flag)[16] instead (Islam 2000). Even after independence was finally attained in 1947 and the tricolour flag became the national flag, the RSS still refused to accept it (Islam 2000). Similarly, the RSS did not hide its dislike of the Constitution, and wanted it replaced by Manusmriti, or Code of Manu.[17] When the Constituent Assembly finalized the Constitution of India, the RSS organ, *Organizer*, complained in an editorial dated 30 November 1949 that there was no mention of Manu's laws – 'the unique constitutional development in ancient Bharat'. It reported, 'To this day his laws as enunciated in the *Manusmriti* excite the admiration of the world and elicit spontaneous obedience and conformity. But to our constitutional pundits that means nothing'. Golwalkar (1966) wrote, 'It has absolutely nothing, which can be called our own. Is there a single word of reference in its guiding principles to what our national mission is and what our keynote in life is? No!'

The RSS aspired for political power within the very constitutional framework it rejected. In October 1951, the RSS floated a full-fledged political party called Bharatiya Jan Sangh (BJS), which could not make any significant mark until the time of the political vortex created by the movement of

Jaiprakash Narayan, a veteran socialist who sought to fight corruption and restore democracy in the public sphere in the context of the increasingly authoritarian rule of Indira Gandhi in the early 1970s. This movement prompted Indira Gandhi to impose a state of emergency on 25 June 1975. In spite of its fascist antecedents, the RSS managed to earn the reputation of a crusader for democracy in the resistance struggle that erupted against the state of emergency. The RSS became part of the post-emergency political constellation, in the form of the Janata Party (People's Party), and tasted political power when this party won the general elections in 1977. However, it brought the rule of the Janata Party to an end in 1979 on the issue of 'duel membership' of the Janasangh members.[18] Soon thereafter, elements of the party organized themselves into the Bharatiya Janata Party (Indian People's Party or BJP). The BJP also languished at the margins of national politics but eventually came to power (albeit through a coalition) on the basis of promoting communalism for the first time in 1996, then in 1998 and in 1999. The demolition of the Babri mosque in 1992 symbolized this great turnaround in the fortunes of the BJP, which became increasingly communal in its political slogans.

It is worth pointing out that the Hindu fundamentalists did not initially develop ideas in the area of economics. As Malik (2003) wrote:

> Under the stewardship of Golwalkar from 1940 to 1973, the RSS saw itself as a sort of Hinduized social service league. It concentrated on issues such as rural development and uplift of aboriginal tribal people. If it had an economic view at all, it was fairly similar to Mahatma Gandhi's cottage industry doctrine. This involved the idea of the self-sufficient village, one that met its own needs and did not need to look to the world beyond. In essence, it was an anti-free trade argument, albeit in an inchoate form.

In the wake of globalization, the RSS floated an outfit called Swadeshi Jagaran Manch (SJM) in 1991[19] to monitor the economic policy of the Congress government. The name itself gives the impression of active opposition to economic neoliberalism, in keeping with the populist and ultra-nationalist rhetoric of Hindu fundamentalists. However, after coming to power, the BJP not only adopted the same neoliberal economic policies, but also accelerated their implementation. It emphasized foreign investment, opened up the insurance sector, sold a number of public sector companies, and removed quantitative restrictions on the import of various products (Basu 2001). The SJM initially voiced stern criticism of these policies, but this was not to last.

Another dimension of Hindu fundamentalist politics extends to the Indian diaspora abroad, particularly in the USA. Its influence has been significant not only in supporting Hindu fundamentalism within India, but also in shaping ties with US imperialism. The 1.5-million-strong

Indian–American community, made up largely of upper caste/privileged class backgrounds, typically subscribes to Hindutva ideology and is interested in the idea of reviving India's 'past glory'. Relatively prosperous, the community has actively contributed considerable funds to the Hindu fundamentalist organizations and has built a formidable international network (Sabrang Communications and The South Asian Citizens Watch 2002). It is also known to have contributed heavily to both the Democratic and Republican Parties in the presidential elections of 2004. The Congressional caucus on India and Indian–Americans has more than 120 members, and is one of the biggest interest groups in the US House of Representatives. In 2001,[20] the community lobbied successfully for the removal of a number of sanctions that were placed on India under the aegis of the US Nuclear Proliferation Prevention Act of 1994 following its nuclear tests in 1998, and pushed hard for President Bill Clinton's visit to India in March 2000 (Cohen and Dasgupta 2001).

BJP rule and imperialism

The environment of communalized politics that allowed the exponents of Hindu fundamentalist politics to retake power was, ironically, largely provided by the actions of their great rival, the Congress Party of Indira Gandhi. Uncertain of her popular standing at the time, Congress attempted to garner the support of the religious majority by casting the Kashmir and Punjab problems in communalistic terms, following Indira Gandhi's second coming to power in 1980 (Frank 2001). The communalization of the Kashmir problem and the insurgency in Punjab that bloodied the decade were harbingers of the further communalization of Indian politics (Jeffrey 1994: 46–7).

When Rajiv Gandhi took over the reins after his mother was assassinated in 1984, simmering communal tensions were exacerbated. His government's policies, for example, contributed to the flare-up of bloody communal violence in Punjab in 1986 (Jeffrey 1994: xxxiii–xxxiv). In February that year, the locks (installed in 1949) were removed from the Ram shrine within the precinct of the Babri mosque in Ayodhya (*The Times of India*, 6 February 1986; Rajgopal 2001: 284–91). In the same month, the government exempted Muslims from the provisions of the Criminal Procedure Code, under which a Muslim woman, Shah Bano, had been granted alimony from her former husband in December 1985 (*The Times of India*, 1 March 1986). As mentioned earlier, the BJP took full advantage of this communalized political context and expanded its campaign for the Ram temple. The BJP's message was conveyed evermore widely due to the expansion of the media industry in the 1980s (Rajgopal 2001; Jeffrey 2002: 281–300). Robin Jeffrey notes a strange correlation between the media revolution and the rise of the BJP: as the number of newspapers trebled and television ownership expanded, the BJP trebled its vote in national elections (Jeffrey 2002: 281–300).

The BJP's traditional social base, comprising the urban middle class, petty traders and industrialists typically belonging to the Dwija (twice-born) castes, had undergone significant expansion and urbanization during the post-Independence period.[21] Although these sectors derived maximum benefit from post-Independence developments, they found that their traditional hegemony was threatened by the rising demands of the lower castes. The slow pace of economic development also failed to meet their growing aspirations, in spite of the economic liberalization drive started by Rajiv Gandhi. Together with a new professional middle class made up of IT professionals and the like, they were attracted to the rhetoric of the BJP and claimed the party's vision of a 'strong India'[22] as their own.

The combination of such developments catapulted the BJP from a mere 'two seats and apparent oblivion in 1984, to 86 seats in 1989 and the capacity to bring down governments' (Jeffrey 2002: 285); in 1991, it won 120 seats and 20.1 per cent of the popular vote. The 'equity boom' and the 'consumer goods revolution' of the 1980s led the urban middle class to discard 'socialist rhetoric and Gandhian temperance' (Hansen 1998: 296). This, after the formal adoption of the reform package in July 1991, exploded into what Corbridge and Harriss (2001: 126) have called an 'elite revolution'. 'The "elite revolt", evident in a growing embrace of both liberalisation and Hindu nationalism, has seen a much stronger assertion of upper-and-middle class interests, encapsulated in opposition to public subsidies for the poor through poverty alleviation programs' (Hill 2002: 156).

The BJP strengthened its position in 1996 to 180 seats and made its first, albeit short-lived, bid for national political power in May 1996. In the 1998 elections, it formed the government, with a coalition of eighteen parties, which lasted thirteen months. In the 1999 elections, the BJP emerged as the biggest party with 182 seats, and formed the government in coalition with twenty-four parties.

While in power, the BJP had to confront the contradiction between the imperatives of its 'strong India' rhetoric, which was to be achieved through engagement in modernization and globalization, and the ideas of purity and pollution that were so important in the *swadeshi* ideology of the RSS. Yet, given that its middle-class base (Dubashi 1992) was increasingly in favour of globalization – and in the context of the triumph of capitalism over the crumbled Soviet bloc – the BJP overcame this its ambivalence and became an aggressive promoter of neoliberal globalization. The BJP also sought an alliance with the USA, which had emerged as the supreme power in the post-Cold-War world order. This move was further fuelled by the party's ideological opposition to communism; its historical opposition to the Congress Party, which was identified with the USSR; and the collapse of Soviet Russia. Other factors, such as pressure from the increasingly globalized middle class and the Indian diaspora in the USA, also pushed it in a direction that was increasingly pro-capitalist, pro-globalization and pro-USA.

Economics

The five years (1999–2004) of the BJP-led National Democratic Alliance rule was characterized by nationalistic and patriotic bravado, while the economy was opened up to the operations of foreign capital through several liberalization measures. As mentioned earlier, these included the removal of quantitative restrictions on imports, the slashing of import tariffs and new regulations that were generally favourable to MNCs and foreign investors. While these measures did not succeed in getting foreign direct investment for productive economic activity (much went into unproductive mergers and acquisitions), they did attract hot money in the form of portfolio investments and NRI deposits, which were essentially a deposit scheme for non-resident Indians, and the like.[23] The deflationary economic policies undertaken by the government under advice from the IMF and World Bank, however, were detrimental to generating jobs as they restricted government expenditure (Patnaik 2002). Unemployment was also exacerbated by privatization policies that were aimed at containing the budget deficit. The annual addition to formal sector employment consistently declined from 1991 to 2000, even becoming negative during the era of the BJP-led government. Equity disinvestment in public sector companies was also accelerated with the institution of a special ministry.[24]

The BJP government shored up the above policies with further economic reforms along neoliberal lines. It altered the Indian Patent Act, opened up the banking sector to foreign capital, opened up capital markets, and set up export-processing zones where Indian laws did not apply. It also provided export subsidies; pursued the devaluation of the rupee; promoted large-scale outsourcing for transnational corporations (TNCs), particularly in the IT sector, where labour costs are internationally low; and also scrapped the public distribution system that provided food security for millions of the poor (Arvind 2002: 82). Other policies, such as allowing bio-engineered agricultural products, were implemented to meet commitments to the World Trade Organization.

In a seeming contradiction, the nominally *swadeshi*-committed BJP government enthusiastically adopted the free market dogma and markedly reduced the state's share of responsibility in running a public health system[25] and providing basic education. The agricultural sector, which sustains more than 70 per cent of the population, was largely neglected by the BJP government. The dual pressure of declining production and falling commodity prices drove thousands of farmers to suicide (RUPE 2004; *Hindu*, 9 December 2002). Control of basic resources such as water and forests was also given to foreign companies in spite of protests from various people's movements. The supply of water from many rivers was contracted out, for example, to MNCs like Coca-Cola.[26] In Kerala, poor Dalits and Adivasis had to launch a bitter struggle against Coca-Cola when the company drew groundwater for its factory, leaving villagers without a water supply (Shiva *et al.* 2002). The government contracted out dams as well, to private companies, for the purpose of building hydro-electric power plants. In one controversial episode, it gave control of the Maheshwar Dam to S. Kumar, an Indian clothing company that had no expertise or experience in constructing hydro-electric plants, thus raising suspicion that the company was working by proxy for foreign firms.[27] So while the emergence of India as a rising economic force is now being widely hailed, there is clearly a much darker side to economic globalization as it has concerned the majority of Indians.

Politics

In politics, Hindu fundamentalist forces have supported the agenda of American Empire because they, too, see Islamic fundamentalism and Chinese communism as threats (Sinha 2000). The government of India has come out on the side of the USA on matters of missile defence, globalization and many other contentious issues of the day (Prashad 2001). Soon after coming to power in 1998, the coalition government led by the Hindutva forces carried out nuclear tests despite international criticism, and proceeded to reach out to both the USA and Israel in an attempt to create a Washington–Tel Aviv–New Delhi *entente* against communism and Islam. Significantly, when the Indian Foreign Minister, Jaswant Singh, visited Israel in July 2000, he said that the relationship between the two countries was strained due to Indian 'domestic policies' resulting from the existence of a 'Muslim vote bank' (Prashad 2001).

India and Israel have, thus, developed an extraordinarily close strategic partnership. Israel has become India's second largest weapons supplier (Bedi 2003) after Russia, and sells military technology that alone is worth US$1.5 billion annually (Kumar 2003). Israel now co-ordinates its political strategies and intelligence with India due to the perception of sharing common adversaries – Pakistan and Islamic terrorism. There were important historical precedents to the close relationship that the BJP has forged with Israel. In January 1963, a few months after India's border war with China, the government of India initiated dialogue with the Israeli military;[28] two years later, Israeli Cabinet Minister Yigal Alon visited India. Mossad and India's Research Analysis Wing (RAW) began sharing information from the late 1970s onwards (Burki 2004) and in 1992, the Congress Party-led government sent an envoy to Israel, and diplomatic relations began in earnest.

During a visit by US President Bill Clinton in March 2000, India demonstrated its new allegiance to the USA by signing a so-called 'vision statement' (prepared by the consultancy firm, McKinsey and Co.) that envisaged 'complementary responsibility for, ensuring regional and international security . . . and strategic stability in Asia and beyond' (Embassy of India 2000). During the period of BJP rule, there were extensive tie-ups between India and the USA in the form of interlocking relations – formal and informal – at the ministerial level, at the top echelons of the bureaucracy, in internal security, and in intelligence and defence. After 9/11, US–Indian military relations grew dramatically closer, allowing India to hope for an Israel-like role in South Asia as a US gendarme. There has been, for example, tacit US acceptance of India's nuclear programme and its supposed need for minimum deterrence. There is also direct US commitment to 'bolster joint efforts to counter terrorism'. On the other hand, India has endorsed the USA's Missile Defence Programme (Ritchie 2003) despite opposition from many of the USA's closest military allies. As indicated by Jaswant Singh to reporters at the end of his five-day visit to Australia in June 2001, the first steps had been taken to allow US military bases on Indian soil (McInerney 2001), despite his pronouncement that 'India's military bases are not accessible to any foreign country' (*Indian Express*, 5 December 2001). After September 11, India was one of the first countries to support the US coalition against terrorism (*Indian Express*, 5 December 2001). It is important to note, however, that close ties with the USA were already being formed during Rajiv Gandhi's government. It was his government, after all, that in 1990 allowed US aircraft to refuel in Mumbai during the Gulf War (Rajghatta 2001).

While the BJP openly represents Hindu fundamentalism, the currently ruling Congress Party has always been an ambivalent supporter. Even in the wake of communal carnage in Gujarat in 2002, in which Muslims and Christians were the victims, it did not come out forcefully against Hindu communalism despite current Congress leader Sonia Gandhi's accusation that BJP leaders were responsible for 'abetting the riots', and that they had failed 'to protect the lives and property of the Muslim community' (*The Tribune*, 1 May 2002). Following the BJP's electoral defeat in 2004, Congress has now formed a government that crucially depends upon the external support of the Marxist parties; however, it is continuing with its predecessor's neoliberal economic policies, many of which it foreshadowed during its previous time in power, albeit in a characteristically muffled manner. Significantly, it is likely that Congress cannot or will not take up a confrontational stance against Hindutva forces in general, for fear of losing electoral support from the majority Hindu population. An early indication of this emerged when a Congress minister was forced to back down during controversy over comments that were deemed harmful to the memory of V. D. Savarkar, regarded by many as a colonial-era Hindutva nationalist hero.

Conclusion

The Hindu fundamentalism that ostensibly originated in the 1920s in response to the anti-colonial struggles of the Indian people and rising assertiveness of the lower castes had a clearly pro-imperialist character. It had inherited this from its ideological source, Brahmanical Hinduism. Its pro-USA proclivities surfaced all throughout the Cold War period, in opposition to the USSR and, domestically, to the pro-Soviet Congress Party. In the 1980s, changing circumstances catapulted the Hindu fundamentalist political party, the BJP, to prominence. The ascent of neoliberal economics was apparently in conflict with its *swadeshi* ideology, but the BJP discarded the latter after coming to power in order to maintain its upper-caste and middle-class support base. During its five-year rule (1999–2004), the BJP promoted economic neoliberal policies with the full support and encouragement of the USA and international development organizations. Moreover, its long-held animosity towards Muslims had become increasingly useful in strengthening ties with Israel and the USA.

Domestically, Hindu fundamentalist politics has caused severe damage to the pluralism of Indian society – the scars from the demolition of the Babri mosque, the communal riots that followed, and the heinous carnage of Muslims in Gujarat are not likely to disappear quickly. The neoliberal economic policies promoted by the BJP, which are likely to be continued by Congress, have arguably caused much suffering to the ordinary people of India, although they are frequently lauded by international development organizations. The Indian people subsequently rejected the BJP, and a Congress-led alliance, swearing by secularist principles, has since come to power. Slogans, however, have been poor solace; given the Congress's soft position on Hindutva, the threat of Hindu fundamentalism still looms in the background.

Notes

1 Dalit is a popular term for the people belonging to the untouchable castes in India's social hierarchy. Although, the Indian Constitution abolished untouchability in 1951, these people continue to suffer discrimination. They are also known as Scheduled Castes and account for 16 per cent of the total population.
2 Adivasis are the aboriginal people who are not a part of the Hindu social order. They are also known as Scheduled Tribes and account for 7.5 per cent of the total population.
3 Amorphousness refers to the pluralistic traditions of Hinduism such as Smarta, Shaiva, Vaishnava, Shakta and others, which defy the precise definition of Hinduism as a political identity.
4 Right from its inception, Hindutva has shown a strong liking for fascism and Nazism. B. S. Moonje, V. D. Savarkar, M. S. Golwalkar, all Hindutva proponents, are well known for their praise of Mussolini and Hitler. For example (Golwalkar 1966: 35), the RSS chief writes in praise of Hitler: 'To keep up the purity of the Race and its culture, Germany shocked the world by her purging the country of the semitic Races – the Jews . . . Germany has also shown how well nigh impossible it is for Races and cultures, having differences going to the root, to be assimilated into one united whole, a good lesson for us in Hindusthan to learn and profit by.'
5 For providing access to and intelligence on Afghanistan, Pakistan had extracted a deep price from the USA: a promise to intervene in the Kashmir dispute, keeping India and Israel out of the coalition, waiver of external debt, and a bail-out financial package (Bothra 2002).
6 This mosque was built by Mir Baqi, a minister of the Mughal emperor, Babar.

7 George W. Bush, during his campaign for the US presidency in 2000, accepted 'the security needs' of India and, therefore, its nuclear programme. He indicated that he was in favour of removing the economic sanctions that had been imposed on India for carrying out nuclear tests as soon as possible (Ramchandran, S. 2000).

8 Computed from the trade statistics taken from various sources (The India One Stop 2004, The US–China Business Council 2004 and The US–Asean Business Council 2004).

9 *Anandmath* was first published in serial form in 1875 in a Bengali magazine, *Bang Darshan*, edited by Sanjib Chandra Chattopadhyay, the elder brother of Bankim Chandra. It was first published in book form in 1882.

10 The second Round Table Conference convened by the British government to frame a constitution for India with a view to satisfying the demands of the people of India, to which fifty-three Indian members were invited.

11 In 1934, Moonje started work for the foundation of his own institution, the Bhonsla Military School. For this, he founded the Central Hindu Military Education Society, whose aim was to provide education in 'Sanatan Dharma' (traditional religion), and training 'in the science and art of personal and national defence' (Moonje 1932–36).

12 Shivaji (1630–80) is a legendary creator of the Maratha Empire with an alleged vision of a Hindu Swarajya, or sovereign Hindu state. He is seen by present-day Hindu fundamentalists as a benevolent dictator.

13 Moonje does not give any clear-cut indication regarding this 'adversary', whether it was the external enemy, the British, or the 'historical' internal enemy – the Muslims. Considering the Hindu nationalists' historical animosity against Muslims, however, it may be well surmised that he meant Muslims as the adversary.

14 In the 1930s, the Hindu Right was ecstatic about the advent of Hitler. One of its founders, V. D. Savarkar, was feted in the Nazi press for his enthusiastic support of the Nazis. Also see note 2.

15 Manu, a mythological figure, is credited with founding the ancient sacred laws of Brahminism, which sanctify the caste system.

16 The saffron flag is identified with Hinduism and signifies renunciation as well as valour. Notably, it was the flag of the Bhakti movement and Shivaji. RSS adopted it as its flag.

17 Manusmriti provides an ancient code for Hindu Social Order based on caste hierarchy.

18 Socialist leaders like Raj Narain in the Janata Party raised this issue – known as the duel membership issue – and asked the Jansangh members in the Janata Party to resign their RSS membership. The RSS made it plain to their members not to resign and planned several communal riots in Aligarh, Varanasi, Jamshedpur, etc., to display its strength.

19 SJM came into existence on 22 November 1991 at Nagpur as decided by five organizations – BMS, ABVP, BKS, Akhil Bharatiya Grahak Panchayat (ABGP) and Sahkar Bharati – within the Sangh Parivar, with the formation of a central committee convened under Dr M.G. Bokare (former Vice-Chancellor, Nagpur University).

20 'U.S. lifts sanctions against India, Pak', *The Hindu*, Chennai, 24 September 2001.

21 The proportion of urban population to the total population has gone up from 17.3 per cent in 1951 to 27.8 per cent in 2001. See eCensusIndia (2003).

22 'Strong India' has been the historical obsession of the Sangh Parivar and integral to the Hindutva ideology (Vanaik 2002).

23 India's share of portfolio investments has been consistently higher than FDI during the 1990s. Out of a capital account balance of US$77.69 billion, the portfolio investment was US$18.50 billion as opposed to US$15.58 billion (*RBI Handbook of Statistics of the Indian Economy* 2000). On 31 March 2001, US$38.1

billion of India's US$42.2 billion in foreign exchange reserves consisted of trade credits, short-term official debt, foreign portfolio investment and non-resident Indian deposits, collectively described by the Centre for Monitoring Indian Economy (CMIE) as 'vulnerable liabilities' (Jha 2001). This trend continued unabated thereafter; in April–June 2003, the growth in NRI deposit and portfolio flows (as a percentage of growth in forex reserves) amounted to a whooping 54.62 per cent (Celestine 2003).

24 Disinvestment proceeds in 1991–2 were Rs.30.38 billion; they remained far below Rs.10.00 billion except for two years, 1992–3 (Rs.19.61 billion) and 1994–5 (Rs.50.78 billion). With the BJP's coming to power, it zoomed in the first year itself (1998–9) to Rs.90.06 billion. Total proceeds up to 2000 came to Rs.22.19 billion (*Hindustan Times*, 10 October 99).

25 The budgetary allocation for the Public Health System had decreased from 1.3 per cent in 1990 to 0.9 per cent in 1999.

26 For example, much of the Ganga water ex-Tehri Dam was contracted out to Ondeo Degre'mont, a subsidiary of Suez Lyonnaise des Eaux Water Division of France, for putting up a drinking water plant at Sonia Vihar in New Delhi on a build–operate–transfer (BOT) basis for ten years. River Bhavani, an important tributary of Cauvery, was sold by the Tamilnadu government to Coca-Cola for its Kinley brand mineral water.

27 The Maheshwar hydro-electric project is the first privatized big dam being built in the country. The total cost includes 66 per cent of the total cost is covered by funds from two German companies, Bayerwerk and VEW. On a short-term basis, Siemens, another German company, has provided 17 per cent additional equity in return for the contract to provide generators and turbines for the hydel project (Deshpande 1999).

28 This story broke in the *Hindustan Times* on 15 May 1980.

Bibliography

Articles and books

Abat, Fortunato (1993) *The Day We Nearly Lost Mindanao: the armed forces of the Philippines Central Command story*, Manila.

Abdul Aziz Nik Mat, Nik (1995) *Kelantan: Universiti Politik Terbuka*, Nilam Puri, Kelantan: Maahad ad-Dakwah Wal-Imamah.

——(1996) *Tafsir Sura Hud*, Nilam Puri, Kelantan: Maahad ad-Dakwah Wal-Imamah.

——(1998) *Tafsir Sura Yunus*, Nilam Puri, Kelantan: Maahad ad-Dakwah Wal-Imamah.

Abdul Hadi Awang (2002) *Amanat Haji Hadi: Penghuraian dan Penjelasan Dato' Seri Tuan Guru Haji Abdul Hadi Awang*, Kuala Lumpur: Jabatan Penerangan PAS Pusat.

Abinales, Patricio N. (1998) 'State leaders, apparatuses and local strongmen: the Philippine military under Marcos', in *Images of State Power: essays on Philippine politics from the margins*, Quezon City: University of the Philippines Press, 64–75.

——(2000a) 'From *orang besar* to colonial big man: Datu Piang of Cotabato and the American colonial state', in Alfred W. McCoy (ed.) *Lives at the Margins: biography of Filipinos obscure, ordinary, and heroic*, Madison, WI: University of Wisconsin Center for Southeast Asian Studies, 193–288.

——(2000b) *Making Mindanao: Cotabato and Davao in the formation of the Philippine nation-state*, Quezon City: Ateneo de Manila University Press.

——(2003) 'Progressive-machine conflict in early-twentieth century US politics and colonial state building in the Philippines', in Julian Go and Anne Foster (eds) *The American Colonial State: global perspectives*, Durham, NC and London: Duke University Press, 148–81.

Abuza, Zachary (2003) 'Al Qaeda in Southeast Asia: exploring the linkages', in Kumar Ramakrishna and See Seng Tan (eds) *After Bali: the threat of terrorism in Southeast Asia*, Singapore: Institute of Defence and Strategic Studies and World Scientific, 133–57.

Acharya, Amitav (2002) 'State-society relations: Asian and world order after September 11', in Ken Booth and Tim Dunne (eds) *Worlds in Collision: Terror and the Future of Global Order*, Basingstoke: Palgrave, 194–204.

——(2004) 'Waging the "war on terror": Singapore's responses and dilemma', Paper prepared for *Singapore Perspectives* 2004, Institute of Policy Studies, Singapore, 13 January.

Adams, Francis, Satya Dev Gupta and Kidane Mengisteab (eds) (1999) *Globalization and the Dilemmas of the State in the South*, New York: St Martin's Press.

Aditjondro, George (n.d.) 'Orang-orang Jakarta di balik tragedi Maluku', Unpublished paper.

Adorno, T. W., Else Frenkel-Brunswik, Daniel J. Levinson and R. Nevitt Sanford (1969) *The Authoritarian Personality,* New York: W.W. Norton.

Aglietta, Michel (2000) *Ein neues Akkumulationsregime. Die Regulationstheorie auf dem Prüfstand,* Hamburg: VSA.

Agnew, J. and S. Corbridge (1995) *Mastering Space: Hegemony, Territory and International Political Economy*, London: Routledge.

Ahmad, A. (1998) 'Right-wing politics, and the cultures of cruelty', Ved Gupta Memorial Lecture 1998. Online. Available: http://www.geocities.com/Indianfascism/fascism/cruality_culture.htm (accessed 30 May 2004).

——(2001) 'Colonialism, fascism and "Uncle Shylock": a reflection on our times–IV', *Frontline* 17: 90 (19 August–19 September).

Ahmad Fauzi Abdul Hamid (2001) 'Islamic resurgence: an overview of causal factors, a review of "Ummatic" linkages', *Jurnal IKIM*, 9(1): 15–47 (January/June).

——(2002) 'The formative years of the *Dakwah* movement: origins, causes and manifestations of Islamic resurgence in Malaysia', *Jurnal IKIM*, 10(2): 87–123 (July/December).

——(2003a) 'The maturation of *Dakwah* in Malaysia: divergence and convergence in the methods of Islamic movements in the 1980s', *Jurnal IKIM*, 11(2): 59–97 (July/December).

——(2003b) 'Inter-movement tension among resurgent Muslims in Malaysia: response to the state clampdown on Darul Arqam in 1994', *Asian Studies Review*, 27(3): 361–87 (September).

Ahmad Hussein, Syed (2002) 'Muslim politics and the discourse on democracy', in Francis Loh Kok Wah and Khoo Boo Teik (eds) *Democracy in Malaysia: Discourses and Practices*, Richmond: Curzon Press, 74–107.

Ahmad Osman (2000) 'AMP drops idea for separate leaders', *Straits Times*, 23 December: 2.

Alden, Edward and Roula Khalaf (2003) 'Mideast trade plan a leap of faith for Bush', *Financial Times*, 10, 11 May: 3.

Alhadar, Smith (2004) 'Aib Abu Ghraib', *Kompas*, 11 May: 4.

Ali, Tariq (1983) *Can Pakistan Survive? The death of a state*, London: Verso.

Allen, W. Kenneth, R. James, David M. Finkelstein, Banning Garrett, Bonnie Glaser, Michael J. Green, Michael Krepon, Michael McDevitt, Eric A. McVadon, Mike M. Mochizuki, Ronald N. Montaperto, James Mulvenon, Benjamin L. Self and David Shambaugh (2000) *Theater Missile Defenses in the Asia–Pacific Region*, Working Report No. 34, June, Washington, DC: The Henry L. Stimson Center.

Altvater, Elmar (2004) 'Inflationäre Deflation oder die Dominanz der globalen Finanzmärkte', *Prokla–Zeitschrift für kritische Sozialwissenschaft*, 134 (March).

Altvater, Elmar and Birgit Mahnkopf (2004) *Globalisierung der Unsicherheit–Arbeit im Schatten, schmutziges Geld und informelle Politik*, 6th edition, Münster: Westfälisches Dampfboot.

Amoroso, Donna J. (2003) 'Inheriting the "Moro problem": Muslim authority and colonial rule in British Malaya and the Philippines', in Julian Go and Anne Foster (eds) *The American Colonial State: global perspectives*, Durham, NC and London: Duke University Press, 118–47.

Anderson, Benedict (1998) 'Cacique democracy in the Philippines', in *Spectre of Comparison: nationalism, Southeast Asia and the world*, London: Verso, 192–226.

Anderson, P. (2002) 'Force and consent', *New Left Review*, 17: 5–30.

Appleyard, Bryan (2004) 'America's most famous thinker', *Straits Times Interactive*, 15 August. Online. Available:http://straitstimes.asia1.com.sg/ (accessed 20 August 2004).

Armstrong, D. (2002) 'Dick Cheney's song of America', *Harper's Magazine*, 76–83.

Aronowitz, Stanley and Heather Gautney (eds) (2003) *Globalization and Resistance in the 21st Century World Order*, New York: Basic Books.

Arvind (2002) *Globalisation: an attack on India's sovereignty*, New Vistas, New Delhi.

Asian Wall Street Journal (1997) Editorial, 'Socialist international', 18 December: 10.

——(1998) 'An $18 billion inoculation', 5 February: 14.

Aspinall, Ed and Mark T. Berger (2001) 'The break-up of Indonesia: nationalisms after decolonisation and the limits of the nation-state in post-cold war Southeast Asia', *Third World Quarterly*, 222(6): 1003–24.

Associated Press (2002) 'Al-Qaida arrests shock Singapore', 9 January.

Bacevich, A. J. (2002) *American Empire: The realities and consequences of US diplomacy*, Cambridge, MA: Harvard University Press.

——(ed.) (2003) *The Imperial Tense: prospects and problems of American empire*, Chicago: Ivan R. Dee.

Baclagon, Uldarico (1988) *Christian-Moslem Guerrillas of Mindanao*, Manila: Lord Avenue.

Baker, Chris (2004) 'Pluto-populism: Thaksin, business and popular politics in post-crisis Thailand', Unpublished paper.

Baker, James III (1991) 'America in Asia: emerging architecture for a Pacific community', *Foreign Affairs*, 70(5): 1–18.

Balais-Serrano, Evelyn (2004) 'Peace and security and the international criminal court: key challenges and issues for civil society in Asia', Paper presented at the Asian Civil Society Forum 2004, UN Conference Center, Bangkok, 21–25 November.

Balakrishnan, Gopal (ed.) (2003) *Debating Empire*, London: Verso.

Balowski, James (2003) 'Indonesian military seeks more power after Marriott bombing', *Green Left Weekly*, 3 September.

Barakwi, T. and M. Laffey (1999) 'The imperial peace: democracy, force and globalisation', *European Journal of International Relations*, 5(4): 403–34.

Barton, Greg (2004) *Indonesia's Struggle: Jemaah Islamiyah and the Soul of Islam*, Sydney: University of New South Wales Press.

Basu, K. (2001) 'Requiem for the QR', *India Today*, 19 March: 48.

Basu, T. P. Datta, S. Sarkar, T. Sarkar and S. Sen (1993) *Khaki Shorts and Saffron Flags*, New Delhi: Orient Longman.

BBC (2003) 'China issues "terrorist" list', *BBC News*, 15 December. Online. Available:http://news.bbc.co.uk/go/pr/fr/-/hi/asia-pacific/3319575.stm (accessed 16 December 2003).

Beckett, Jeremy (1975) 'The datus of Rio Grande de Cotabato', *Asian Studies*, 15 (April–August).

Bedi, R. (2003) 'Moving closer to Israel', *Frontline*, 20(4) (15–28 February). Online. Available: http://www.flonnet.com/fl2004/stories/20030228002005500.htm (accessed 25 July 2004).

Beeson, Mark (2001) 'Globalization, governance, and the political-economy of public policy reform in East Asia', *Governance*, 14(4): 481–502.

——(2002) 'Southeast Asia and the politics of vulnerability', *Third World Quarterly*, 23(3): 549–64.

——(2003) 'ASEAN plus three and the rise of reactionary regionalism', *Contemporary Southeast Asia*, 25(2): 251–68.

——(2004) 'The United States and Southeast Asia: change and continuity in American hegemony', in K. Jayasuriya (ed.) *Crisis and Change in Regional Governance*, London: Routledge, 213–29.

——(forthcoming) 'Re-thinking regionalism: Europe and East Asia in comparative historical perspective', *Journal of European Public Policy*, 12 (6):959–985.

Beeson, Mark and Richard Robison (2000) 'Introduction: interpreting the crisis', in Richard Robison, Mark Beeson, Kanishka Jayasuriya and Hyuk-Rae Kim (eds) *Politics and Markets in the Wake of the Asian Crisis*, London: Routledge, 3–24.

Bellow, Saul (2000) *Ravelstein*, Harmondsworth: Penguin, 58–9.

Bentley, G. Carter (1985) 'Dispute, authority and Maranao social order', in Resil Mojares (ed.) *Dispute Processing in the Philippines*, Quezon City: Ministry of Local Government, 69–75.

——(1993) 'Mohamad Ali Dimaporo: a modern Maranao datu', in Alfred W. McCoy (ed.) *An Anarchy of Families: state and family in the Philippines*, Madison, WI: University of Wisconsin Center for Southeast Asian Studies, 243–84.

Bernhard, Michael and John Ravenhill (1995) 'Beyond product cycles and flying geese: regionalization, hierarchy, and the industrialization of East Asia', *World Politics*, 47(2): 171–209.

Bhagwati, Jagdish and Arvind Panagariya (2003) 'Bilateral trade treaties are a sham', *Financial Times*, 14 July: 13.

Bhumiputra (2004) *106 Dead Bodies: living deaths*, Bangkok: Khien Paen Din. (In Thai)

Bliss, Tasker (1909) 'The government of the Moro province and its problems', *Mindanao Herald*, 3 February.

Blood, Archer K. (1971) Memo No. 00959, Declassified State Department information.

Blum, W. (2000) *Rogue State*, Monroe, ME: Common Courage Press.

Bobbio, Norberto (1987) *The Future of Democracy: a defence of the rules of the game*, trans. Roger Griffin, Cambridge: Polity Press.

Bobbitt, Philip (2003) *The Shield of Achilles: war, peace and the course of history*, London: Penguin.

Boey, David (2004) 'S'pore take note: strikes may fail but terrorists don't forget', *Straits Times Interactive*, 14 September.

Boggs, Carl (ed.) (2003) *Masters of War: militarism and blowback in the era of American empire*, New York: Routledge.

Bonner, Raymond (2003) 'Thailand tiptoes in step with the American antiterror effort', *New York Times*, 8 June: 1, 29.

Boot, Max (2004) 'Neocons', *Foreign Policy*, January: 20–8.

Borradori, G. (2003) *Philosophy in a Time of Terror,* Chicago: The University of Chicago Press.

Bothra, R. (2002) 'India-US relations in the aftermath of September 11, 2001', Prepared by American Association of Physicians from India (AAPI), March. Online. Available: http://www.ccsindia.org/Indous.htm (accessed 4 October 2004).

Bourchier, David and Vedi R. Hadiz (2003) *Indonesian Politics and Society: A Reader*, London: RoutledgeCurzon.

Bowden, B. (2002) 'Reinventing imperialism in the wake of September 11', *Alternatives: Turkish Journal of International Relations*. Online. Available: http://www.alternativesjournal.net/volume1/number2/bowden-1.pdf (accessed 12 December 2004).

Bowring, B. (2002) 'The degradation of international law', in John Strawson (ed.) *Law After Ground Zero*, London: Glasshouse Press, 3–19.

Bowring, Philip (2004) 'Thailand only feeds Muslim discontent', *International Herald Tribune*, 28 October.

Breslin, S. (2002) 'IR, area studies and IPE: rethinking the study of China's international relations' CSGR Working Paper No. 94/02. Online. Available: http://www.warwick.ac.uk/fac/soc/CSGR/publications.html (accessed 13 July 2005).

Brown, David (1994) *The State and Ethnic Politics in Southeast Asia*, London: Routledge.

——(2000) *Contemporary Nationalism*, London: Routledge.

Brown, W. N. (1972) *The United States and India, Pakistan and Bangladesh*, Cambridge, MA: Harvard University Press.

Brzezinski, Zbigniew (1997) *The Grand Chessboard: American primary and its geostrategic imperatives*, New York: Basic Books.

Burke, S. M. (1973) *Pakistan's Foreign Policy*, London: Oxford University Press.

Burki, S. J. (2004) 'The question of "location"', *Dawn – The Internet Edition*, 29 January. Online. Available: http://dawn.com/2002/01/29/op.htm (accessed 25 July 2004).

Bush, George (1991) 'Remarks to the Asia Society in New York City', New York: Asia Society, 12 November.

——(2002) Graduation speech, West Point, 1 June.

Bush, George W. and Thaksin Shinawatra (2001) 'Joint statement between the United States of America and the Kingdom of Thailand', *Weekly Compilation of Presidential Documents*, Washington, 37(50), 17 December.

Bush, George W. (2002) Graduation speech, West Point, 1 June.

Callinicos, Alex (2003) *An Anti-Capitalist Manifesto*, Cambridge: Polity Press.

Camdessus, Michel (1997) 'Asia will survive with realistic economic policies,' *Jakarta Post*, 8 and 9 December: 5.

——(1998a) 'The IMF and good governance', Address at Transparency International, Paris, France, 21 January. Online. Available: http://imf.org/external/np/speeches/1998/012198.htm (accessed 25 June 1998).

——(1998b) 'From the Asian crisis towards a new global architecture', Speech to the Parliamentary Assembly of the Council of Europe, Strasbourg, France, 23 June. Online. Available: http://www.imf.org/external/np/speeches/1998/062398.HTM (accessed 25 June 1998).

——(1998c) 'The IMF and its programs in Asia', Remarks by the Managing Director of the International Monetary Fund at the Council on Foreign Relations, New York, 6 February. Online. Available: http://www.imf.org/external/np/speeches/1998/020698.htm (accessed 29 May 1999).

Cammack, P. (2001) 'Making the poor work for globalisation?', *New Political Economy*, 6(3): 397–408.

Campbell, Colin and Jean H. Laherrère (1998) 'The end of cheap oil', *Scientific American*, March. Online. Available: http://dieoff.org/page140.htm.

Carlucci, Frank, Robert Hunter and Zalmay Khalilzad (co-chairs) (2000) *Taking Charge: A Bipartisan Report to the President Elect on Foreign Policy and National Security–Discussion Papers*, Santa Monica, CA: Rand.

Carothers, Thomas (2003) 'Promoting democracy and fighting terror', *Foreign Affairs*, 82(1): 84–97.

Cassese, Antonio (2001) *International Law*, Oxford: Oxford University Press.

Cassolari, M. (2000) 'Foreign tie-up in the 1930s – archival evidence', *Economic and Political Weekly*, 22 January: 218–28.

Castles, F. (2004) *The Future of the Welfare State*, Oxford: Oxford University Press.

Cavallar, Georg (2001) 'Kantian perspective on democratic peace: alternatives to Doyle', *Review of International Studies*, 27: 233.

Celestine, Avinash (2003) 'The "Hot Money" worries', *Business World*, 29 September.

Center for Anti-Imperialist Studies (2002) *Unmasking the US War on Terror: US imperialist hegemony and crisis*, Quezon City: Center for Anti-Imperialist Studies.

Cerny, Philip (2004) 'Mapping varieties of neo-liberalism', IPEG Papers in Global Political Economy, 12 May.

Chaiwat Satha-Anand (2002) 'Understanding the success of terrorism', *Inter-Asia Cultural Studies*, 3(1): 157–59 (April).

——(2003) *Living Weapons? Critical perspectives on violence*, Bangkok: Fa Diew Kan. (In Thai)

——(2004a) 'Facing the demon within', *Seeds of Peace*, 20(2): 11–14 (May–August).

——(2004b) 'Praying in the rain: the politics of engaged Muslims in anti-war protest in Thai society', *Global Change, Peace & Security*, 16(2): 151–67 (June).

Chan Heng Chee (1971) *The Politics of Survival, 1965–1967*, Singapore: Oxford University Press.

Chandhoke, N. (2000) 'The tragedy of Ayodhya', *Frontline*, 17(13), 24 June–7 July. Online. Available: http://www.hinduonnet.com/fline/fl1713/17130170.htm (accessed 25 September 2004).

Chang, Dae-oup (2001) 'Bringing class struggle back in the economic crisis', *Historical Materialism*, 8.

Chang, Michael (1989) *Social Movements and Political Transition*, Taipei: Institute for National Policy Research (INPR).

channelnewsasia.com (2004) 'Rumsfeld justifies war on terror after ally says US is part of problem', 5 June.

Chatterjee, B. C. (2000) *Anandmath (Abbey of Delights)*, trans. A. Das, Calcutta: Bandana Das.

Che Man, W. K. (1990) *Muslim Separatism: the Moros of southern Philippines and the Malays of Southern Thailand*, Manila: Ateneo de Manila University Press.

——(2003b) 'Crackdown on the Internet by the Singapore government', E-mail (12 November 2003).

Cheney Report (2001) *National Energy Policy – Reliable, Affordable, and Environmentally Sound Energy for America's Future. Report of the National Energy Development Group*, Washington, DC: The Vice-President.

Chesnais, François and Claude Serfati (2003) 'Les conditions physiques de la reproduction sociale', in J.-M. Harribey and Michael Löwy (eds) *Capital contre nature*, Collection Actuel Marx Confrontation, Paris: Presse universitaires de France, 69–105.

Chirmsak Pintong (2004) 'Truth at Tak Bai: inhumanity, loss of legitimacy', Bangkok: Kor Khid Duey Kon. (In Thai)

Chu, Yun-han (1992) *Crafting Democracy in Taiwan*, Taipei: Institute for National Policy Research (INPR).

Chu, Yun-han and Chia-lung Lin (1998) 'The construction of Taiwanese identity and cross-Strait relations', Paper presented at the Conference on The Development of Contemporary Taiwan, Taipei, 16–17 December 1998. Online: http://www.taiwansecurity.org/TS/TS-Lin.htm (accessed 20 March 2004).

Chua Beng Huat (1995) *Communitarian Ideology and Democracy in Singapore*, London: Routledge.

Chua Lee Hoong (2002) '13 suspected terrorists to be detained 2 years', *Straits Times*. Cited at sg_daily<\\>@>yahoogroups.com. Online posting (11 January).

Clark, Donald (ed.) (1988) *The Kwangju Uprising: shadow over the regime in South Korea*, Boulder, CO: Westview Press.

Clark, John G. (1991) *The Political Economy of World Energy*, Chapel Hill, NC and London: The University of North Carolina Press.

Clarke, R. A. (2004) *Against all enemies: inside America's war on terror*, New York: Free Press.

CNN.com (2004) 'Concern over ASEAN Anti-terror Treaty', 29 July.

Cockett, R. (1994) *Thinking the Unthinkable: think-tanks and the economic counter-revolution 1931–1983*, London: Harper Collins.

Cohen, S. P. (1999) 'The United States, India, and Pakistan: retrospect and prospect', in Selig S. Harrison, P. H. Kreisberg and D. Kux (eds) *India and*

Pakistan: the first fifty years, Cambridge: Cambridge University Press, 189–205.

Cohen, S. P. and S. Dasgupta (2001) 'US-South Asia: relations under Bush', *Bharat Rakshak Monitor*, 4 (July–August). Online. Available: http://www.stratmag.com/issue2Sep-1/page06.htm (accessed 4 August 2004).

Cooper, R. (2002) 'Why we still need empires', *Observer*, 7 April.

Corbridge, S. and J. Harriss (2001) *Reinventing India: liberalization, Hindu nationalism and popular democracy*, Delhi: Oxford University Press.

Cowen, Myron (1950) 'Telegram to the Secretary of State, American Embassy, Manila, April, 1950', in US State Department Central Files *The Philippine Republic: internal and foreign affairs, 1950–4*.

Cribb, Robert (ed.) (1990) *The Indonesian Killings of 1965–66: studies from Java and Bali*, Monash Papers on Southeast Asia No. 21, Clayton: Centre of Southeast Asian Studies, Monash University.

Crispin, Shawn W. (2003a) 'Thai-US relations fray on terror – Washington is said to seek quick arrests of suspects; Bangkok eager for caution', *Wall Street Journal*, 6 February: A14.

——(2003b) 'US, Thailand start trade talks; negotiations reflect effort By Washington to enhance Asian economic relations', *Asian Wall Street Journal*, 20 October: A3.

——(2004) 'Torture in Thailand', *Far Eastern Economic Review*, 12 August: 12–15.

Cronin, A. K. (2002) 'Rethinking sovereignty: American strategy in the age of terrorism', *Survival*, 44: 119–39.

Crook, Stephen (1994) 'Introduction: Adorno and authoritarian irrationalism', in Theodor W. Adorno, *The Stars Down to Earth: and other essays on the irrational in culture*, London and New York: Routledge, 1–33.

Cui, Zhiyuan (2004) 'The Bush Doctrine: a Chinese perspective', in David Held and Mathias Koenig-Archibugi, *American Power in the Twenty-First Century*, Cambridge: Polity Press.

——(2005) 'Liberal socialism and the future of China: a petty-bourgeois manifesto', in Cao Tianyu (ed.) *The Chinese Model of Modern Development*, London: Routledge.

Cumings, Bruce (1987) 'The origins and development of the northeast Asian political economy: industrial sectors, product cycles, and political consequences', in Frederic C. Deyo (ed.) *The Political Economy of the New Asian Industrialism*, Ithaca, NY: Cornell University Press, 44–83.

——(1997) *Korea's Place in the Sun*, New York: W.W. Norton.

——(1998) 'The "Korean crisis" and the end of late development', *New Left Review*, 231 (September/November).

Daadler, I. H. and J. M. Lindsay (2003) *America Unbound: The Bush revolution in foreign policy*, Washington, DC: Brookings Institution.

DAWN.com (2004) 'US is part of the problem: Singapore PM', 6 June.

De Angelis, Massimo (2004) 'Separating the doing and the deed: capital and the continuous character of enclosures', *Historical Materialism. Research in Critical Marxist Theory*, 12(2): 57–8.

de Luna Martinez, José (2002) *Die Herausforderungen der Globalisierung für die Schwellenländer: Lehren aus den Finanzkrisen von Mexiko und Südkorea*, Berlin: Logos Verlag.

Denizer, Cevdet, Raj M. Desai and Nikolay Gueorguiev (1998) 'The political economy of financial repression in transition economies', World Bank Paper. Online. Available: http://www.econ.worldbank.org/docs/400.pdf.

Dent, C. (2004) 'The new economic bilateralism and the Southeast Asia: region-convergent or region-divergent', *IPEG Papers in Global Political Economy* No. 7, April. Online. Available: http://www.bisa.ac.uk/groups/ ipeg/papers/7%20Christopher%20Dent.pdf (accessed 13 July 2005).

Desai, Radhika (2004) 'From national bourgeoisie to rogues, failure and bullies: 21st century imperialism and the unravelling of the third world', *Third World Quarterly*, 25(1): 169–85.

Deshpande, Vidya (1999) 'The muddy waters of Maheshwar', *Indian Express*, 15 August. Online. Available: http://www.expressindia.com/fe/ daily/19990815/fec15025p.html (accessed 3 August 2004).

Desker, Barry (2003) 'The Jemaah Islamiyah', *Contemporary Southeast Asia*, 25(3): 489–507.

Deyo, Frederic C. (1987) 'State and labor: modes of political exclusion in East Asian development', in Frederic C. Deyo (ed.) *The Political Economy of the New Asian Industrialism*, Ithaca, NY: Cornell University Press, 182–202.

Deyo, Frederic C. (ed.) (1987) *The Political Economy of the New Asian Industrialism*, Ithaca, NY: Cornell University Press.

Dinsman (ed.) (2000) *Sepuluh Tahun Membangun Bersama Islam: Kelantan di bawah pimpinan Ulamak*, Kota Bharu: Pusat Kajian Strategik.

Dobriansky, Paula (2003) 'Democracy promotion: explaining the Bush administration's position', *Foreign Affairs*, 82(3): 141–5.

DoD (Department of Defense) (1995) *US Security Strategy for the East Asia-Pacific Region*, DoD: Office of International Security Affairs FRUS (Foreign Relations of the United States), February.

Dorrien, G. (1993) *The Neoconservative Mind: politics, culture and the war of ideology,* Philadelphia: Temple University Press.

Doyle, Michael (1986) 'Liberalism and world politics', *American Political Science Review*, 80: 1151–69.

——(1997) *Ways of War and Peace*, New York: W.W. Norton.

Dubashi, J. (1992) *Organiser*, 15 March.

Dye, R. W. (1965) 'The Jakarta Faculty of Economics', Ford Foundation Report.

Easterlin, Richard A. (1998) *Growth Triumphant: the twenty-first Century in Historical perspective*, Ann Arbor, MI: University of Michigan Press.

Eccleston, R. (2002) 'Bush orders US security revolution', *The Australian*, 8–9 June: 1.

eCensusIndia (2003) 'eCensusIndia', 14. Online. Available: http://www.censusindia.net/results/eci14_page2.html (accessed 16 September 2004).

Ecip, Sinansari S. (ed.) (1998) *Kronologi Situasi Penggulingan Soeharto*, Bandung: Mizan.

Embassy of India (2000) 'India–US relations: a vision for the 21st century, joint India–US statement'. Online. Available: http://www.indiagov.org/ indusrel/clinton_india/joint_india_us_statement_mar_21_2000.htm (accessed 20 July 2004).

Enquete Kommission (2002) 'Deutscher Bundestag (2002): Schlussbericht der Enquete-Kommission "Globalisierung der Weltwirtschaft – Herausforderungen und Antworten"', Drucksache 14/9200, 12 June.

Esping-Anderson, Gosta (1980) *The Three Worlds of Welfare Capitalism*, Princeton, NJ: Princeton University Press.

Esposito, John L. (1998) *Islam: the straight path*, 3rd edn, New York: Oxford University Press.

Euayporn Taechootrakul (2004) 'Farewell . . . Charoen Wataksorn', *Sekiyadhamma*, 14(61): 14–17, 45 (July–September). (In Thai)

European Commission (2003) *The Social Situation in the European Union*, Brussels: EU.

Evans, Peter (1995) *Embedded Autonomy*, Princeton, NJ: Princeton University Press.

Fa Diew Kan (Under the Same Sky) (2004) 2(3): 120–164 (July–September). (In Thai)

Fanon, Franz (1965) *The Wretched of the Earth*, New York: Grove Press.

Farish A. Noor (2002) *The Other Malaysia: writings on Malaysia's subaltern history*, Kuala Lumpur: Silverfishbooks.

——(2003) 'The localization of Islamist discourse in the *Tafsir* of Tuan Guru Nik Aziz Nik Mat, *Murshid'ul Am* of PAS', in Virgina Hooker and Norani Othman (eds) *Malaysia: Islam, society and politics*, Singapore: Institute of Southeast Asian Studies, 195–235.

Felix, David (2002) 'The rise of real long-term interests rates since the 1970s: comparative trends, causes and consequences. Gutachten für die Enquete-Kommission "Globalisierung der Weltwirtschaft"', Berlin: Deutscher Bundestag (AU-Stud 14/26).

Ferguson, N. and L. J. Kotlikoff (2003) 'Going critical: American power and the consequences of fiscal overstretch', *The National Interest*, 73: 22–32.

——(2004a) *Colossus: the rise and fall of the American empire*, London: Allen Lane.

——(2004b) *Colossus: the price of America's empire*, London: Penguin.

Fernandez, Warren (2003) 'Busy evening in Singapore', *Straits Times Interactive*, 21 October.

Fidler, S. and G. Baker (2003) 'America's democratic imperialists: how the neo-conservatives rose from humility to empire in two years', *Financial Times*, 6 March: 11.

Fine, Ben (2001) *Social Capital versus Social Theory*, London, Routledge.

——(2002) 'The World Bank's speculation on social capital', in Jonathan R. Pincus and Jeffrey A. Winters (eds) *Reinventing the World Bank*, Ithaca, NY: Cornell University Press, 203–21.

Fine, Ben, Costas Lapavitsas and Jonathan Pincus (eds) (2001) *Development Policy in the Twenty-First Century: beyond the Washington Consensus*, London, Routledge.

Ford Foundation (2003) *Celebrating Indonesia: Fifty Years with the Ford Foundation 1953–2003*, Jakarta: Ford Foundation and Equinox Publishing.

Ford, Michele (2003) 'NGO as outside intellectual: a history of non-governmental organisations' role in the Indonesian labour movement', PhD thesis, School of History and Politics, University of Wollongong.

Frank, K. (2001) *Indira*, London, Harper Collins.

FRUS (Foreign Relations of the United States) (1947I) *Selected extracts from the Foreign Relations of the United States series*, 1947, Vol. I, General; United Nations. Published in 1973 by the US Department of State.

——(1948I) *Selected extracts from the Foreign Relations of the United States series*, 1948, vol. I, General; United Nations. Published in 1975 by the US Department of State.

Friedman, Thomas (1997) 'Quit the whining: globalisation isn't a choice', *International Herald Tribune*, 9 January: 8.

——(2000) *The Lexus and the Olive Tree*, New York: Harper Collins.

Fuentes, Winston Jay (1998) 'Negotiating an agenda for peace and self-rule in Moroland', *Mindanao Focus*, 4.

Fukuyama, Francis (1989) 'The end of history?', *The National Interest* (Summer).

——(1992) *The End of History and the Last Man*, New York: Avalon Books.

Funston, John (1980) *Malay Politics in Malaysia: a study of the United Malay National Organization and Party Islam*, Kuala Lumpur: Heinemann.

——(2004) 'The Mahathir years: the rural Malay heartland', in Bridget Welsh (ed.) *Reflections: The Mahathir Years*, Washington, DC: Southeast Asia Studies Program, Johns Hopkins University, 168–76.

Gaddis, J. L. (1982) *Strategies of Containment: a critical appraisal of postwar American security policy*, Oxford: Oxford University Press.

Ganesan, N. (2004) 'Thaksin and the politics of domestic and regional consolidation', *Contemporary Southeast Asia*, 26(1): 26–44.

Ganguly, Sumit (1999) 'India: policies, past and future', in Selig S. Harrison, P. H. Kreisberg and D. Kux (eds) *India and Pakistan: the first fifty years*, Cambridge: Cambridge University Press, 155–69.

Garrison, J (2004) *America as Empire*, San Francisco: Berrett-Koehler.

Gazali, Effendi (2003) 'SARS dan politik nostalgi', *Kompas*, 27 December.

Gelbard, Robert (2001) 'United State-Indonesia relations in 2001', Council of American Ambassadors. Online. Available: http://www.americanambassadors.org/index.cfm?fuseaction= Publications.article&articleid = 42 (accessed 1 July 2004).

George, T. J. S. (1980) *Revolt in Mindanao: the rise of Islam in Philippine politics*, Kuala Lumpur: Oxford University Press.

Georgescu-Roegen, Nicholas (1971) *The Entropy Law and the Economic Process*, Cambridge, MA and London: Harvard University Press.

Giesenfeld, Günter (2004) 'Im Sumpf. Das Scheitern der USA von Vietnam bis Irak', *Blätter für deutsche und internationale Politik*, 11: 1323–34.

Gill, Stephen (1998) 'New constitutionalism, democratisation and global political economy', *Pacifica Review*, 10(1): 23–38.

Gills, Barry (2000) 'American power, neo-liberal economic globalisation, and low intensity democracy: an unstable trinity', in Michael Cox, G. John Ikenberry and Takashi Inoguchi (eds) *American Democracy Promotion: impulses, strategies and impacts*, Oxford: Oxford University Press, 326–44.

Glang, Alunan (1969) *Muslim Secession or Integration?*, Quezon City: R.P. Garcia.

Global Challenge Network (2002) *Ölwechsel. Das Ende des Erdölzeitalters und die Weichenstellung für die Zukunft*, dtv premium, München.

Global Security (2003) *Taiwan Strait 21 July 1995 to 23 March 1996*. Online: http://www.globalsecurity.org/military/ops/taiwan_strait.htm (accessed 12 April 2004).

——(2004) 'Thailand Islamic insurgency'. Online. Available: http://www.globalsecurity.org/military/world/war/thailand2.htm (accessed 10 November 2004).

Golwalkar, M. S. (1966) *The Bunch of Thoughts*, Bangalore: Vikrama Prakashan.

Gonzales, Francisco (2000) 'Sultans of a violent land', in Kristina Gaerlan and Mara Stankovich (eds) *Rebels, Warlords and Ulama: A reader on Muslim separatism and the war in Southern Philippines*, Quezon City: Institute for Popular Democracy, 114–20.

Goodenough, Patrick (2004) 'Indonesian campaigners still believe military murdered Americans'. Online. Available: http://www.cnsnews.com/ViewForeignBureaus.asp?Page%5CForeignBureaus%5Carchive%5C200408%5CFOR20040805b.html (accessed 1 September 2004).

Goodman, Matthew (2004) 'America must show its lasting interest in Asia policy', *Financial Times*, 19 November: 13.

Gordon, P. H. (2003) 'Bush's Middle East vision', *Survival*, 45: 155–65.

Gore, Lance (2000) 'A meltdown with Chinese characteristics?', in Richard Robison, Mark Beeson, Kanishka Jayasuriya and Hyuk-Rae Kim, *Politics and Markets in the Wake of the Asian Crisis*, London: Routledge, 130–50.

Government of Pakistan (1998) *Pakistan Chronology: 1947–1997*, Pakistan: Ministry of Information and Media Development.

Government Printing Office (1907) *Report of the Philippine Commission*, Washington, DC: Government Printing Office.

Gowan, Peter (2004a) 'Triumphing toward international disaster: the impasse in American grand strategy', *Critical Asian Studies*, 36(1): 3–36.

——(2004b) 'The American campaign for global sovereignty', in Leo Panitch, Colin Leys, Alan Zuege and Martijn Konings (eds) *The Globalisation Decade: A Critical Reader*, London: Merlin Press, 295–321.

Gowing, Peter (1977) *Mandate in Moroland: the American government of Muslim Filipinos, 1899–1920*, Quezon City: New Day.

Gramsci, Antonio (1971) *Selections from the Prison Notebooks*, trans. Q. Hoare and G. Nowell Smith, New York: International.

Gray, J. (1998) *False Dawn: the delusions of global capitalism*, London: Granada.

Gutierrez, Eric (2000) 'In the battlefields of the warlord', in Kristina Gaerlan and Mara Stankovich (eds) *Rebels, Warlords and Ulama: A reader on Muslim separatism and the war in Southern Philippines*, Quezon City: Institute for Popular Democracy, 64–77.

——(2001) 'From Ilagas to Abu Sayaf: new entrepreneurs of violence and their impact on local politics in Mindanao', Unpublished manuscript, September.

Habermas, Jurgen (2003) '*Was bedeutet der Denkmalsturz?*', *Frankfurter Allgemeine Zeitung*, 17 April: 33.

Hadar, Leon (2002) 'S'pore Caucus formed in US Congress', *Business Times Weekly*, 11 October.

Hadiz, Vedi R. (1997) *Workers and the State in New Order Indonesia*, London: Routledge.

——(2004a) 'The rise of "neo-third worldism"? The Indonesian trajectory and the consolidation of illiberal democracy', *Third World Quarterly*, Special 25th Anniversary Issue, 25(1):55–71.

——(2004b) 'Decentralisation and democracy in Indonesia: a critique of neo-institutionalist perspectives', *Development and Change*, 35(4): 697–718 (September).

——(2004c) 'Indonesian local party politics: a site of resistance to neo-liberal reform', *Critical Asian Studies*, 36(4): 615–35 (December).

Hafidz, Tatik (2003) 'The war on terror and the future of Indonesian democracy', No. 46 (March), Singapore: Institute of Defence and Strategic Studies.

Haggard, Stephan (2000) *The Political Economy of the Asian Financial Crisis*, Washington, DC: Institute for International Economics.

Hale, David (2003) 'The Manchurian candidate', *Financial Times*, 29 August: 11.

Halim Salleh (1981) *Bureaucrats, Petty Bourgeois and Townsmen: an observation on status identification in Kota Bharu*, Monash Paper on Southeast Asia, No. 8, Clayton, Victoria: Monash University Centre of Southeast Asian Studies.

——(1992) 'Peasants, proletarianization and the state: FELDA settlers in Pahang', in Joel S. Kahn and Francis Loh Kok Wah (eds) *Fragmented Vision: culture and politics in contemporary Malaysia*, Sydney: Allen & Unwin, 107–32.

——(1999) 'Development and the politics of social stability in Malaysia', *Southeast Asian Affairs 1999*, Singapore: Institute of Southeast Asian Studies, 185–203.

——(2000) 'PAS and UMNO in Kelantan and Trengganu', Paper presented at the Workshop on the Malaysian General Election of 1999, Universiti Sains Malaysia, Penang, 1–2 April.

Hamilton, Clive (1986) *Capitalist Industrialization in Korea*, Boulder, CO: Westview Press.

Hansen, T. B. (1998) 'The ethics of Hindutva and the spirit of capitalism', in Thomas Blom Hansen and Christophe Jeffrelot (eds) *The BJP and the Compulsions of Politics in India*, Delhi: Oxford University Press, 296.

Hardt, Michael and Antonio Negri (2000) *Empire*, Cambridge, MA: Harvard University Press.

Harney, Robert A. (2004) 'Thai coalition engineer unit supports operation enduring freedom', *Army Logistician*, 36(1): 26–30.

Harper, T. N. (1999) The *End of Empire and the Making of Malaya*, Cambridge: Cambridge University Press.

Harriss, John (2002) *Depoliticizing Development: The World Bank and Social Capital*, Wimbledon: Anthem Press.

Hartley, Douglas Thompson Kellie (1983) 'American participation in the economic development of Mindanao and Sulu, 1899–1930', PhD dissertation, James Cook University of North Queensland.

Harvey, David (1996) *Justice, Nature & the Geography of Difference*, Cambridge, MA and Oxford: Blackwell.

—— (2003a) *The New Imperialism*, Oxford: Oxford University Press.

——(2003b) 'The "new" imperialism: accumulation by dispossession', in Leo Panitch and Colin Leys (eds) *The New Imperial Challenge, Socialist Register 2004*, London: Merlin Press/Fernwood Publishing/Monthly Review Press, 63–87.

Hathaway, Robert M. (1984) 'Economic diplomacy in a time of crisis', in William Becker and Samuel F. Wells (eds) *Economics and World Power: an assessment of American diplomacy since 1789*, New York: Columbia University Press.

Hayase, Shinzo (1984) 'Tribes, settlers, and administrators on a frontier: economic development and social change in Davao, Southeastern Mindanao, the Philippines, 1899–1941', PhD dissertation, Murdoch University.

Hefner, Robert (1993) 'Islam, state and civil society: ICMI and the struggle for the Indonesian middle class', *Indonesia*, 56: 1–35 (October).

Helleiner, E. (1994) *States and the Reemergence of Global Finance*, Ithaca, NY: Cornell University Press.

Hemmer, C. and P. J. Katzenstein (2002) 'Why is there no NATO in Asia? Collective identity, regionalism, and the origins of multilateralism', *International Organization*, 56: 575–607.

Henderson, Jeffrey and R. P. Appelbaum (eds) (1992) *States and Development in the Asian Pacific Rim*, Newbury Park, CA: Sage.

Hersh, Seymour (1983) *The Price of Power*, New York: Summit Books.

Hewison, Kevin (1989) *Bankers and Bureaucrats: Capital and State in Thailand*, Yale University Southeast Asian Monographs, No. 34, New Haven, CT: Yale Center for International and Area Studies.

——(2000) 'Resisting globalization: a study of localism in Thailand', *Pacific Review*, 13(2): 279–96.

——(2002) 'The World Bank and Thailand: crisis and safety nets', *Public Administration and Policy*, 11(1): 1–21.

——(2004) 'Pathways to recovery: bankers, business, and nationalism in Thailand', in E. T. Gomez and Hsin-Huang Michael Hsiao (eds) *Chinese Enterprise, Transnationalism, and Identity*, London: RoutledgeCurzon, 232–77.

——(2005) 'Neo-liberalism and domestic capital: the political outcomes of the economic crisis in Thailand', *Journal of Development Studies*, 41(2): 310–30.

Hewison, Kevin, Richard Robison and Garry Rodan (eds) (1993) *Southeast Asia in the 1990s: Authoritarianism, Democracy and Capitalism*, Sydney: Allen & Unwin.

Higgott, R. (2003a) 'American unilateralism: foreign economic policy and the "securitization" of globalisation', CSGR Working Paper 124/03. Online. Available: http://www.csr.og (accessed 13 July 2005).

——(2003b) 'A battle of ideas: globalisation, nation states and alternatives to neo-liberalism', Paper presented to the Conference on Globalisation, Conflict and Political Regimes in Southeast Asia, Asia Research Centre,

Murdoch University and Southeast Asian Research Centre, City University, Hong Kong, Fremantle, 15–16 August.

——(2004) 'After neoliberal globalization: the "securitization" of US foreign economic policy in East Asia', *Critical Asian Studies*, 36(3): 425–44.

Higgott, R. and R. Stubbs (1995) 'Competing conceptions of economic regionalism: APEC versus EAEC', *Review of International Political Economy*, 2(3): 516–35.

Hill, D. (2002) 'Food security, governance and rural development under the BJP', *South Asia*, XXXV(3): 156 (December).

Hilley, John (2001) *Malaysia: Mahathirism, hegemony and the new opposition*, London and New York: Zed Books

Hirsch, J. (1995) *Der nationale Wettbewerbstaat. Staat, Demokratie und Politik im globalem Kapitalismus*, Berlin: Edition ID-Archiv.

Hogan, M. J. (1998) *A Cross of Iron: Harry S. Truman and the origins of the national security state 1945–1954*, Cambridge: Cambridge University Press.

Holley, Joe (2004) 'Archer K. Blood: dissenting diplomat', *Washington Post*, 23 September.

Holstrom, N. and R. Smith (2000) 'The necessity of gangster capitalism: primitive accumulation in Russia and China', *Monthly Review*, February.

Hooker, M. B. (2003) 'Submission to Allah? The Kelantan Syariah Criminal Code (II) 1993', in Virgina Hooker and Norani Othman (eds) *Malaysia: Islam, society and politics*, Singapore: Institute of Southeast Asian Studies, 80–98.

Hoyt, Ralph (1909) *Report of the Governor of the Moro Province*, Washington, DC: Government Printing Office.

Hubbert, Marion King (1972) *Structural Geology*, New York: Hafner.

Hund, M. (2003) 'ASEAN plus three: towards a new age of pan-East Asian regionalism? A sceptic's appraisal', *Pacific Review*, 16(3): 383–418.

Hunt, M. H. (1987) *Ideology and US Foreign Policy*, New Haven, CT: Yale University Press.

Huntington, Samuel (1968) *Political Order in Changing Societies*, New Haven, CT: Yale University Press.

——(1993) 'The clash of civilizations', *Foreign Affairs*, Summer: 22–49.

Husam Musa (2003) *Malaysia Darul Kasino*, Kuala Lumpur: Lajnah Penerangan PAS Pusat.

Husin Ali, Syed (1978) *Kemiskinan dan Kelaparan Tanah di Kelantan*, Petaling Jaya, Selangor: Karangkraf.

Ibrahim Syukri (1985) *History of the Malay Kingdom of Patani*, trans. Conner Bailey and John N. Miksic, Athens, OH: Ohio University Center for International Studies.

IEA (2004) 'International Energy Agency: analysis of high oil prices on the global economy', May. Online. Available: http://library.iea.org/dbtw-wpd/textbase/papers/2004/high_oil_prices.pdf (accessed 26 May 2004).

Ignatieff, M. (2003) 'The burden', *New York Times*, 5 January, Sunday Magazine, 22–54.

Ikenberry, G. J. (2001) 'American power and the empire of capitalist democracy', *Review of International Studies*, 27: 191–212.

Ikenberry, J and M. Mastanduno (2003) *International Relations Theory and the Asia Pacific*, New York: Columbia University Press.

ILO (2000) *World Labour Report 2000*, Geneva: ILO. Online. Available: http://www.ilo.org./public/english/protection/socfas/research/stat/table14.htm.

Inglehart, R., M. Basanez, J. Diez-Madrano, L. Halman and R. Luijkx (eds) (2004) *Human Beliefs and Values*, Mexico: Siglo XXI.

International Council on Human Rights Policy (2002) *Human Rights After September 11*, Versoix: International Council on Human Rights Policy.

International Crisis Group (2001) 'Indonesia: violence and radical Muslims', Indonesian Briefing, Jakarta/Brussels, 10 October.

——(2002) 'Al-Qaeda in Southeast Asia: the case of the Ngruki network in Indonesia', Jakarta/Brussels, 8 August. Online. Available: www.crisisweb.org (accessed 14 January 2003).

——(2003) 'Jemaah Islamiyah in Southeast Asia: damaged but still dangerous', ICG Asia Reports No. 63, Jakarta/Brussels, 26 August.

International Herald Tribune (2004) 'Musharraf repackaged', 13 July.

International Monetary Fund (2003) *World Economic Outlook Database*. Online. Available: http://www.imf.org/external/pubs/ft/weo/2003/02/data/index.htm.

IPCC (Intergovernmental Panel on Climate Change) (ed.) (2001) *Climate Change 2001: The Scientific Basis. IPCC Third Assessment Report. Summary for Policymakers*, Cambridge and New York: Cambridge University Press.

Iriye, Akira (1967) *Across the Pacific: an inner history of American-East Asian relations*, New York: Harcourt, Brace, and World.

Islam, S. (2000) 'Call off the RSS bluff'. Online. Available: http://www.truthindia.com/page33.html, posted 12 October 2000 (accessed 5 August 2004).

Ismail bin Wan Jusoh, Wan (ed.) (1999) *Koleksi Ucapan Rasmi YAB Tuan Guru Dato'Haji Nik Abdul Aziz bin Nik Mat, Menteri Besar Kelantan*, Kota Bharu, Kelantan: Dian Darulnaim.

Janjira Sombatpoonsiri (2004) 'Data collection on the April 28, 2004 incident', Bangkok: Peace Information Center, Foundation for Democracy and Development Studies. (In Thai)

Jayasuriya, K. (1999) 'Globalization, law, and the transformation of sovereignty: the emergence of global regulatory governance', *Indiana Journal of Global Legal Studies*, 6(2): 425–55 (Spring).

——(2001a) 'Globalization and the changing architecture of the state: regulatory state and the politics of negative coordination', *Journal of European Public Policy*, 8(1): 101–23.

——(2001b) 'Globalisation, sovereignty, and the rule of law: from political to economic constitutionalism?', *Constellations*, Special Issue, 8(4): 442–60.

——(2004) 'Introduction: the vicissitudes of Asian regional governance', in K. Jayasuriya (ed.) *Asian Regional Governance: Crisis and Change*, London: Routledge, 1–19.

Jeffrey, R. (1994) *What's Happening to India?*, 2nd edn, London: Macmillan.

——(2002) 'Grand canyon, shaky bridge: media revolution and the rise of "Hindu" politics', *South Asia*, XXXV(3): 281–300 (December).

Jervis, Robert (2003) 'Understanding the Bush Doctrine', *Political Science Quarterly*, 118(3): 365–88.

Jessop, Bob (2002) *The Future of the Capitalist State*, Cambridge: Polity Press.

Jha, Prem Shankar (2001) 'Time has run out Mr. Vajpayee', *The Hindu*, 18 September.

Joaquin, Nick (2003) *A Kadre's Road to Damascus: the Ruben Torres story*, Quezon City: Milflores.

Johnson, Chalmers (2000) *Blowback: the costs and consequences of American empire*, New York: Metropolitan Books.

——(2004) *The Sorrows of Empire*, New York: Henry Holton Company, Metropolitan Books.

——(2005) 'The scourge of militarism: Rome and America'. Online. Available:http://www.tomdispatch.com/index.mhtml?pid = 3178 (accessed 6 July 2005).

Jomo, K. S. and Ahmad Shabery Cheek (1992) 'Malaysia's Islamic movements', in Joel S. Kahn and Francis Loh Kok Wah (eds) *Fragmented Vision: culture and politics in contemporary Malaysia*, Sydney: Allen & Unwin, 79–106.

Jones, Sidney (2004) 'Political update 2003: terrorism, nationalism and disillusionment with reform', in M. Chatib Basri and Pierre van der Eng (eds) *Business in Indonesia: New Challenges, Old Problems*, Singapore: Institute of Southeast Asian Studies, 23–38.

Judt, Tony (2004) 'Dreams of empire', *New York Review of Books*, 51(17), 4 November. Online: http://www.nybooks.com/articles/17518?email (accessed 13 March 2005).

Kagan, R. (1998) 'The benevolent empire', *Foreign Policy*, 111: 24–35.

——(2003) *Of Paradise and Power: America and Europe in the new world order*, New York: Knopf.

——(n.d.) 'American as global hegemon', *In the National Interest*. Online. Available: http://www.inthenationalinterest.com/Articles/Vol2Issue29/Vol2 Issue29Kagan.html (accessed 12 June 2005).

Kagan, R. and W. Kristol (2000a) 'The present danger', *The National Interest*, 57–69.

Kagan, R. and W. Kristol (2000b) *Present Dangers: Crisis and Opportunity in American Foreign Policy*, (eds) San Francisco: Encounter Books.

Kahin, Audrey R. and George McT. Kahin (1995) *Subversion as Foreign Policy: the secret Eisenhower and Dulles debacle in Indonesia*, New York: The New Press.

Kalaw, Maximo M. (1931) 'The Moro Bugaboo', *Philippine Social Science Review*, 3(4): 34–8 (September).

Kammen, Douglas (1997) 'A time to strike: industrial strikes and changing class relations in New Order Indonesia', PhD thesis, Cornell University.

Kang, Davis (2002) *Crony Capitalism: corruption and development in South Korea and the Philippines*, Cambridge: Cambridge University Press.

Kant, I. (1991) *Political Writing*, ed. H. S. Reiss, Cambridge: Cambridge University Press.

Kapila, S. (2000) 'India-USA strategic partnership: the advent of the inevitable', South Asia Analysis Group. Online. Available: http://www. saag.org/papers2/paper120.html (accessed 4 October 2004).

——(2001) 'United States policies in South Asia under Bush: continuity is expected', South Asia Analysis Group No. 181. Online. Available: http://www.saag.org/papers2/paper181.htm (accessed 16 September 2004).

Kaplan, Lawrence and William Kristol (2003) *The War over Iraq: Saddam's tyranny and America's mission*, California: Encounter Books.

Kasian Tejapira (2004) *Bush and Thaksin: Thai and US Neoconservative Authoritarianism*, Bangkok: Kobfai. (In Thai)

Kasilag, Marcial (1938) 'Policy of the Commonwealth government towards the non-Christians in Mindanao and Sulu', in *The Development of Mindanao and the Future of Non-Christians*, Manila: Philippine Council, Institute of Pacific Relations, 12–23.

Katsiaficas, George (ed.) (2003) 'Special edition: the Kwangju uprising and the creation of South Korean democracy', *New Political Science*, 25: 2 (June).

Kautsky, K. (1970) 'Ultra-imperialism', *New Left Review*, 1(59): 41–6 (January–February).

Kavi Chongkittavorn (2004) 'Thailand: international terrorism and the Muslim south', in Daljit Singh and Chin Kin Wah (eds) *Southeast Asian Affairs 2004*, Singapore: Institute of Southeast Asian Studies, 267–75.

Keller, Bill (2002) 'The sunshine warrior', *New York Times*, 22 September.

Kemfert, Claudia (2004) 'Die ökonomischen Kosten des Klimawandels', *DIW-Wochenbericht* (Weekly Report of the German Institute for Economic Research), 42/2004.

Keohane, R and J. Nye (1977) *Power and Interdependence: world politics in transition*, Boston, MA: Little Brown.

Kershaw, Roger (1969) 'Politics in Kelantan, West Malaysia: parochial integrity versus national integration?', in Lucy Mair *et al.* (eds) *Autonomy and Dependence in 'Parochial' Politics*, Institute of Commonwealth Studies, ICS Collected Seminar Papers 7, London: University of London, 50–66.

Kessler, Clive (1978) *Islam and Politics in a Malay State: Kelantan 1838–1969*, Ithaca, NY and London: Cornell University Press.

——(2004) 'The mark of the man: Mahathir's Malaysia after Dr. Mahathir', in Bridget Welsh (ed.) *Reflections: the Mahathir years*, Washington, DC: Southeast Asia Studies Program, Johns Hopkins University, 15–27.

Khalidi, Rashid (2004) *Resurrecting Empire: western footprints and America's perilous path in the Middle East*, Boston, MA: Beacon Press.

Khoo Boo Teik (2003) *Beyond Mahathir: Malaysian politics and its discontents*, London and New York: Zed Books

Kilusan (2002) *Kilusan: A Movement of News and Views*, 3: 2–3.

Kim, Dae Jung (1985) *Mass Participatory Economy: a democratic alternative for Korea,* Cambridge, MA: Center for International Affairs, Harvard University.

Kim, Song-koo (2000) 'Restructuring policy of citizen's movement and the 2000 general election', *Monthly PSSP* (Peoples' Solidarity for Social Progress), April. (In Korean)

Kim Sunhyuk (2000) *The Politics of Democratization in Korea: The Role of Civil Society*, Pittsburgh: University of Pittsburgh Press.

Kingsbury, Damien and Lesley McCulloch (2004) 'Military business in Aceh and East Timor: a comparative study', Unpublished paper.

Klare, M.T. (2002) 'Endless military superiority', *The Nation*, 15 July. Online edition. Available: http://www.thenation.com/doc.mhtml?i = 20020715&s = klare (accessed 18 December 2005).

——(2004) *Blood and Oil: the dangers and consequences of America's growing dependency on petroleum*, New York: Metropolitan Books Henry Holt.

Kleveman, Lutz (2004) *The New Great Game: blood and oil in central Asia*, London: Atlantic Books.

Kohli, Atul (1990) *Democracy and Discontent: India's growing crisis of governability*, Cambridge: Cambridge University Press.

Koo, Hagen (1993) 'The state, Minjung, and the working class in Korea', in Hagen Koo (ed.) *State and Society in Contemporary Korea*, Ithaca, NY: Cornell University Press, 163–96.

——(2001) *Korean Workers: the culture and politics of class formation*, Ithaca, NY: Cornell University Press.

——(2002) 'Engendering civil society: the role of the labor movement', in Charles Armstrong (ed.) *Korean Society: Civil Society, Democracy, and the State*, London: Routledge, 109–31.

Krauthammer, Charles (1991) 'The unipolar moment', *Foreign Affairs*, 70(1): 23–33.

Kristol, Irving (1995) *Neoconservative: the autobiography of an idea*, New York: Free Press.

——(2003) 'The neoconservative persuasion', *Weekly Standard*, 23–5.

Kumar, D. (2003) 'Ariel Sharon's successful India visit'. Online. Available: http://www.westerndefense.org/bulletins/Sept1-03.htm   (accessed   14 September 2004).

Kumar Ramakrishna (2003) 'The US foreign policy of praetorian unilateralism and the implications for Southeast Asia', in Uwe Johannen, Alan Smith and James Gomez (eds) *September 11 & Political Freedom: Asian perspectives*, Singapore: Select Books: 116–41.

Kumar Ramakrishna and See Seng Tan (eds) (2004) *After Bali: The threat of terrorism in Southeast Asia*, Singapore: Institute of Defence and Strategic Studies, Nanyang University of Technology and World Scientific.

Kunz, D. B. (1997) *Butter and Guns: America's Cold War economic diplomacy*, New York: Free Press.

Kurniawan Moch, N. (2003) 'Polls to disappoint reformists', *Jakarta Post*, 23 December.

Kux, D. (1993) *India and the United States: estranged democracies*, Washington, DC: National Defense University Press.

——(2001) *The United States and Pakistan, 1947–2000*, Baltimore, MD: Johns Hopkins University Press.

Lafer, Gordon (2004) 'Neoliberalism by other means: the "war on terror" at home and abroad', *New Political Science*, 26(3): 323–46.

Lake, D. A. (1999) *Entangling Relations: America's foreign policy and its century*, Princeton, NJ: Princeton University Press.

Lal, Deepak (2004) *In Praise of Empires: globalization and order*, London: Palgrave Macmillan.

Lampton, David M. (1994) 'America's China policy in the age of the finance minister: Clinton ends linkage', *China Quarterly*, 139: 597–621.

Lasswell, Harold (1941) 'The garrison state', *American Journal of Sociology*, 46: 455–68.

Latham, R. (1997) *The Liberal Moment: modernity, security, and the making of postwar international order*, New York: Columbia University Press.

Lauridson, L. S. (1998) 'The financial crisis in Thailand: conduct and consequences', *World Development*, 26(8): 1575–93.

Lavin, Franklin (2003) 'Building on success: adjoining the Singapore model', Remarks to Young Entrepreneurs Organization, 28 May. Online. Available: http://singapore.usembassy.gov/speeches/2003/may28.shtml (accessed 15 June 2003).

Lee Kim Chew (2003) 'Iraq must disarm now or face war', *Straits Times Interactive*, 15 March.

Lee Kuan Yew (2004a) 'Terrorism escalates worldwide', *Forbes Magazine*, 18 October. Online. Available: http://www.singapore-window.org/sw04/041018fo.htm (accessed 12 June 2005).

——(2004b) 'The world after Iraq', Speech by Senior Minister Lee Kuan Yew at the Thammasat Unversity Graduate School of Business International Forum 2003, Bangkok, 16 December 2003. Online. Available: http://app.mfa.gov.sg/pr/read_content.asp?View,3875 (accessed 10 May 2005).

Lee, Lai To (2001) '*China's relations with ASEAN: partners in the 21st century?*', *Pacific Review*, 13(1): 61–71.

Lee Siew Hua (2002) 'Security the focus of talks with Bush', *StraitsTimes*, 2 May: 2.

Lee, Teng-hui (2000) *Asia's Strategy*, Taipei: Yuan-Liou.

Lee, Wen-Chih (1988) 'What's the matter with politics? A structural perspective on the discourses of unification and independence', *Wen-Shin*, March: 19–31.

——(1996) 'The Asia-Pacific strategy of China: the challenges to build a sea power', in Chyuan-jenq Shiau and Wen-Chih Lee (eds) *The Grand Transition: the Dynamic Relationships of Asia-Pacific and Taiwan Strait*, Taipei: Ya-Chiang, 91–154.

——(2001) 'Under the struggle of the sea power and land power, the Asia-Pacific strategic development and Taiwan's security strategy', *Soochow Journal of Political Science*, 13: 129–72 (September).

——(2003) 'The construction of Taiwan's "Go-South" worldview: the vantage point of struggle of sea power and land power in Asia-Pacific', in Hsin-Huang Michael Hsiao (ed.) *Taiwan and Southeast Asia: Go-south policy and Vietnamese brides,* Taipei: Center for Asia-Pacific Area Studies Academic Sinica, 1–41.

Lee Yock Suan (2002) 'East Asia Post 9-11', Ministerial Speech, Houston, 28 October. Available at http://www.asiasociety.org/speeches/suan.html (accessed 1 December 2002).

Lefebvre, H. (1991) *The Production of Space*, Oxford: Blackwell.

Leffler, M. P. (1992) *A Preponderance of Power: national security, the Truman administration, and the Cold War*, Stanford, CA: Stanford University Press.

Leifer, Michael (2000) *Singapore's Foreign Policy: Coping with Vulnerability*, London: Routledge.

Leinin, Jennifer (2003) 'S'pore firms set to reap s$200m a year from US trade pact', *Business Times*, 8 May: 1–2.

Leonard, M. (2004) 'The US heads home: will Europe regret it?', *Financial Times*, 26–27 June: W1, W2.

Leys, Colin (1996) *The Rise and Fall of Development Theory*, Bloomington, IN: Indiana University Press.

Lieberthal, Kenneth (1994) 'A new China strategy', *Foreign Affairs*, 74(6): 35–49.

Lim, L. (2002) 'JI members: not poor, not stupid, not marginalised', *Straits Times Weekly*, 28 September: 1.

Lin, Cheng-yi (2002) 'Cross-strait military balance and the security of Taiwan', Paper presented at Japan-Taiwan Research Forum, Keio University and Taiwan Security Research Center, Taipei, 22 January.

Lipschutz, R. (2002) 'The clash of governmentalities: the fall of the UN republic and America's reach for imperium'. Online. Available: www-bib: (accessed 12 December 2004).

Lipset, S. M. (1996) *American Exceptionalism: a double-edged sword,* New York: W.W. Norton.

Lobe, J. (2002) 'Neoconservatives consolidate control over US Mideast policy', *Foreign Policy in Focus*, Washington, DC: Institute for Policy Studies.

Lohr, Steve (1998) 'Business, Asian style: a revaluing of values; some say market collapse shows democracy is key to growth, after all', *New York Times*, 7 February: 9.

Lopez, Leslie and Shawn W. Crispin (2003) 'A Thai-CIA antiterrorism team', *Wall Street Journal*, 1 October: A17.

Low, Eugene (2004) 'PM calls for unity in war on terror', *Straits Times Interactive*, 5 June.

Lugard, F. (1929) *The Dual Mandate in British Tropical Africa*, London: William Blackwood.

Luttwak, Edward (1994) *Weltwirtschaftskrieg. Export als Waffe – aus Partnern werden Gegner*, Reinbek bei Hamburg: Rowohlt.

Madale, Nagasura (1984) 'The future of the Moro National Liberation Front (MNLF) as a separatist movement in Southern Philippines', in Lim Joo-Jock and S. Vani Singapore (eds) *Armed Separatism in Southeast Asia*, Singapore: Institute for Southeast Asian Studies.

Maddison, Angus (2001) *The World Economy: a millennial perspective*, Paris: Development Centre Studies, OECD.

Mahathir Mohamad (1998) Speech at the 52nd UMNO General Assembly, Kuala Lumpur, 19 June. Reprinted as 'All Malaysians should defend their sovereignty', *New Straits Times*, 20 June.

Mahbubani, Kyshore (1993) 'The dangers of decadence', *Foreign Affairs*, 72(4): 10–14.

Malcolm, George (1936) *The Commonwealth of the Philippines*, New York and London: D. Appleton-Century.

Malik, A. (2003) 'The BJP, the RSS family and globalization in India', *Harvard Asia Quarterly*, 16 September.

Mallaby, Sebastian (2002) 'The reluctant imperialist: terrorism, failed states, and the case for American empire', *Foreign Affairs*, 81(2): 2–7.

Malthus, Thomas Robert (1970) *An Essay on the Principle of Population and a Summary View of the Principle of Population*, Harmondsworth: Penguin.

Mann, J. (2004) *Rise of the Vulcans: the history of Bush's war cabinet,* New York: Viking.

Mann, Michael (2001) 'Globalisation and September 11', *New Left Review*, 12: 51–72 (November/December).

——(2003) *The Incoherent Empire*, London: Verso.

Manupipatpong, W. (2002) 'The ASEAN surveillance process and the East Asian Monetary Fund', *ASEAN Economic Bulletin*, 19(1): 111–22.

Marable, Manning (2003) '9/11: racism in a time of terror', in Stanley Aronowitz and Heather Gautney (eds) *Globalization and Resistance in the 21st Century World Order*, New York: Basic Books, 1–14.

Marcos, Subcommandante (2002) 'The fourth world war has begun', in Tom Hayden (ed.) *The Zapatista Reader*, New York: Nation Books, 270–84.

Martin, L. L. (2003) 'Multilateral Organizations after the US-Iraq War of 2003' Unpublished paper.

Martinez, Patricia (2004) 'Perhaps he deserved better: the disjuncture between vision and reality in Mahathir's Islam', in Bridget Welsh (ed.) *Reflections: the Mahathir years*, Washington, DC: Southeast Asia Studies Program, Johns Hopkins University, 28–39.

Marx, Karl (1970) *Das Kapital*, Vol. I, MEW 23, Berlin.

——(1972) *On Colonialism*, New York: International.

Marx, Karl and Friedrich Engels (1969), Manifest der Kommunistischen Partei', *Werke*, MEW IV: 461–93, Berlin.

Mastanduno, M. (1998) 'Economics and security in statecraft and scholarship', *International Organization*, 52: 825–54.

Maznah Mohamad (2004) 'Mahathir's Malay question', in Bridget Welsh (ed.) *Reflections: the Mahathir years*, Washington, DC: Southeast Asia Studies Program, Johns Hopkins University, 162–3.

McCormack, Gavan (2003) 'Sunshine, containment, war: options on Korea', The Australia Institute. Online. Available: http://www.tai.org.au/Publications_Files/Papers&Sub_Files/Pyongyang2.pdf (accessed 6 July 2005).

McCoy, Alfred W. (ed.) (1993) *An Anarchy of Families: state and family in the Philippines*, Madison, WI: University of Wisconsin Center for Southeast Asian Studies.

McDougall, W. A. (1997) *Promised Land, Crusader State: the American encounter with the world since 1776,* Boston: Mariner Books.

McHenry, D. and K. Bird (1977) 'Food bugle in Bangladesh', *Foreign Policy*, 27: 72–88.

McInerney, M. (2001) 'India does not rule out US military base access', 22 June. Online. Available: http://www.freerepublic.com/forum/a3b3372f813a0.htm (accessed 2 July 2004).

McKenna, Thomas M. (1998) *Muslim Rulers and Rebels: everyday politics and armed separatism in the Southern Philippines*, Berkeley, CA and London: University of California Press.

McLeod, Ross (2000) 'Soeharto's Indonesia: a better class of corruption', *Agenda*, 7(2): 99–112.

——(2004) 'After Soeharto: prospects for reform and recovery in Indonesia', Indonesia Project,   Australian National University.

Merry, Robert W. (2003) 'Rome on the Potomac', *International Economy*, Summer: 12–15, 94–9.

Micklethwaite, John and Adrian Wooldridge (2004) *The Right Nation: Conservative Power in America*, New York: Penguin.

Mietzner, Marcus (2003) 'Business as usual? The Indonesian armed forces and local politics in the post-Soeharto era', in Ed Aspinall and Greg Fealy (eds) *Local Power and Politics in Indonesia: Democratisation and Decentralisation*, Canberra and Singapore: Australian National University and Institute of Southeast Asian Studies, 245–58.

Migdal, Joel (1988) *Strong Societies and Weak States*, Princeton, NJ: Princeton University Press.

Milbank, Dana (2001) '1975 East Timor invasion got US go-ahead: Ford, Kissinger told Indonesian leader they would not object, documents show', *Washington Post*, 7 December: A38.

Mill, John Stuart (1871) *Principals of Political Economy*, London: Longman.

Misra, Amalendu (2001) 'Shanghai 5 and the emerging alliance in Central Asia: the closed society and its enemies', *Central Asian Survey*, 20(3): 305–21.

Mogato, Manny (2002) 'America's agenda', *Newsbreak*, 13 February: 7–9.

Mohammad Agus Yusoff (1994) *Politik Kelantan Selepas Pilihanraya Umum 1990*, Bangi, Selangor: Institut Alam dan Tamadun Melayu, Universiti Kebangsaan Malaysia, Terbitan Tak Berkala No. 13.

Mohammad, Goenawan and Laksmi Pamuntjak (2004) 'Indonesia: corruption notebook', The Center for Public Integrity, 21 May. Online. Available: http://www.publicintegrity.org/ga/country.aspx?cc=id&act= notebook (accessed 2 May 2004).

Mohd Amin Yaakub, Haji (2001) *Sejarah Pemerintahan PAS Kelantan 1959–1990*, Kota Bharu, Kelantan: Pusat Kajian Strategik.

Moon, Chung-In and David Steinberg (eds) (1999) *Kim Dae-Jung Government and Sunshine Policy*, Seoul: Yonsei University Press.

Moonje, B. S. (1932–36) 'The Central Military Education Society', in Moonje Papers, Microfilm m1, 1932–36, New Delhi: Nehru Memorial Museum and Library.

Mortimer, Rex (1974) *Indonesian Communism Under Sukarno: ideology and politics, 1959–1965*, Ithaca, NY: Cornell University Press.

Muhammad Ikmal Said (1996) 'Malay nationalism and national identity', in Muhammad Ikmal Said and Zahid Emby (eds) *Malaysia: critical perspectives. Essays in Honour of Syed Husin Ali*, Kuala Lumpur: Malaysian Social Science Association, 34–73.

Müller, Friedemann (2004) *Klimapolitik und Energieversorgungssicherheit*, Berlin: SWP-Studie.

Nadzru B. Azhari (2004) 'The crisis in the south: a Kelantanese perspective', *The Nation*, 14 May.

National Security Coordination Centre (2004) *The Fight against Terror: Singapore's national security strategy*, Singapore: National Security Coordination Centre.

National Security Strategy of the United States of America (2004) Online. Available: www.whitehouse.gov/nsc/nss (accessed 8 November 2004).

Nau, H. R. (2002) *At Home Abroad: identity and power in American foreign policy*, Ithaca, NY: Cornell University Press.

NCCU (National Chengchi University) (2004) 'The Central Election Commission (CEC) & *National Chengchi University* (NCCU) Election Databank', online categories and results of elections in Taiwan, the legislators elections: 1995, 1998 and 2001. Online. Available: http://vote.nccu.edu.tw/engcec/vote4.asp (accessed 15 April 2004).

Nehru, J. (1946) *Discovery of India*, Calcutta: The Signet Press.

NEPDG (2001) *National Energy Policy,* Washington, DC: White House.

Norani Othman (2003) 'Islamization and democratization in Malaysia in regional and global contexts', in Ariel Heryanto and Sumit K. Mandal (eds) *Challenging Authoritarianism in Southeast Asia: comparing Indonesia and Malaysia*, New York and London: RoutledgeCurzon, 117–44.

Nuruzzaman, Mohammed (2004) 'Neoliberal economic reforms, the rich and the poor in Bangladesh', *Journal of Contemporary Asia*, 34(1): 33–54.

Nye, Joseph S., Jr (1995) 'The case for deep engagement', *Foreign Affairs*, 74(4): 90–102.

——(2002) *The Paradox of American Power,* Oxford: Oxford University Press.

——(2004a) *Soft Power: the means to success in world politics*, New York: Public Affairs.

——(2004b) 'Is America really an empire?', *Straits Times Interactive*, 28 January. Online. Available: http://straitstimes.asia1.com.sg/ (accessed 4 February 2004).

Oakeshott, Michael (1962) On being conservative. Online. Available: http://www.geocities.com/Heartland/4887/conservative.html (accessed 6 July 2005).

Odom, William E. and Robert Dujarric (2004) *America's Inadvertent Empire*, Yale, CT: Yale University Press.

Ohmae, Kenichi (1990) *The Borderless World: power and strategy in the inter-linked economy*, London: Collins.

Ong, A. (1999) *Flexible Citizenship: the Cultural Logics of Transnationality*, Durham, NC: Duke University Press.

——(2002) 'A multitude of spaces: radical versus moderate Islam', Paper presented at Panel on 9/11 and the Risks of Hegemony: Global Emergency or False Alarm?, AAA Meetings, New Orleans, 21 November 2002. Online. Available: http://www.emory.edu/college/anthropology/faculty/antbk/pdfs/AAA%20Ong%20Revised.PDF (accessed 20 October 2003).

——(2004) 'The Chinese axis: zoning technologies and variegated sovereignty', *Journal of East Asian Studies*, 4: 69–96.

Panitch, L. (2000) 'The new imperial state', *New Left Review*, 2, March-April: 5–20.

Panitch, L. and S. Gindin (2004) 'Global capitalism and American empire', *Socialist Register 2004*, Monthly Review Press.

Paris, R. (2002) 'International peace building and the mission civilisatrice', *Review of International Studies*, 28: 637–58.

Parti Islam SeMalaysia (PAS) (2003) *Negara Islam*, Bangi, Selangor. Trans. *The Islamic State Document*. Online. Available: http://www.parti-pas.org/IslamicStateDocument.php (accessed 18 June 2004).

Passerin d'Entreves, Alexander (1967) *The Notion of the State: An Introduction to Political Theory,* London: Clarendon Press.

Pasuk Phongpaichit and Chris Baker (2004) *Thaksin: The Business of Politics in Thailand*, Chiang Mai: Silkworm Books.

Patnaik, P. (2002) 'Swayed by the "humbug of finance": economic policy under the BJP-led government', *South Asia*, XXV(3): 131–46 (December).

Payne, A. (2000) 'Rethinking United States-Caribbean relations: toward a new mode of transterritorial governance', *Review of International Studies*, 26: 69–82.

——(ed.) (2004) *The New Regional Politics of Development*, London: Palgrave.

Pempel, T. J. (2004) 'Challenges to bilateralism: changing foes, capital flows, and complex forums', in E. S. Krauss and T. J. Pempel (eds) *Beyond Bilateralism: US-Japan Relations in the New Asia-Pacific*, Stanford, CA: Stanford University Press, 1–33.

Peoples' Solidarity for Social Progress (PSSP) (2000) 'Victory of small stock holders is a despair of people', *Weekly Socialization and Labor*, 13 March.

Pereira, Brendan and Abu Bakar Zuraidah (2004) 'Pas will work to counter "fear" factor', *New Sunday Times*, 30 May.

Peri, Yoram (2002) *The Israeli Military and Israel's Palestinian Policy: from Oslo to the Al Aqsa Intifada* (Peaceworks No. 47), Washington, DC: United States Institute of Peace.

Perrin, Andrew (2002) 'Thailand's terror', *Time Asia*, 25 November.

Peters, Michael (2004) 'Neo-liberalism'. Online. Available: http://www.vusst.hr/encyclopaedia/neoliberalism.htm (accessed 24 August 2004).

Petras, James (2001) 'The Ford Foundation and the CIA: a documented case of philanthropic collaboration with the secret police'. Online. Available: http://www.ratical.org/ratville/CAH/FordFandCIA.html (accessed 2 May 2004).

Petras, James and Henry Veltmeyer (2001) 'NGOs in the service of imperialism', in James Petras and Henry Veltmeyer, *Globalization Unmasked: imperialism in the 21st century*, London: Zed, 128–38.

Philippine Social Weather Station (2002a) Special Media Release, 30 January.

——(2002b) Special Institutional Sponsor Release, 6 August.

Phillips, N. (2004) 'The dynamics of "linkage": the economic-security nexus in contemporary US trade strategies', Paper presented at the Conference on Asia Pacific Economies: Multilateral vs. Bilateral Relationships, Hong Kong, 19–21 May 2004.

Picciotto, S. (1996) 'The regulatory crisis-cross: interaction between jurisdictions and the construction of global regulatory networks', in W. Bratton. J. McCahery, S. Picciotto and C. Scott (eds) *International Regulatory Competition and Coordination: perspective on economic regulation in Europe and the United States*, Oxford: Clarendon Press, 89–127.

Pieterse, Jan Nederveen (2004) *Globalization or Empire?*, London: Routledge.

Podhoretz, N. (1980) *The Present Danger: do we have the will to reverse the decline of American power?*, New York: Simon & Schuster.

Poggi, G. (1978) *The Development of the Modern State: a sociological intro-duction*, London: Hutchinson.

Pollard, R. A. (1985) *Economic Security and the Origins of the Cold War, 1945–1950,* New York: Columbia University Press.

Posen, B. R. and A. L. Ross (1996–97) 'Competing visions of US grand strategy', *International Security*, 21: 5–53.

Poulantzas, N. (1978a) *Classes in Contemporary Capitalism*, London: New Left Books.

——(1978b) *State, Power and Socialism*, London: New Left Books.

Prair Sirisakdumkeong (2003) 'The interrelationship between Malay Muslims and the Chinese in the market place "Sai Klang" in Yala province', Masters thesis, Department of Anthropology, Silpakorn University. (In Thai)

Prashad, V. (2001) 'Hindutva and Zionism: comprador states of Pentagon, Inc', *Z-Net Magazine*, 8 August. Online. Available: http://www.zmag.org/sustainers/content/2001-08/08prashad.htm (accessed 3 August 2004).

PRC (2004) *A Year After the Iraq War,* Washington, DC: Pew Research Center.

Puniyani, R. (2003a) 'Distorting history of freedom struggle', *Countercur-rents.org*, 11 September. Online. Available: http://www.countercurrents.org/comm-puniyani110903.htm (accessed 30 May 2004).

——(2003b) 'Complimenting imperialist designs', *Kashmir Telegraph*, II(I) (May). Online. Available: http://www.kashmirtelegraph.com/0503/ram.htm (accessed 30 May 2004).

——(2003c) 'From culture to politics: RSS bares its fangs (review of the book – RSS's tryst with politics by Pralay Kanungo, Manohar, Delhi)', *Milli Gazette*, 19 September. Online. Available: http://www.milligazette.com/Archives/1511200218.htm.

Quadir, M. N. (1997) *Dusho Chheshatti Dine Swadhinata*, Dhaka: Mukto.

Quirino, Carlos (1984) *Chick Parson: master spy of the Philippines,* Quezon City: New Day.

Rahim, Lilly (1998) *The Singapore Dilemma: the political and educational marginality of the Malay community*, Kuala Lumpur: Oxford University Press.

Rajghatta, C. (2001) 'US revokes minor defence sanctions as DoD steps up quake relief effort', *Indian Express*, 3 February.

Rajgopal, A. (2001) *Politics after Television*, Cambridge: Cambridge University Press.

Ramakrishna, K. (2004) 'US strategy on Southeast Asia: counterterrorist or counterterrorism?', in K. Ramakshina and S. S. Tan (eds) *After Bali: the threat of terrorism in Southeast Asia*, Singapore: World Scientific, 305–7.

Ramchandran, S. (2000), 'Indian analysts see advantages in Bush victory', CNS News.Com, 6 November. Online. Available: http://www.cnsnews.com/ViewForeignBureaus.asp?Page=\ForeignBureaus\archive\200011\For20001106a.html (accessed 2 August 2004).

Ramo, Joshua Cooper (2004) 'The Beijing Consensus', The Foreign Policy Centre. Online. Available:http://fpc.org.uk/fsblob/244.pdf (accessed 6 July 2005).

Randall, Doug and Peter Schwartz (2003) *An Abrupt Climate Change Scenario and Its Implications for United States National Security*. Online. Available: http://www.ems.org/climate/pentagon_climatechange.pdf (accessed 26 May 2004).

Ransom, David (1970) 'The Berkeley Mafia and the Indonesian massacre', *Ramparts*, 27–9, 40–9.

Ravenhill, J. (2004) 'The new bilateralism in the Asia-Pacific', in K. Jayasuriya (ed.) *Regional Governance: Crisis and Change*, London: RoutledgeCurzon, 61–82.

——(2006) 'US Economic Relations with East Asia: from hegemony to complex interdependence?', in M. Beeson (ed.) *Bush and Asia: America's Evolving Relations with East Asia*, London: Routledge.

Regnier, P. (2001) 'Reform in post-crisis Thailand (1997–2001): exploring the contribution of small entrepreneurs to socio-economic change, democratization and emerging populist governance', Draft paper presented to the EUROSEAS Conference, London, School of Oriental and African Studies, 6–8 September.

Reinicke, W. (1998) *Global Public Policy*, Washington, BC: Brookings Institution.

Reuters (2003) 'Singapore clamps down on hackers', 13 November. Online. Available: http//:www.ThinkCentre.org/article.cfm?ArticleID=229 (accessed 19 November 2003).

Rhodes, E. (2003) 'The imperial logic of Bush's liberal agenda', *Survival*, 45: 131–54.

Rice, Condoleezza (2000) 'Promoting the national interest', *Foreign Affairs*, 79(1): 45–62.

Ritchie, N. (2003) 'Notes on missile defence', Oxford Research Group, May. Online. Available: http://www.mdwg.org.uk/notesonmissiledefence.htm (accessed 3 July 2004).

Roberts, Dexter (2002) *China Journal*, 29 May. Online. Available: http://www.businessweek.com/bwdaily/dnflash/may2002/nf20020529_1844.htm (accessed 3 June 2004).

Roberts, John (2003) 'Thailand sends troops to bolster US occupation of Iraq', World Socialist Web Site, 1 October. Online. Available: http://www.wsws.org/articles/2003/oct2003/thai-o01.shtml (accessed 7 November 2004).

Robertson, S., X. Bonal and R. Dale (2002) 'GATS and the educational service industry: the politics of scale and global re-territorialization', *Comparative Education Review*, 46(4): 472–96.

Robinson, William (2004) *A Theory of Global Capitalism: Production, Class, and State in a Transnational World*, Baltimore, MD: Johns Hopkins University Press.

Robinson, W. I. (1996) *Promoting Polyarchy: Globalisation, US Intervention, and Hegemony,* Cambridge: Cambridge University Press.

Robison, Richard (1987) 'After the Gold Rush: the politics of economic restructuring in Indonesia in the 1980s', in Richard Robison, Kevin Hewison and Richard Higgot (eds) *Southeast Asia in the 1980s: the politics of economic crisis*, Sydney: Allen & Unwin, 16–51.

——(1996) 'The politics of "Asian values"', *Pacific Review*, 9(3): 309–27.

——(2001) 'Indonesia: crisis, oligarchy and reform' in Garry Rodan, Kevin Hewison and Richard Robison (eds) *The Political Economy of South East Asia: Conflicts, Crisis and Change*, Melbourne: Oxford University Press, 104–37.

——(2004) 'Neoliberalism and the future world: markets and the end of politics', *Critical Asian Studies*, 36(3): 405–23.

Robison, Richard and Vedi R. Hadiz (2004) *Reorganising Power in Indonesia: the politics of oligarchy in an age of markets*, London: RoutledgeCurzon.

Robison, Richard and Andrew Rosser (1998) 'Contesting reform: Indonesia's New Order and the IMF', *World Development*, 26(8): 1593–1609.

Rodan, Garry (1996a) 'State-society relations and political opposition in Singapore', in Garry Rodan (ed.) *Political Oppositions in Industrialising Asia*, London: Routledge, 95–127.

——(1996b) 'The internationalization of ideological conflict: Asia's new significance', *Pacific Review*, 9(3): 328–51.

——(2001) 'Singapore: globalisation and the politics of economic restructuring' in Garry Rodan, Kevin Hewison and Richard Robison (eds) *The Political Economy of Southeast Asia: conflicts, crises and change*, Melbourne: Oxford University Press, 138–77.

——(2004) *Transparency and Authoritarian Rule in Southeast Asia: Singapore and Malaysia*, London: Routledge.

Rodan, Garry and Kevin Hewison (2004) 'Closing the circle? Globalisation, conflict and political regimes', *Critical Asian Studies*, 36(3): 383–404.

Rodan, Garry, Kevin Hewison and Richard Robison (2001) 'Theorising Southeast Asia's Boom Bust and Recovery', in Garry Rodan, Kevin Hewison and Richard Robison (eds) *The Political Economy of Southeast Asia: conflicts, crises and change*, Melbourne: Oxford University Press, 1–41.

Rubin, Robert E. (1998) 'The Asian financial situation', Address to Georgetown University (Treasury News), 21 January. Online. Available: http://www.usia.gov/regional/ea/asiafin/rubnasia.htm (accessed 1 August 1998).

Rudolph, Jürgen (2000) 'The political causes of the Asian crisis', in Uwe Johannen, Jürgen Rudolph and James Gomez (eds) *The Political Dimensions of the Asian Crisis*, Singapore: Select Books and Friedrich Naumann Foundation, 13–94.

Ruggie, J. (1983) 'International regimes, transactions, and change: embedded liberalism in the postwar economic order', in S. Krasner (ed.) *International Regimes*, Ithaca, NY: Cornell University Press, 195–231.

RUPE (Research Unit for Political Economy) (2004) *Aspects of India's Economy*, 36 & 37: 56–7 (March).

Rupert, Mark (1995) *Producing Hegemony: The politics of mass production and American global power*, Cambridge: Cambridge University Press.

Saber, Mamitua (1962) 'The Muslim minority in the Philippines', Unpublished manuscript.

Sabrang Communications and The South Asian Citizens Watch (2002) 'The foreign exchange of hate: the IDRF (India Development and Relief Fund) (a report by 11 NRIs)', Mumbai, India: Sabrang Communications

& Publishing; France: The South Asia Citizens Web. Online. Available: http://www.zmag.org/southasia/stopfundinghate/part3.html (accessed 4 August 2004).

Sachs, Jeffrey and Thye Woo Wing (1994) 'Structural factors in the economic reforms of China, Eastern Europe and the former Soviet Union,' *Economic Policy*, April: 102–45.

——(1997) 'Understanding China's economic performance', Development Discussion Paper No. 575, Harvard Institute of International Development, Harvard University.

Said, Edward (1978) *Orientalism*, New York: Pantheon Books.

Salas, Rafael (1961) 'Development plans for Mindanao', *Sunday Times Magazine*, 2 February.

Santos, Soliman (2003) 'Malaysia's role in the peace negotiations between the Philippine government and the Moro Islamic Liberation Front', Unpublished manuscript, 26 May.

Schaller, Michael (1985) *The American Occupation of Japan: the Origins of the Cold War in Asia*, New York: Oxford University Press.

Scheer, Herrmann (1999) *Solare Weltwirtschaft. Strategien für die ökologische Moderne,* München: Kunstmann Verlag.

Schmitt, Gary (2003) 'Power & duty: US action is crucial to maintaining world order', *Los Angeles Times*, March 23. Reproduced in 'Project for the New American Century'. Online. Available: http://www.newamerican-century.org/global-032303.htm (accessed 3 June 2004).

Schoppa, L. J. (1997) *Bargaining with Japan: what American pressure can and cannot do,* New York: Columbia University Press.

Schwenniger, S. R. (2003) 'Revamping American grand strategy,' *World Policy Journal*, 20: 25–44.

Scupin, Raymond (1998) 'Muslim accommodation in Thai society', *Journal of Islamic Studies*, 9(2): 229–58.

Sebastian, Leonard C. (2003) 'The Indonesian dilemma: how to participate in the war and terror without becoming a national security state', in Kumar Ramakrishna and See Seng Tan (eds) *After Bali: the threat of terrorism in Southeast Asia*, Singapore: Institute of Defence and Strategic Studies and World Scientific, 357–81.

Selden, Mark and Alvin Y. So (eds) (2003) *War and State Terrorism: The United States, Japan and the Asia Pacific in the long twentieth century*, Lanham, MD: Rowman and Littlefield.

Senate Foreign Committee, The Thai Senate (2004) 'Statement on deaths and excessive violence in suppressing demonstration at the provincial police station, Tak Bai, Narathiwat on October 25, 2004', Bangkok, 3 November.

Seow, Francis T. (2004) *Beyond Suspicion? The Singapore judiciary*, New Haven, CT: Yale University Press.

Serfati, Claude (2002) 'War drive: armed globalization', *International Viewpoint*, IV: 344 (October). Online. Available: http://212.67.202.147/~ivnet05/article.php3?id_article = 332 (accessed 10 June 2005).

Shambaugh, David (1995) 'The United States and China: a new Cold War?' *Current History*, September.

——(2004/5) 'China engages Asia', *International Security*, 29: 64–99.

Shanker, T. (2005) 'Rumsfeld issues a sharp rebuke to China on arms', *New York Times*, 4 June.

Shaw, M. (2000) *Theory of the Global State: globality as an unfinished revolution*, Cambridge: Cambridge University Press.

Shiva, V., A. Jafri and K. Jalees (2002) '"Ganga" is not for sale: Suez-Degre'mont and the privatization of Ganga water', *In Motion Magazine*, 20 October. Online. Available: http://www.inmotionmagazine.com/global/vshiva2.html (accessed 4 August 2004).

Shue, Vivienne B. (1988) *Reach of the State: sketches of the Chinese body politic*, Stanford, CA: Stanford University Press.

Sidel, John T. (2003) 'Other schools, other pilgrimages, other dreams: the making and unmaking of *Jihad* in Southeast Asia', in James T. Siegel and Audrey R. Kahin (eds) *Southeast Asia over Three Generations: Essays Presented to Benedict R. O'G. Anderson*, Ithaca, NY: Cornell University, Southeast Asia Program, 347–81.

Sinha, R. (2000) 'Stigmatising the Sangh', *Indian Express*, 16 May.

Slaughter, Anne-Marie (1997) 'The real new world order', *Foreign Affairs*, 76(5): 183–97.

Smith, T. (1994) *America's Mission: the United States and the worldwide struggle for democracy in the twentieth century,* Princeton, NJ: Princeton University Press.

——(2000) 'National security liberalism and American foreign policy', in M. Cox, G. J. Ikenberry and T. Inoguchi (eds) *American Democracy Promotion: impulses, strategies, and impacts*, Oxford: Oxford University Press, 85–102.

Sobhan, R. (1979) 'Politics of food and famine in Bangladesh', *Economic and Political Weekly* (Bombay), 14: 1973–80.

Soederberg, Susan (2004) 'American empire and "excluded states": the millennium challenge account and the shift to pre-emptive development', *Third World Quarterly*, 25(2): 279–302.

Solan, G. R. (1988) *Geopolitics in United States Strategic Policy: 1890–1987*, Brighton: Wheatsheaf Books.

Solans, Eugenio Domingo (2004) 'The international role of the Euro. Its impact on economic relations between Asia and Europe', *Asia Europe Journal*, 2(1): 7–14.

Sonn Hochul (1987) 'Towards a synthetic approach of third world economy: the case of South Korea', Dissertation, University of Texas at Austin.

——(1995) 'State and "civil society" in Korea: a reappraisal', Paper presented at Georgetown Conference on Korean Society, Georgetown University, Washington, DC May.

——(1997) 'Late blooming of South Korean labor movement', *Monthly Review*, June.

——(2003a) 'Sunshine policy and south-south conflict', in Sonn Hochul, *Modern Korean Politics, 1945–2003*, Seoul: Sahoipyungryun. (In Korean)

——(2003b) 'Regional cleavage in Korean politics and elections', *Korean Journal*, 43: 2 (Summer).

——(2004) 'Are anti-globalization struggles reactionary?', *Studies in Marxism*, 1. (In Korean)

——(2005) 'Characteristics of welfare reform of the Kim Dae Jung government', *Korean Political Science Review*, 1. (In Korean)

Spain, J. W. (1954) 'Military assistance for Pakistan', *American Political Science Review*, 48(3): 738–51.

Spanier, J. (1985) *American Foreign Policy Since World War*, Fort Worth, TX: The Dryden Press.

Stark, Jan (2003) 'The Islamic debate in Malaysia: the unfinished project', *South East Asia Research*, 11(2): 173–201.

——(2004) 'Constructing an Islamic model in two Malaysian states: PAS rule in Kelantan and Terengganu', *Sojourn*, 19(1): 51–75 (April).

Steinmetz, George (2003) 'The state of emergency and the revival of American imperialism: towards an authoritarian Fordism', *Public Culture*, 15(2): 323–45.

Stiglitz, Joseph (1998) 'More instruments and broader goals: moving towards the post-Washington Consensus', The 1998 WIDER Annual Lecture, Helsinki.

——(2003) *Globalization and Its Discontents*, New York: W.W. Norton.

Straits Times (2004) 'We must show terrorists we won't be cowed', 31 July: H8.

Strange, S. (1994) *States and Markets*, 2nd edn, London: Pinter.

Stubbs, Richard (1994) 'The political economy of the Asia-Pacific region', in Richard Stubbs and Geoffrey Underhill (eds) *The Political Economy of the Chaning Global Order*, London: Macmillan, 366–77.

——(1999) 'War and economic development: expert-oriented industrialization in East and Southeast Asia', *Comparative Politics*, 31: 337–55.

Sudha Ramachandran (2004) 'Divisions over terror threat in Malacca Straits', *Asia Times Online*, 16 June.

Sugianto Tandra (2004) 'People yearn for a strong leader, but not an authoritarian regime', *Jakarta Post*, 30 April.

Sum Ngai-Ling (2003) 'An integral approach to the Asian "crisis": the disarticulation of the production and financial (dis)orders', *Capital and Class*, 74: 141–66.

Sutter, Robert G. (1991) *The United States and the Changing East Asia Order: implication for Taiwan's ability to deter possible treats from the mainland*, Congressional Research Service, July.

Tabb, William (2002) 'The face of empire', *Monthly Review*, November. Online. Available: http://www.monthlyreview.org/1102tabb.htm (accessed 17 January 2003).

——(2005) 'Capital, class and the state in the global political economy', *Globalizations*, 2 (1): 47–60.

Tan, Kenneth Paul (2003) 'Crisis, self-reflection and rebirth in Singapore's national life cycle', *Southeast Asian Affairs*, 241–58, Singapore: Institute of Southeast Asian Studies.

Tempo Interaktif (2005) 'Pemilihan Kepala Daerah Langsung: Panglima Tetap Izinkan TNI Aktif Dicalonkan', 27 April. Online, Available HTTP: http://www.tempointeraktif.com/hg/nasional/2005/04/27/brk,20050427-17,id.html (accessed 27 April 2005).

Thaksin Shinawatra (2002) 'Keynote speech' to the 2nd International Conference of Asian Political Parties, Bangkok, 23 November. Online.

Available: http://www.thaigov.go.th/news/speech/thaksin/sp23nov02-2.htm (accessed 26 November 2002).

The Ministry of Planning and Budget (2002) *The White Papers of the Korean Government Reform*. (In Korean)

The World Bank Group (ed.) (2003) 'The extractive industries review (EIR)', Final Workshop Report, Lisbon, December.

Therborn, Goran (1995) *European Modernity and Beyond: The Trajectory of European Societies, 1945–2000*, London: Sage.

——(2002) 'The world's trader, the world's lawyer: Europe and global processes', *European Journal of Social Theory*, 5(4): 403–18.

——(2004) *Between Sex and Power: family in the world, 1900–2000*, London: Routledge.

Thitinan Pongsudhirak (2003a) 'Behind Thaksin's war on terror', *Far Eastern Economic Review*, 25 September: 29.

——(2003b) 'Thailand: democratic authoritarianism', in Daljit Singh and Chin Kin Wah (eds) *Southeast Asian Affairs 2003*, Singapore: Institute of Southeast Asian Studies, 277–90.

Thompson, Wayne W. (1975) 'Governors of the Moro province: Wood, Bliss and Pershing in the Southern Philippines', PhD dissertation, University of California, San Diego.

Thornton, Thomas P. (1999) 'Pakistan: fifty years on insecurity', in Selig S. Harrison, P. H. Kreisberg and D. Kux (eds) *India and Pakistan: the first fifty years*. Cambridge: Cambridge University Press, 170–88.

Thubron, Colin (1995) *The Lost Heart of Asia*, London: Penguin.

Tjhin, Christine Susanna (2004) 'The return of the old New Order measures', *Jakarta Post*, 1 June.

Tocqueville, Alexis de (1956) *Democracy in America*, ed. Richard D. Hefner, New York: Mentor.

Treanor, Paul (2004) 'Neoliberalism: origins, theory and definition' Online. Available: http://web.inter.nl/users/paultreanor/neoliberalism.htm (accessed 24 August 2004).

Tremewan, Christopher (1994) *The Political Economy of Social Control in Singapore*, Oxford: St Martin's Press.

Tuck, Richard (1999) *The Rights of War and Peace*, Oxford: Oxford University Press.

Tyler, Patrick E. (2002) 'US strategy plan calls for insuring no rivals develop', *New York Times*, 8 March.

UNCTAD (2002) *World Investment Report 2002*, New York and Geneva: UN.

——(2004) *World Investment Report 2004*, New York and Geneva: UN.

UNDP (2003) *Human Development Report 2003*, Geneva: UNDP.

US Chamber of Commerce (2003) 'Singapore FTA – almost concluded – with free flow of capital caveat'. Online. Available HTTP: http//:www.uschamber.com/international/regional/asia/0212aisingfta.htm (accessed 12 January).

Vanaik, Achin (2002) 'Making India strong: the BJP-led government's foreign policy perspectives', *South Asia, New Series*, XXV(3): 320–41.

Virilio, Paul and Sylvere Lotringer (1983) *Pure War*, trans. M. Polizzotti. New York: Semiotext(e).

Virtual Information Center (2002) 'Primer: Muslim separatism in Southern Thailand', USPACOM. Online. Available: http://www.vic-info.org/SEAsia/ThailandPage.htm (accessed 10 November 2004).

Vitug, Marites and Glenda Gloria (2000) *Under the Crescent Moon: Rebellion in Mindanao,*   Quezon City: Ateneo Center for Social Policy and Public Affairs and the Institute for   Popular Democracy.

Wade, Robert (1988) 'The Asian crisis: the high debt model versus the Wall Street-Treasury-IMF complex', *New Left Review*, 231: September/November.

——(1998a) 'The Asian crisis and the global economy: causes, consequences, and cure', *Current History*, November: 361–73.

——(1998b) 'The Asian debt-and-development crisis of 1997: causes and consequences', *World Development*, 26(8): 1535–54.

——(2002) 'America's empire rules an unbalanced empire', *Counterpunch*, 2 January. Online. Available: http://www.counterpunch.org/wade1.html (accessed 16 December 2003).

Wade, Robert and Frank Venoroso (1998) 'The Asian Crisis: the high debt model versus the Wall Street–Treasury–IMF complex', *New Left Review*, 228: 3–23.

Wall Street Journal (1997) 'The emerging American imperium', 18 August.

Waltz, Kenneth (2002) 'Structural realism after the Cold War', in G. John Ikenberry (ed.) *American Unrivaled: the future of the balance of power*, Ithaca, NY: Cornell University Press, 34.

Wardell, Jane (2004) 'In Britain, Big Brother's always watching', *Bangkok Post*, 16 August.

Watson, A. (1992) *The Evolution of International Society,* London: Routledge.

Weber, H. (2002) 'The imposition of a global development architecture: the example of micro credit', *Review of International Studies*, 28(3): 537–55.

Weber, Max (1978) *Economy and Society,* Berkeley, CA: University of California Press.

Weber, S. (1993) 'Shaping the postwar balance of power: multilateralism in NATO', in J. G. Ruggie (ed.) *Multilateralism Matters: the theory and praxis of an institutional form*, New York: Columbia University Press.

Weiss, Linda (1998) *The Myth of the Powerless State*, Ithaca, NY: Cornell University Press.

White, Gordon (ed.) (1988) *Developmental States in East Asia*, New York: St Martin's Press.

White House (2002) *The National Security Strategy of the United States,* Washington, DC: White House.

Williams, Appleman (1972) *The Tragedy of American Diplomacy*, New York: Dell.

Williams, Clive M. G. (2003) 'The question of "links" between Al Qaeda and Southeast Asia', in Kumar Ramakrishna and See Seng Tan (eds) *After Bali: the threat of terrorism in Southeast Asia*, Singapore: Institute of Defence and Strategic Studies and World Scientific, 83–95.

Williamson, John (2000) 'What should the World Bank think about the Washington Consensus?', *World Bank Research Observer*, 15(2): 251–64 (August), Washington, DC: The International Bank for Reconstruction and Development.

——(2002) 'Did the Washington Consensus fail?', Outline of remarks at CSIS, Washington, DC: Institute for International Economics, 6 November.

Winik, J. (1996) *On the Brink,* New York: Simon & Schuster.

Winters, Jeffrey A. (1996) *Power in Motion: capital mobility and the Indonesian state*, Ithaca, NY: Cornell University Press.

——(2000) 'The financial crisis in Southeast Asia', in Richard Robison, Mark Beeson, Kanishka Jayasuriya and Hyuk-Rae Kim (eds) *Politics and Markets in the Wake of the Asian Crisis*, London: Routledge, 34–52.

Wolf, M. (2003) 'Why Europe was the past, the US is the present and a China-dominated Asia is the future', *Financial Times*, 23 September: 13.

Wolfson, A. (2004) 'Conservatives and neoconservatives', *The Public Interest*, 32–48.

Wood, Ellen Meiksins. (2003) *Empire of Capital*, London: Verso.

Wood, Leonard (1904) 'Report of the governor of the Moro province', *Annual Report of the War Department*, Washington, DC: General Printing Office.

Woods, N. (2003) 'The United States and the international financial institutions: power and influence within the World Bank and the IMF', in R. Foot. S. Neil MacFarlane and Michael Mastanduno (eds) *US Hegemony and International Organizations*, Oxford: Oxford University Press, 92–114.

Woodward, B. (2003) *Bush at War,* London: Pocket Books.

——(2004) *Plan of Attack,* New York: Simon & Schuster.

World Bank (1997) *World Development Report: the state in a changing world*, Washington, DC: Oxford University Press.

——(2000) Poverty in an Age of Globalization, Washington, DC: World Bank.

——(2000/01) *World Development Report: attacking poverty*, Washington, DC: Oxford University Press.

——(2003) *World Development Report 2003*, New York: Oxford University Press.

——(n.d.) 'Decentralization net', Online. Available: http://www1.worldbank.org/publicsector/decentralization/Different.htm (accessed 5 December 2003).

Wright-Neville, David (2004) 'Dangerous dynamics: activists, militants and terrorists in Southeast Asia', *Pacific Review*, 17(1): 27–46.

WTO (2001) *World Trade Report 2001*, Geneva and New York: UN.

——(2004) *World Trade Report 2004*, Geneva and New York: UN.

Wu, Nai-teh (2002) 'Identity conflict and political trust: ethnic politics in contemporary Taiwan', *Taiwanese Sociology*, 4: 75–118.

Zakaria, Fareed (1994) 'Culture is destiny: a conversation with Lee Kuan Yew', *Foreign Affairs*, 73(2): 109–26.

——(1997) 'The rise of illiberal democracy', *Foreign Affairs*, 76(6): 22–43 (November/December).

Zaring, D. (1998) 'International law by other means: the twilight existence of international financial regulatory organisation', *Texas International Law Journal*, 33(2): 281–330.

Zingales, Luigi and Robert McCormack (2003) 'A choice between the rich and the markets', *Financial Times*, 3 March: 13.

Zulfikar Shariff Mohamad (2002) 'Terrorism and Singapore', Press release, 19 January, Online. Available: http:/ fateha.com (accessed 21 January 2002).

Newspaper/magazine resources

A Day Weekly (2004) (26) November 12–18.
Bangkok Post (2004) 16 July.
Bangkok Post (2004) 19 July.
Bangkok Post (2004) 21 July.
Bangkok Post (2004) 23 July.
Bangkok Post (2004) 28 July.
Bangkok Post (2004) 17 November.
Bangkok Post (2004) 19 November.
Bangkok Post (2004) 21 November.
Bengali Weekly (2004) 3(13): 5 July. Dhaka.
China Times (2004) 22 May: A13. Taiwan.
China Times (2000) 14 July: A14. Taiwan.
China Times (2000) 26 November: A3. Taiwan.
Daily News (2004) 17 November. (In Thai)
Jakarta Post (2003) 21 November.
Jakarta Post (2004) 19 May.
Matichon (2004) 9 April. (In Thai)
Matichon (2004) 29 April. (In Thai)
Matichon (2004) 5 April. (In Thai)
Matichon (2004) 6 October. (In Thai)
Mindanao Herald, Zamboanga City.
Taipei Times (1999) 19 December: 1.
Tempo (2003), No. 46, 13 January.
The Budapest Times (2004) 28 June–4 July.
The Daily Star (2004) 29 June. Dhaka.
United Daily News (2004) 5 May: A4.

Index

9/11 1, 4, 5, 10, 13, 16, 38, 39, 47–50, 62, 73, 78, 80, 121, 132, 136, 166, 190, 222, 227, 234, 246, 258
Abu Ghraib 32, 34, 136
Abu Sayyaf 164, 165
Adivasis 247, 256, 259
Afghanistan 2, 5, 6, 23, 28–29, 84, 98, 100, 115–16, 121, 165, 167, 183, 186, 202, 204, 233, 234, 237, 249, 259
Al Qaeda 6, 15, 116, 123, 166
American exceptionalism 72–73, 79, 196, 197,
Anderson, Perry 38, 124
anti-Americanism 4, 13–14, 74, 213–15
Anwar Ibrahim 145, 153
APEC (Asia-Pacific Economic Cooperation) 2, 52, 63, 64, 107, 116, 119
Aquino, Corazon 164
ASEAN 25, 30, 31, 44, 64, 115, 221, free trade agreement with China 24; and APEC 107; US-ASEAN Business Council 109, 260
ASG *see* Abu Sayyaf
Asian economic crisis *see* Asian financial crisis
Asian financial crisis 5, 12–13, 17, 53, 55, 63, 64–65, 67, 105, 107, 114–15, 127, 129, 139, 153, 189, 190, 204–7, 209–10, 213, 217, 230, 245
Asian Monetary Fund 64, 115
authoritarianism: authoritarian regime 7–8, 98, 105, 106, 108, 110, 120, 130, 131, 223–24, 234–35; authoritarian democracy 17, 169–70, 183–7; post-authoritarian 106
Awami League 236, 240–41, 243, 245
Ayodhya 249, 254

Bagram 28, 32, 34
Bali bombings 66, 123, 135

Bangladesh independence war 234, 242, 244, 245
Beijing Consensus 188, 191–92, 200–201
Bengali nationalism 232
Berkeley Mafia in Indonesia 128
bilateralism 44–46, 70
BJP (Bharatiya Janata Party) 248–49, 253–59, 261
'blowback' 6, 137, 234–35, 245
BN (Barisan Nasional) 140, 142, 144, 145, 146–47, 149, 154, 155
Bretton Woods 13, 56, 57, 70, 89
BTA (bilateral trade agreement) 60, 64, 117
Buddhism 31, 179
Bush Sr., George 220–21
Bush, George W.: administration 10–11, 15, 59–60, 62, 70, 72, 76–79, 82, 83, 136, 192, 207, 219; and American neoconservatives 74, 78, 120; Doctrine 74, 192–98, 200

capitalism: American 3, 27; political 59, 64; Asian 105; crony 129, 205
Central Asia 16, 29–31, 60–61, 79, 84, 97, 98, 196, 227, 248, 250
chaebol 206, 213, 217
Chaturon Chaisaeng 175–76
Chen Shui-Bian 219, 227–28, 229
China: as economic superpower 30, 36, 60, 188–89, 192, 219, 221; as rival to USA 12, 17, 24, 63, 64, 218, 221, 248; model of development 12; economic problems 31, 92, 200, 225; economic growth 13, 16, 17, 31, 57, 77, 115, 190–95
'China threat' 226, 228
Christianity 33, 34, 37, 73

civil society 11, 13, 54, 59, 106, 113, 119,
  125, 127, 169, 180, 183, 215, 249
clash of civilizations 55
climate change 92–93
Clinton, Bill 10, 33, 194, 195–98, 214,
  227, 254, 257
Cold War: post-1–3, 5, 7, 8, 14–18,
  202–16, 255; era 12, 18, 19, 126, 128,
  136, 195, 218, 222, 245; agenda 192;
  order 40; politics 3, 127–28
communism 5, 12, 23, 75, 120, 126–27,
  129, 130, 142, 203, 220, 239, 242, 245,
  255, 257
complex sovereignty 42, 51
congagement 221, 226
Congress Party in India 248, 252,
  254–55, 257–59
Containment policy, doctrine of 74,
  221–22, 235, 239
Council of Europe 26

dakwah 141, 147
Dalits 247–48, 251, 256, 259
Darul Arqam in Malaysia 141
datus in Mindanao 157–60
democracy movement; in Taiwan 219,
  223
democracy: despotic 185; liberal 4, 17,
  32, 35–36, 126; authoritarian 169,
  170, 183, 184–87 *see also*
  democratization
democratization 7, 16, 66, 124, 127, 131,
  200, 203, 209, 212, 224, 226
doctrine of pre-emption 74, 79
Doyle, Michael 198–200
DPP (Democratic Progress Party) in
  Taiwan 218–19, 224–25, 227–28, 230

economic: militarization 47; technocrats
  52, 126, 128
Empire: American 2–4, 6, 7–8, 9, 14, 26,
  123, 136, 139, 156, 169, 219, 247–49,
  257; of capital 233; British 24, 237 *see
  also* imperialism
environmentalists: in Thailand 178; in
  Taiwan 225
EOI (export-oriented industrialization)
  12, 217
EU (European Union) 24–27, 96, 197
euro 26, 98–99, 101, 196

failed state 124, 130
Felda (Federal Land Development
  Authority) in Malaysia 141, 143

financialization: of modern capitalism
  88, 90, 91
Ford Foundation 128, 137
foreign direct investment 205, 216, 256
fossil energy regime 7, 15, 16, 83–85, 88,
  91–92, 96, 100
fossil fuel *see* fossil energy regime
Friedman, Thomas 9, 19, 32, 53, 54, 62
FTA (foreign trade agreement) 45–47,
  107, 114, 117, 120, 121, 211, 205, 216,
  256
Fukuyama, Francis 4, 53, 180, 202

Gandhi, Indira 242, 248, 253, 254
Gandhi, Rajiv 248, 254–55
GATT (General Agreement on Tariffs
  and Trade) 70
Gini coefficients *see* Gini index
Gini index 27, 31, 190, 207–8
Gini ratio *see* Gini index
GLC (government-linked companies) in
  Singapore 107, 109
globality 40
globalization: armed 202, 204–5, 213–16
  see also neoliberal economic
  globalization
globalizing bureaucrats 43–44
Goh Chok Tong 108, 112
governance: global 15, 26, 32, 48, 52, 81,
  197; transnational regulatory 38–46,
  48, 50, 51
Gowan, Peter 3, 10, 60–61, 64, 67
graduated sovereignty 48–49
Guantanamo 5, 28, 32, 136

Hambali 116, 119
Hardt and Negri 9, 42 204
Harvey, David 2–3, 56–57, 59–1, 86, 88,
  106, 233
Heritage Foundation 76, 109
Hindu fundamentalism 18, 247, 253; in
  politics 248, 250–52; influence of
  fascism on 18, 251, 259 *see also*
  Hindutva
Hindu Rashtra 247, 252
Hinduism 31, 247, 251, 258, 259, 260
Hindutva 247, 254, 257–59, 260
holo lang (Hokkien speakers) in Taiwan
  218
Huntington, Samuel 4, 20, 55, 125

ICC (International Criminal Court) 26,
  181
illiberalism 19, 64, 126, 137

IMF (International Monetary Fund)
44, 52, 24–25, 57, 59–60, 62–64,
114–15, 129, 139, 205, 206–9, 216,
249, 256
imperialism: capitalist 3, 39; US 6–7, 17,
25, 35, 80, 156, 192, 232, 253; ultra-
15; new 7, 15, 38–41, 43, 45–47,
49–50, 63, 233
Indonesian military 126–27, 130,
132–36
industrialization: in Korea 48, 71, 203,
217
industrial–military complex in USA *see*
military–industrial complex
Internal Security Act: in Malaysia 4,
134, 139; in Singapore 110, 134
Iraq war 28, 84, 97, 195, 215
irredentism in Taiwan 222–26
Islam: in Malaysia 139–55; and the state
8; political 8, 16, 132; militant 120;
separatist 16–17, 117, 196, 221, 227;
and politics 140; as political idiom
139, 140, 152
Islamic: radicalism 4, 8, 15, 18, 78,
123–26, 132, 165, 237;
fundamentalism 66, 120, 152, 232,
235, 248–49, 257
Islamization 139, 141, 245, 286
Isolationism: American 3, 60
Israel 20, 29, 34, 77–78, 82, 135, 182,
248, 257–59

Japan 5–6, 17, 24, 30–31, 33, 35–36, 45,
61, 63–64, 70, 72, 87, 99, 156, 160,
180,195, 203, 220–22, 226, 231, 233
JI (Jemaah Islamiyah) 112, 116, 121,
123, 133
Johnson, Chalmers *see* 'blowback'

Kagan, Robert 4, 6, 193, 201
Kant, Immanuel 199–200
Kashmir 238, 254, 259
Kautsky, Karl 39
Kazakhstan 97, 101, 196, 221
Kelantan 140–55, 172
Kim Dae-Jung 206, 216
Kim Young Sam 205–9, 217
Korean War 203, 219
Krauthammer, Charles 76, 83
Kristol, Irving 75, 193–94, 198
Kuomintang 195, 218–19, 222–31

labour disputes: in South Korea 209–10,
China 190

labour movements and rights 26, 203,
209–10
law: soft 181; international 26, 79, 195,
230; martial 124, 127, 134, 163, 224,
239
Lee Deng-Hui 225–30
Lee Kuan Yew 3, 55, 113, 126, 137
liberalism 33, 35, 48, 55, 58, 195, 197,
202; political 13, 105, 117, 137;
constitutional 186; economic 13
Likud Party 34, 77

Mahathir Mohamad 4, 55, 63, 139, 153
Mann, Michael 2–4, 6, 9, 20, 56, 233
Marcos, Ferdinand 157, 162–65
market: capitalism 13, 53, 59, 62;
fundamentalism 59, 62
Middle East 5, 61, 67, 77–80, 95, 112,
141–42, 163, 238, 248
MILF (Moro Islamic Liberation Front)
163, 164, 165
military–industrial complex 10, 71
MIM (Mindanao Independence
Movement) 162–63
Mindanao: Spanish colonialism 157–58
US colonialism 17, 157
minjung (people's) movement in Korea
203, 212–14
Moro Province 157–58
Mujibur Rahman, Sheikh 236, 245
multilateralism 40, 46–48, 76, 78
Muslims: in Thailand 117–19, 139, 169,
170–78; in the Philippines 156–57,
159, 160–62

NAFTA (North American Free Trade
Agreement) 24, 25
national identity 72, 74, 176, 225–26,
229
NATO (North Atlantic Treaty
Organization) 28, 43, 96–97, 100,
117, 181
neocon (neoconservative) 6–7, 10, 11,
15, 60, 67, 69, 74, 75, 77–78, 82, 97,
106, 167, 194, 196, 201, 246, *see also*
neoconservatism
neoconservatism 17, 60, 66, 67, 75, 188,
192, 195, 197–99, 201
neoliberalism 1, 7, 18, 27, 42, 46–47, 52,
53, 60, 63, 66, 67, 105–6, 157, 167,
190–91, 205–6, 212, 217, 249, 253;
neoliberal economic globalization
1–3, 8, 13–15, 19, 190, 202, 207, 208

NEP (New Economic Policy) in
Malaysia 140–45
New Order (in Indonesia) 123, 124, 126,
127–35
Nik Abdul Aziz Nik Mat 142, 147–53
Nixon, Richard 33, 220, 239, 240, 242–44
Nur Misuari 163, 164
Nye, Joseph 6, 9, 40, 51, 81, 105, 136;
Nye Report 221

occidental despotism 15, 32, 35
oil 11, 25, 59, 61, 63, 79, 83–84, 88,
91–95; politics of 3, 15; rent 29;
deposits 29; and gas 16, 29, 93, 196,
248; imperialism 84, 96–99; revenue
95, 101, 128
One-China policy 219, 227
OPEC 94, 96, 98
Osama Bin Laden 82, 123, 165

PAP (People's Action Party) in
Singapore 111, 113; ideology 113
Park Chung Hee 205, 206–7, 212–13, 217
PAS (Malaysian Islamic Party) 139–53,
154, 155
Patriot Act 9
Pattani 117, 169, 170, 172–74, 177
Pax Americana 1, 7, 15, 52–53, 56–57,
59–64
peakoil' 93–94, 99
PKI (Indonesian Communist Party) 127
populism 13, 53, 72, 114, 127; capitalist
180
'pure war' 183–84,

Reagan, Ronald 33, 77, 223
Reformasi: in Indonesia 131—2; in
Malaysia 153
regime: Indonesian 124, 129–31;
democratic 8, 12, 165, 217
religious fundamentalism 35
Rice, Condoleezza 83, 134, 221
Roh Mu-hyun 212, 213—14
RSS (Rashtriya Swayansewak Sangh)
247, 251, 252–53, 259, 260
Russia (or Soviet Union) 1, 11, 12, 24,
25, 28, 29, 33, 36, 58—61, 76, 83, 88,
91, 95, 96—9, 100, 101, 196—7, 189,
203, 219—20, 221, 233—5, 238—42,
248, 249, 255, 257

Second World War 23, 26, 35, 38, 56, 71,
82, 160, 161, 182, 203, 218, 220,
236–37, 241

separatists: in Thailand 17, 117, 170,
187; in Indonesia 124, 128, 134, 136;
in the Philippines 16, 156, 159–60,
163; in China 196, 219, 221, 222, 224,
226, 227, 231
Serfati, Claude 90, 202–3
social conservatism 56, 62, 106, 120
Soeharto 68, 123–25, 127–33, 135–36,
137; rise to power 127
Soekarno 127–28
'soft power' 9, 81, 136
Songkhla 172, 173, 177
Southern Thailand 7, 17, 66, 169–73, 183
STEER (Singapore–Thailand Enhanced
Economic Relationship) 45
Stiglitz, Joseph 54, 59, 206
Sunshine Policy 204, 214, 215
surplus-value production 84, 86, 88–89,
90, 100
swadeshi 248, 255, 256, 259

Tak Bai incident/demonstration 175,
177–79
terrorism 2, 4, 7, 16, 31, 34, 49, 61, 80,
84, 106, 108–12, 116–20, 123, 134,
181–83, 187, 219, 257; counter 49,
108, 115–16, 258
Thaksin Shinawatra 16, 63, 64, 114–20,
121, 122, 175, 178, 180
Third Worldism 8, 23
Tocqueville, Alexis de 170, 184–86
trade liberalization 44–45, 47, 107, 236
transnational state 40, 42
Trengganu 140, 145–52, 153, 154, 155,
160
TRT (Thai Rak Thai) Party 114–15,
118–20, 170

UMNO (United Malays National
Organization) 139, 142–53, 154, 155
unilateralism 40, 46, 49, 69, 76, 82, 195,
196–97
unipolarity *see* unilateralism
USAID 66, 125
USSFTA (United States Singapore Free
Trade Agreement) 107–10

Vietnam War 23, 71, 121, 128, 219, 220,
242

waisheng ren (mainlanders) in Taiwan
218, 219
Wall Street–Treasury-IMF complex 206,
214

War on Terror 1, 2, 5, 7, 8, 11, 13, 16–17, 38, 43, 45, 71, 73, 78–79, 105–17, 120, 126, 130, 132, 136, 139, 157, 165, 182, 222, 227, 232, 248

Washington Consensus 67, 188–91, 200–201

(WMD) weapons of mass destruction 28, 37, 108, 121, 227

Westphalian: framework, state, model 15, 40, 42, 47, 50

Wolfowitz, Paul 10–11, 76–78, 82, 137, 192, 193, 201

Wood, Ellen Meiksins 2, 3, 11, 39, 124, 233

World Bank 11, 13, 52, 53, 55, 66, 70, 77, 88, 125, 256

WTO (World Trade Organization) 26, 52, 57, 60, 64, 190, 196, 211, 221, 256

For Product Safety Concerns and Information please contact our EU
representative GPSR@taylorandfrancis.com
Taylor & Francis Verlag GmbH, Kaufingerstraße 24, 80331 München, Germany

9 7 8 0 4 1 5 3 9 0 8 1 1